ADDISON-WESLEY
MATHEMATICS

Robert E. Eicholz

Phares G. O'Daffer

Charles R. Fleenor

Randall I. Charles

Sharon Young

Carne S. Barnett

Addison-Wesley Publishing Company

Menlo Park, California   Reading, Massachusetts   London   Amsterdam   Don Mills, Ontario   Sydney

ILLUSTRATION ACKNOWLEDGMENTS

Frank Ansley 6–7, 20–21, 32, 72–73, 87, 134–135, 190, 240, 242, 326–327

Sherry Balestra 8–9, 30–31, 40–41, 51, 114, 117, 136–137, 160–161, 177, 184, 199, 218–219, 250–251, 302–303, 318–319, 336–337, 355

Ellen Blonder 50, 84, 116, 146, 176, 196, 220, 244, 264, 288, 310, 330–331, 338, 354

Cindy Brodie 19, 53, 75, 76, 85, 122–123 (clock faces), 124–125 (clock faces), 130–131, 140–141, 147, 149, 202–203, 212, 265, 272, 276–277, 280–281, 284–285, 291, 306–307, 320–321, 339, 348–349

Kirk Caldwell 10–11, 44, 97, 104–105, 124–125, 154–155, 170, 182–183, 197, 216–217, 229 (lower right), 232–233, 308–309, 322–323, 350–351, 357

Liz Callen 27, 46–47, 52, 68–69, 78, 93, 112–113, 132, 148, 150–151, 158–159, 203, 208–209, 222, 224–225, 234–235, 245, 256–257, 262–263, 270–271, 290, 292–293, 304–305, 311, 328–329, 334–335, 342–343, 346–347, 356

Maxie Chambliss 4–5, 18, 22, 38–39, 43, 54–55, 100–101, 118–119, 123, 139, 144, 164–165, 179, 186, 198, 206–207, 231, 252–253, 260–261, 266–267, 296–297, 332–333, 340, 352–353

Randy Chewning 12, 65, 70–71, 102–103, 162–163, 169, 171, 189, 195, 241, 254, 273

Myron Grossman 48–49

Roberta Holmes 36–37, 115, 341

Glenn Iwasaki 34–35, 95, 106–107, 168, 172–173, 214–215, 258–259

Susan Jaekel 59, 86, 166–167, 178, 194, 246, 312

Jane McCreary 14–15, 23, 26, 42, 58, 60–61, 62, 74, 90, 92, 94, 96, 110–111, 126–127, 130 (upper right), 133, 138, 142–143, 183 (lower right), 188, 191, 205, 210, 228–229, 236–237, 255, 274–275, 278–279, 286–287, 300–301, 313, 316–317, 324–325

Yoshi Miyake 1, 25, 57, 89, 121, 153, 181, 201, 227, 249, 269, 295, 315, 345

Deborah Morse (money) 33, 34–35, 36–37, 51, 155, 167

Susan Nelson 156–157, 174–175, 230, 298–299

Dennis Nolan 66, 185, 187

Valerie Randall 64, 78 (graph), 82–83, 128, 145, 192–193, 243, 282–283, 289, 359–362

Judy Sakaguchi 16, 247

Ed Taber 2–3, 80–81, 98–99, 108–109, 238–239

Cover Photograph © **Bill Ross/West Light**

ISBN 0-201-24300-8

Contents

CHAPTER 1 ADDITION AND SUBTRACTION FACTS, 1

2   Sums Through 10
4   Differences Through 10
6   Sums Through 18
8   Differences Through 18
10 Fact Families
12 Practice the Facts
14 Problem Solving: The 5-Point Checklist
16 Three Addends
18 Problem Solving: Understanding the Question
19 Problem Solving: Using Data from a Picture
20 Problem Solving: Choose the Operations
21 CHAPTER REVIEW/TEST
22 ANOTHER LOOK
23 ENRICHMENT: Logical Reasoning
24 CUMULATIVE REVIEW

CHAPTER 2 PLACE VALUE, 25

26 Tens and Ones
28 Hundreds, Tens, and Ones
30 Counting and Order
32 Skip Counting
33 Counting Money
34 Counting Change
36 Dollars and Cents
38 Rounding to the Nearest Ten
40 More About Rounding
42 Thousands
44 Comparing Numbers
46 More About Thousands
48 Ordinal Numbers
50 Problem Solving: Guess and Check
51 CHAPTER REVIEW/TEST
52 ANOTHER LOOK
53 ENRICHMENT: Roman Numerals
54 TECHNOLOGY: Using a Calculator
56 CUMULATIVE REVIEW

CHAPTER 3 ADDITION, 57

58 Trading 10 Ones for 1 Ten
60 Adding 2-Digit Numbers: Trading Ones
62 Adding 2-Digit Numbers: Trading 10 Tens
64 Problem Solving: Using Data from a Graph
65 Problem Solving: Choose the Operations
66 Adding 3-Digit Numbers: Trading Once
68 Adding 3-Digit Numbers: Two or More Trades
70 Adding Amounts of Money
71 Problem Solving: Using Data from an Advertisement
72 Special Sums: Mental Math
74 Estimating Sums
76 Adding: Mental Math
78 Column Addition
80 Adding 4-Digit Numbers
82 Problem Solving: Using the 5-Point Checklist
84 Problem Solving: Use Logical Reasoning
85 CHAPTER REVIEW/TEST
86 ANOTHER LOOK
87 ENRICHMENT: Finding Patterns
88 CUMULATIVE REVIEW

CHAPTER 4 SUBTRACTION, 89

90 Trading 1 Ten for 10 Ones
92 Subtracting 2-Digit Numbers: Trading Tens
94 Problem Solving: Understanding the Question
95 Subtraction Practice
96 Subtracting 3-Digit Numbers: Trading Hundreds
98 Subtracting 3-Digit Numbers: Two Trades
100 Checking Subtraction
102 Problem Solving: Using Data from a Map
103 Problem Solving: Using Data from a Table

104 Subtracting Across a Middle Zero
106 Subtracting Amounts of Money
108 Special Differences: Mental Math
110 Estimating Differences
112 Subtracting 4-Digit Numbers
114 Problem Solving: Using Data from a Catalog

115 Problem Solving: Practice
116 Problem Solving: Draw a Picture
117 CHAPTER REVIEW/TEST
118 ANOTHER LOOK
119 ENRICHMENT: Making Predictions
120 CUMULATIVE REVIEW

CHAPTER 5   MEASUREMENT: Metric Units, 121

122 Hour, Half-Hour, and Quarter-Hour
124 Minutes
126 a.m. and p.m.
127 Problem Solving: Practice
128 Reading the Calendar
130 Units for Measuring
131 Using the Centimeter Unit
132 Measuring to the Nearest Centimeter
134 Meters and Kilometers
135 Problem Solving: Using Data from a Picture
136 Perimeter
138 Area

140 Volume
142 Liquid Measure
143 Weight
144 Temperature
145 Problem Solving: Using Data from a Graph
146 Problem Solving: Make a List
147 CHAPTER REVIEW/TEST
148 ANOTHER LOOK
149 ENRICHMENT: Estimation in Measurement
150 TECHNOLOGY: Flowcharts
152 CUMULATIVE REVIEW

CHAPTER 6   MULTIPLICATION FACTS, 153

154 Addition and Multiplication
156 Understanding Multiplication
158 2 as a Factor
160 3 as a Factor
162 Problem Solving: Choose the Operations
163 Practice the Facts
164 4 as a Factor
166 5 as a Factor
168 Problem Solving: Using Data from an Advertisement
169 Practice the Facts

170 0 and 1 as Factors
171 Practice the Facts
172 Order in Multiplication
174 Problem Solving: Using the 5-Point Checklist
176 Problem Solving: Make a Table
177 CHAPTER REVIEW/TEST
178 ANOTHER LOOK
179 ENRICHMENT: Finding Patterns
180 CUMULATIVE REVIEW

CHAPTER 7   MORE MULTIPLICATION FACTS, 181

182 6 as a Factor
184 7 as a Factor
186 8 and 9 as Factors
188 Problem Solving: Practice
189 Practice the Facts
190 Multiplying Three Numbers
191 Missing Factors
192 Problem Solving: Using Data from a Table

193 Problem Solving: Identifying Needed Data
194 Problem Solving: Practice
195 Practice the Facts
196 Problem Solving: Choose the Operations
197 CHAPTER REVIEW/TEST
198 ANOTHER LOOK
199 ENRICHMENT: Space Perception
200 CUMULATIVE REVIEW

CHAPTER 8 GEOMETRY AND GRAPHING, 201

202 Space Figures
204 Plane Figures
206 Segments
208 Angles
210 Congruent Figures
212 Lines of Symmetry
214 Tallies and Bar Graphs
216 Picture Graphs

218 Number Pairs on a Graph
220 Problem Solving: Find a Pattern
221 **CHAPTER REVIEW/TEST**
222 **ANOTHER LOOK**
223 **ENRICHMENT: Moving Figures on a Graph**
224 **TECHNOLOGY: Using Flowcharts**
226 **CUMULATIVE REVIEW**

CHAPTER 9 DIVISION FACTS, 227

228 Understanding Division
230 Dividing by 2 and 3
232 Multiplication and Division are Related
234 Dividing by 4
236 Dividing by 5
238 Problem Solving: Understanding
     the Operation
239 A New Sign for Division
240 Problem Solving: Identifying
     Unneeded Data

241 Practice the Facts
242 Problem Solving: Estimation
243 Problem Solving: Practice
244 Problem Solving: Using the Strategies
245 **CHAPTER REVIEW/TEST**
246 **ANOTHER LOOK**
247 **ENRICHMENT: Probability Zoo Game**
248 **CUMULATIVE REVIEW**

CHAPTER 10 MORE DIVISION FACTS, 249

250 Dividing by 6
252 Dividing by 7
254 Practice the Facts
255 Problem Solving: Choose
     the Operations
256 Dividing by 8
258 Dividing by 9
260 More about Division

261 Problem Solving: Practice
262 Problem Solving: Using Data
     from a Table
264 Problem Solving: Using the Strategies
265 **CHAPTER REVIEW/TEST**
266 **ANOTHER LOOK**
267 **ENRICHMENT: Negative Numbers**
268 **CUMULATIVE REVIEW**

CHAPTER 11 MULTIPLICATION, 269

270 Special Products: Mental Math
272 Multiplication and Addition
273 Problem Solving: Choose the Operations
274 Multiply and Then Add: Mental Math
276 Multiplying: Trading Ones
278 Multiplying: Trading Ones and Tens
280 Multiplying with Money
282 Problem Solving: Using Data from a
     Picture Graph
283 Multiplication Practice
284 Estimating Products with Money:
     Mental Math

285 Problem Solving: Estimating to
     Check Answers
286 Problem Solving: Practice
288 Applied Problem Solving
289 **CHAPTER REVIEW/TEST**
290 **ANOTHER LOOK**
291 **ENRICHMENT: Estimation and
     Mental Math**
292 **TECHNOLOGY: Using a Computer**
294 **CUMULATIVE REVIEW**

CHAPTER 12 DIVISION, 295

296 Showing Remainders
298 Finding Quotients and Remainders
300 Problem Solving: Understanding the Answer
302 Checking Divsion
303 Problem Solving: Practice
304 2-Digit Quotients
306 2-Digit Quotients and Remainders
308 Estimating Quotients with Money: Mental Math
309 Problem Solving: Using Data from an Advertisement
310 Applied Problem Solving
311 CHAPTER REVIEW/TEST
312 ANOTHER LOOK
313 ENRICHMENT: Logical Reasoning
314 CUMULATIVE REVIEW

CHAPTER 13 FRACTIONS AND DECIMALS, 315

316 Naming Parts of a Whole
318 Finding Fractions of a Whole
320 Finding Fractional Parts of a Set
322 Fractions of a Set
323 Problem Solving: Practice
324 Equivalent Fractions
326 Comparing Fractions
327 Problem Solving: Practice
328 Fractions and Decimals
330 Larger Decimals
332 Adding Decimals
334 Subtracting Decimals
336 Problem Solving: Using Data from a Map
337 Problem Solving: Using a Calculator
338 Applied Problem Solving
339 CHAPTER REVIEW/TEST
340 ANOTHER LOOK
341 ENRICHMENT: Magic Squares with Your Calculator
342 TECHNOLOGY: More About Computers
344 CUMULATIVE REVIEW

CHAPTER 14 MEASUREMENT: Customary Units, 345

346 Customary Units for Length
348 Measuring with Inch Units
350 Cups, Pints, Quarts, and Gallons
352 Weight: Ounces and Pounds
353 Temperature
354 Applied Problem Solving
355 CHAPTER REVIEW/TEST
356 ANOTHER LOOK
357 ENRICHMENT: Area Using Half Units
358 CUMULATIVE REVIEW

APPENDIX

359 Data Bank
363 More Practice
385 Table of Measures
386 Glossary
389 Index

Julie belongs to the 4-H Club. 4-H stands for head, hands, heart, and health. Julie has many 4-H projects. One project is to train guide-dog puppies. She teaches puppies how to be "eyes" for blind people. Julie trains the puppies to be good in stores. She teaches them to ride on buses. Julie has trained 4 German shepherds. She has also trained 3 golden retrievers.

Sums Through 10

How many bugs are there in all?

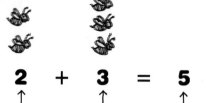

$$2 + 3 = 5$$

Addend Addend Sum

$$2 \leftarrow \text{Addend}$$
$$+ 3 \leftarrow \text{Addend}$$
$$5 \leftarrow \text{Sum}$$

There are 5 bugs in all.

Warm Up Add.

1. 4
    $+ 2$

2. 3
    $+ 3$

3. 3
    $+ 1$

Read each number sentence aloud and give the sum.

Example We read $5 + 4 = 9$ as **"Five plus four equal nine."**

4. $2 + 6 =$ ___   5. $2 + 8 =$ ___   6. $5 + 3 =$ ___   7. $2 + 2 =$ ___

8. $1 + 7 =$ ___   9. $4 + 3 =$ ___   10. $7 + 0 =$ ___   11. $1 + 8 =$ ___

12. $1 + 6 =$ ___   13. $2 + 4 =$ ___   14. $3 + 6 =$ ___   15. $4 + 6 =$ ___

16. $4 + 1 =$ ___   17. $7 + 2 =$ ___   18. $1 + 2 =$ ___   19. $2 + 5 =$ ___

20. $3 + 4 =$ ___   21. $0 + 9 =$ ___   22. $6 + 2 =$ ___   23. $3 + 3 =$ ___

Add.

1. $\begin{array}{r} 6 \\ +\ 2 \\ \hline \end{array}$ 2. $\begin{array}{r} 3 \\ +\ 7 \\ \hline \end{array}$ 3. $\begin{array}{r} 4 \\ +\ 2 \\ \hline \end{array}$ 4. $\begin{array}{r} 5 \\ +\ 4 \\ \hline \end{array}$ 5. $\begin{array}{r} 5 \\ +\ 2 \\ \hline \end{array}$ 6. $\begin{array}{r} 9 \\ +\ 1 \\ \hline \end{array}$ 7. $\begin{array}{r} 2 \\ +\ 7 \\ \hline \end{array}$

8. $\begin{array}{r} 3 \\ +\ 2 \\ \hline \end{array}$ 9. $\begin{array}{r} 8 \\ +\ 2 \\ \hline \end{array}$ 10. $\begin{array}{r} 1 \\ +\ 2 \\ \hline \end{array}$ 11. $\begin{array}{r} 0 \\ +\ 9 \\ \hline \end{array}$ 12. $\begin{array}{r} 2 \\ +\ 2 \\ \hline \end{array}$ 13. $\begin{array}{r} 4 \\ +\ 1 \\ \hline \end{array}$ 14. $\begin{array}{r} 6 \\ +\ 1 \\ \hline \end{array}$

15. $\begin{array}{r} 4 \\ +\ 6 \\ \hline \end{array}$ 16. $\begin{array}{r} 3 \\ +\ 4 \\ \hline \end{array}$ 17. $\begin{array}{r} 5 \\ +\ 3 \\ \hline \end{array}$ 18. $\begin{array}{r} 2 \\ +\ 4 \\ \hline \end{array}$ 19. $\begin{array}{r} 2 \\ +\ 8 \\ \hline \end{array}$ 20. $\begin{array}{r} 4 \\ +\ 5 \\ \hline \end{array}$ 21. $\begin{array}{r} 6 \\ +\ 3 \\ \hline \end{array}$

22. $\begin{array}{r} 3 \\ +\ 3 \\ \hline \end{array}$ 23. $\begin{array}{r} 8 \\ +\ 0 \\ \hline \end{array}$ 24. $\begin{array}{r} 7 \\ +\ 1 \\ \hline \end{array}$ 25. $\begin{array}{r} 5 \\ +\ 5 \\ \hline \end{array}$ 26. $\begin{array}{r} 4 \\ +\ 3 \\ \hline \end{array}$ 27. $\begin{array}{r} 1 \\ +\ 5 \\ \hline \end{array}$ 28. $\begin{array}{r} 7 \\ +\ 3 \\ \hline \end{array}$

29. $7 + 2$ 30. $5 + 1$ 31. $2 + 5$ 32. $3 + 6$

33. $2 + 3$ 34. $2 + 6$ 35. $1 + 3$ 36. $4 + 4$

Find the sum for each pair of addends.

37.

5 4

38.
3 7

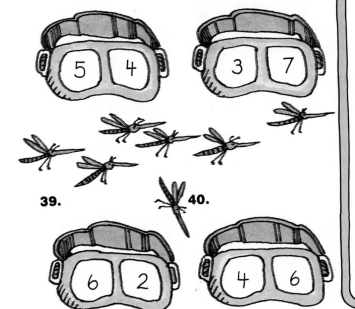

39.
6 2

40.
4 6

THINK

Patterns

Write as many more sums as you can.

Sums of 8

$\begin{array}{r} 0 \\ +\ 8 \\ \hline 8 \end{array}$ $\begin{array}{r} 1 \\ +\ 7 \\ \hline 8 \end{array}$ $\begin{array}{r} 2 \\ +\ 6 \\ \hline 8 \end{array}$ $\begin{array}{r} 3 \\ +\ 5 \\ \hline 8 \end{array} \cdots$

Sums of 9

$\begin{array}{r} 0 \\ +\ 9 \\ \hline 9 \end{array}$ $\begin{array}{r} 1 \\ +\ 8 \\ \hline 9 \end{array}$ $\begin{array}{r} 2 \\ +\ 7 \\ \hline 9 \end{array}$ $\begin{array}{r} 3 \\ +\ 6 \\ \hline 9 \end{array} \cdots$

MATH

Differences Through 10

How many carrots are left?

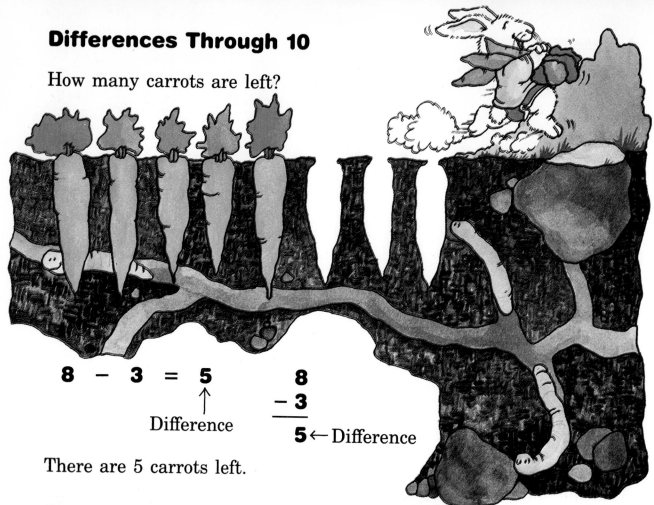

$$8 - 3 = 5$$

↑
Difference

$$\begin{array}{r} 8 \\ -3 \\ \hline 5 \end{array} \leftarrow \text{Difference}$$

There are 5 carrots left.

Warm Up Subtract.

1. $\begin{array}{r} 5 \\ -2 \\ \hline \end{array}$

2. $\begin{array}{r} 10 \\ -2 \\ \hline \end{array}$

Read each number sentence aloud and give the difference.

Example We read $9 - 4 = 5$ as **"Nine minus four equal five."**

3. $9 - 3 =$ ___   4. $3 - 1 =$ ___   5. $8 - 4 =$ ___   6. $10 - 8 =$ ___

7. $2 - 2 =$ ___   8. $8 - 6 =$ ___   9. $10 - 4 =$ ___   10. $7 - 3 =$ ___

11. $5 - 5 =$ ___   12. $9 - 7 =$ ___   13. $5 - 1 =$ ___   14. $4 - 2 =$ ___

15. $4 - 1 =$ ___   16. $7 - 5 =$ ___   17. $10 - 2 =$ ___   18. $9 - 5 =$ ___

19. $8 - 2 =$ ___   20. $10 - 9 =$ ___   21. $9 - 1 =$ ___   22. $6 - 3 =$ ___

Subtract.

1. 5 − 3	**2.** 9 − 3	**3.** 10 − 3	**4.** 4 − 2	**5.** 7 − 3	**6.** 10 − 5	**7.** 8 − 6
8. 6 − 2	**9.** 9 − 7	**10.** 7 − 4	**11.** 10 − 1	**12.** 8 − 3	**13.** 9 − 6	**14.** 6 − 3
15. 8 − 5	**16.** 10 − 7	**17.** 9 − 9	**18.** 7 − 2	**19.** 9 − 4	**20.** 10 − 8	**21.** 8 − 7
22. 10 − 2	**23.** 5 − 5	**24.** 9 − 2	**25.** 8 − 4	**26.** 6 − 4	**27.** 10 − 0	**28.** 4 − 3

29. 10 − 9   **30.** 6 − 1   **31.** 8 − 2   **32.** 9 − 8

33. 7 − 5   **34.** 8 − 8   **35.** 10 − 4   **36.** 6 − 0

Find the difference for each pair of numbers.

37.

38.

39.

40.

THINK

Logical Reasoning

There are 7 rabbits altogether.
How many rabbits are inside the house?

➤ MATH ◄

Sums Through 18

How many toys are there in all?

8 + 5 = 13

THINK
8 and 5
10 and 3

There are 13 toys in all.

Warm Up   Give each sum.

1.   9   🍞🍞🍞🍞🍞🍞🍞🍞🍞
    + 5   🍞🍞🍞🍞🍞

2.   8   🍞🍞🍞🍞🍞🍞🍞🍞
    + 4   🍞🍞🍞🍞

Give each sum aloud.

3. 8 + 3 = ___   **4.** 9 + 4 = ___   **5.** 9 + 3 = ___   **6.** 6 + 5 = ___

7. 4 + 8 = ___   **8.** 4 + 7 = ___   **9.** 7 + 5 = ___   **10.** 9 + 6 = ___

11. 5 + 8 = ___   **12.** 8 + 8 = ___   **13.** 5 + 9 = ___   **14.** 3 + 8 = ___

15. 9 + 2 = ___   **16.** 4 + 9 = ___   **17.** 7 + 4 = ___   **18.** 7 + 9 = ___

19. 7 + 6 = ___   **20.** 3 + 9 = ___   **21.** 5 + 7 = ___   **22.** 5 + 6 = ___

Add.

1. 4 + 9	**2.** 7 + 9	**3.** 2 + 9	**4.** 8 + 9	**5.** 7 + 7	**6.** 5 + 9	**7.** 7 + 5
8. 4 + 8	**9.** 8 + 6	**10.** 6 + 7	**11.** 3 + 9	**12.** 3 + 8	**13.** 9 + 6	**14.** 7 + 4
15. 6 + 6	**16.** 5 + 6	**17.** 9 + 4	**18.** 7 + 8	**19.** 9 + 9	**20.** 4 + 7	**21.** 8 + 5
22. 5 + 7	**23.** 9 + 8	**24.** 9 + 5	**25.** 7 + 6	**26.** 9 + 2	**27.** 9 + 7	**28.** 9 + 3

29. 6 + 9   **30.** 8 + 4   **31.** 8 + 8   **32.** 5 + 8

33. 6 + 8   **34.** 8 + 3   **35.** 3 + 9   **36.** 4 + 7

SKILLKEEPER

Add or subtract.

1. 5 − 2	**2.** 8 + 1	**3.** 4 + 3	**4.** 10 − 6	**5.** 7 + 2	**6.** 9 − 0
7. 8 − 5	**8.** 6 + 4	**9.** 2 + 3	**10.** 1 + 0	**11.** 10 − 8	**12.** 7 − 6

Differences Through 18

How many grapes are left
in the bunch?

THINK
12 in all
3 taken away

$12 - 3 = 9$

There are 9 grapes left in the bunch.

Warm Up   Give each difference.

1. $\begin{array}{r} 11 \\ -\ 4 \\ \hline \end{array}$ 2. $\begin{array}{r} 13 \\ -\ 5 \\ \hline \end{array}$ 3. $\begin{array}{r} 14 \\ -\ 8 \\ \hline \end{array}$

Give each difference aloud.

4. $15 - 7 =$ ___   5. $12 - 8 =$ ___   6. $13 - 9 =$ ___   7. $14 - 8 =$ ___

8. $10 - 7 =$ ___   9. $16 - 8 =$ ___   10. $11 - 7 =$ ___   11. $13 - 5 =$ ___

12. $7 - 0 =$ ___   13. $9 - 5 =$ ___   14. $11 - 5 =$ ___   15. $17 - 8 =$ ___

16. $11 - 3 =$ ___   17. $14 - 6 =$ ___   18. $11 - 9 =$ ___   19. $13 - 7 =$ ___

20. $8 - 8 =$ ___   21. $12 - 9 =$ ___   22. $14 - 9 =$ ___   23. $16 - 7 =$ ___

8   (eight)

Subtract.

1. 14 − 9	**2.** 11 − 5	**3.** 17 − 8	**4.** 13 − 5	**5.** 12 − 4	**6.** 11 − 6
7. 15 − 9	**8.** 12 − 5	**9.** 18 − 9	**10.** 14 − 5	**11.** 11 − 3	**12.** 15 − 6
13. 13 − 6	**14.** 12 − 7	**15.** 16 − 8	**16.** 11 − 9	**17.** 13 − 8	**18.** 14 − 8
19. 12 − 3	**20.** 11 − 7	**21.** 13 − 9	**22.** 15 − 7	**23.** 12 − 8	**24.** 14 − 7

25. 14 − 6   **26.** 17 − 9   **27.** 11 − 4   **28.** 15 − 8

29. 13 − 4   **30.** 11 − 3   **31.** 12 − 6   **32.** 16 − 8

Find the difference for each pair of numbers.

33.

34.

35.

36.

37.

38.

THINK

A Strategy Game

1. Each player writes the numbers 2 through 12.
2. In turn, each player tosses two cubes numbered 1 through 6.
3. Add the top numbers.
4. Cross out your sum or any numbers that add up to your sum.
5. Continue until you cannot cross out a number.
6. The player with the most crossed out numbers wins.

MATH

Fact Families

$$7 + 6 = 13$$

Because I know this fact, I know another addition fact and two subtraction facts.

Fact Family

$$7 + 6 = 13$$
$$6 + 7 = 13$$
$$13 - 6 = 7$$
$$13 - 7 = 6$$

Warm Up Solve.

1.

13

8   5

Fact-Family
Numbers

$8 + 5 =$ ___

$5 + 8 =$ ___

$13 - 5 =$ ___

$13 - 8 =$ ___

2.

16

9   7

Fact-Family
Numbers

$9 + 7 =$ ___

$7 + 9 =$ ___

$16 - 7 =$ ___

$16 - 9 =$ ___

3.

14

5   9

Fact-Family
Numbers

$5 + 9 =$ ___

$9 + 5 =$ ___

$14 - 9 =$ ___

$14 - 5 =$ ___

4.

15

8   7

Fact-Family Numbers

$$\begin{array}{r} 8 \\ + 7 \\ \hline \end{array} \qquad \begin{array}{r} 7 \\ + 8 \\ \hline \end{array}$$

$$\begin{array}{r} 15 \\ - 7 \\ \hline \end{array} \qquad \begin{array}{r} 15 \\ - 8 \\ \hline \end{array}$$

5.

12

3   9

Fact-Family Numbers

$$\begin{array}{r} 3 \\ + 9 \\ \hline \end{array} \qquad \begin{array}{r} 9 \\ + 3 \\ \hline \end{array}$$

$$\begin{array}{r} 12 \\ - 9 \\ \hline \end{array} \qquad \begin{array}{r} 12 \\ - 3 \\ \hline \end{array}$$

Find the sums and differences.

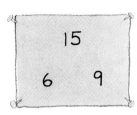

1.

15

6   9

```
   6        9
 + 9      + 6
```

```
  15       15
 - 9      - 6
```

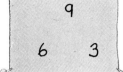

2.

9

6   3

```
   6        3
 + 3      + 6
```

```
   9        9
 - 6      - 3
```

3.
```
   7
 + 5
```

4.
```
   4
 + 6
```

5.
```
   7
 + 7
```

6.
```
   3
 + 5
```

7.
```
   4
 + 9
```

8.
```
   7
 + 4
```

9.
```
  12
 - 5
```

10.
```
  10
 - 6
```

11.
```
  14
 - 7
```

12.
```
   8
 - 5
```

13.
```
  13
 - 9
```

14.
```
  11
 - 4
```

★ Write four number sentences for each set of fact-family numbers.

15.

11

8   3

16.

17

9   8

THINK

Logical Reasoning

I'm the smallest number in my family. The other two numbers are 13 and 9.
WHO AM I?

MATH

Practice the Facts

Add.

1. 8 + 7	**2.** 4 + 9	**3.** 8 + 8	**4.** 3 + 9	**5.** 9 + 5	**6.** 7 + 5	**7.** 8 + 9
8. 6 + 8	**9.** 6 + 6	**10.** 9 + 6	**11.** 9 + 2	**12.** 5 + 8	**13.** 8 + 4	**14.** 7 + 8
15. 7 + 7	**16.** 9 + 9	**17.** 6 + 9	**18.** 6 + 7	**19.** 9 + 8	**20.** 8 + 5	**21.** 8 + 3
22. 7 + 4	**23.** 7 + 9	**24.** 9 + 4	**25.** 8 + 6	**26.** 6 + 5	**27.** 5 + 9	**28.** 9 + 3

Subtract.

29. 11 − 2	**30.** 15 − 7	**31.** 11 − 5	**32.** 18 − 9	**33.** 14 − 6	**34.** 17 − 8
35. 12 − 4	**36.** 14 − 9	**37.** 16 − 7	**38.** 11 − 8	**39.** 12 − 3	**40.** 13 − 8
41. 15 − 8	**42.** 12 − 7	**43.** 12 − 5	**44.** 16 − 8	**45.** 14 − 8	**46.** 13 − 5
47. 15 − 9	**48.** 11 − 4	**49.** 13 − 4	**50.** 13 − 7	**51.** 14 − 5	**52.** 16 − 9

Add or subtract.

1. $\begin{array}{r} 4 \\ + 7 \\ \hline \end{array}$
2. $\begin{array}{r} 5 \\ + 7 \\ \hline \end{array}$
3. $\begin{array}{r} 11 \\ - 5 \\ \hline \end{array}$
4. $\begin{array}{r} 15 \\ - 7 \\ \hline \end{array}$
5. $\begin{array}{r} 9 \\ + 7 \\ \hline \end{array}$
6. $\begin{array}{r} 14 \\ - 5 \\ \hline \end{array}$

7. $\begin{array}{r} 12 \\ - 4 \\ \hline \end{array}$
8. $\begin{array}{r} 8 \\ + 6 \\ \hline \end{array}$
9. $\begin{array}{r} 9 \\ + 5 \\ \hline \end{array}$
10. $\begin{array}{r} 16 \\ - 7 \\ \hline \end{array}$
11. $\begin{array}{r} 9 \\ + 4 \\ \hline \end{array}$
12. $\begin{array}{r} 13 \\ - 6 \\ \hline \end{array}$

13. $\begin{array}{r} 6 \\ + 5 \\ \hline \end{array}$
14. $\begin{array}{r} 5 \\ + 8 \\ \hline \end{array}$
15. $\begin{array}{r} 11 \\ - 7 \\ \hline \end{array}$
16. $\begin{array}{r} 14 \\ - 7 \\ \hline \end{array}$
17. $\begin{array}{r} 3 \\ + 9 \\ \hline \end{array}$
18. $\begin{array}{r} 7 \\ + 6 \\ \hline \end{array}$

19. $\begin{array}{r} 13 \\ - 4 \\ \hline \end{array}$
20. $\begin{array}{r} 3 \\ + 8 \\ \hline \end{array}$
21. $\begin{array}{r} 12 \\ - 7 \\ \hline \end{array}$
22. $\begin{array}{r} 11 \\ - 8 \\ \hline \end{array}$
23. $\begin{array}{r} 8 \\ + 7 \\ \hline \end{array}$
24. $\begin{array}{r} 12 \\ - 9 \\ \hline \end{array}$

25. $13 - 5$ 26. $9 + 8$ 27. $9 + 9$ 28. $16 - 8$

29. $9 + 5$ 30. $9 + 6$ 31. $12 - 3$ 32. $13 - 5$

33. $14 - 6$ 34. $6 + 6$ 35. $16 - 7$ 36. $7 + 5$

THINK

Patterns

Guess each rule. Then give the missing numbers.

Gina said	Mike answered
4	13
6	15
2	11
1. 9	▦
2. ▦	14

Mike said	Gina answered
8	1
7	0
10	3
3. 9	▦
4. ▦	6

Gina said	Mike answered
1	2
2	4
3	6
4	8
5. 5	▦

MATH

PROBLEM SOLVING ⭐ The **5**-Point Checklist

To solve a problem
⭐ 1. **Understand the Question**
⭐ 2. **Find the needed Data**
⭐ 3. **Plan what to do**
⭐ 4. **Find the Answer**
⭐ 5. **Check back**

QUESTION
DATA
PLAN
ANSWER
CHECK

Use the 5-Point Checklist to help you solve the following problem.

Sally took 8 pictures at the park.
She took 7 more pictures at the beach.
How many pictures did Sally take?

1. Understand the QUESTION
What is the total number of pictures?

2. Find the needed DATA
Park: 8 pictures   Beach: 7 pictures

3. PLAN what to do
We want the total number.
We should add.

4. Find the ANSWER
$8 + 7 = 15$ Sally took 15 pictures.

5. CHECK back
Read the problem again.
15 seems about right.

Solve. Use the 5-Point Checklist.

1. Sally put some pictures in a book. She put 6 on one page and 8 on another. How many pictures are on both pages?

2. Only 13 of Sally's pictures were good. She gave 5 of them to friends. How many does she have left?

Solve.

1. Tom took 9 pictures of his friends. He took 8 more of his family. How many pictures did Tom take in all?

2. Betty has 6 pictures of her brother. She has 7 pictures of her sister. How many does she have of both of them?

3. Yuri had 14 animal pictures. He lost 6 of them. How many animal pictures does Yuri have left?

4. Kay had 17 pictures in her picture book. She took 8 of them to school. How many did she leave in the book?

5. Dan took 5 pictures of his dog to school. He left 8 more of them at home. How many pictures of his dog does Dan have?

6. Maria bought a roll of film for 16 pictures. She has taken 8 of them. How many does she have left to take?

7. Dom sent these pictures to his grandmother: 4 of himself and 5 of the whole family. How many did he send?

8. Carla had 12 pictures of a family party. She sent 4 of them to her uncle Joe. How many does she have left?

Three Addends

Maria put 4 small striped fish in the tank. Ben put 5 small goldfish in the tank. Rita put 3 large goldfish in the tank. How many fish are now in the tank?

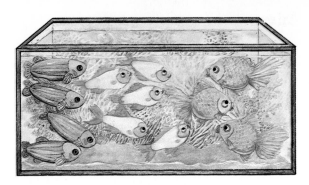

(4 + 5) + 3   **4 + (5 + 3)**

9 + 3 = 12   **4 + 8 = 12**

↑ Small fish   ↑ Large fish   ↑ Fish in all   ↑ Striped fish   ↑ Goldfish   ↑ Fish in all

12 fish are in the tank.

When you add, you can change the grouping and get the same sum.

Other Examples

3 + 4 = 7 and 2 more make 9

3 + 4 + 2 = _9_

4 + 2 = 6
3 + 6 = 9

3 + 4 + 2 = _9_

Adding down

5
2
+ 4
———
11

7 and 4 more make 11

Adding up

5
2
4
+
———
11

6 and 5 more make 11

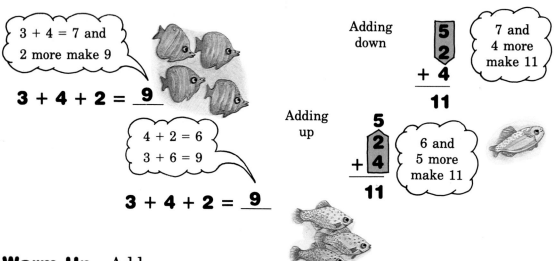

Warm Up   Add.

1. $6 + 2 + 4 =$ ___   **2.** $3 + 5 + 2 =$ ___   **3.** $2 + 7 + 3 =$ ___

4. 6   **5.** 1   **6.** 5   **7.** 8   **8.** 3   **9.** 5   **10.** 4
    3   7   2   1   7   4   1
 + 2   + 2   + 4   + 1   + 2   + 5   + 3

Add.

1. 2
   3
  +1

2. 5
   1
  +6

3. 2
   3
  +2

4. 4
   2
  +3

5. 5
   3
  +2

6. 2
   5
  +3

7. 6
   2
  +1

8. 7
   1
  +4

9. 6
   3
  +5

10. 2
    8
   +1

11. 3
    4
   +3

12. 4
    5
   +3

13. 8
    2
   +4

14. 7
    2
   +3

15. 6
    3
   +5

16. 3
    6
   +2

17. 4
    5
   +4

18. 6
    1
   +4

19. 5
    2
   +5

20. 8
    2
   +8

21. 8
    1
   +6

22. 3
    7
   +2

23. 3
    3
   +3

24. 4
    2
   +6

25. $2 + 7 + 2$

26. $5 + 5 + 4$

27. $3 + 7 + 1$

28. $5 + 3 + 4$

29. $8 + 2 + 7$

30. $4 + 4 + 6$

31. $3 + 7 + 2$

32. $2 + 3 + 5$

33. $5 + 3 + 5$

34. $4 + 2 + 5$

35. $6 + 1 + 8$

36. $7 + 3 + 5$

SKILLKEEPER

Add.

1. 8
  +3

2. 6
  +9

3. 9
  +8

4. 7
  +6

5. 8
  +7

6. 4
  +4

7. 5
  +2

8. 1
  +7

9. 4
  +9

10. 5
   +8

11. 6
   +5

12. 8
   +4

PROBLEM SOLVING
Understanding the Question

Short story problems let you think mostly about the **question.**

Solve.

1. Music:
   6 old songs
   4 new songs
   How many songs
   are there?

2. Spelling:
   10 words
   Missed 2
   How many
   were right?

3. Reading:
   Red book—8 pages
   Blue book—7 pages
   How many pages
   are in both?

4. Lunch:
   12 children at a table
   3 left the table
   How many are
   still there?

5. Recess:
   8 large swings
   4 small swings
   How many swings
   are there?

6. Math:
   12 problems
   9 right
   How many were
   missed?

7. Game:
   4 players on Team A
   5 players on Team B
   4 players on Team C
   How many are there
   in all?

8. Science:
   13 white mice
   4 got away
   How many
   are left?

PROBLEM SOLVING
Using Data from a Picture

Use the data in the pictures to solve these problems.

1. How many shells did Sally and Sam find together?

Ted

2. Pam gave 5 of her shells to a friend. How many does she have left?

Pam

3. Al broke 2 of his shells. How many does he have now?

Sally

4. Sally and Jane put their shells together. How many did they have then?

Sam

5. Ted lost 4 of his shells. How many does he have now?

Al

6. Sam found 5 more shells. How many does he have now?

Jane

PROBLEM SOLVING
Choose the Operations

There are 4 frogs in a pond.
7 ladybugs are on a limb.

How many animals is this in all?

PUT TOGETHER

7 + 4 = 11

Each frog ate a bug.
How many bugs were left?

How many more bugs
are there than frogs?

TAKE AWAY

7 − 4 = 3

COMPARE

7 − 4 = 3

▷ PUT TOGETHER ⟶ Choose addition.
▷ TAKE AWAY ⟶ Choose subtraction.
▷ COMPARE (more or fewer) ⟶ Choose subtraction.

Solve.

1. There were 12 birds in a
   tree. 9 of the birds flew
   away. How many of the birds
   were still in the tree?

2. There are 7 bugs on a leaf.
   There are 8 more on another
   leaf. How many bugs are on
   the two leaves?

3. There are 15 fish in the
   pond. 6 turtles are in the
   pond. How many more fish
   are there than turtles?

4. There are 14 tadpoles in the
   pond. 5 frogs are on the
   bank. How many fewer frogs
   are there than tadpoles?

CHAPTER REVIEW/TEST

Find the sum or difference.

1.	2.	3.	4.	5.	6.	7.
4 + 5	3 + 2	6 − 3	5 + 3	2 − 1	8 − 4	2 + 7

8.	9.	10.	11.	12.	13.	14.
2 + 8	7 − 3	4 − 3	3 + 4	5 − 2	6 + 2	7 − 5

Add or subtract.

15.	16.	17.	18.	19.	20.	21.
7 + 5	7 + 7	12 − 3	11 − 7	12 − 4	9 + 6	8 + 5

22.	23.	24.	25.	26.	27.	28.
15 − 7	7 + 6	14 − 8	9 + 9	13 − 9	7 + 9	17 − 8

Find the sums.

29.	30.	31.	32.	33.
4 2 + 4	6 2 + 4	3 2 + 3	5 2 + 3	7 1 + 4

Solve.

34. Anita took 12 pictures of her kitten. She gave 4 of them away. How many did she keep?

35. Ted has 5 pictures of his dog. He has 9 pictures of his cat. How many pictures does Ted have?

36. Jan found 8 shells. Jo found 7 shells. They put them together. How many did they have then?

37. There were 14 ducks on the pond. 8 frogs were in the pond. How many more ducks were there than frogs?

ANOTHER LOOK

$$\begin{array}{r} 8 \\ +\ 3 \\ \hline 11 \end{array}$$

Start with **8**.

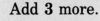

Add **3** more.

Get **11** in all.

Find the sums.

1. $\begin{array}{r} 7 \\ +\ 5 \\ \hline \end{array}$ **2.** $\begin{array}{r} 6 \\ +\ 8 \\ \hline \end{array}$ **3.** $\begin{array}{r} 5 \\ +\ 3 \\ \hline \end{array}$

4. $\begin{array}{r} 7 \\ +\ 9 \\ \hline \end{array}$ **5.** $\begin{array}{r} 4 \\ +\ 3 \\ \hline \end{array}$ **6.** $\begin{array}{r} 7 \\ +\ 6 \\ \hline \end{array}$

$$\begin{array}{r} 12 \\ -\ 5 \\ \hline 7 \end{array}$$

Start with **12**.

Take away **5**.
7 are left.

Find the differences.

7. $\begin{array}{r} 11 \\ -\ 7 \\ \hline \end{array}$ **8.** $\begin{array}{r} 16 \\ -\ 8 \\ \hline \end{array}$ **9.** $\begin{array}{r} 7 \\ -\ 5 \\ \hline \end{array}$

10. $\begin{array}{r} 8 \\ -\ 3 \\ \hline \end{array}$ **11.** $\begin{array}{r} 13 \\ -\ 8 \\ \hline \end{array}$ **12.** $\begin{array}{r} 10 \\ -\ 4 \\ \hline \end{array}$

$6 + 2 = 8$
and 3 more
make 11.

$$\begin{array}{r} 6 \\ 2 \\ +\ 3 \\ \hline 11 \end{array}$$

Find the sums.

13. $\begin{array}{r} 5 \\ 1 \\ +\ 3 \\ \hline \end{array}$ **14.** $\begin{array}{r} 6 \\ 4 \\ +\ 2 \\ \hline \end{array}$ **15.** $\begin{array}{r} 3 \\ 5 \\ +\ 2 \\ \hline \end{array}$

16. $\begin{array}{r} 5 \\ 3 \\ +\ 6 \\ \hline \end{array}$ **17.** $\begin{array}{r} 5 \\ 4 \\ +\ 5 \\ \hline \end{array}$ **18.** $\begin{array}{r} 4 \\ 5 \\ +\ 3 \\ \hline \end{array}$

Logical Reasoning

Try a game of Nim with a friend.

1. Start with 11 counters.

2. When it is your turn, you must pick up 1, 2, or 3 counters.

3. To win, make your friend have to pick up the last counter.

Hints for Reasoning

1. It is your turn. There are 2 counters left. How can you be sure to win?

2. It is your turn. There are 4 counters left. How can you be sure to win?

3. It is your turn. There are 6 counters left. How can you be sure to win?

Give the letter for the correct answer.

1. $2 + 4 = $ _____
- **A** 2
- **B** 8
- **C** 6
- **D** not given

2. $5 + 3 = $ _____
- **A** 6
- **B** 8
- **C** 2
- **D** not given

3. $9 - 4 = $ _____
- **A** 6
- **B** 13
- **C** 5
- **D** not given

4. $4 + 4 = $ _____
- **A** 0
- **B** 9
- **C** 8
- **D** not given

5. $6 - 5 = $ _____
- **A** 2
- **B** 1
- **C** 11
- **D** not given

6. $8 + 1 = $ _____
- **A** 6
- **B** 7
- **C** 8
- **D** not given

7. $\begin{array}{r} 3 \\ + 3 \\ \hline \end{array}$
- **A** 0
- **B** 3
- **C** 6
- **D** not given

8. $\begin{array}{r} 10 \\ - 5 \\ \hline \end{array}$
- **A** 5
- **B** 15
- **C** 6
- **D** not given

9. $\begin{array}{r} 3 \\ + 2 \\ \hline \end{array}$
- **A** 1
- **B** 5
- **C** 7
- **D** not given

10. $\begin{array}{r} 8 \\ + 0 \\ \hline \end{array}$
- **A** 0
- **B** 16
- **C** 8
- **D** not given

11. $\begin{array}{r} 2 \\ - 1 \\ \hline \end{array}$
- **A** 3
- **B** 1
- **C** 2
- **D** not given

12. $\begin{array}{r} 5 \\ - 0 \\ \hline \end{array}$
- **A** 10
- **B** 0
- **C** 5
- **D** not given

13. Amy had 7 stamps. She used 5. How many were left?
- **A** 12
- **B** 7
- **C** 2
- **D** not given

14. Jim caught 3 fish. Then he caught 1 more. How many fish did he catch?
- **A** 3
- **B** 4
- **C** 2
- **D** not given

Josh was once in a book-reading contest called a "Read-A-Thon." He asked people to give money for each book he read. In thirty-one days Josh read twenty-three books. Josh's mother gave seventy-five cents for each book he read. His neighbor gave fifteen cents for each book. The money went to help people who have multiple sclerosis.

Tens and Ones

Jeff is gluing ten cubes together. He is showing that ten ones equal **one ten.**

 ⟶

ten ones   **one ten (10)**

0, 1, 2, 3, 4, 5, 6, 7, 8, and 9 are called **digits.** We use digits and **place value** to write larger numbers.

Examples

2 tens and **3 ones = 23**
We read, "**twenty-three.**"

3 tens and **5 ones = 35**
We read, "**thirty-five.**"

Warm Up   Give the number for each picture.

1.

2 tens and 4 ones = ____

2.

4 tens and 1 one = ____

3.

4.

Write the number for each picture.

1.   **2.**

Write the number. Be careful!

3. 6 tens and 8 ones   **4.** 4 tens and 0 ones

5. 3 ones and 1 ten   **6.** 9 tens and 7 ones

7. 3 ones and 7 tens   **8.** 1 ten and 0 ones

9. 5 ones and 2 tens   **10.** 2 ones and 6 tens

Write the number.

11. twenty-three   **12.** thirty-six   **13.** seventy-five

14. ninety-two   **15.** eighty   **16.** fifty-one

17. seventeen   **18.** forty-eight   **19.** thirteen

20. sixty-seven   **21.** twelve   **22.** eighty-four

23. forty-one   **24.** sixty-six   **25.** nineteen

THINK

Place Value

1. Guess how many cubes are in the picture.

2. Check your guess *without counting higher than ten.*

Hint: How many tens could you make?

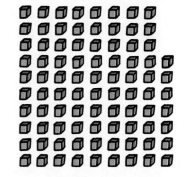

MATH

Hundreds, Tens, and Ones

Jean is gluing blocks together to show that ten tens are equal to **one hundred.**

ten tens	one hundred (100)

We use hundreds, tens, and ones to write larger numbers.

Examples

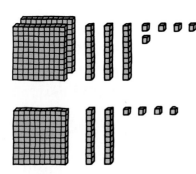

2 hundreds, 3 tens, and 5 ones = **235**
We read, **"two hundred thirty-five."**

1 hundred, 2 tens, and 4 ones = **124**
We read, **"one hundred twenty-four."**

Warm Up   Give the number for each picture.

1.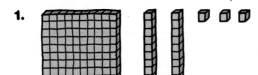

2.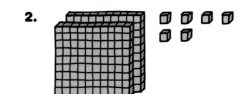

3.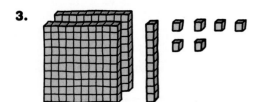

4.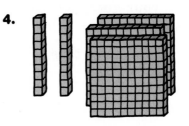

Write the number.

Example

Hundreds	Tens	Ones
3	4	8

Answer   348

1.

Hundreds	Tens	Ones
3	2	4

2.

Hundreds	Tens	Ones
5	9	1

3.

Hundreds	Tens	Ones
2	0	7

4.

Hundreds	Tens	Ones
6	4	7

5.

Hundreds	Tens	Ones
1	2	5

6.

Hundreds	Tens	Ones
4	0	7

7.

Hundreds	Tens	Ones
5	3	0

8.

Hundreds	Tens	Ones
6	0	0

9.

Hundreds	Tens	Ones
7	5	3

10.

Hundreds	Tens	Ones
8	0	4

11.

Hundreds	Tens	Ones
2	6	0

12.

Hundreds	Tens	Ones
9	4	1

13. 6 tens
2 ones
7 hundreds

14. 4 hundreds
0 ones
2 tens

15. 5 ones
3 hundreds
9 tens

16. 7 ones
0 tens
6 hundreds

17. five hundred sixty-seven

18. three hundred twenty-nine

19. nine hundred forty-one

20. six hundred eighty

21. two hundred five

22. four hundred

THINK

Patterns

Make a copy of this figure.
Put the numbers 1, 2, 3, 4, 5,
and 6 in the circles so that
the sum along each line is 14.
Use each number only once.

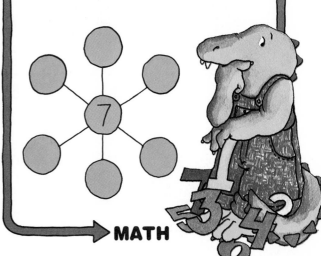

MATH

(twenty-nine) **29**

Counting and Order

Numbers have an order. The pages of a book are numbered. This gives an order to the pages. Page 48 comes **before** page 49. Page 50 comes **after** page 49.

A number line shows the order of numbers.

5   6   7   8   9   10   11   12

45   46   47   48   49   50   51   52

695   696   697   698   699   700   701   702

Warm Up   Give the next four numbers.

1.   13   14   15   16   17   18   19

2.   71   72   73   74   75   76   77

3.   91   92   93   94   95   96   97

4.   392   393   394   395   396   397   398

Write the number of the "next" page.

1.

2.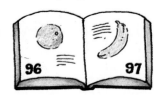

3.

4.

5.

6.

Write the number that comes after.

7. 37   **8.** 58   **9.** 79   **10.** 90   **11.** 19   **12.** 39

13. 126   **14.** 129   **15.** 350   **16.** 499   **17.** 659   **18.** 399

Give the number that comes before.

19. 23   **20.** 41   **21.** 50   **22.** 69   **23.** 70   **24.** 40

25. 134   **26.** 130   **27.** 151   **28.** 670   **29.** 500   **30.** 380

★ Write the number that is between.

31. 329 and 331   **32.** 209 and 211   **33.** 619 and 621

34. 729 and 731   **35.** 846 and 848   **36.** 499 and 501

Skip Counting

Skip count by 2s beginning with 0. You get the even numbers.

Skip count by 2s beginning with 1. You get the odd numbers.

Skip count by 5s beginning with 0. You get numbers that end in 0 or 5.   0, 5, 10, 15, 20, 25, 30, . . .

Count by twos.

1. Begin at 20. Stop at 30.

2. Begin at 41. Stop at 51.

3. Begin at 85. Stop at 95.

Count by fives.

4. Begin at 30. Stop at 80.

5. Begin at 100. Stop at 150.

6. Begin at 210. Stop at 260.

Is the number even or odd?

7. 68   8. 75   9. 39   10. 124   11. 357   12. 1,283

Count by tens. Give the next four numbers.

13. 40, 50, 60, ▥, ▥, ▥, ▥   14. 230, 240, 250, 260, ▥, ▥, ▥, ▥

More Practice, page 365, Set C

Counting Money

penny	nickel	dime	quarter	half dollar
1 cent	5 cents	10 cents	25 cents	50 cents
1¢	5¢	10¢	25¢	50¢

Skip counting can help you count money.

Example

Lay out these coins.

Skip Count.

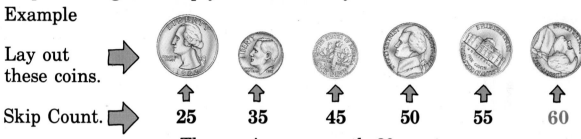

| 25 | 35 | 45 | 50 | 55 | 60 |

These coins are worth **60 cents.**

Give the value of each set of coins.

1.

2.

3.

4.

5.

6.

7.

8.

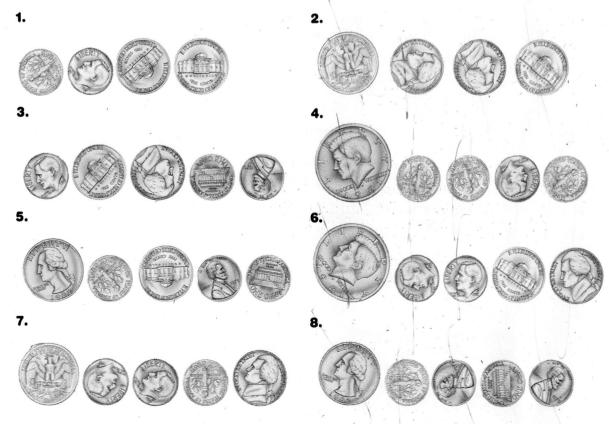

Counting Change

Tina bought a birthday card for 37¢. She gave the clerk 50¢. The clerk counted out her change. He started with the cost of the card and stopped at 50¢. Tina counted with him to make sure the change was correct.

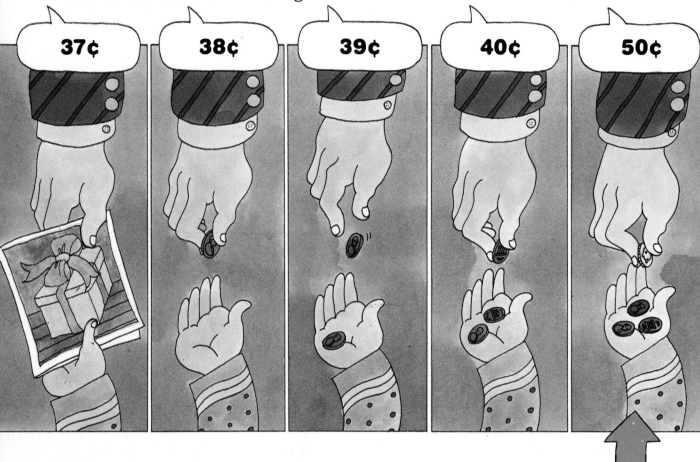

Count the change out loud. Start counting with the cost of the card. Stop with the amount of money handed to the clerk.

Tina's change is correct.

1. Andrea handed the clerk 50¢.

2. Mark handed the clerk $1.00.

Count the change below out loud. Write the numbers the clerk would say.

1. James handed the clerk 50¢.

2. Sue handed the clerk 50¢.

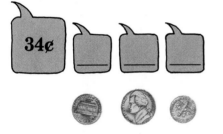

3. Janet handed the clerk 75¢.

4. Sam handed the clerk 75¢.

5. Lisa handed the clerk $1.00.

6. Dana handed the clerk $1.00.

7. Gene handed the clerk $1.00.

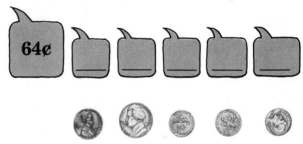

THINK

Logical Reasoning

Marcia handed the clerk $1.00 to buy a card for 74¢. When the clerk counted the change, this is what she said:

| 74¢ | 75¢ | 80¢ | 90¢ | $1.00 |

What coins did she get back in change?

➡ **MATH** ⬅

Dollars and Cents

dollar
100 cents
100¢

dime
10 cents
10¢

penny
1 cent
1¢

3 dollars
300 cents

2 dimes
20 cents

4 pennies
4 cents

324 cents
We write, **$3.24**
We read, **"three dollars and twenty-four cents."**

Other Examples

We write, **$0.32**
We read, **"32 cents."**

We write, **$0.03**
We read, **"3 cents."**

Read each amount aloud.

1. $4.38   2. $9.80   3. $7.98   4. $0.65   5. $2.95   6. $5.00   7. $0.08

8. $3.88   9. $0.75   10. $2.16   11. $7.04   12. $1.00   13. $8.05   14. $2.39

15. $8.01   16. $3.90   17. $0.98   18. $1.69   19. $9.85   20. $6.75   21. $0.01

22. $3.95   23. $0.05   24. $6.00   25. $9.50   26. $0.49   27. $4.87   28. $5.25

The money shows the price of the toy. What amount should be on the price tag?

1.

2.

3.

4.

Write each amount.

5. 2 dollars, 4 dimes, 6 pennies

6. 5 dollars, 7 dimes

7. 4 dollars, 3 pennies

8. 6 dollars

9. 3 dollars and 27 cents

10. 57 cents

11. 5 dollars, 6 dimes, 3 pennies

12. 8 dollars, 2 dimes

13. 2 dollars, 5 pennies

14. 7 dollars and 95 cents

15. 75 cents

More Practice, page 366, Set A

THINK

Place-Value Game

Make two sets of digit cards.

Each player makes a place-value chart.

Hundreds	Tens	Ones

1. Mix the cards and turn them face down.

2. On your turn, draw the top card. Show the digit.

3. Write that digit in any place on your chart.

4. Take turns until each chart is full.

5. The greatest number wins.

MATH

Rounding to the Nearest Ten

We **round** numbers to tell **about** how many. 68 is between 60 and 70.

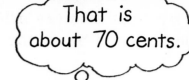

That is about 70 cents.

60 61 62 63 64 65 66 67 68 69 70

68 is nearer 70 than 60.
68 rounded to the nearest 10 is 70.

85 is between 80 and 90.

80 81 82 83 84 85 86 87 88 89 90

When a number is halfway between, round to the larger number.

85 rounded to the nearest 10 is 90.

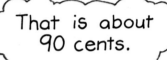

That is about 90 cents.

Warm Up Where is the number? Use the number line.

Example   53 is between ||||| and |||||.

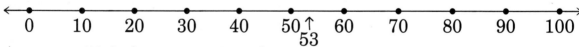

0   10   20   30   40   50↑   60   70   80   90   100
                           53

Answer   53 is between 50 and 60.

1. 77 is between ||||| and |||||.   2. 42 is between ||||| and |||||.

3. 63 is between ||||| and |||||.   4. 17 is between ||||| and |||||.

5. 88 is between ||||| and |||||.   6. 49 is between ||||| and |||||.

7. 24 is between ||||| and |||||.   8. 95 is between ||||| and |||||.

9. 31 is between ||||| and |||||.   10. 85 is between ||||| and |||||.

Round to the nearest ten. Which red number is the better choice?

1. 28 → 20 or 30   **2.** 44 → 40 or 50   **3.** 75 → 70 or 80

4. 82 → 80 or 90   **5.** 36 → 30 or 40   **6.** 61 → 60 or 70

7. 77 → 70 or 80   **8.** 25 → 20 or 30   **9.** 54 → 50 or 60

10. 45 → 40 or 50   **11.** 63 → 60 or 70   **12.** 89 → 80 or 90

Round to the nearest ten.

Examples   36 ▯   Answer 40   53 ▯   Answer 50

13. 29 ▯   **14.** 81 ▯   **15.** 36 ▯   **16.** 44 ▯

17. 52 ▯   **18.** 79 ▯   **19.** 67 ▯   **20.** 45 ▯

21. 13 ▯   **22.** 77 ▯   **23.** 24 ▯   **24.** 61 ▯

Give the price to the nearest ten cents.

25.

26.

THINK

Rounding

What numbers can you find for the ▯?

▯ rounded to the nearest ten is 60.

Which two numbers have digits that add to the same sum?

MATH

27.

More about Rounding

Sometimes you want to round to the
nearest hundred.

230 is between 200 and 300

That is about 200 dollars.

230 rounded to the nearest hundred is 200.

Sometimes you want to round
to the nearest dollar.

$2.79 is between $2.00 and $3.00.

$2.79 is nearer to $3.00.

$2.79 rounded to the nearest dollar is $3.00

That is about 3 dollars.

Warm Up   Where is the number? Use the number line.

Example   675 is between ▦ and ▦.

| 100 | 200 | 300 | 400 | 500 | 600 | ↑700 | 800 | 900 | 1,000 |

675

Answer   675 is between 600 and 700.

1. 231 is between ▦ and ▦.

2. 880 is between ▦ and ▦.

3. 524 is between ▦ and ▦.

4. 650 is between ▦ and ▦.

5. 449 is between ▦ and ▦.

6. 362 is between ▦ and ▦.

7. $6.29 is between $▦ and $▦.

8. $4.75 is between $▦ and $▦.

9. $8.98 is between $▦ and $▦.

10. $7.19 is between $▦ and $▦.

11. $6.54 is between $▦ and $▦.

12. $3.48 is between $▦ and $▦.

Round to the nearest hundred or dollar.
Which red number is the better choice?

1. 769→700 or 800   **2.** 427→400 or 500   **3.** 562→500 or 600

4. 850→800 or 900   **5.** 539→500 or 600   **6.** 728→700 or 800

7. $3.98→$3.00 or $4.00   **8.** $4.29→$4.00 or $5.00

9. $6.15→$6.00 or $7.00   **10.** $3.85→$3.00 or $4.00

Round to the nearest hundred.

11. 244 ▓   **12.** 685 ▓   **13.** 437 ▓   **14.** 552 ▓

15. 579 ▓   **16.** 708 ▓   **17.** 650 ▓   **18.** 376 ▓

Round to the nearest dollar.

19. $4.85 $▓   **20.** $9.25 $▓   **21.** $2.37 $▓   **22.** $6.95 $▓

23. $6.48 $▓   **24.** $1.98 $▓   **25.** $4.77 $▓   **26.** $3.29 $▓

27. $5.64 $▓   **28.** $8.13 $▓   **29.** $3.50 $▓   **30.** $7.39 $▓

Give the price to the nearest dollar.

31.

$2.89

32. $5.25

33. $8.39

```
╔══════════ THINK ══════════╗
        Place Value

  These are my digits:    [ 6 ]

  When you round me to
  the nearest hundred,    [ 4 ]
  you get 500.

  WHO AM I?               [ 3 ]

╚════════════ MATH ═════════╝
```

Thousands

Ten, hundred pieces can be glued together to make **one thousand.**

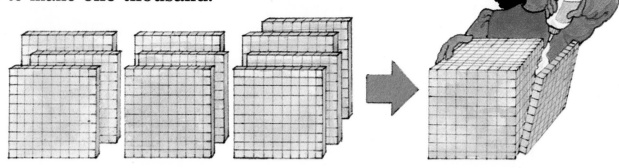

ten hundreds   **one thousand (1,000)**

We use thousands, hundreds, tens, and ones to write larger numbers.

Example

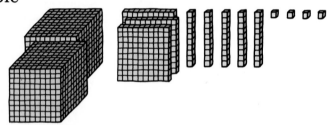

2 thousands, **3** hundreds, **5** tens, and **4** ones = **2,354**
We read, **"two thousand, three hundred fifty-four."**

Warm Up   Read each number aloud.

1. 4,751	2. 2,029	3. 5,846	4. 1,975	5. 6,152
6. 8,010	7. 1,002	8. 3,678	9. 6,027	10. 7,843
11. 8,942	12. 2,000	13. 1,391	14. 5,300	15. 3,012
16. 7,924	17. 8,516	18. 9,406	19. 2,345	20. 6,532
21. 1,058	22. 7,643	23. 9,999	24. 4,251	25. 4,726
26. 5,301	27. 2,640	28. 8,765	29. 5,206	30. 1,001
31. 9,779	32. 8,007	33. 2,443	34. 7,038	35. 5,549

Write the number.

1.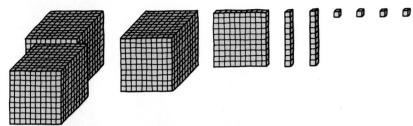

2.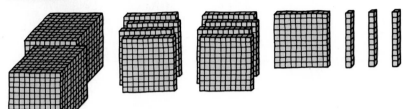

3.

Thousands	Hundreds	Tens	Ones
2	6	8	3

4.

Thousands	Hundreds	Tens	Ones
3	0	9	4

5.

Thousands	Hundreds	Tens	Ones
5	0	7	3

6.

Thousands	Hundreds	Tens	Ones
8	4	0	6

What does the 5 mean in each number? Write
thousands, hundreds, tens, or **ones.**

7. 3,506   **8.** 2,785   **9.** 5,264   **10.** 3,750

11. 4,605   **12.** 2,582

13. 5,807   **14.** 9,562

Write the number.

15. 2 tens   **16.** 5 tens

6 thousands   0 ones

3 ones   0 hundreds

5 hundreds   3 thousands

THINK

Place Value

How many 4-digit
numbers can you
find that have only
0s and 1s?
What are they?

MATH

Comparing Numbers

Which distance is greater?
New York to Washington by air—223 mi.
New York to Washington by road—231 mi.
To find which of two numbers is greater,
you compare them.

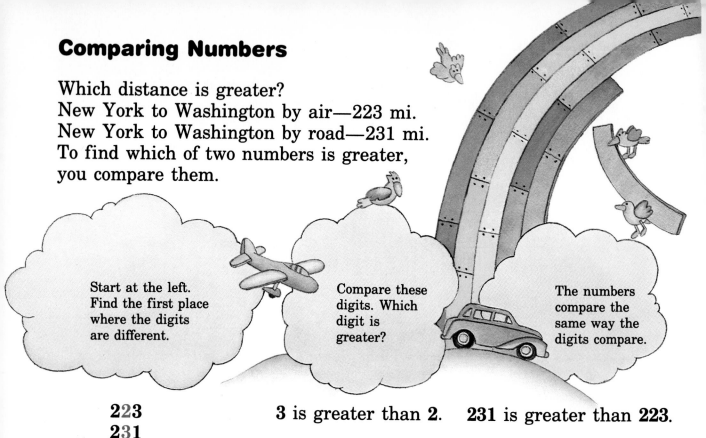

Start at the left.
Find the first place
where the digits
are different.

Compare these
digits. Which
digit is
greater?

The numbers
compare the
same way the
digits compare.

223
231

3 is greater than 2.   231 is greater than 223.

The road distance is greater.

231 is greater than 223.   223 is less than 231.

231 > 223   223 < 231

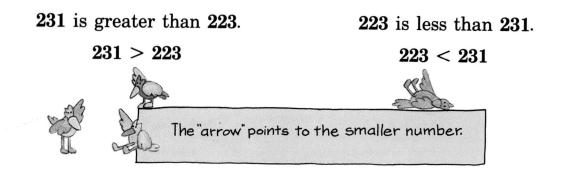

The "arrow" points to the smaller number.

Other Examples   5,236 is less than 5,273.   43 is greater than 39.

5,236 < 5,273   43 > 39

Warm Up   Which of the two numbers is greater?

1. 67   2. 426   3. 692   4. 3,629   5. 5,280   6. 7,268
   63   423   598   3,630   5,340   7,264

Write > or < for each ◍.

1. 8 ◍ 3
2. 7 ◍ 9
3. 20 ◍ 40
4. 60 ◍ 30
5. 300 ◍ 500
6. 700 ◍ 400
7. 900 ◍ 800
8. 3,000 ◍ 2,000
9. 4,000 ◍ 7,000
10. 36 ◍ 38
11. 47 ◍ 37
12. 59 ◍ 62
13. 75 ◍ 68
14. 234 ◍ 236
15. 754 ◍ 750
16. 623 ◍ 643
17. 874 ◍ 774
18. 396 ◍ 412
19. 2,834 ◍ 2,831
20. 4,675 ◍ 4,679
21. 3,260 ◍ 3,250

★ Give the number that is 1,000 more.

22. 3,000
23. 4,765
24. 2,843
25. 6,400
26. 5,628

★ Give the number that is 100 more.

27. 200
28. 428
29. 7,643
30. 2,480
31. 3,657

★ Give the number that is 1,000 less.

32. 3,000
33. 8,432
34. 7,651
35. 3,281
36. 9,467

SKILLKEEPER

Add.

	1.	2.	3.	4.	5.	6.
	2	4	7	1	2	4
	1	3	6	2	5	3
	+ 5	+ 5	+ 3	+ 6	+ 5	+ 3

	7.	8.	9.	10.	11.	12.
	4	3	7	6	8	5
	3	5	1	2	2	3
	+ 6	+ 3	+ 3	+ 2	+ 7	+ 2

More About Thousands

The red digits tell the number of thousands.

   4,000   four thousand
  40,000   forty thousand
400,000   four hundred thousand

Read these numbers aloud.

1. 6,000	**2.** 20,000	**3.** 400,000

1. 6,000   **2.** 20,000   **3.** 400,000

4. 50,000   **5.** 800,000   **6.** 2,000

7. 100,000   **8.** 200,000   **9.** 4,000

Read these numbers aloud.
Example   We read **654,000** as

"six hundred fifty-four thousand."

10. 23,000   **11.** 423,000   **12.** 68,000   **13.** 168,000

14. 480,000   **15.** 327,000   **16.** 562,000   **17.** 34,000

18. 17,000   **19.** 170,000   **20.** 642,000   **21.** 308,000

22. 999,000   **23.** 19,000   **24.** 99,000   **25.** 709,000

Read these numbers aloud.

Example We read **465,281** as

"four hundred sixty-five thousand, two hundred eighty-one."

1. 751,324   2. 28,600   3. 369,070   4. 115,280

5. 37,008   6. 269,095   7. 481,300   8. 7,604

9. 692,000   10. 840,035   11. 31,007   12. 111,224

13. 751,217   14. 684,500   15. 95,090   16. 327,006

17. 816,400   18. 92,328   19. 4,007   20. 300,600

21. 802,325   22. 26,781   23. 384,000   24. 975,617

25. 9,287   26. 384,651   27. 765,567   28. 60,283

Write the number. Use a comma to separate thousands.
Example Write six hundred twelve thousand as 612,000.

29. forty-two thousand, eight hundred eighty

30. forty-two thousand, eight hundred eighty-eight

31. seventy-eight thousand

32. nine thousand, four hundred

33. one hundred twenty thousand

34. fifty-two thousand, ninety

35. fifty-two thousand, nine

36. fifty-two thousand, nineteen

37. seven thousand, sixteen

38. nine hundred ninety thousand

THINK

Patterns

Give the next two numbers in
each column. Read down.

1.	269	2.	4,158
	369		4,257
	469		4,356
	569		4,455
	669		4,554
	769		4,653

 MATH

Ordinal Numbers

We can use numbers to tell order.
The Galaxians are in line for tickets.

TICKETS FOR PLANET EARTH

EARTH SHIP

BEP — first 1st

POL — second 2nd

DIM — third 3rd

SUD — fourth 4th

LOP — fifth 5th

REL — sixth 6th

VAR — seventh 7th

JET — eighth 8th

KEL — ninth 9th

NAC — tenth 10th

Other numbers we use
to tell order are

11th	eleventh
12th	twelfth
13th	thirteenth
14th	fourteenth
15th	fifteenth
16th	sixteenth
⋮	
20th	twentieth
21st	twenty-first
⋮	
30th	thirtieth
31st	thirty-first

Use the pictures on page 48 to answer questions 1–7.

1. Bep is first. Who is last?

2. Where is Dim in line?

3. How many are ahead of Jet?

4. What place is next to last?

5. How many are behind Lop?

Solve.

8. Chris is 12th in line. How many are ahead of him?

9. Terri is 16th in line. How many are ahead of her?

10. There are 20 people in a race. Sandy is 4th. How many are behind her?

11. There are 14 cars in a race. The red car is 12th. How many cars are in front?

12. There are 20 people in line. Tim is next to last. Name his place in line.

★ 13. How many days are between the 13th day and the 19th day of the month?

★ 14. If Mike is next to last in line and he is also third from first place, how many people are in line?

6. After Bep and Pol get tickets, who is third in line?

7. If everyone turned around so Nac was first, who would be in fourth place?

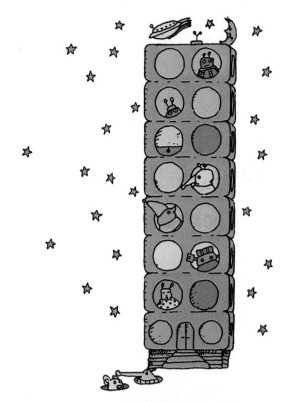

┌─ THINK ─┐

Ordinal Numbers

What is one of the tallest buildings in the world?

First Word	*Second Word*
Second letter E	Third letter W
Fifth letter S	Fifth letter R
First letter S	Second letter O
Fourth letter R	First letter T
Third letter A	Fourth letter E

→ **MATH** ←

PROBLEM SOLVING
Guess and Check

To solve a problem like this, you must do more than just quickly add or subtract. A strategy that can help you with this kind of problem is given below.

Try This Two families went on a picnic together. There were 13 people at the picnic. Which families went on the picnic?

Family	Number of People
	9
Clark	5
Ross	6
Hart	8
Hill	

GUESS AND CHECK

First Guess: Try Clark (9) and Ross (5).
Check 9 + 5 = 14

Too many. Only 13 went on the picnic.

Second Guess: Try Ross (5) and Hart (6).
Check 5 + 6 = 11

Too few. There were 13 at the picnic.

Third Guess: Try Ross (5) and Hill (8).
Check 5 + 8 = 13

Just right!

The Ross and Hill families went on the picnic.

Solve.

1. Ann has \$8. Jan has \$5. Fay has \$7. Sue has \$3. Two of the girls put their money together. Then they had \$11. Who were the girls?

2. Bert has 6 cards. Joe has 4 cards. Tom has 7 cards. Fred has 8 cards. Cal has 9 cards. Three boys put their cards together. Then they had 17 cards. Who were the boys?

Write the number.

1.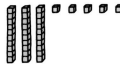

2.

3.

Tens	Ones
5	6

4.

Hundreds	Tens	Ones
8	0	5

Give the next four numbers.

5. 56 57 58 ▓ ▓ ▓ ▓

6. 0, 5, 10, 15, 20, ▓, ▓, ▓, ▓.

How much money?

7.

8.

Round to the nearest ten.   Round to the nearest hundred.

9. 26   **10.** 75   **11.** 83   **12.** 139   **13.** 365   **14.** 850

15. Write the number.
six thousand, seven hundred eighty-five

Write > or < for each ▓.

16. 76 ▓ 81   **17.** 324 ▓ 298   **18.** 1,267 ▓ 1,272

19. Write the number.
seven hundred twenty-eight thousand

20. Jesse is eighth in line. How
many people are in front
of him?

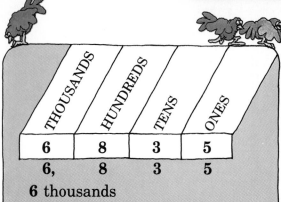

6, 8 3 5

6 thousands
8 hundreds
3 tens
5 ones

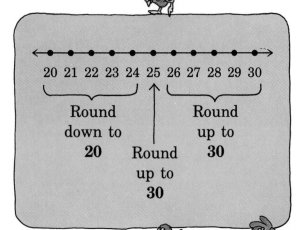

Round
down to
20

Round
up to
30

Round
up to
30

83 > 78

The smaller side
The larger side
83 is greater than **78**

Write the numbers.

1.

Tens	Ones
6	2

2.

Hundreds	Tens	Ones
4	7	5

3.

Thousands	Hundreds	Tens	Ones
3	9	8	4

Round to the nearest ten.

4. 23　　**5.** 29　　**6.** 25　　**7.** 83

8. 89　　**9.** 85　　**10.** 46　　**11.** 42

Round to the nearest hundred.

12. 685　　**13.** 624　　**14.** 650

15. 316　　**16.** 392　　**17.** 348

Write > or < for each .

18. 32 ● 36　　**19.** 43 ● 33

20. 75 ● 72　　**21.** 68 ● 78

22. 59 ● 62　　**23.** 71 ● 69

24. 235 ● 241　　**25.** 368 ● 361

Roman Numerals

The Romans used letters to write their numbers. Three of the letters were I, V, and X.

$$I = 1$$
$$V = 5$$
$$X = 10$$

The chart shows the first twenty **Roman Numerals.** Give the Roman Numeral for each number.

1. 3   **2.** 6   **3.** 9

4. 14   **5.** 17   **6.** 19

Give the number for each Roman Numeral.

7. II   **8.** IV   **9.** XI

10. XVI   **11.** XVIII   **12.** XX

13. Draw a clock face. Put Roman Numerals on it.

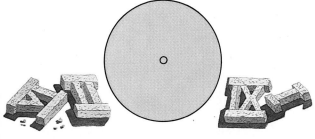

★ **14.** Write the Roman Numerals from 20 to 31. Here is a start. XX, XXI, XXII, . . .

★ **15.** Copy the calendar for this month. Use Roman Numerals.

NUMBER	ROMAN NUMERAL	
1	I	
2	II	1 + 1
3	III	1 + 1 + 1
4	IV	5 - 1
5	V	
6	VI	5 + 1
7	VII	5 + 2
8	VIII	5 + 3
9	IX	10 - 1
10	X	
11	XI	10 + 1
12	XII	10 + 2
13	XIII	10 + 3
14	XIV	10 + 4
15	XV	10 + 5
16	XVI	10 + 6
17	XVII	10 + 7
18	XVIII	10 + 8
19	XIX	10 + 9
20	XX	10 + 10

Using a Calculator

Entering and Erasing Numbers

Press ON to make your calculator work.
Then press the key for your number.
Press CLEAR to erase the number.

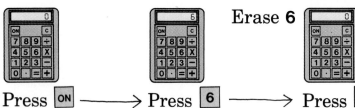

Enter **6**   Erase **6**

Press ON ⟶ Press 6 ⟶ Press C

Entering Large Numbers

Enter **806**.   Press C 8 0 6 ⟶ See 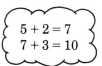 806

Adding Numbers

Clear the calculator. Enter each number
and the + key. Press the = key
for the answer. Add $5 + 2 + 3$.

First add the numbers in your head.
Now check your answer.

$$5 + 2 = 7$$
$$7 + 3 = 10$$

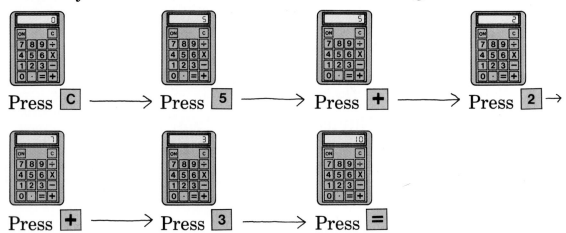

Press C ⟶ Press 5 ⟶ Press + ⟶ Press 2 →

Press + ⟶ Press 3 ⟶ Press =

Sue went birdwatching. She counted 8 sparrows, 9 robins, 8 bluejays, and 7 hawks. What is the total number of birds she saw?

A calculator can help you find the answer.

Write the problem.

$$\begin{array}{r} 8 \\ 9 \\ 8 \\ + 7 \\ \hline \end{array}$$

Which answer would make sense?

More than 100? No.

Less than 50? Yes.

More than 0? Yes.

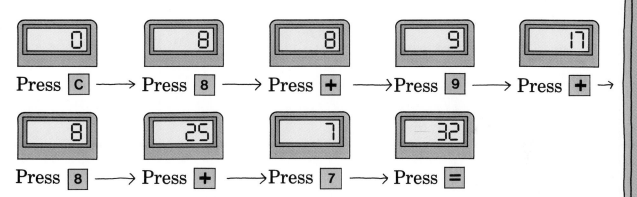

Press **C** ⟶ Press **8** ⟶ Press **+** ⟶ Press **9** ⟶ Press **+** →

Press **8** ⟶ Press **+** ⟶ Press **7** ⟶ Press **=**

The answer is 32 birds. That answer makes sense. It is less than 50 and more than 0.

Solve. Use the calculator to find the sums. Think what answer would make sense. Less than 50? More than 0?

1.
$$\begin{array}{r} 8 \\ 9 \\ 9 \\ + 7 \\ \hline \end{array}$$

2.
$$\begin{array}{r} 4 \\ 9 \\ 6 \\ 8 \\ + 5 \\ \hline \end{array}$$

3.
$$\begin{array}{r} 7 \\ 8 \\ 6 \\ 6 \\ + 8 \\ \hline \end{array}$$

4.
$$\begin{array}{r} 6 \\ 4 \\ 2 \\ 0 \\ + 9 \\ \hline \end{array}$$

Give the letter for the correct answer.

1. $14 - 8 =$ _____
  A 7   **B** 9
  C 12   **D** not given

2. $9 + 8 =$ _____
  A 1   **B** 17
  C 16   **D** not given

3. $11 - 9 =$ _____
  A 10   **B** 5
  C 2   **D** not given

4. $12 - 5 =$ _____
  A 17   **B** 6
  C 7   **D** not given

5. $8 + 7 =$ _____
  A 15   **B** 17
  C 16   **D** not given

6. $9 + 5 =$ _____
  A 4   **B** 14
  C 13   **D** not given

7. $\begin{array}{r} 7 \\ + 9 \\ \hline \end{array}$
  A 15
  B 16
  C 17
  D not given

8. $\begin{array}{r} 16 \\ - 8 \\ \hline \end{array}$
  A 8
  B 7
  C 14
  D not given

9. $\begin{array}{r} 12 \\ - 3 \\ \hline \end{array}$
  A 7
  B 15
  C 8
  D not given

10. $\begin{array}{r} 9 \\ + 4 \\ \hline \end{array}$
  A 13
  B 5
  C 12
  D not given

11. $\begin{array}{r} 8 \\ + 3 \\ \hline \end{array}$
  A 5
  B 11
  C 10
  D not given

12. $\begin{array}{r} 18 \\ - 9 \\ \hline \end{array}$
  A 9
  B 8
  C 17
  D not given

13. Sonja needs 8 clams to make soup. She has 6 clams. How many more clams does Sonja need to make soup?
  A 3   **B** 14
  C 2   **D** not given

14. Raoul caught 6 fish. Then he caught 5 more fish. How many fish did he catch?
  A 11   **B** 10
  C 1   **D** not given

Billy was making a robot from a kit. He needed to buy flashlight batteries to make it run. Billy wanted to get the best kind of batteries. He tested two kinds to see which one would last longer. He put a silver battery into one flashlight. He put a black battery into another flashlight. Then he left them on until the batteries died. The silver battery lasted 8 hours. The black battery lasted 3 more hours than the silver one.

Trading 10 Ones for 1 Ten

Bev has 2 tens and 15 ones. If she trades 10 ones for 1 ten,

1. how many tens will Bev have?
2. how many ones will she have?

Bev will have 3 tens and 5 ones.

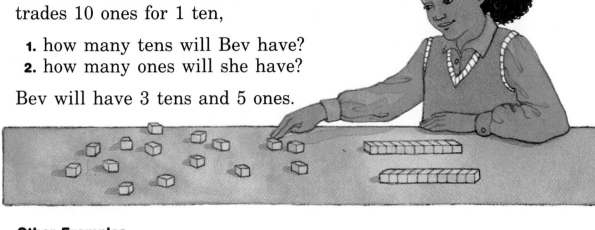

Other Examples

Trade 10 ones for 1 ten.

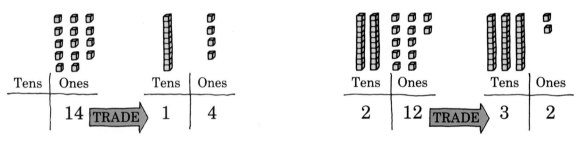

Tens	Ones		Tens	Ones
	14	TRADE	1	4

Tens	Ones		Tens	Ones
2	12	TRADE	3	2

Give the numbers of tens and ones after a trade.

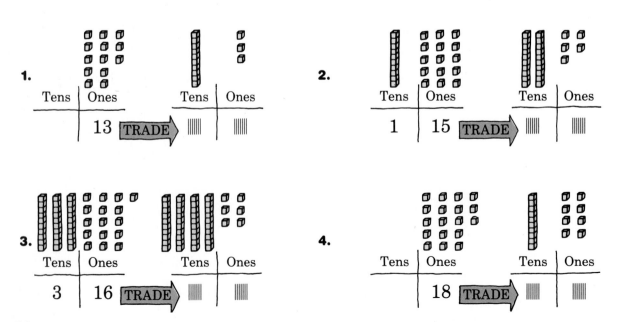

1.

Tens	Ones		Tens	Ones
	13	TRADE		

2.

Tens	Ones		Tens	Ones
1	15	TRADE		

3.

Tens	Ones		Tens	Ones
3	16	TRADE		

4.

Tens	Ones		Tens	Ones
	18	TRADE		

Trade 10 ones for 1 ten.

Example

Tens	Ones
	17

TRADE

Tens	Ones
1	7

1.

Tens	Ones
1	15

TRADE

Tens	Ones

2.

Tens	Ones
3	12

TRADE

Tens	Ones

3.

Tens	Ones
2	16

TRADE

Tens	Ones

4.

Tens	Ones
	11

TRADE

Tens	Ones

5.

Tens	Ones
4	12

TRADE

Tens	Ones

6.

Tens	Ones
5	14

TRADE

Tens	Ones

7.

Tens	Ones
3	10

TRADE

Tens	Ones

8.

Tens	Ones
	16

TRADE

Tens	Ones

9.

Tens	Ones
4	13

TRADE

Tens	Ones

10.

Tens	Ones
5	18

TRADE

Tens	Ones

THINK

Logical Reasoning

Give the missing numbers.

1.
$$\begin{array}{r} 7 \\ + \\ \hline 12 \end{array}$$

2.
$$\begin{array}{r} \\ + 6 \\ \hline 15 \end{array}$$

3.
$$\begin{array}{r} \\ - 4 \\ \hline 9 \end{array}$$

4.
$$\begin{array}{r} 6 \\ + \\ \hline 14 \end{array}$$

MATH

Adding 2-Digit Numbers: Trading Ones

Jill weighs 35 kg. Jan weighs
29 kg. What is their total weight?

Since we want their total weight, we add.

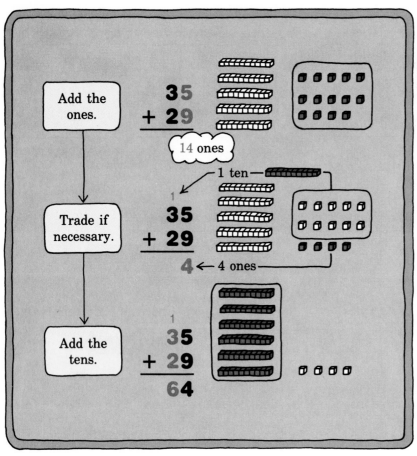

Add the
ones.

$$\begin{array}{r} 3\,5 \\ +\,2\,9 \end{array}$$

14 ones

1 ten

Trade if
necessary.

$$\begin{array}{r} 1 \\ 3\,5 \\ +\,2\,9 \\ \hline 4 \end{array}$$

4 ones

Add the
tens.

$$\begin{array}{r} 1 \\ 3\,5 \\ +\,2\,9 \\ \hline 6\,4 \end{array}$$

Their total weight is 64 kg.

Other Examples

$$\begin{array}{r} 1 \\ 2\,7 \\ +\,4\,8 \\ \hline 7\,5 \end{array} \qquad \begin{array}{r} 5\,3 \\ +\,3\,4 \\ \hline 8\,7 \end{array} \qquad \begin{array}{r} 1 \\ 3\,9 \\ +4 \\ \hline 4\,3 \end{array} \qquad \begin{array}{r} 3\,0 \\ +\,6\,8 \\ \hline 9\,8 \end{array} \qquad \begin{array}{r} 1 \\ 7 \\ +\,3\,5 \\ \hline 4\,2 \end{array}$$

NO TRADE
NECESSARY

NO TRADE
NECESSARY

Warm Up Add.

1. $\begin{array}{r} 2\,4 \\ +\,1\,7 \end{array}$
2. $\begin{array}{r} 3\,6 \\ +\,4\,2 \end{array}$
3. $\begin{array}{r} 5\,4 \\ +\,2\,9 \end{array}$
4. $\begin{array}{r} 6\,8 \\ +7 \end{array}$
5. $\begin{array}{r} 9 \\ +\,3\,5 \end{array}$
6. $\begin{array}{r} 2\,0 \\ +\,1\,5 \end{array}$

Find the sums.

1.	26 + 37	**2.**	24 + 15	**3.**	47 + 25	**4.**	29 + 55
5.	36 + 51	**6.**	18 + 27	**7.**	7 + 64	**8.**	75 + 3
9.	62 + 28	**10.**	46 + 8	**11.**	16 + 50	**12.**	19 + 54
13.	48 + 20	**14.**	8 + 23	**15.**	67 + 21	**16.**	82 + 11
17.	19 + 24	**18.**	32 + 41	**19.**	45 + 36	**20.**	73 + 18

21. 14 + 85　　　**22.** 35 + 36　　　**23.** 20 + 52　　　**24.** 59 + 7

25. Add 23 to 18　　　**26.** Add 56 to 27　　　**27.** Add 39 to 7

Solve.

28. Sandy weighs 28 kg. Pat weighs 34 kg. How much do Sandy and Pat weigh together?

29. Don weighs 32 kg. Rob weighs 36 kg. How much do both Don and Rob weigh?

30. DATA HUNT Find out your weight and the weight of a friend. Altogether how much do the two of you weigh?

THINK

Money Puzzle

Jane has 2 coins in her hand. Give the name of the coins if their value is:

1. 2¢　　**2.** 6¢　　**3.** 10¢

4. 15¢　　**5.** 20¢　　**6.** 26¢

7. 30¢　　**8.** 35¢　　**9.** 50¢

MATH

Adding 2-Digit Numbers: Trading 10 Tens

Joan checked her pulse rate after riding her bicycle. The first minute it beat 92 times. The second minute her pulse rate slowed to 83 beats. How many times did it beat in the two minutes?

Since we want the total number of beats, we add.

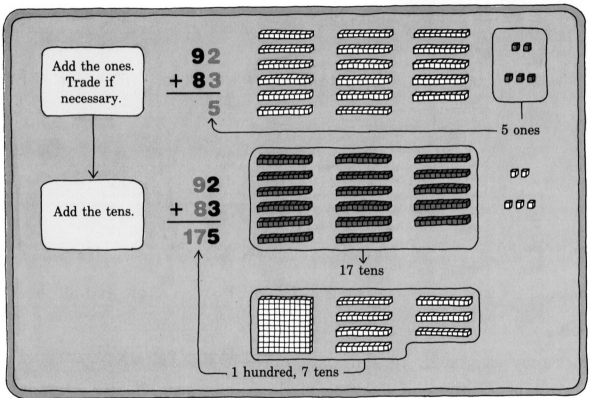

Add the ones. Trade if necessary.

$$
\begin{array}{r} 9\,2 \\ +\ 8\,3 \\ \hline 5 \end{array}
$$

— 5 ones

Add the tens.

$$
\begin{array}{r} 9\,2 \\ +\ 8\,3 \\ \hline 1\,7\,5 \end{array}
$$

17 tens

1 hundred, 7 tens

Joan's pulse beat 175 times in the two minutes.

Other Examples

$$
\begin{array}{r} 85 \\ +\ 42 \\ \hline 127 \end{array}
\qquad
\begin{array}{r} \overset{1}{5}6 \\ +\ 84 \\ \hline 140 \end{array}
\qquad
\begin{array}{r} 90 \\ +\ 62 \\ \hline 152 \end{array}
\qquad
\begin{array}{r} \overset{1}{4}7 \\ +\ 58 \\ \hline 105 \end{array}
$$

Warm Up Add.

1. $\begin{array}{r} 74 \\ +\ 64 \end{array}$
2. $\begin{array}{r} 85 \\ +\ 31 \end{array}$
3. $\begin{array}{r} 96 \\ +\ 56 \end{array}$
4. $\begin{array}{r} 72 \\ +\ 80 \end{array}$
5. $\begin{array}{r} 46 \\ +\ 84 \end{array}$
6. $\begin{array}{r} 95 \\ +\ 47 \end{array}$

Find the sums.

1.	75 + 86	**2.**	35 + 94	**3.**	87 + 83	**4.**	68 + 73	**5.**	83 + 54	**6.**	45 + 26
7.	86 + 30	**8.**	72 + 98	**9.**	64 + 68	**10.**	85 + 64	**11.**	69 + 53	**12.**	94 + 96
13.	91 + 23	**14.**	74 + 36	**15.**	82 + 18	**16.**	47 + 21	**17.**	98 + 83	**18.**	40 + 72

19. 95 + 68   **20.** 58 + 67   **21.** 75 + 13   **22.** 93 + 40

23. 85 + 49   **24.** 95 + 85   **25.** 84 + 21   **26.** 58 + 96

27. Find the sum of 68 and 72.   **28.** Find the sum of 96 and 27.

Solve.

29. Tim checked his pulse after running. The first minute it beat 97 times. The second minute it slowed to 84. Find the total number of beats.

30. DATA HUNT Check your own pulse rate for each of the first two minutes after running. Find the total number of beats for the two minutes.

SKILLKEEPER

Round to the nearest hundred or dollar.

1. 325 → ||||| **2.** 550 → ||||| **3.** 892 → ||||| **4.** 764 → |||||

5. $2.59 → ||||| **6.** $5.25 → ||||| **7.** $8.50 → ||||| **8.** $3.49 → |||||

Write > or < for each ◍.

9. 28 ◍ 37   **10.** 65 ◍ 55   **11.** 439 ◍ 388   **12.** 638 ◍ 645

PROBLEM SOLVING
Using Data from a Graph

The graph shows some of the tickets sold for the school play. The dashed line helps you see that Carla sold 12 tickets.

Solve. Use the graph.

1. Who sold the same number of tickets as Carla?

2. Who sold 15 tickets?

3. Who sold the most tickets?

4. How many did Greg sell?

5. How many did José sell?

6. How many tickets did Carla and José sell together?

7. Greg sold 8 more tickets after the graph was made. How many did he sell in all?

8. How many tickets did Fran and Nita sell together?

9. José said, "If I sell 6 more tickets, I will sell the same number as Nita." Check to see if he is right.

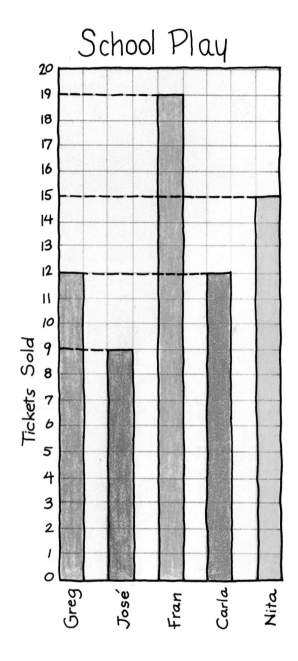

School Play

Tickets Sold

Greg José Fran Carla Nita

10. *Try This* Tickets cost $4, $6, $7, and $9. Amy bought two tickets for $11. What price tickets did she buy? Hint: Guess and check.

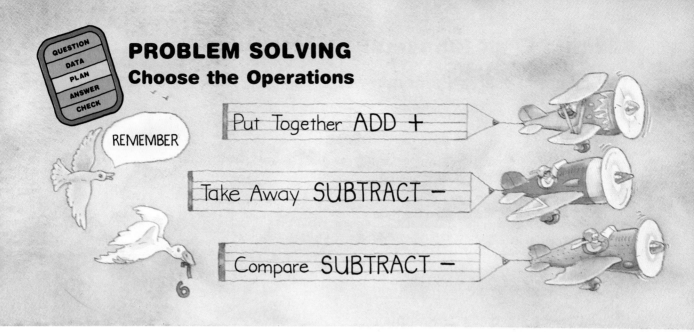

REMEMBER

Put Together ADD +

Take Away SUBTRACT −

Compare SUBTRACT −

Choose the operations and then solve.

1. There were 17 students from one class and 18 from another class who tried out for the school play. How many students tried out?

2. There were 12 students who got parts in the play. 5 of them were boys. How many were girls?

3. There were 14 students who helped paint. 6 helped clean. How many more students helped paint than clean?

4. There were 17 boys and 8 girls who helped people find seats. How many more boys than girls helped with the seating?

5. The first act was 35 minutes long. The second act lasted for 25 minutes. How long were the two acts?

6. Ann had 15 tickets left to sell. She sold 6 tickets. How many does she have left?

7. On the first night, 96 adults came to the play. On the second night, there were 87. How many adults came altogether?

8. *Try This* The first row had 11 seats. The second had 12. The third row had 13 and the fourth had 14. Which two rows could 26 people just fill?

Adding 3-Digit Numbers: Trading Once

How much do the two animals weigh together?

376 kg

182 kg

Since we want the total weight for both, we add.

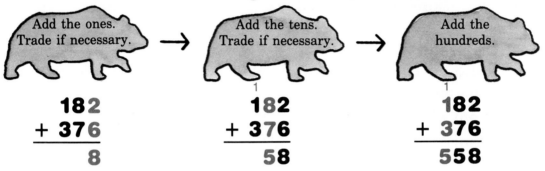

Add the ones.
Trade if necessary.

```
  182
+ 376
─────
    8
```

→

Add the tens.
Trade if necessary.

```
  ¹
  182
+ 376
─────
   58
```

→

Add the
hundreds.

```
  ¹
  182
+ 376
─────
  558
```

The two animals weigh a total of 558 kg.

Other Examples

trading ones	trading tens	trading hundreds
¹	¹	
249	346	634
+ 38	+ 281	+ 720
287	627	1,354

13 hundreds is
1 thousand and 3 hundreds

Warm Up Add.

1.	535	2.	487	3.	734	4.	234	5.	59
	+ 338		+ 262		+ 520		+ 283		+ 713

Find the sums.

1. 575
    + 802

2. 526
    + 446

3. 166
    + 253

4. 817
    + 46

5. 173
    + 183

6. 216
    + 635

7. 543
    + 76

8. 933
    + 346

9.   72
    + 672

10. 284
    + 800

11. 467
    + 517

12. 302
    + 433

13. 678
    + 51

14. 284
    + 181

15. 776
    + 14

16. 325
    + 591

17. 408
    + 79

18. 213
    + 904

19. 625
    + 281

20. 175
    + 42

21. 134 + 718

22. 492 + 497

23. 844 + 93

24. 548 + 327

25. 58 + 327

26. 151 + 681

27. 632 + 293

28. 903 + 755

29. Add 731 and 226.

30. Add 729 and 550.

Solve.

31. Find the total weight of these
    two animals.
    Tiger: 182 kg   Deer: 125 kg

32. Look at page 66. If the bear
    weighed 309 kg, how much
    would the bear and tiger weigh
    together?

33. **DATA BANK** See page 359.
    Find the total weight of the
    buffalo and the camel.

THINK

Logical Reasoning

Find the missing digits.

1.   7▮▮▮
    + ▮▮▮3
    ‾‾‾‾‾‾
      159

2.   ▮▮▮8
    + 7▮▮▮
    ‾‾‾‾‾‾
      143

3.   3▮▮▮
    + ▮▮▮2
    ‾‾‾‾‾‾
      119

4.   ▮▮▮6
    + 4▮▮▮
    ‾‾‾‾‾‾
      101

5.   7▮▮▮
    + ▮▮▮2
    ‾‾‾‾‾‾
      130

MATH

Adding 3-Digit Numbers: Two or More Trades

Emil's collie needs 596 grams of dry dog food each day. His sister's cocker spaniel needs 355 grams each day. How many grams do both dogs need in one day?

Since we want the total number of grams, we add.

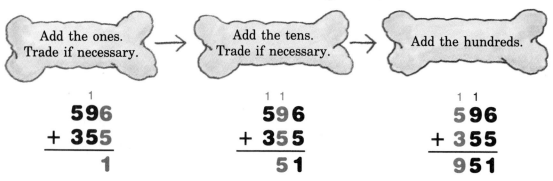

Add the ones. Trade if necessary. → Add the tens. Trade if necessary. → Add the hundreds.

$$
\begin{array}{r}
\overset{1}{5}96 \\
+\ 355 \\
\hline
1
\end{array}
\qquad
\begin{array}{r}
\overset{1}{5}\overset{1}{9}6 \\
+\ 355 \\
\hline
51
\end{array}
\qquad
\begin{array}{r}
\overset{1}{5}\overset{1}{9}6 \\
+\ 355 \\
\hline
951
\end{array}
$$

The two dogs need a total of 951 grams in one day.

Other Examples

$$
\begin{array}{r}
\overset{1}{4}72 \\
+\ 856 \\
\hline
1{,}328
\end{array}
\qquad
\begin{array}{r}
\overset{1}{7}\overset{1}{6}5 \\
+\ 847 \\
\hline
1{,}612
\end{array}
\qquad
\begin{array}{r}
\overset{1}{9}\overset{1}{7}5 \\
+\ \ 96 \\
\hline
1{,}071
\end{array}
$$

Warm Up Add.

1. $\begin{array}{r} 784 \\ +\ 752 \\ \hline \end{array}$
2. $\begin{array}{r} 256 \\ +\ \ 68 \\ \hline \end{array}$
3. $\begin{array}{r} 247 \\ +\ 946 \\ \hline \end{array}$
4. $\begin{array}{r} 765 \\ +\ 840 \\ \hline \end{array}$
5. $\begin{array}{r} 324 \\ +\ 170 \\ \hline \end{array}$

6. $\begin{array}{r} 649 \\ +\ \ 87 \\ \hline \end{array}$
7. $\begin{array}{r} 764 \\ +\ 478 \\ \hline \end{array}$
8. $\begin{array}{r} 615 \\ +\ 239 \\ \hline \end{array}$
9. $\begin{array}{r} 559 \\ +\ 614 \\ \hline \end{array}$
10. $\begin{array}{r} 279 \\ +\ 978 \\ \hline \end{array}$

Find the sums.

1. 238 + 195	**2.** 764 + 482	**3.** 953 + 649	**4.** 287 + 954	**5.** 855 + 792
6. 742 + 682	**7.** 758 + 428	**8.** 327 + 610	**9.** 87 + 863	**10.** 483 + 462
11. 657 + 648	**12.** 686 + 921	**13.** 493 + 976	**14.** 76 + 556	**15.** 507 + 758

16. 516 + 230   **17.** 756 + 58   **18.** 351 + 284   **19.** 840 + 585

20. 61 + 279   **21.** 964 + 320   **22.** 720 + 393   **23.** 369 + 543

24. Find the sum of 399 and 208.   **25.** Find the sum of 871 and 371.

26. Find the sum of 285 and 199.   **27.** Find the sum of 76 and 385.

Solve.

28. Jay's dog needs 156 grams of dog food each day. Tom's dog needs 255 grams. How many grams do both dogs need?

29. A poodle needs 198 grams of dog food each day. Sue has 2 poodles. How many grams do both dogs need?

30. **DATA BANK** See page 360. Find the total number of grams of dry dog food needed by a bulldog and a German shepherd in one day.

THINK

Using a Calculator

Show 806 on your calculator. Now show 876 by **adding one** number.

Now try these the same way.

1. 908 → 928

2. 704 → 754

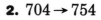

3. 8,064 → 8,364

4. 7,086 → 7,986

MATH

Adding Amounts of Money

GIGANTIC TAPE SALE!!

COUNTRY WESTERN $3.49   EASY LISTENING $3.88   CLASSICAL $4.98   ROCK $6.75   JAZZ $4.40

How much would it cost for a Country Western tape and an Easy Listening tape?

Since we want the total cost for the tapes, we add the prices.

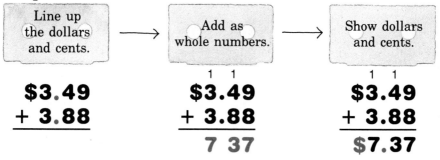

Line up the dollars and cents.	→	Add as whole numbers.	→	Show dollars and cents.

$3.49
+ 3.88

1 1
$3.49
+ 3.88
7 37

1 1
$3.49
+ 3.88
$7.37

The total cost for both tapes is $7.37.

Find the total amounts.

1. $6.43 + 5.76	**2.** $3.85 + 4.29	**3.** $7.86 + 9.00	**4.** $0.69 + 1.56	**5.** $8.15 + 7.35
6. $6.59 + 3.98	**7.** $7.50 + 5.50	**8.** $0.78 + 0.57	**9.** $8.75 + 6.98	**10.** $3.75 + 2.98

11. $4.85 + $3.49   **12.** $6.50 + $5.90   **13.** $2.49 + $9.00

14. $1.98 + $0.75   **15.** $8.35 + $6.75   **16.** $0.59 + $0.63

17. $6.75 + $5.95   **18.** $7.50 + $9.95   **19.** $0.08 + $0.69

More Practice, page 369, Set B

PROBLEM SOLVING
Using Data from an Advertisement

Use the advertisement on page 70 to help you answer the questions on this page. Find the cost for each pair of tapes.

1. Rock
   Classical

2. Rock
   Country Western

3. Jazz
   Classical

4. Rock
   Easy Listening

5. Jazz
   Easy Listening

6. Classical
   Country Western

7. Jazz
   Country Western

8. Classical
   Easy Listening

9. Rock
   Jazz

10. Kay bought some tape cleaner for $1.95. She also bought an Easy Listening tape. How much did she pay?

11. Don bought a record for $7.95. He also bought a Classical tape. How much did he spend for both?

12. Mr. Hernández wants to buy one of each kind of tape. How much money will he spend for all of them?

13. Ms. Tanaka bought a record for $8.87 and a Jazz tape. The tax was $0.86. How much money did she pay?

14. *Try This* Some special tapes were on sale for $4, $5, $6, and $7. Jeanna bought two of them for $13. What price was on each tape?

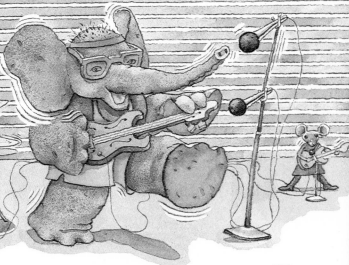

Special Sums: Mental Math

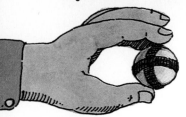

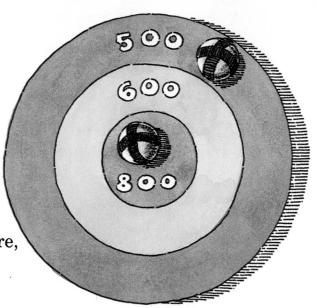

First, Jerry scored 800 points.
Then he scored 500 points. What
was his total score?

Since we want to know the total score,
we need to add.

Think about hundreds.

      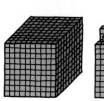

8 hundreds	**+**	**5 hundreds**	**=**	**13 hundreds**
800	**+**	**500**	**=**	**1,300**

Other Examples   **40 + 30 = 70**   **700 + 500 = 1,200**

> THINK
> 4 tens + 3 tens = 7 tens

> THINK
> 7 hundreds + 5 hundreds = 12 hundreds

Warm Up

Give the sums aloud.

1. 50 + 20   **2.** 80 + 60   **3.** 80 + 30   **4.** 30 + 50

5. 50 + 50   **6.** 70 + 30   **7.** 60 + 10   **8.** 70 + 60

9. 50 + 60   **10.** 60 + 30   **11.** 80 + 40   **12.** 50 + 40

13. 900 + 200   **14.** 800 + 700   **15.** 400 + 400   **16.** 400 + 900

17. 700 + 200   **18.** 200 + 800   **19.** 500 + 800   **20.** 600 + 600

72   (seventy-two)

Find the sums. Write answers only.

1. 30 + 80   **2.** 90 + 50   **3.** 70 + 20

4. 70 + 90   **5.** 40 + 30   **6.** 80 + 20

7. 80 + 90   **8.** 40 + 40   **9.** 70 + 40

10. 40 + 50   **11.** 90 + 70   **12.** 30 + 90

13. 60 + 90   **14.** 50 + 50   **15.** 90 + 40

16. 70 + 60   **17.** 50 + 20   **18.** 30 + 30

19. 700 + 500   **20.** 600 + 100   **21.** 800 + 900

22. 500 + 300   **23.** 800 + 700   **24.** 200 + 400

25. 600 + 600   **26.** 600 + 900   **27.** 300 + 600

28. 900 + 900   **29.** 200 + 500   **30.** 900 + 100

31. 800 + 400   **32.** 600 + 400   **33.** 800 + 800

34. 600 + 800   **35.** 400 + 900   **36.** 700 + 600

Solve.

37. Cindy scored 600 points. Then she scored 500. What was her total score?

38. Ted scored 1,300 points. One score was 500. What was the other score?

★ **39.** Nancy scored 400, 500, and 400 in three turns. What was her total score?

More Practice, page 370, Set A

THINK

Patterns

Give the next number.

1. 200, 400, 600, 800, ▨.

2. 10, 30, 50, 70, ▨.

3. 10, 20, 40, 80, ▨.

4. 100, 200, 400, 700, ▨.

MATH

Estimating Sums

Sometimes you want an answer that is only close to the exact answer. To **estimate** how much the sweater and jeans will cost, we round and add.

About how much would both cost?

$$\begin{array}{c} \$19 \\ +\ 32 \end{array} \quad \boxed{\text{nearest ten}} \quad \begin{array}{c} \$20 \\ +\ 30 \\ \hline \$50 \end{array}$$

The sweater and jeans cost about $50.

Other Examples

nearest ten	nearest hundred	nearest dollar

$$\begin{array}{c} 48 \rightarrow 50 \\ +\ 53 \rightarrow +\ 50 \\ \hline 100 \end{array} \qquad \begin{array}{c} 296 \rightarrow 300 \\ +\ 412 \rightarrow +\ 400 \\ \hline 700 \end{array} \qquad \begin{array}{c} \$3.98 \rightarrow \$4.00 \\ +\ 2.25 \rightarrow +\ 2.00 \\ \hline \$6.00 \end{array}$$

Warm Up Estimate by rounding to the nearest ten.

1. $\begin{array}{r} 41 \\ +\ 18 \end{array}$
2. $\begin{array}{r} 38 \\ +\ 29 \end{array}$
3. $\begin{array}{r} 48 \\ +\ 33 \end{array}$
4. $\begin{array}{r} 27 \\ +\ 52 \end{array}$

Estimate by rounding to the nearest hundred.

5. $\begin{array}{r} 199 \\ +\ 289 \end{array}$
6. $\begin{array}{r} 396 \\ +\ 402 \end{array}$
7. $\begin{array}{r} 511 \\ +\ 295 \end{array}$
8. $\begin{array}{r} 195 \\ +\ 604 \end{array}$

Estimate by rounding to the nearest dollar.

9. $\begin{array}{r} \$3.89 \\ +\ 1.20 \end{array}$
10. $\begin{array}{r} \$5.75 \\ +\ 4.98 \end{array}$
11. $\begin{array}{r} \$3.88 \\ +\ 4.25 \end{array}$
12. $\begin{array}{r} \$1.29 \\ +\ 3.69 \end{array}$

Estimate by rounding to the nearest ten.

1. 68
    + 24

2. 51
    + 23

3. 47
    + 34

4. 65
    + 23

5. 78
    + 69

6. 64
    + 38

7. 55
    + 25

8. 81
    + 56

9. 72
    + 43

10. 59
    + 34

Estimate by rounding to the nearest hundred or dollar.

11. 280
    + 390

12. 412
    + 167

13. 289
    + 427

14. 350
    + 137

15. $7.89
    + 1.25

16. $2.75
    + 3.89

17. $4.15
    +1.95

18. $2.78
    + 3.35

Use the catalog below.
Estimate the total cost by rounding to the nearest dollar.

19. How much for D and A?

20. How much for C and D?

21. How much for B and A?

22. How much for E and B?

A. $2.98
B. $5.25
E. $4.95
C. $1.75
D. $3.10

Adding: Mental Math

Look at the map. How far is it from Hope to Mills?

Since we want the total of the three distances, we add.

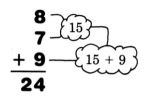

$$
\begin{array}{r}
8 \\
7 \\
+\ 9 \\
\hline
24
\end{array}
$$

15
15 + 9

It is 24 miles from Hope to Mills.

Sometimes when you add three or more numbers, you need to find sums such as **15 + 9** "in your head."

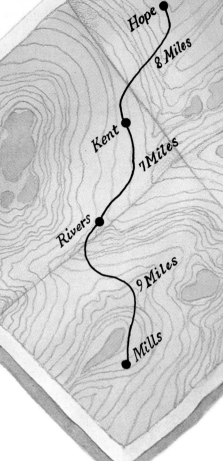

Hope
8 Miles
Kent
7 Miles
Rivers
9 Miles
Mills

Other Examples

13 + 4

THINK
Since 3 + 4 = 7,
I know 13 + 4 = 17.

28 + 5

THINK
Since 8 + 5 = 13,
I know 28 + 5 = 33.

17 + 8

THINK
Since 7 + 8 = 15,
I know 17 + 8 = 25.

Warm Up Give each sum aloud.

1. 16 + 3
2. 14 + 2
3. 18 + 3
4. 17 + 6

5. 12 + 8
6. 22 + 9
7. 19 + 5
8. 24 + 3

9. 15 + 7
10. 18 + 3
11. 25 + 2
12. 13 + 9

13. 23 + 6
14. 11 + 8
15. 15 + 6
16. 14 + 6

17. 12 + 3
18. 12 + 9
19. 27 + 7
20. 25 + 8

Find the sums. Write answers only.

1. $16 + 5$ 2. $16 + 4$ 3. $12 + 6$ 4. $11 + 7$

5. $14 + 9$ 6. $13 + 2$ 7. $18 + 5$ 8. $27 + 8$

9. $19 + 2$ 10. $24 + 3$ 11. $18 + 4$ 12. $14 + 5$

13. $12 + 6$ 14. $11 + 9$ 15. $21 + 8$ 16. $17 + 7$

17. $26 + 6$ 18. $28 + 5$ 19. $17 + 4$ 20. $13 + 3$

21.
$$\begin{array}{r} 8 \\ 6 \\ + 7 \\ \hline \end{array}$$
14    $14 + 7$

22.
$$\begin{array}{r} 9 \\ 6 \\ + 8 \\ \hline \end{array}$$
15    $15 + 8$

23.
$$\begin{array}{r} 6 \\ 7 \\ + 4 \\ \hline \end{array}$$
13    $13 + 4$

24.
$$\begin{array}{r} 8 \\ 9 \\ + 7 \\ \hline \end{array}$$
17    $17 + 7$

25.
$$\begin{array}{r} 6 \\ 9 \\ + 7 \\ \hline \end{array}$$

26.
$$\begin{array}{r} 4 \\ 7 \\ + 8 \\ \hline \end{array}$$

27.
$$\begin{array}{r} 7 \\ 7 \\ + 7 \\ \hline \end{array}$$

28.
$$\begin{array}{r} 9 \\ 8 \\ + 6 \\ \hline \end{array}$$

29.
$$\begin{array}{r} 6 \\ 5 \\ + 8 \\ \hline \end{array}$$

30.
$$\begin{array}{r} 8 \\ 8 \\ + 8 \\ \hline \end{array}$$

Solve.

31. Joe rode his bicycle 17 miles one day. He rode 8 miles the next day. How many miles did he ride in the two days?

32. Sally walked 8 miles one day, 7 miles the second day, and 8 miles the third day. How many miles did Sally walk in the three days?

Column Addition

How many children voted in the "Favorite Wheels" poll?

Since we want the total number of children, we add the numbers.

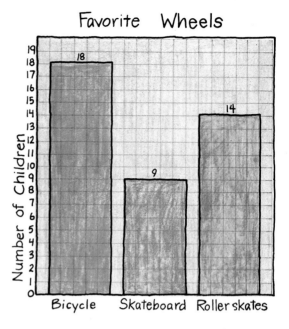

Favorite Wheels

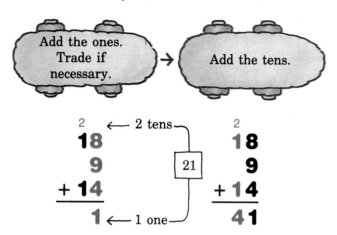

```
  2
  18  ←── 2 tens ──┐
   9      ┌────┐    │
+ 14      │ 21 │    
   1  ←── 1 one ──┘
```

```
  2
  18
   9
+ 14
  41
```

41 children voted.

Other Examples

```
  1
  32
  27
+ 16
  75
```

```
  2
  28
   7
+ 39
  74
```

```
  1
  46
  37
  52
+ 21
 156
```

```
 2 1
 276
 477
+ 84
 837
```

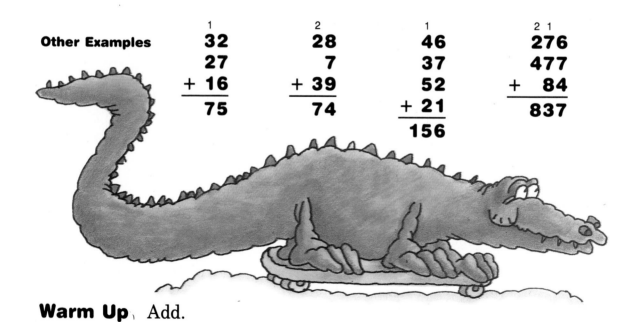

Warm Up Add.

1.
```
  34
  26
+ 13
```

2.
```
  57
  34
+ 65
```

3.
```
  19
   8
+ 17
```

4.
```
  48
  36
  55
+ 32
```

5.
```
 123
  48
+ 307
```

6.
```
 485
 534
 627
+ 102
```

Find the sums.

1.	2.	3.	4.	5.
26	48	32	57	8
15	7	41	24	42
+ 34	+ 14	+ 10	+ 35	+ 68

6.	7.	8.	9.	10.
325	371	418	371	82
105	256	375	486	671
+ 246	+ 30	+ 186	+ 721	+ 389

11.	12.	13.	14.	15.
37	65	684	817	143
29	42	93	695	287
18	79	765	283	651
+ 20	+ 32	+ 421	+ 140	+ 830

16. 24 + 37 + 16

17. 327 + 408 + 75

18. 43 + 24 + 55 + 62

19. 327 + 146 + 83 + 276

Solve.

20. There were 28 votes for roller skates, 17 for skateboards, and 15 for bicycles. How many votes were there?

21. In one class, 8 children voted for skateboards. 9 voted for bicycles. 7 voted for roller skates. 2 did not vote. How many are in the class?

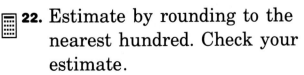 22. Estimate by rounding to the nearest hundred. Check your estimate.

287 + 539 + 496

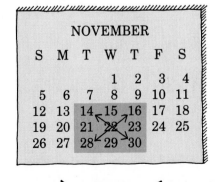

THINK

Patterns

Look at the calendar. Find the sum along each arrow. What do you notice? Try this with another "square" of numbers on the calendar.

NOVEMBER

S	M	T	W	T	F	S
			1	2	3	4
5	6	7	8	9	10	11
12	13	14	15	16	17	18
19	20	21	22	23	24	25
26	27	28	29	30		

MATH

Adding 4-Digit Numbers

Look at the table. How many people attended the first two games?

Since we want the total number of people, we add the two numbers.

BASKETBALL ATTENDANCE	
First game	1,928
Second game	2,306
Third game	3,265
Fourth game	1,876

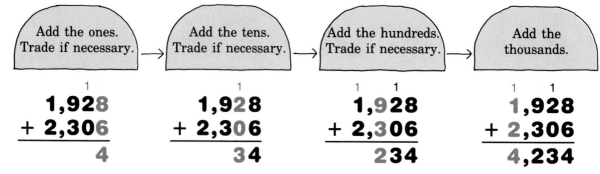

Add the ones. Trade if necessary.	Add the tens. Trade if necessary.	Add the hundreds. Trade if necessary.	Add the thousands.

$$
\begin{array}{r} \overset{1}{1{,}92\mathbf{8}} \\ +\ 2{,}30\mathbf{6} \\ \hline 4 \end{array}
\qquad
\begin{array}{r} \overset{1}{1{,}9\mathbf{2}8} \\ +\ 2{,}3\mathbf{0}6 \\ \hline 34 \end{array}
\qquad
\begin{array}{r} \overset{1\ \ 1}{1{,}\mathbf{9}28} \\ +\ 2{,}\mathbf{3}06 \\ \hline 234 \end{array}
\qquad
\begin{array}{r} \overset{1\ \ 1}{\mathbf{1}{,}928} \\ +\ \mathbf{2}{,}306 \\ \hline 4{,}234 \end{array}
$$

4,234 people attended the first two games.

Other Examples

$$
\begin{array}{r} \overset{1\ 1}{3{,}287} \\ +\ 4{,}165 \\ \hline 7{,}452 \end{array}
\qquad
\begin{array}{r} \overset{1\ 1}{5{,}672} \\ +\ \ \ 495 \\ \hline 6{,}167 \end{array}
\qquad
\begin{array}{r} \overset{1\ \ 1\ 1}{5{,}875} \\ +\ 1{,}659 \\ \hline 7{,}534 \end{array}
$$

Warm Up   Add.

1. 4,236
    + 1,357

2. 2,173
    + 4,592

3. 6,713
    + 2,940

4. 3,627
    + 1,809

5. 3,247
    + 1,485

6. 2,761
    + 3,783

7. 4,653
    + 178

8. 6,275
    + 980

9. 3,679
    + 1,856

10. 2,037
    + 1,590

Find the sums.

1. 3,729
 + 5,549

2. 6,751
 + 2,684

3. 1,254
 + 3,298

4. 472
 + 6,089

5. 4,290
 + 4,841

6. 5,761
 + 4,086

7. 2,463
 + 562

8. 5,668
 + 1,246

9. 4,662
 + 4,791

10. 1,824
 + 5,567

11. 3,124
 + 488

12. 3,750
 + 5,775

13. 7,772
 + 1,473

14. 3,393
 + 5,870

15. 7,858
 + 1,954

16. 7,624 + 1,294

17. 3,765 + 3,052

18. 3,908 + 465

19. 2,853 + 5,677

20. 385 + 2,367

21. 5,841 + 3,628

22. Add 3,251 and 4,009.

23. Add 1,265 and 8,308.

24. Add 2,725 and 5,304.

25. Add 6,060 and 3,783.

Use the table on page 80 for problems 26–28.

26. How many people attended the third and fourth games?

27. Which two games had the highest attendance? How many came to these two games?

28. How many attended all four games?

THINK

Estimation

Two of these numbers have a sum of exactly 1,400. Use **estimation** to find them. Check by adding.

816 952
698 286
508 584

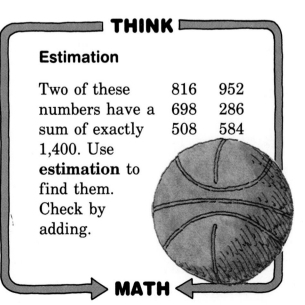

MATH

PROBLEM SOLVING ★ Using the 5-Point Checklist

To solve a problem

☆ 1. Understand the Question
☆ 2. Find the needed Data
☆ 3. Plan what to do
☆ 4. Find the Answer
☆ 5. Check back

An adult has about 206 bones. A baby may have as many as 144 more bones than an adult. How many bones could a baby have?

Use the 5-Point Checklist to help you solve the problem.

1. Understand the QUESTION
What is the total number of bones a baby could have?

2. Find the needed DATA
An adult has 206 bones. A baby has 144 more.

3. PLAN what to do
Since we want to increase 206 by 144, we must add.

4. Find the ANSWER

```
  1
  206    A baby has
+ 144    350 bones.
  350
```

5. CHECK back

```
  206    nearest hundred    200
+ 144    nearest hundred  + 100
                           300
```

350 seems about right.

Solve. Use the 5-Point Checklist.

1. The face has 14 bones. The spinal column has 26 bones. How many bones is this altogether?

2. There are 28 bones in the fingers. There are 28 bones in the toes. How many bones are in both?

Where Your Bones Are Found

Head		Trunk		Limbs	
Cranium	8	Spinal column	26	Arms	60
Face	14	Ribs	24	Legs	60
Ears	6	Breast bone	1		
Throat	1	Collar bones	2		
		Shoulder bones	2		
		Hip bones	2		

Solve.

1. How many bones are in the arms and legs?

2. What is the total number of bones in the spinal column and ribs?

3. How many more bones are in the face than in the cranium?

4. What is the total number of bones in the head?

5. How many more bones are in the face than the ears?

6. How many more bones are in the arms than in the face?

7. There are 8 bones in a wrist, 5 in a palm, and 14 bones in the fingers. How many is this in all?

8. The arm has 3 large bones. How many fewer is this than the 8 bones in the wrist?

9. How many bones are in the trunk?

10. *Try This* The dentist cleaned the teeth of 12 people Monday, 10 people Tuesday, 8 people Thursday, and 11 people Friday. Which two days did he clean the teeth of 21 people?

PROBLEM SOLVING
Use Logical Reasoning

QUESTION
DATA
PLAN
ANSWER
CHECK

To solve this problem, you may need to organize your work in a different way. You cannot just quickly add or subtract. A strategy that can help you is given below.

Try This Melinda was asked how old she is. She said, "I am less than 12 years old. My age is more than 9. I have lived an even number of years." How old is Melinda?

USE LOGICAL REASONING

Listing what you know helps you to reason logically.

Melinda's age is less than 12.

First, list the numbers less than 12.

0 1 2 3 4 5 6 7 8 9 10 11

It is more than 9.

Second, cross out all numbers on the list that are **not** greater than 9.

0̸ 1̸ 2̸ 3̸ 4̸ 5̸ 6̸ 7̸ 8̸ 9̸ 10 11

It is even.

Third, cross out all **odd** numbers still on the list.

0̸ 1̸ 2̸ 3̸ 4̸ 5̸ 6̸ 7̸ 8̸ 9̸ 10 1̸1̸

Melinda must be 10 years old because 10 is the only number left on the list.

Solve.

1. Doug said, "The number of goldfish I have is between 25 and 35. It is more than 32. I have an odd number of goldfish." How many goldfish does Doug have?

2. Candy said, "The number of people in my family is more than 3 and less than 4 and 4. It is an odd number and it is not 7." How many are in Candy's family?

Add.

1.	16 + 25	**2.**	42 + 13	**3.**	84 + 65	**4.**	36 + 47	**5.**	28 + 59

6.	370 + 985	**7.**	567 + 242	**8.**	475 + 68	**9.**	933 + 474	**10.**	165 + 237

11.	$5.26 + 3.15	**12.**	$1.02 + 3.98	**13.**	$3.87 + 1.64	**14.**	$2.79 + 8.56	**15.**	$7.95 + 4.69

Estimate by rounding to the nearest ten or dollar.

16.	17 + 23	**17.**	34 + 65	**18.**	$7.09 + 2.98	**19.**	$6.81 + 3.22

Add.

20.	23 18 + 31	**21.**	2,476 + 1,282	**22.**	6,417 + 1,958	**23.**	42 65 28 + 19	**24.**	276 128 + 315

Use the table to solve problems 25–26.

25. How much more did Sue grow than Jo?

26. What was Jo's height at the end of the year?

Name	Height	Growth in 1 year
Ben	118 cm	13 cm
Jo	124 cm	9 cm
Sue	119 cm	12 cm

Solve.

27. How much do both A and B cost?

A.

B.

ANOTHER LOOK

$$\begin{array}{r}\overset{1}{3}6\\ +\ 27\\ \hline 63\end{array}$$

← 1 ten
13 = 1 ten and 3 ones
← 3 ones

6 tens

$$\begin{array}{r}\overset{1}{3}72\\ +\ 485\\ \hline 857\end{array}$$

THINK
8 + 7 = 15
I'll need to trade.

$$\begin{array}{r}\overset{1}{2}8\\ 35\\ +\ 24\\ \hline 87\end{array}$$

13
13 + 4

Find the sums.

1. $\begin{array}{r}26\\ +\ 48\end{array}$ **2.** $\begin{array}{r}58\\ +\ 15\end{array}$ **3.** $\begin{array}{r}67\\ +\ 24\end{array}$

4. $\begin{array}{r}79\\ +\ 46\end{array}$ **5.** $\begin{array}{r}37\\ +\ 99\end{array}$ **6.** $\begin{array}{r}89\\ +\ 64\end{array}$

7. $\begin{array}{r}274\\ +\ 372\end{array}$ **8.** $\begin{array}{r}640\\ +\ 185\end{array}$ **9.** $\begin{array}{r}394\\ +\ 350\end{array}$

10. $\begin{array}{r}193\\ +\ 179\end{array}$ **11.** $\begin{array}{r}246\\ +\ 465\end{array}$ **12.** $\begin{array}{r}348\\ +\ 57\end{array}$

13. $\begin{array}{r}367\\ +\ 249\end{array}$ **14.** $\begin{array}{r}158\\ +\ 472\end{array}$ **15.** $\begin{array}{r}647\\ +\ 275\end{array}$

16. $\begin{array}{r}25\\ 17\\ +\ 46\end{array}$ **17.** $\begin{array}{r}24\\ 28\\ +\ 23\end{array}$ **18.** $\begin{array}{r}16\\ 35\\ +\ 28\end{array}$

19. $\begin{array}{r}57\\ 8\\ +\ 76\end{array}$ **20.** $\begin{array}{r}29\\ 87\\ +\ 46\end{array}$ **21.** $\begin{array}{r}36\\ 69\\ +\ 56\end{array}$

Finding Patterns

Fold a piece of paper like the one shown below.

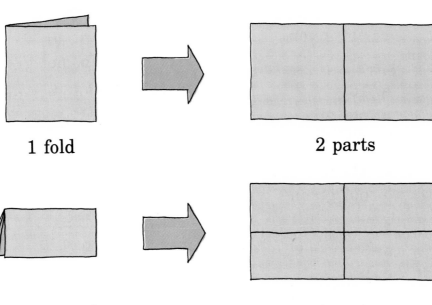

1 fold

2 parts

2 folds

4 parts

3 folds

How many parts?

Copy the following table. Put your answer in. Then complete the table. Use a calculator if you need help.

Folds	1	2	3	4	5	6	7	8	9	10
Parts	2	4								

Give the letter for the correct answer.

1. 3 + 4 + 6 = ____

- **A** 14
- **B** 12
- **C** 13
- **D** not given

2. 5 + 1 + 9 = ____

- **A** 14
- **B** 16
- **C** 15
- **D** not given

3. 3 + 2 + 6 = ____

- **A** 9
- **B** 11
- **C** 10
- **D** not given

4.
```
   3
   4
 + 5
```
- **A** 7
- **B** 8
- **C** 9
- **D** not given

5.
```
   3
   3
 + 7
```
- **A** 7
- **B** 8
- **C** 9
- **D** not given

6.
```
   8
   2
 + 5
```
- **A** 14
- **B** 15
- **C** 16
- **D** not given

7. 6 tens and 7 ones

- **A** 76
- **B** 77
- **C** 67
- **D** not given

8. 7 hundreds, 3 tens, 2 ones

- **A** 372
- **B** 732
- **C** 273
- **D** not given

9. What is the next number?
26, 27, 28, 29, ▌▌▌

- **A** 20
- **B** 40
- **C** 30
- **D** not given

10. What is the next number?
96, 97, 98, 99, ▌▌▌

- **A** 100
- **B** 80
- **C** 90
- **D** not given

11. What is the next number?
127, 128, 129, ▌▌▌

- **A** 148
- **B** 120
- **C** 130
- **D** not given

12. What is the next number?
396, 397, 398, 399, ▌▌▌

- **A** 200
- **B** 400
- **C** 300
- **D** not given

13. Mariko has 2 guppies and 1 angel fish. She bought 2 zebra fish. How many fish does she have?

- **A** 2
- **B** 5
- **C** 3
- **D** not given

14. Allen bought 6 bananas, 4 oranges, and 3 apples. How many pieces of fruit did he buy?

- **A** 13
- **B** 11
- **C** 12
- **D** not given

SUBTRACTION

Dan lives in Alaska. He is 15 years old.
Dan carves totem poles like the Alaskan
Indians once did. The Indians carved poles
when a chief died. They carved poles after
winning a battle. Poles were even used to
make fun of people. Dan knows many
legends about the animals he carves. A
legend is an old story. The eagle on the
top is 55 cm high. The beaver on the
bottom is 42 cm high.

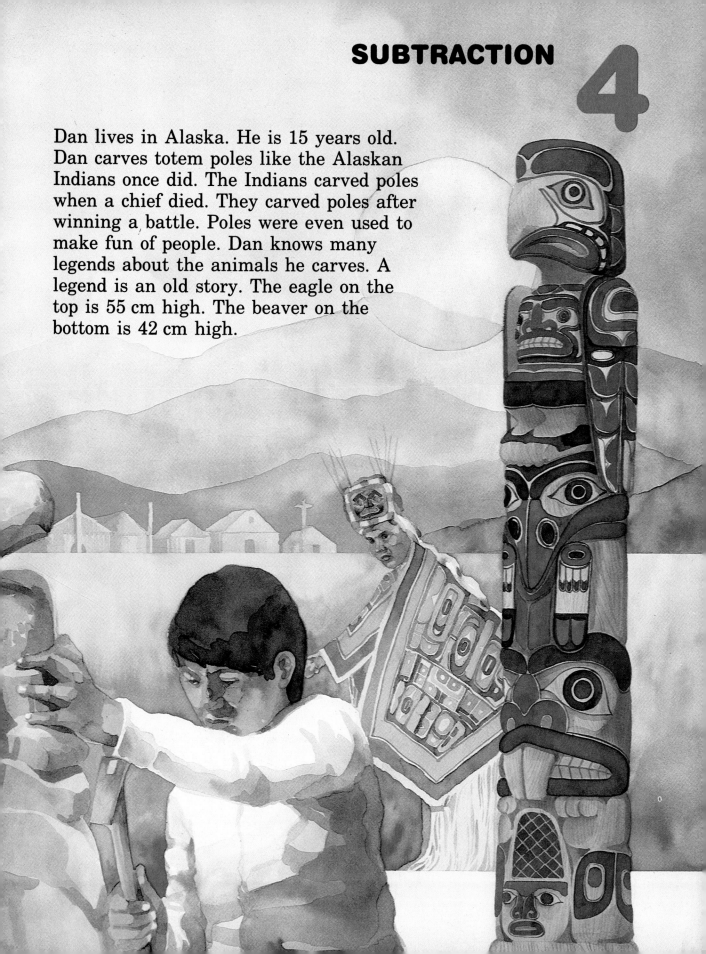

Trading 1 Ten for 10 Ones

Mark has 4 tens and 3 ones. If he trades 1 ten for 10 ones,

1. how many tens will Mark have?
2. how many ones will Mark have?

Mark will have 3 tens and 13 ones.

Other Examples

Trade 1 ten for 10 ones.

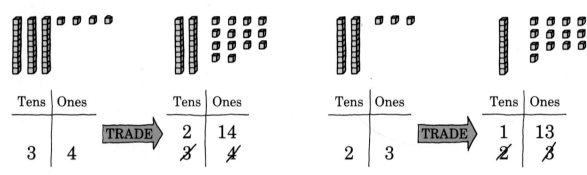

Tens	Ones		Tens	Ones
3	4	TRADE	2 ~~3~~	14 ~~4~~

Tens	Ones		Tens	Ones
2	3	TRADE	1 ~~2~~	13 ~~3~~

Give the numbers of tens and ones after a trade.

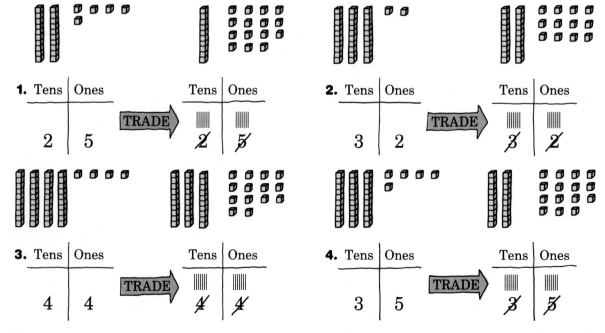

1.

Tens	Ones		Tens	Ones
2	5	TRADE	~~2~~	~~5~~

2.

Tens	Ones		Tens	Ones
3	2	TRADE	~~3~~	~~2~~

3.

Tens	Ones		Tens	Ones
4	4	TRADE	~~4~~	~~4~~

4.

Tens	Ones		Tens	Ones
3	5	TRADE	~~3~~	~~5~~

Trade 1 ten for 10 ones.

Example

Tens	Ones
6	7

TRADE ➤

Tens	Ones
5	17
6̸	7̸

1.

Tens	Ones
4	7

TRADE ➤

Tens	Ones
4̸	7̸

2.

Tens	Ones
5	5

TRADE ➤

Tens	Ones
5̸	5̸

3.

Tens	Ones
7	2

TRADE ➤

Tens	Ones
7̸	2̸

4.

Tens	Ones
3	6

TRADE ➤

Tens	Ones
3̸	6̸

5.

Tens	Ones
2	1

TRADE ➤

Tens	Ones
2̸	1̸

6.

Tens	Ones
5	0

TRADE ➤

Tens	Ones
5̸	0̸

7.

Tens	Ones
8	3

TRADE ➤

Tens	Ones
8̸	3̸

Copy the number. Trade 1 ten
for 10 ones.

Example $56 \rightarrow \overset{4\ 16}{5̸6̸}$

8. 76   **9.** 36   **10.** 47

11. 60   **12.** 15   **13.** 92

14. 24   **15.** 67   **16.** 80

17. 86   **18.** 73   **19.** 66

20. 29   **21.** 82   **22.** 55

THINK

Place Value

Each stick is made up of ten
cubes. Which numbers can you
pick up without trading?

1. 23   **2.** 31   **3.** 6   **4.** 15

If you trade a ten-stick for
ten single cubes, which
numbers can you pick up?

5. 9   **6.** 29   **7.** 5   **8.** 18

➤ **MATH** ◂

Subtracting 2-Digit Numbers: Trading Tens

Carla and Paul were trying to guess one minute (60 seconds). Carla guessed 48 seconds. By how much did she miss?

Since we want the difference between 48 and 60, we subtract.

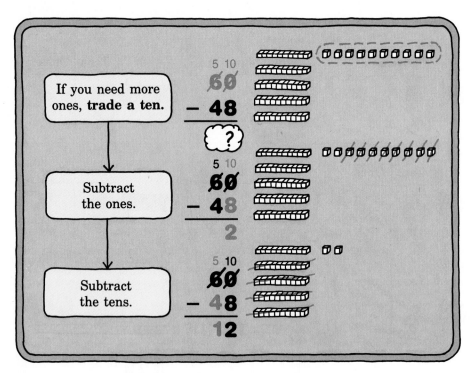

Carla missed by 12 seconds.

Other Examples

$$\overset{5\ 15}{\cancel{65}} - 28 = 37$$

$$\overset{6\ 15}{\cancel{75}} - 69 = 6$$

$$68 - 27 = 41 \quad \text{(NO TRADE NECESSARY)}$$

$$\overset{7\ 15}{\cancel{85}} - 7 = 78$$

$$54 - 3 = 51 \quad \text{(NO TRADE NECESSARY)}$$

Warm Up Subtract.

1. 74 − 18

2. 80 − 26

3. 72 − 8

4. 76 − 34

5. 57 − 49

92 (ninety-two)

Find the differences.

1. 72
  − 18

2. 62
  − 34

3. 58
  − 22

4. 64
  − 58

5. 52
  − 7

6. 70
  − 22

7. 48
  − 3

8. 95
  − 56

9. 43
  − 15

10. 72
  − 63

11. 71
  − 9

12. 44
  − 19

13. 50
  − 35

14. 79
  − 36

15. 71
  − 14

16. 46
  − 28

17. 76
  − 67

18. 37
  − 29

19. 80
  − 42

20. 64
  − 29

21. 97
  − 49

22. 95
  − 70

23. 56
  − 37

24. 55
  − 28

25. 83 − 56

26. 64 − 8

27. 51 − 34

28. 43 − 12

29. 63 − 27

30. 90 − 78

31. 75 − 7

32. 85 − 65

33. Subtract 25 from 33.

34. Subtract 19 from 32.

Solve.

35. Salvador tried to guess one minute. His guess was 75 seconds. By how much did Salvador miss 60 seconds?

36. **DATA HUNT** Have a friend time you with a stopwatch. Close your eyes and try to guess one minute. Find the difference between your guess and one minute.

THINK

Patterns

Pretend today is Wednesday, the 10th of December.

1. What is the date next Wednesday?
2. What is the date in two weeks?

MATH

PROBLEM SOLVING
Understanding the Question

The data in the following problems is given in
"short form" to help you think about the **question.**

1. Running once
around the track:
Jan: 59 seconds
Tom: 72 seconds
How many more seconds did
Tom take than Jan?

2. Sit-ups:
Rob: 41
Ben: 27
How many fewer sit-ups did
Ben do than Rob?

3. Push-ups:
Pam on first try: 17
Pam on second try: 15
How many push-ups did Pam
do in two tries?

4. Baseball throw:
First try: 28 yards
Second try: 46 yards
How much longer was the
second try than the first?

5. Four-person relay race:
1st: 17 seconds
2nd: 18 seconds
3rd: 18 seconds
4th: 16 seconds
What was the total time for
the relay?

6. *Try This* School record baseball
throw: 47 yards
Sally's own record baseball
throw: 36 yards
Sally broke her own record
but not the school record. Her
throw ends in 0. How far was
her throw? Hint: Use logical
reasoning.

Subtraction Practice

Find the differences.

1. 63
    − 15

2. 84
    − 16

3. 52
    − 34

4. 81
    − 16

5. 38
    − 9

6. 26
    − 18

7. 79
    − 46

8. 95
    − 7

9. 80
    − 29

10. 76
     − 21

11. 55
     − 47

12. 49
     − 39

13. 64
     − 37

14. 70
     − 55

15. 48
     − 3

16. 91
     − 68

17. 52
     − 37

18. 71
     − 36

19. 46
     − 22

20. 63
     − 49

21. 47
     − 18

22. 52 − 17

23. 63 − 24

24. 75 − 18

25. 37 − 29

26. Joanne's paper has three mistakes. Which problems have the mistakes?

Add.

1.   25
    + 74

2.   63
    + 28

3.   56
    + 95

4. 321
    + 69

5. 684
    + 352

6. 366
    + 642

7. 193
    + 408

8. 579
    + 847

9. 908
    + 214

10. 788
     + 556

Subtracting 3-Digit Numbers: Trading Hundreds

Brian works in a bicycle store. In March, the store sold 132 bicycles. In April, the store sold 315 bicycles. How many fewer bicycles did the store sell in March?

To find out how many fewer bicycles, we subtract.

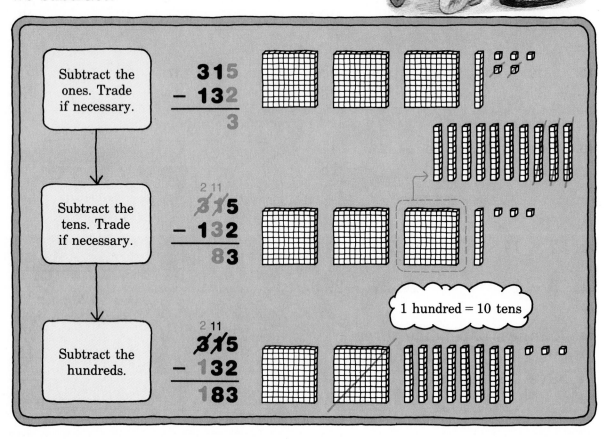

Subtract the ones. Trade if necessary.

$$\begin{array}{r} 315 \\ -\,132 \\ \hline 3 \end{array}$$

Subtract the tens. Trade if necessary.

$$\begin{array}{r} {}^{2\ 11}\!\!\not{3}\not{1}5 \\ -\,132 \\ \hline 83 \end{array}$$

Subtract the hundreds.

$$\begin{array}{r} {}^{2\ 11}\!\!\not{3}\not{1}5 \\ -\,132 \\ \hline 183 \end{array}$$

1 hundred = 10 tens

The store sold 183 fewer bicycles in March.

Other Examples

$$\begin{array}{r} {}^{6\ 12}\!\!\not{7}\not{2}6 \\ -\,251 \\ \hline 475 \end{array} \qquad \begin{array}{r} {}^{5\ 10}\!\!\not{6}\not{0}5 \\ -\,183 \\ \hline 422 \end{array} \qquad \begin{array}{r} {}^{3\ 12}\!\!\not{4}\not{2}8 \\ -\,375 \\ \hline 53 \end{array} \qquad \begin{array}{r} {}^{2\ 15}\!\!\not{3}\not{5}6 \\ -\,92 \\ \hline 264 \end{array} \qquad \begin{array}{r} 138 \\ -\,53 \\ \hline 85 \end{array}$$

Warm Up Subtract.

1.
$$\begin{array}{r} 837 \\ -\,372 \end{array}$$

2.
$$\begin{array}{r} 708 \\ -\,156 \end{array}$$

3.
$$\begin{array}{r} 643 \\ -\,560 \end{array}$$

4.
$$\begin{array}{r} 725 \\ -\,81 \end{array}$$

5.
$$\begin{array}{r} 127 \\ -\,82 \end{array}$$

Find the differences.

1. 716 − 231	2. 417 − 83	3. 603 − 420	4. 154 − 70	5. 516 − 432
6. 168 − 95	7. 819 − 168	8. 127 − 92	9. 435 − 240	10. 524 − 71
11. 904 − 312	12. 418 − 24	13. 156 − 72	14. 768 − 692	15. 544 − 281
16. 854 − 648	17. 708 − 49	18. 135 − 127	19. 624 − 65	20. 312 − 187

21. 307 − 172   **22.** 424 − 70

23. 738 − 474   **24.** 136 − 85

25. How much greater is 823 than 170?

26. How much less is 271 than 348?

Solve.

27. In December, the bicycle store sold 714 bicycles. In January, the store sold 180. How many fewer bicycles did the store sell in January?

★ **28.** Use the following data to write your own question. Then solve it. The bicycle store had 183 girl's bicycles and 327 boy's bicycles.

THINK

Using a Calculator

Show 582 on your calculator. Now show 502 by **subtracting one** number.

Now try these the same way.

  1. 573 → 503

  2. 924 → 904

  3. 8,267 → 8,067

  4. 9,146 → 9,046

MATH

Subtracting 3-Digit Numbers: Two Trades

One of the larger jet airplanes carries
374 people. A new smaller plane carries
197 people. How many more people
can the larger plane carry?

To find how many more people,
we find the difference
between the two
numbers.

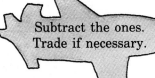

$$\begin{array}{r} \overset{6\ 14}{3\cancel{7}\cancel{4}} \\ -\ 197 \\ \hline 7 \end{array}$$

$$\begin{array}{r} \overset{2\ 16\ 14}{\cancel{3}\cancel{7}\cancel{4}} \\ -\ 197 \\ \hline 77 \end{array}$$

$$\begin{array}{r} \overset{2\ 16\ 14}{\cancel{3}\cancel{7}\cancel{4}} \\ -\ 197 \\ \hline 177 \end{array}$$

The larger plane carries 177 more people.

Other Examples

$$\begin{array}{r} \overset{6\ 10\ 14}{\cancel{7}\cancel{1}\cancel{4}} \\ -\ 189 \\ \hline 525 \end{array}$$

$$\begin{array}{r} \overset{8\ 13\ 13}{\cancel{9}\cancel{4}\cancel{3}} \\ -\ 878 \\ \hline 65 \end{array}$$

$$\begin{array}{r} \overset{5\ 12\ 14}{\cancel{6}\cancel{3}\cancel{4}} \\ -\ 89 \\ \hline 545 \end{array}$$

$$\begin{array}{r} \overset{3\ 12}{1\cancel{4}\cancel{2}} \\ -\ 68 \\ \hline 74 \end{array}$$

Warm Up Subtract.

1. $\begin{array}{r} 324 \\ -\ 167 \end{array}$
2. $\begin{array}{r} 854 \\ -\ 175 \end{array}$
3. $\begin{array}{r} 712 \\ -\ 638 \end{array}$
4. $\begin{array}{r} 126 \\ -\ 88 \end{array}$
5. $\begin{array}{r} 927 \\ -\ 258 \end{array}$

6. $\begin{array}{r} 228 \\ -\ 79 \end{array}$
7. $\begin{array}{r} 437 \\ -\ 359 \end{array}$
8. $\begin{array}{r} 516 \\ -\ 97 \end{array}$
9. $\begin{array}{r} 135 \\ -\ 77 \end{array}$
10. $\begin{array}{r} 643 \\ -\ 578 \end{array}$

Find the differences.

1.	743 − 555	**2.**	154 − 86	**3.**	654 − 590

4. 123
 − 87   **5.** 324
 − 68

6. 815
 − 337   **7.** 483
 − 45   **8.** 530
 − 364   **9.** 327
 − 213   **10.** 122
 − 24

11. 435
 − 267   **12.** 311
 − 172   **13.** 462
 − 325   **14.** 146
 − 73   **15.** 654
 − 88

16. 627 − 463   **17.** 153 − 78   **18.** 412 − 385   **19.** 567 − 234

20. How much less is 69 than 835? **21.** How much less is 57 than 124?

22. A large jet plane carried 254 people. A small jet carried 96 people. How many more did the larger jet carry?

23. A jet plane has 214 seats. 167 people get on. How many seats are empty?

24. DATA BANK See page 361. Find how many people the largest jet can carry. Find how many people another jet can carry. What is the difference between your choice and the largest jet?

More Practice, page 373, Set A

> ## THINK
>
> ### Using a Calculator
>
> Start with a 3-digit number.   287
>
> Reverse the digits and subtract the smaller number from the larger number.
>
> 782
 − 287
 ——
 495
>
> Reverse the digits and add.
>
> + 594
 ——
 1,089
>
> Try this with other 3-digit numbers. What do you notice?
>
> ➡ **MATH** ◀

Checking Subtraction

You can check subtraction by adding.

$$\begin{array}{r} {\scriptstyle 6\ 13\ 12} \\ \not{7}\not{4}\not{2} \\ -\ 285 \\ \hline 457 \end{array}$$

CHECK

$$\begin{array}{r} {\scriptstyle 1\ 1} \\ 457 \\ +\ 285 \\ \hline 742 \end{array}$$

Janet missed two subtraction problems. **Check** her problems for her. Which ones did she miss? What are the correct answers?

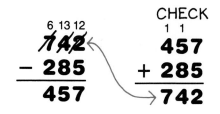

Janet

1. $\begin{array}{r} {\scriptstyle 5\ 12} \\ \not{6}\not{2} \\ -27 \\ \hline 35 \end{array}$ CHECK $\begin{array}{r} 35 \\ +27 \end{array}$

2. $\begin{array}{r} 56 \\ -32 \\ \hline 24 \end{array}$ CHECK $\begin{array}{r} 24 \\ +32 \end{array}$

3. $\begin{array}{r} {\scriptstyle 1\ 13} \\ 1\not{2}\not{3} \\ -\ 56 \\ \hline 67 \end{array}$ CHECK $\begin{array}{r} 67 \\ +56 \end{array}$

4. $\begin{array}{r} {\scriptstyle 4\ 10} \\ 1\not{5}\not{0} \\ -\ 73 \\ \hline 77 \end{array}$ CHECK $\begin{array}{r} 77 \\ +\ 73 \end{array}$

5. $\begin{array}{r} {\scriptstyle 3\ 12} \\ \not{4}\not{2}8 \\ -172 \\ \hline 246 \end{array}$ CHECK $\begin{array}{r} 246 \\ +172 \end{array}$

6. $\begin{array}{r} {\scriptstyle 4\ 13} \\ 7\not{5}\not{3} \\ -128 \\ \hline 625 \end{array}$ CHECK $\begin{array}{r} 625 \\ +128 \end{array}$

7. $\begin{array}{r} {\scriptstyle 8\ 11\ 12} \\ \not{9}\not{2}\not{2} \\ -437 \\ \hline 485 \end{array}$ CHECK $\begin{array}{r} 485 \\ +437 \end{array}$

8. $\begin{array}{r} {\scriptstyle 7\ 12\ 15} \\ \not{8}\not{3}\not{5} \\ -379 \\ \hline 556 \end{array}$ CHECK $\begin{array}{r} 556 \\ +379 \end{array}$

Warm Up   Subtract. Check each answer.

1. $\begin{array}{r} 85 \\ -28 \end{array}$

2. $\begin{array}{r} 62 \\ -57 \end{array}$

3. $\begin{array}{r} 78 \\ -24 \end{array}$

4. $\begin{array}{r} 120 \\ -36 \end{array}$

5. $\begin{array}{r} 141 \\ -75 \end{array}$

6. $\begin{array}{r} 382 \\ -158 \end{array}$

7. $\begin{array}{r} 436 \\ -285 \end{array}$

8. $\begin{array}{r} 724 \\ -76 \end{array}$

9. $\begin{array}{r} 840 \\ -175 \end{array}$

10. $\begin{array}{r} 927 \\ -869 \end{array}$

Find the differences. Check your answers.

1. $\begin{array}{r} 72 \\ -\ 25 \\ \hline \end{array}$
2. $\begin{array}{r} 64 \\ -\ 56 \\ \hline \end{array}$
3. $\begin{array}{r} 92 \\ -\ \ 7 \\ \hline \end{array}$
4. $\begin{array}{r} 76 \\ -\ 34 \\ \hline \end{array}$
5. $\begin{array}{r} 40 \\ -\ 25 \\ \hline \end{array}$

6. $\begin{array}{r} 136 \\ -\ 63 \\ \hline \end{array}$
7. $\begin{array}{r} 152 \\ -\ 76 \\ \hline \end{array}$
8. $\begin{array}{r} 124 \\ -\ 80 \\ \hline \end{array}$
9. $\begin{array}{r} 116 \\ -\ 39 \\ \hline \end{array}$
10. $\begin{array}{r} 130 \\ -\ 52 \\ \hline \end{array}$

11. $\begin{array}{r} 827 \\ -\ 153 \\ \hline \end{array}$
12. $\begin{array}{r} 706 \\ -\ 284 \\ \hline \end{array}$
13. $\begin{array}{r} 657 \\ -\ 583 \\ \hline \end{array}$
14. $\begin{array}{r} 948 \\ -\ 83 \\ \hline \end{array}$
15. $\begin{array}{r} 765 \\ -\ 290 \\ \hline \end{array}$

16. $\begin{array}{r} 824 \\ -\ 175 \\ \hline \end{array}$
17. $\begin{array}{r} 623 \\ -\ 564 \\ \hline \end{array}$
18. $\begin{array}{r} 726 \\ -\ 87 \\ \hline \end{array}$
19. $\begin{array}{r} 650 \\ -\ 188 \\ \hline \end{array}$
20. $\begin{array}{r} 514 \\ -\ 257 \\ \hline \end{array}$

21. $83 - 47$
22. $60 - 8$
23. $67 - 21$
24. $124 - 76$

25. $832 - 280$
26. $643 - 129$
27. $644 - 389$

28. Find the difference between 68 and 136.

29. Subtract 79 from 624.

30. How much more is 726 than 581?

31. How much less is 295 than 632?

SKILLKEEPER

Subtract.

1. $\begin{array}{r} 15 \\ -\ 9 \\ \hline \end{array}$
2. $\begin{array}{r} 16 \\ -\ 8 \\ \hline \end{array}$
3. $\begin{array}{r} 14 \\ -\ 6 \\ \hline \end{array}$
4. $\begin{array}{r} 13 \\ -\ 4 \\ \hline \end{array}$
5. $\begin{array}{r} 11 \\ -\ 8 \\ \hline \end{array}$

6. $\begin{array}{r} 16 \\ -\ 7 \\ \hline \end{array}$
7. $\begin{array}{r} 17 \\ -\ 9 \\ \hline \end{array}$
8. $\begin{array}{r} 10 \\ -\ 3 \\ \hline \end{array}$
9. $\begin{array}{r} 15 \\ -\ 7 \\ \hline \end{array}$
10. $\begin{array}{r} 12 \\ -\ 4 \\ \hline \end{array}$

PROBLEM SOLVING
Using Data from a Map

QUESTION
DATA
PLAN
ANSWER
CHECK

Use the map to answer questions 1–10. Give each distance.

1. Indianapolis to St. Louis

2. Indianapolis to Detroit

3. Cleveland to Pittsburgh

4. Cincinnati to St. Louis

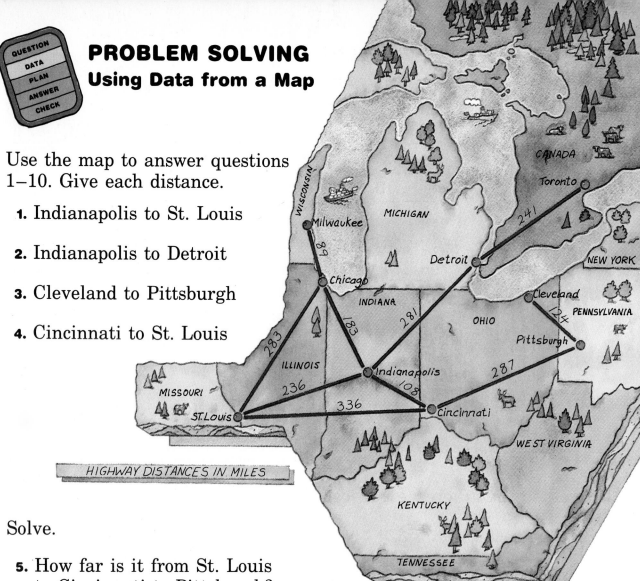

HIGHWAY DISTANCES IN MILES

Solve.

5. How far is it from St. Louis to Cincinnati to Pittsburgh?

6. How much farther is it from St. Louis to Chicago than from St. Louis to Indianapolis?

7. How far is it from Indianapolis to Detroit to Toronto?

8. How much shorter is the trip from Chicago to Milwaukee than from Chicago to Indianapolis?

9. DATA BANK See page 362. How far is it from Tampa to Atlanta to Birmingham?

10. *Try This* Pretend you take one of the trips on the map above. Your trip is more than 200 miles and less than 300 miles. You go an even number of miles. What two cities do you visit?

PROBLEM SOLVING
Using Data from a Table

The yellow shading shows you
how to read the table.
The distance from New York
to Pittsburgh is 384 miles.

Other Examples

Philadelphia to Buffalo: 381 miles

Boston to Washington: 437 miles

	Boston	Buffalo	New York	Philadelphia	Pittsburgh	Washington
Boston	—	454	212	302	593	437
Buffalo	454	—	434	381	217	384
New York	212	434	—	93	384	227
Philadelphia	302	381	93	—	302	139
Pittsburgh	593	217	384	302	—	240
Washington	437	384	227	139	240	—

Mileage Table

Use the table to answer
questions 1–8.

Give each distance.

1. Pittsburgh to Buffalo

2. New York to Washington

3. Buffalo to New York

4. Philadelphia to Boston

Solve.

5. What is the distance from
Boston to Buffalo and then
to Pittsburgh?

6. How much farther is the
distance from Buffalo to
Philadelphia than the
distance from Pittsburgh to
Philadelphia?

7. How far is it from Boston to
Washington to Buffalo to
Pittsburgh to Philadelphia to
Boston?

8. **Try This** Joe lives less than
500 miles from Boston. It is
an odd number of miles.
Where does Joe live?

(one hundred three) **103**

Subtracting Across a Middle Zero

How many more cars passed Main Street between 7:00 a.m. and 8:00 a.m. than between 9:00 a.m. and 10:00 a.m.?

To find how many more cars, we subtract.

Monday Car Count - Main Street	
Time	Number of cars
7:00-8:00 a.m.	405
8:00-9:00 a.m.	302
9:00-10:00 a.m.	128
10:00-11:00 a.m.	137

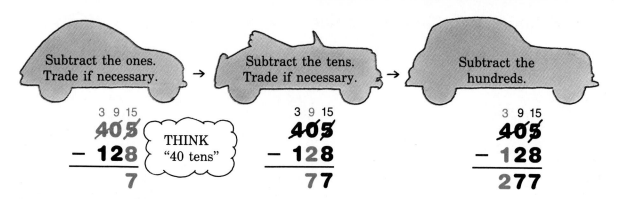

Subtract the ones. Trade if necessary.

$$\begin{array}{r} {}^{3\ 9\ 15}\!\!\not{4}\not{0}\not{5} \\ -\ 128 \\ \hline 7 \end{array}$$

THINK "40 tens"

Subtract the tens. Trade if necessary.

$$\begin{array}{r} {}^{3\ 9\ 15}\!\!\not{4}\not{0}\not{5} \\ -\ 128 \\ \hline 77 \end{array}$$

Subtract the hundreds.

$$\begin{array}{r} {}^{3\ 9\ 15}\!\!\not{4}\not{0}\not{5} \\ -\ 128 \\ \hline 277 \end{array}$$

277 more cars passed Main Street between 7:00 a.m. and 8:00 a.m. than between 9:00 a.m. and 10:00 a.m.

Other Examples

$$\begin{array}{r} {}^{6\ 9\ 10}\!\!\not{7}\not{0}\not{0} \\ -\ 367 \\ \hline 333 \end{array} \qquad \begin{array}{r} {}^{7\ 9\ 16}\!\!\not{8}\not{0}\not{6} \\ -\ 759 \\ \hline 47 \end{array} \qquad \begin{array}{r} {}^{5\ 9\ 15}\!\!\not{6}\not{0}\not{5} \\ -\ 88 \\ \hline 517 \end{array} \qquad \begin{array}{r} {}^{9\ 13}\!\!1\not{0}\not{3} \\ -\ 76 \\ \hline 27 \end{array} \qquad \begin{array}{r} {}^{6\ 10}\!\!\not{7}\not{0}5 \\ -\ 382 \\ \hline 323 \end{array}$$

Warm Up   Subtract.

1. 602
   − 273

2. 906
   − 528

3. 401
   − 89

4. 504
   − 392

5. 703
   − 634

6. 104
   − 36

7. 502
   − 287

8. 703
   − 59

9. 800
   − 342

10. 605
    − 416

Find the differences.

1. 702 − 237	**2.** 504 − 146	**3.** 400 − 164	**4.** 623 − 508	**5.** 904 − 627
6. 506 − 458	**7.** 712 − 285	**8.** 309 − 142	**9.** 600 − 536	**10.** 805 − 723
11. 803 − 439	**12.** 107 − 29	**13.** 435 − 67	**14.** 205 − 76	**15.** 900 − 285

16. 204 − 154   **17.** 600 − 316   **18.** 906 − 78   **19.** 746 − 359

20. 304 − 168   **21.** 503 − 188   **22.** 705 − 627   **23.** 108 − 59

24. Subtract 275 from 704.

25. Subtract 364 from 907.

26. Look at the table on page 104. How many more cars passed between 8:00 a.m. and 9:00 a.m. than between 10:00 a.m. and 11:00 a.m.?

27. On Sunday, only 29 cars passed between 7:00 a.m. and 8:00 a.m. How many fewer is this than 405 cars?

★ **28.** Make up the missing data and solve this problem. How many more cars passed Elm Street between 6:00 a.m. and 7:00 a.m. than between 1:00 p.m. and 2:00 p.m.?

THINK

Smallest Difference Game

1. Make this set of cards.

2. Mix the cards face down.

3. Give each player four cards.

4. Each player makes a subtraction problem.

Example

7   3 ←Winner

5. Smallest difference wins.

MATH

Subtracting Amounts of Money

How much more money does the book about robots cost than the book about dinosaurs?

To find out how much more money, we subtract the smaller amount from the larger amount.

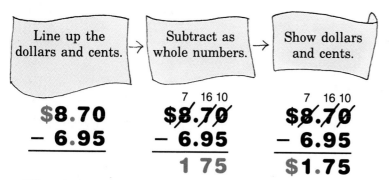

Line up the dollars and cents.	→	Subtract as whole numbers.	→	Show dollars and cents.

$$\begin{array}{r} \$8.70 \\ -\ 6.95 \\ \hline \end{array} \qquad \begin{array}{r} {}^{7\ 16\ 10} \\ \$\cancel{8.70} \\ -\ 6.95 \\ \hline 1\ 75 \end{array} \qquad \begin{array}{r} {}^{7\ 16\ 10} \\ \$\cancel{8.70} \\ -\ 6.95 \\ \hline \$1.75 \end{array}$$

The book about robots costs $1.75 more than the book about dinosaurs.

Other Examples

$$\begin{array}{r} {}^{7\ 11\ 15} \\ \$\cancel{8.25} \\ -\ 2.49 \\ \hline \$5.76 \end{array} \qquad \begin{array}{r} {}^{4\ 9\ 10} \\ \$\cancel{5.00} \\ -\ 0.98 \\ \hline \$4.02 \end{array} \qquad \begin{array}{r} {}^{9\ 10} \\ \$\cancel{1.00} \\ -\ 0.69 \\ \hline \$0.31 \end{array}$$

Warm Up   Subtract.

1. $6.15 − 1.30	**2.** $7.25 − 2.50	**3.** $5.00 − 2.47	**4.** $7.50 − 0.75	**5.** $8.00 − 6.25

6. $1.00 − 0.49	**7.** $5.00 − 1.75	**8.** $3.69 − 1.25	**9.** $5.00 − 2.75	**10.** $8.50 − 1.75

Find the differences in the amounts.

1. $6.25
  − 1.50

2. $5.50
  − 1.70

3. $7.42
  − 0.98

4. $5.00
  − 2.25

5. $1.00
  − 0.75

6. $4.25
  − 0.75

7. $8.00
  − 3.50

8. $1.00
  − 0.45

9. $7.50
  − 0.98

10. $5.00
  − 2.89

11. $8.25
  − 6.75

12. $4.00
  − 0.95

13. $6.32
  − 4.44

14. $3.09
  − 1.99

15. $1.36
  − 1.27

16. $4.35 − $2.50

17. $6.50 − $3.75

18. $7.25 − $0.79

19. $4.00 − $1.25

20. $5.00 − $2.65

21. $6.00 − $1.98

Solve each problem.

22. How much for A and B?

23. How much more is B than C?

24. How much for B and C?

25. How much less is C than A?

26. How much more is A than B?

27. How much for A and C?

28. How much for A, B, and C?

A $8.50
B $5.95
C $2.75

Special Differences: Mental Math

It is 1,100 yards from the Tree to the Treasure if you go past Big Rock. It is only 800 yards if you cross the Dangerous Bridge. How much farther is it to go past Big Rock?

Since we are comparing, we subtract.

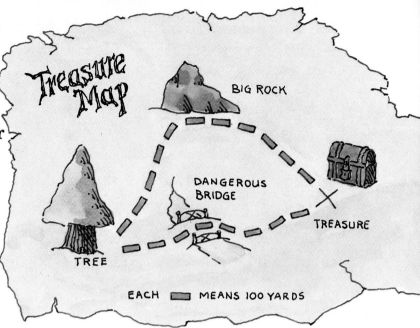

Think about hundreds.
11 hundreds − 8 hundreds = 3 hundreds

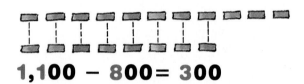

1,100 − 800 = 300

It is 300 yards farther to go past Big Rock.

Other Examples

1,300 − 600 = 700

THINK
13 hundreds − 6 hundreds = 7 hundreds

150 − 80 = 70

THINK
15 tens − 8 tens = 7 tens

Warm Up Give the differences aloud.

1. 110 − 50   2. 80 − 30   3. 1,200 − 600   4. 100 − 20

5. 130 − 40   6. 1,700 − 900   7. 900 − 500   8. 1,400 − 800

9. 120 − 70   10. 1,000 − 400   11. 140 − 60   12. 1,100 − 200

Find the differences. Write answers only.

1. $90 - 10$
2. $1,400 - 800$
3. $120 - 60$
4. $60 - 50$

5. $160 - 80$
6. $800 - 600$
7. $1,500 - 600$
8. $1,000 - 700$

9. $1,200 - 900$
10. $50 - 20$
11. $150 - 90$
12. $100 - 40$

13. $80 - 30$
14. $1,100 - 600$
15. $1,400 - 700$
16. $700 - 100$

17. $900 - 700$
18. $130 - 90$
19. $70 - 20$
20. $1,300 - 800$

21. $1,400 - 600$
22. $70 - 40$
23. $1,600 - 900$
24. $120 - 50$

25. $130 - 60$
26. $150 - 80$
27. $1,700 - 800$
28. $90 - 30$

Solve.

29. It is 600 yards from Big Rock to the Treasure. It is 400 yards from Dangerous Bridge to the Treasure. How much farther is the Treasure from Big Rock than from Dangerous Bridge?

30. The Tree is 20 yards tall. Big Rock is 70 yards tall. How much taller is Big Rock than the Tree?

Use the map on page 108.

31. Jan started at the Tree and walked 300 yards toward Big Rock. She rested and then walked 400 yards more. How much farther does she have to go to get to the Treasure?

THINK

Patterns

Give the next number.

1. 120, 100, 80, 60, 40, ▓
2. 1,800, 1,400, 1,000, 600, ▓
3. 170, 140, 110, 80, 50, ▓
4. 1,500, 1,400, 1,200, 900, 500, ▓

MATH

Estimating Differences

Sometimes you want an answer that is only close to the exact answer.

To estimate how much less the blue car is than the yellow car, we round and subtract.

About how much less is the blue car?

$$\begin{array}{r} \$7.98 \\ - 5.19 \\ \end{array} \quad \boxed{\text{nearest dollar}} \rightarrow \begin{array}{r} \$8.00 \\ - 5.00 \\ \hline \$3.00 \end{array}$$

The blue car is about $3.00 less than the yellow car.

Other Examples

nearest ten	nearest hundred	nearest dollar

$$\begin{array}{r} 72 \rightarrow 70 \\ - 29 \rightarrow - 30 \\ \hline 40 \end{array} \qquad \begin{array}{r} 518 \rightarrow 500 \\ - 195 \rightarrow - 200 \\ \hline 300 \end{array} \qquad \begin{array}{r} \$6.95 \rightarrow \$7.00 \\ - 4.29 \rightarrow - 4.00 \\ \hline \$3.00 \end{array}$$

Warm Up Estimate by rounding to the nearest ten.

1. $\begin{array}{r}92 \\ -48 \\ \hline\end{array}$	2. $\begin{array}{r}59 \\ -13 \\ \hline\end{array}$	3. $\begin{array}{r}67 \\ -39 \\ \hline\end{array}$	4. $\begin{array}{r}81 \\ -33 \\ \hline\end{array}$

Estimate by rounding to the nearest hundred.

5. $\begin{array}{r}789 \\ -207 \\ \hline\end{array}$	6. $\begin{array}{r}617 \\ -321 \\ \hline\end{array}$	7. $\begin{array}{r}575 \\ -187 \\ \hline\end{array}$	8. $\begin{array}{r}921 \\ -498 \\ \hline\end{array}$

Estimate by rounding to the nearest dollar.

9. $\begin{array}{r}\$7.95 \\ -1.29 \\ \hline\end{array}$	10. $\begin{array}{r}\$5.08 \\ -1.95 \\ \hline\end{array}$	11. $\begin{array}{r}\$6.98 \\ -1.99 \\ \hline\end{array}$	12. $\begin{array}{r}\$8.19 \\ -3.25 \\ \hline\end{array}$

Estimate by rounding to the nearest ten.

1. 87
   − 19

2. 63
   − 39

3. 79
   − 42

4. 67
   − 38

5. 92
   − 43

6. 56
   − 17

7. 73
   − 27

8. 45
   − 21

9. 89
   − 19

10. 58
    − 27

Estimate rounding to the nearest hundred or dollar.

11. 921
    − 196

12. 804
    − 295

13. 795
    − 319

14. 817
    − 595

15. $7.25
    − 3.19

16. $5.98
    − 2.79

17. $9.20
    − 4.39

18. $4.79
    − 0.95

Estimate by rounding to the nearest dollar.

19. A 🧦 costs $3.95.

A 🧤 costs $2.15.
How much for both?

20. A ✂️ costs $2.98.
How much change should
you get from a 5-dollar
bill?

21. A ▨ costs $6.95.

A 🪁 costs $1.98.
How much less is
the 🪁 ?

22. A ⏰ costs $8.89.
Judy has only $6.05.
How much more does she

need to buy the ⏰ ?

23. A 🪀 costs $4.98.

A 🦸 costs $7.95.
How much for both?

24. Alex had $5.00.

He bought a 📖 for $2.79.
How much money is left?

Subtracting 4-Digit Numbers

Guess the number of beads.

Student	Guess
Ken	4,800
Lynn	8,307
Janet	5,675
Juan	6,992

The actual number was 6,354.

Whose guess was closest?

Since we are comparing numbers, we subtract.

The smallest difference wins.

Ken	Lynn	Janet	Juan
$\begin{array}{r} {\scriptstyle 5\ \ 13} \\ \cancel{6},\cancel{3}54 \\ -\ 4,800 \\ \hline 1,554 \end{array}$	$\begin{array}{r} {\scriptstyle 7\ \ 12\ 10} \\ \cancel{8},\cancel{3}\cancel{0}7 \\ -\ 6,354 \\ \hline 1,953 \end{array}$	$\begin{array}{r} {\scriptstyle 5\ \ 12\ 14\ 14} \\ \cancel{6},\cancel{3}\cancel{5}\cancel{4} \\ -\ 5,675 \\ \hline 679 \end{array}$	$\begin{array}{r} {\scriptstyle 8\ 12} \\ 6,9\cancel{9}\cancel{2} \\ -\ 6,354 \\ \hline 638 \end{array}$

Juan's guess was closest to 6,354.

Warm Up Subtract.

1. $\begin{array}{r} 7,287 \\ -\ 1,532 \\ \hline \end{array}$

2. $\begin{array}{r} 5,759 \\ -\ 4,287 \\ \hline \end{array}$

3. $\begin{array}{r} 8,746 \\ -\ \ \ 578 \\ \hline \end{array}$

4. $\begin{array}{r} 9,314 \\ -\ 8,487 \\ \hline \end{array}$

5. $\begin{array}{r} 9,538 \\ -\ 5,675 \\ \hline \end{array}$

6. $\begin{array}{r} 7,620 \\ -\ 6,341 \\ \hline \end{array}$

7. $\begin{array}{r} 6,504 \\ -\ 3,257 \\ \hline \end{array}$

8. $\begin{array}{r} 4,313 \\ -\ 2,765 \\ \hline \end{array}$

Find the differences.

1. 5,628
    − 1,375

2. 7,605
    − 1,238

3. 6,304
    − 1,765

4. 7,628
    − 403

5. 4,130
    − 786

6. 8,683
    − 4,362

7. 6,247
    − 768

8. 6,832
    − 5,460

9. 7,204 − 6,487

10. 7,620 − 307

11. 6,800 − 2,375

12. 7,186 − 549

13. 6,473 − 3,284

14. 9,327 − 58

📧 **Check** your answers to exercises 15–18.

15. How much more is 7,234 than 4,760?

16. How much more is 4,823 than 975?

17. How much more is 6,408 than 3,769?

18. How much more is 8,213 than 2,765?

19. Ilene guessed there were 5,683 beads in the jar. By how much did Ilene miss the total of 6,354?

20. Luis guessed 6,703 beads. Joanne guessed 4,675 beads. How many more did Luis guess than Joanne?

21. Not enough data is given in this problem. Make up the needed data and solve. Betty and Hans put 2,356 beans in a jar. Jerry's guess was closest. By how much did Jerry miss the total amount?

┌ THINK ┐

Logical Reasoning

Find the missing digits.

1. ▓▓2
    − 3▓▓
    ─────
      3 4

2. 7▓▓▓
    − ▓▓9
    ─────
      4 6

3. 8▓▓▓
    − 4 6
    ─────
    ▓▓▓7

➤ MATH ◄

PROBLEM SOLVING
Using Data from a Catalog

QUESTION
DATA
PLAN
ANSWER
CHECK

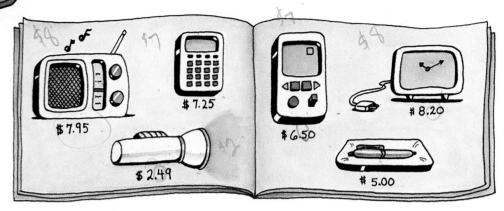

Use the catalog page to solve the problems.
Be sure to **estimate** to see if your answer
makes sense.

1. How much are the calculator and flashlight?

2. How much more is the clock than the flashlight?

3. How much less is the calculator than the clock?

4. How much are the radio and the game?

5. How much more is the pen than the flashlight?

6. How much less is the game than the clock?

7. How much are the radio, the flashlight, and the game?

8. How much are the calculator, the game, and the clock?

9. Round to the nearest dollar and **estimate** the cost of the radio and the clock.

10. **DATA HUNT** Choose one of these gifts that you would like. Look up the price somewhere else. Find the difference in your price and the price given here.

11. *Try This* Ria saw some gifts in another catalog for $13, $17, $19, and $25. She bought two of them for $38. How much was each gift?

PROBLEM SOLVING
Practice

QUESTION
DATA
PLAN
ANSWER
CHECK

These buildings are called skyscrapers. The height to the roof is given for each one.

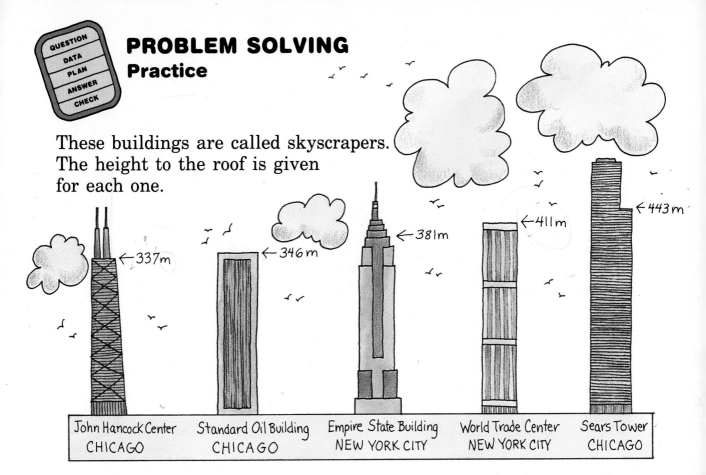

←337m	←346m	←381m	←411m	←443m
John Hancock Center CHICAGO	Standard Oil Building CHICAGO	Empire State Building NEW YORK CITY	World Trade Center NEW YORK CITY	Sears Tower CHICAGO

Use the pictures for problems 1–6.

1. How much shorter is the John Hancock Center than the Standard Oil Building?

2. The tower on top of the Sears Tower is 107 meters. What is the building's total height?

3. How much taller is the World Trade Center than the Empire State Building?

4. How much shorter is the Standard Oil Building than the Sears Tower?

5. **DATA BANK** See page 361. How many more stories does the World Trade Center have than the Chrysler Building?

6. *Try This* The number of stories in the Hillview Palace Hotel is more than 45 and less than 65. The two digits in the number are the same. How many stories does the Hillview Palace Hotel have? Hint: Use logical reasoning.

PROBLEM SOLVING
Draw a Picture

There are no numbers in this problem so you cannot just add or subtract. A **strategy** that can help you is given below.

Try This Ada is between Bend and Dale. Ely is between Ada and Dale. Dale is between Ely and Cody. All the towns are on the same road. Give the order of the towns starting at Bend.

DRAW A PICTURE

1. Draw the road.

2. Ada is between **Bend** and **Dale**.

B   A   D

3. Ely is between Ada and Dale.

B   A   E   D

4. Dale is between Ely and Cody.

B   A   E   D   C

Now read the order of the towns from your picture.

Solve.

1. The red snake is longer than the green snake. The blue snake is shorter than the green snake. Which is longer, the red or the blue snake?

2. Cindy lives on the floor under Don. Ben lives on the floor under Cindy. Gail lives on a floor higher than Ben. Each child lives on a different floor. Who lives on the highest floor?

CHAPTER REVIEW/TEST

Subtract.

1.	76 − 15	2.	83 − 56	3.	95 − 58	4.	90 − 53	5.	68 − 46

6.	138 − 95	7.	924 − 657	8.	124 − 78	9.	657 − 589	10.	135 − 86

11.	304 − 127	12.	608 − 239	13.	$8.32 − 2.70	14.	$6.23 − 2.57	15.	$7.50 − 3.90

Estimate by rounding to the nearest hundred or dollar.

16.	795 − 213	17.	604 − 379	18.	$4.28 − 1.96	19.	$5.80 − 3.87

Find the differences.

20.	6,594 − 3,276	21.	5,042 − 1,864	22.	2,710 − 2,654	23.	4,100 − 2,973

Solve.

24. How much less is B than A?

A

25. How much for both A and B?

B

26. How much farther is it from Hilltop to Lake than from Home to Lake?

27. The IDS Center is 57 stories. The Sears Tower is 110. How many stories are in both?

DO YOU NEED MORE ONES?

Answer YES or NO.

1. 76 − 24	**2.** 83 − 14	**3.** 95 − 32
no	yes	no

Do you need more ones?
Answer YES or NO.

1. 78 − 19	**2.** 84 − 36	**3.** 92 − 71

4. 56 − 28	**5.** 65 − 36	**6.** 43 − 12

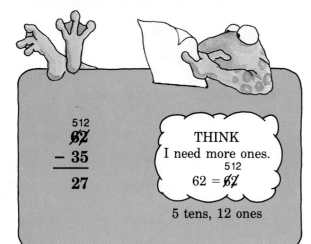

512
$\cancel{62}$
− 35
―――
27

THINK
I need more ones.
512
62 = $\cancel{62}$

5 tens, 12 ones

Subtract.

7. 58 − 23	**8.** 61 − 44	**9.** 93 − 52

10. 50 − 36	**11.** 86 − 45	**12.** 75 − 37

7 915
$\cancel{805}$
− 268
―――
537

THINK
I need more ones.
7915
805 = $\cancel{805}$

79 tens, 15 ones

13. 902 − 235	**14.** 604 − 316	**15.** 803 − 527

16. 724 − 652	**17.** 653 − 428	**18.** 924 − 276

Making Predictions

To get your score, spin both spinners and add the two numbers. The score shown is 9.

1. What is the greatest sum you can spin?

2. What is the least?

3. How many ways can you spin a sum of 7?

Make a table like this one. Finish it.

Sum	Different ways to spin the sum
6	5 + 1,
7	5 + 2, 6 + 1
8	5 + 3, 6 + 2, 7 +
9	5 + 4,
10	

4. When you spin the spinners, what sum do you think you would get most often?

5. What sums do you think you would get least often?

6. Use two spinners like these. Take 50 turns. Keep a record of your sums. Were your predictions right?

CUMULATIVE REVIEW

Give the letter for the correct answer.

1.   35   **A** 58   **B** 69
       + 24   **C** 59   **D** not given

2.   68   **A** 94   **B** 22
       + 26   **C** 84   **D** not given

3.   78   **A** 135   **B** 125
       + 57   **C** 145   **D** not given

4.   355   **A** 771   **B** 781
       + 426   **C** 761   **D** not given

5. $7.49   **A** $14.74
       + 6.25   **B** $13.64
                C $13.74
                D not given

6.   367   **A** 921
       + 554   **B** 811
               C 911
               D not given

Give the number.

7. 8 tens   **A** 88
     3 ones   **B** 38
              C 83
              D not given

8. 2 hundreds   **A** 624
     4 tens   **B** 426
     6 ones   **C** 264
                  D not given

9. 7 hundreds   **A** 207
     0 tens   **B** 720
     2 ones   **C** 702
                  D not given

Which number sentence is correct?

10. A $52 < 41$ **B** $52 > 32$
    C $52 > 108$ **D** not given

11. A $325 > 400$ **B** $325 < 250$
    C $325 < 500$ **D** not given

12. A $6,508 > 6,500$
    B $6,508 > 7,296$
    C $6,508 < 3,454$
    D not given

13. Tondi had $2.75. She earned $1.50. How much did she have then?
    A $3.25   **B** $3.17
    C $4.25   **D** not given

14. Erin paid $9.98 for a puppet. He paid $4.75 for a stage. How much did he pay for both?
    A $5.23   **B** $14.63
    C $14.73   **D** not given

Dana wanted to make a cage for her guinea pig. She made a plan. She needed two pieces of wood 61 cm long and 38 cm wide. First she would nail four wood posts to the corners of the cage bottom. Next she would nail on the top. Then she would staple wire mesh around the sides. The door would be cut from one of the sides. Then it would be clipped back on. Dana made a list of what she needed. She looked at the clock. Dana had just enough time to go to the store.

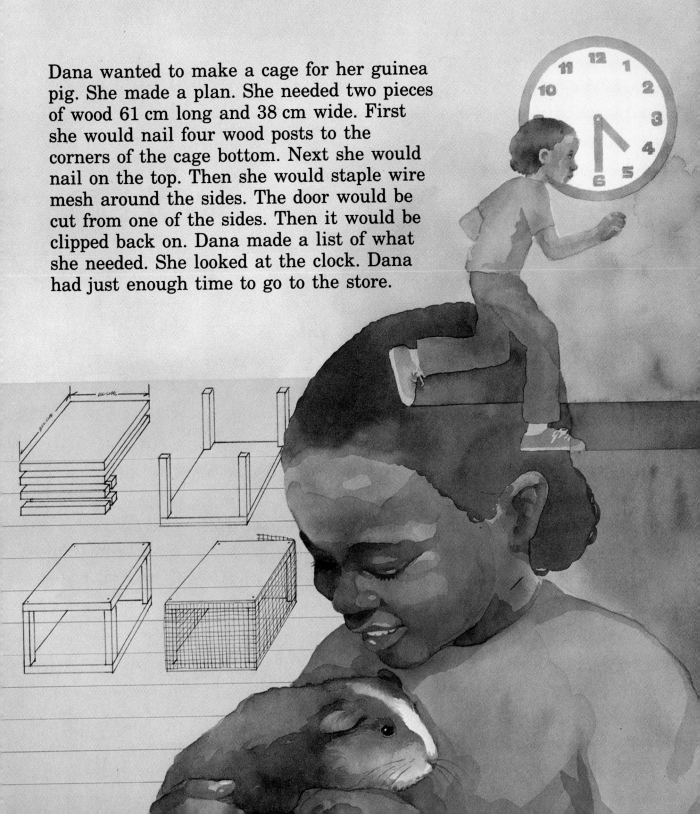

Hour, Half-Hour, and Quarter-Hour

There are 60 minutes in 1 hour.
The minute hand goes around once in 1 hour.
The hour hand goes from one number to the next in 1 hour.
The long hand is the minute hand. The short hand is the hour hand.

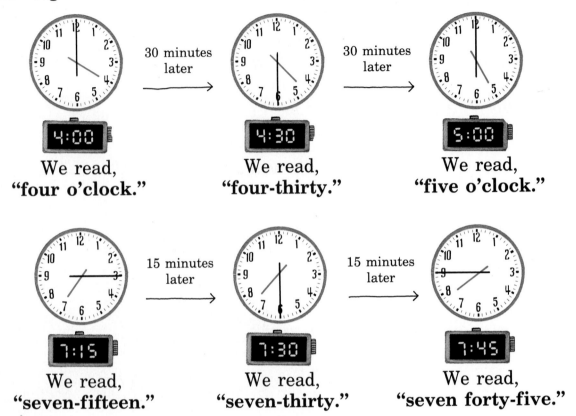

We read,
"four o'clock."

We read,
"four-thirty."

We read,
"five o'clock."

We read,
"seven-fifteen."

We read,
"seven-thirty."

We read,
"seven forty-five."

Write each time as you would see it on a digital clock.

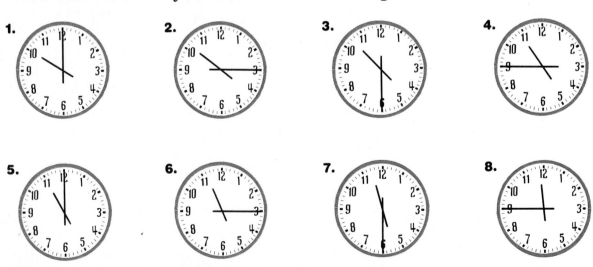

Write each time.

1.

2.

3.

4.

5.

6.

7.

8.

9.

10.

11.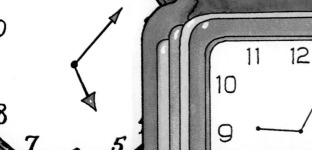

12.

13. Barb looked at the clock. It was 2:30. School is out in 15 minutes. What time is school out?

14. The train came in at 4:15. It was 30 minutes late. What time should the train have come in?

15. Mike said, "I'll be there in 30 minutes." It was 5:00. What time will he be there?

THINK

Guess and Check

Guess the answer before you try this one.

1. Open a book. Add the two page numbers.

2. Turn one page and add the two page numbers.

3. Find the difference in the two sums. Try this with other pages. What do you notice?

MATH

Minutes

School is out at 3:15. Bev said, "In 10 minutes, we will be out of school." What time is it now?

Time now
10 minutes
← School is out

The time is 3:05. The minute hand moves from one number to the next in 5 minutes and from one mark to the next in 1 minute.

5 minutes later

1 minute later

7:15   7:20   7:21

Write each time. Use the numbers around each clock to help you.

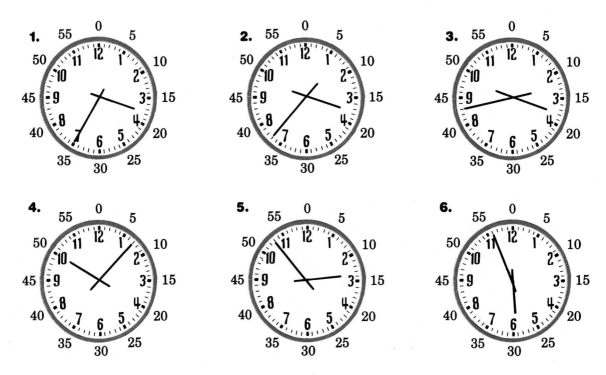

1.

2.

3.

4.

5.

6.

Give the letter of the digital clock that shows the same time as the clock face.

1.

2.

3.

4.

5.

6.

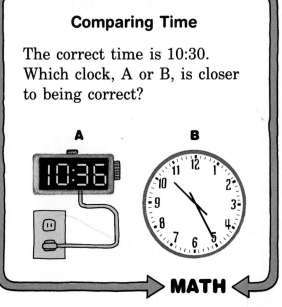

A 3:13

B 3:56

C 3:23

D 3:25

E 3:48

F 3:34

7. The race started at 1:00. The winner finished in one hour and 38 minutes. What time did the winner finish?

8. Art class is right after lunch. It lasts 30 minutes. Lunch is over at 12:25. What time is art over?

9. School is out at 3:00. Bob said, "In 8 minutes we will be out of school." What time is it now?

THINK

Comparing Time

The correct time is 10:30. Which clock, A or B, is closer to being correct?

A 10:36

B

MATH

a.m. and p.m.

The times from 12:00 midnight to 12:00 noon are a.m. times.
8:30 a.m.

The times from 12:00 noon to 12:00 midnight are p.m. times.
8:30 p.m.

Give each time. Be sure to give a.m. or p.m.

1.

Sunrise

2.

Supper

3.

School starts

4.

Bedtime

5. What time do you get out of school?

6. What time do you get up in the morning?

PROBLEM SOLVING
Practice

Jane got up at 7:00 a.m. She took 45 minutes to get ready for school and eat breakfast. What time did she leave for school?

THINK

45 minutes later

Jane got up.

Jane left for school.

Jane left for school at 7:45 a.m.

Solve. Be sure to give a.m. or p.m.

1. Jane's school starts at 8:30 a.m. Recess starts one hour later. What time does recess start?

2. Music class is 30 minutes long. It is over at 10:30 a.m. What time does the music class begin?

3. School lunch starts at 12:00 noon. Lunch time is 50 minutes. What time is lunch over?

4. Science class starts at 1:00 p.m. It is over at 1:45 p.m. How long is the science class?

5. School is out at 2:45 p.m. Jane gets home by 3:15 p.m. How long does it take Jane to get home from school?

6. Jane is ready to play at 3:30 p.m. She plays for two hours. What time does Jane finish playing?

7. **DATA HUNT** What time do you go to lunch? What time is lunch over? How long do you have for lunch?

8. *Try This* Reading is right after math. Science is right before math. Which class is first? Hint: Draw a picture.

Reading the Calendar

MAY

Sunday	Monday	Tuesday	Wednesday	Thursday	Friday	Saturday
		1	2	3	4	5
6	7	8	9	10	11	12
13	14	15	16	17	18	19
20	21	22	23	24	25	26
27	28	29	30	31		

May 16 is on Wednesday.
It is the third Wednesday in May.
The second Tuesday is May 8.

Use the calendar page for problems 1–14.
Give the number of

1. days in May

2. Wednesdays in this month

3. Sundays in this month

4. days in one week

Give the date for

5. the first Saturday

6. the fourth Monday

7. the fifth Thursday

8. the second Friday

Give the day of the week for

9. May 14

10. May 26

11. May 30

12. May 20

13. John's birthday is 5 days before the 31st. What is his birth date?

14. Jan's birthday is 6 days after the 16th. What is Jan's birth date?

JANUARY	FEBRUARY	MARCH	APRIL
S M T W T F S	S M T W T F S	S M T W T F S	S M T W T F S
1 2 3 4 5	1 2	1 2	1 2 3 4 5 6
6 7 8 9 10 11 12	3 4 5 6 7 8 9	3 4 5 6 7 8 9	7 8 9 10 11 12 13
13 14 15 16 17 18 19	10 11 12 13 14 15 16	10 11 12 13 14 15 16	14 15 16 17 18 19 20
20 21 22 23 24 25 26	17 18 19 20 21 22 23	17 18 19 20 21 22 23	21 22 23 24 25 26 27
27 28 29 30 31	24 25 26 27 28	24 25 26 27 28 29 30	28 29 30
		31	

MAY	JUNE	JULY	AUGUST
S M T W T F S	S M T W T F S	S M T W T F S	S M T W T F S
1 2 3 4	1	1 2 3 4 5 6	1 2 3
5 6 7 8 9 10 11	2 3 4 5 6 7 8	7 8 9 10 11 12 13	4 5 6 7 8 9 10
12 13 14 15 16 17 18	9 10 11 12 13 14 15	14 15 16 17 18 19 20	11 12 13 14 15 16 17
19 20 21 22 23 24 25	16 17 18 19 20 21 22	21 22 23 24 25 26 27	18 19 20 21 22 23 24
26 27 28 29 30 31	23 24 25 26 27 28 29	28 29 30 31	25 26 27 28 29 30 31
	30		

SEPTEMBER	OCTOBER	NOVEMBER	DECEMBER
S M T W T F S	S M T W T F S	S M T W T F S	S M T W T F S
1 2 3 4 5 6 7	1 2 3 4 5	1 2	1 2 3 4 5 6 7
8 9 10 11 12 13 14	6 7 8 9 10 11 12	3 4 5 6 7 8 9	8 9 10 11 12 13 14
15 16 17 18 19 20 21	13 14 15 16 17 18 19	10 11 12 13 14 15 16	15 16 17 18 19 20 21
22 23 24 25 26 27 28	20 21 22 23 24 25 26	17 18 19 20 21 22 23	22 23 24 25 26 27 28
29 30	27 28 29 30 31	24 25 26 27 28 29 30	29 30 31

January is the first month.
The seventh month is July.

1. Give the months in order from first to twelfth.

Give the name of the day of the week.

2. July 4

3. February 14

4. October 31

5. January 1

6. February 22

7. December 31

Give the date.

Example   first Sunday of the third month → March 3

8. second Tuesday of the seventh month

9. third Friday of the tenth month

10. first Monday of the ninth month

11. last Monday of the fifth month

Units for Measuring

Laura is making a ruler. She is using a paper clip as her unit for measuring. Each unit is one paper clip. About how many paper clips long is the brush?

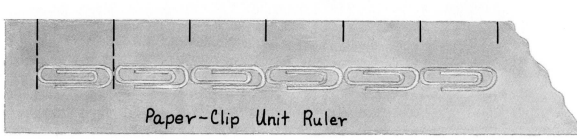

Paper-Clip Unit Ruler

The length of the brush is about 6 paper-clip units.

Give the length of each pencil. Use the paper-clip unit ruler below.

1.

2.

3.

4.

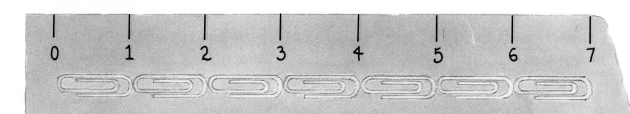

Using the Centimeter Unit

This is a **centimeter** (cm) unit. → ■
Give the length of each object.
Use the centimeter ruler below.

1.

2.

3.

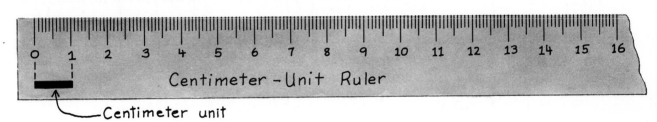

Centimeter–Unit Ruler

Centimeter unit

Use your centimeter ruler. Give the length of each object.

4.

5.

6.

7.

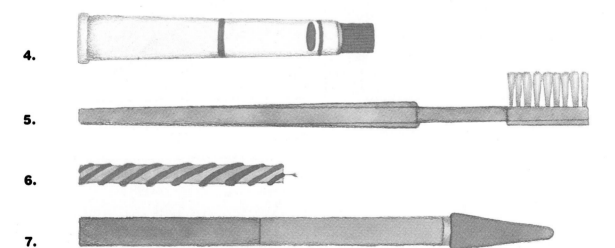

Use your centimeter ruler. Draw some lines that have these lengths.

8. 10 cm   **9.** 7 cm   **10.** 15 cm

Measuring to the Nearest Centimeter

Sometimes measures are not exact. Then you give the measure to the **nearest unit.**

The width of Maria's wrist is closer to 5 cm than to 6 cm. The width to the nearest centimeter is 5 cm.

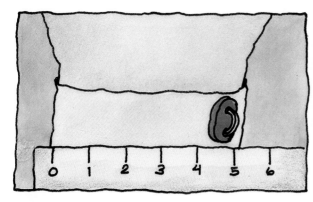

The length of Ted's finger is closer to 6 cm than to 5 cm. The length to the nearest centimeter is 6 cm.

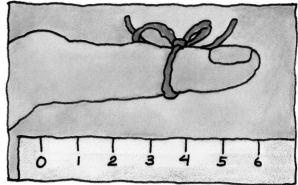

Give each measure to the nearest centimeter.

1. Sue's hand width

2. Larry's thumb length

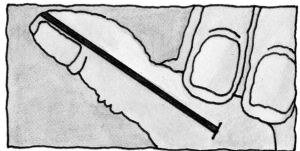

3. Ben's little finger length

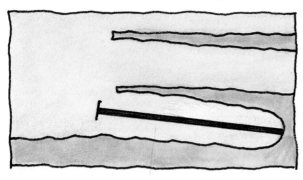

4. Patty's wrist width

This is a picture of Jo's hand.

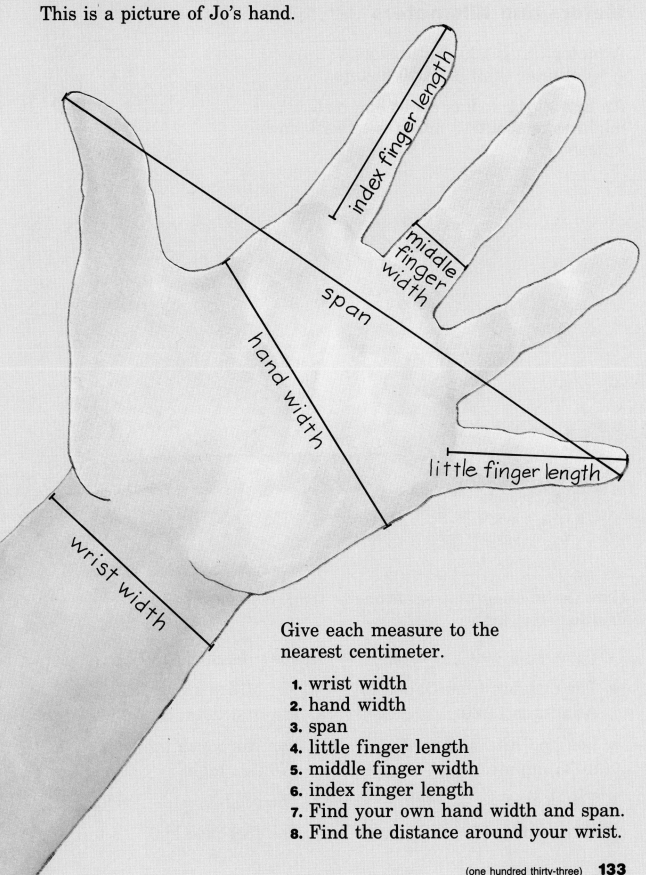

Give each measure to the nearest centimeter.

1. wrist width
2. hand width
3. span
4. little finger length
5. middle finger width
6. index finger length
7. Find your own hand width and span.
8. Find the distance around your wrist.

Meters and Kilometers

A **meter** (m) is 100 centimeters.
A **kilometer** (km) is 1,000 meters.

An extra long step is about one meter. You might take about 10 minutes to walk one kilometer.

1 METER

Give the missing unit—centimeter (cm), meter (m), or kilometer (km).

1. Pam ran a 400 ___ race.

2. Joe's height is 150 ___.

3. The distance from Dallas to Atlanta is 1,160 ___.

4. Mr. Miller drove 75 ___ the first hour.

5. Len and Rita walked 3 ___ in 35 minutes.

6. Ron can touch the wall 176 ___ high.

7. The door is 2 ___ high.

8. The room is 6 ___ wide.

9. Mia's foot is 17 ___ long.

10. The flag pole is 6 ___ tall.

PROBLEM SOLVING
Using Data from a Picture

1. How far is it from Dale to Brook to Troy?

2. How much taller is the building than it is wide?

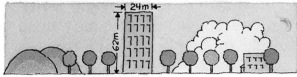

3. How much wider is the brick wall than it is tall?

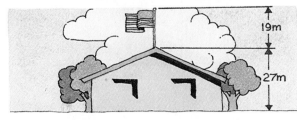

4. How far is it from the ground to the top of the flagpole?

5. How long is the wire holding the birdhouse?

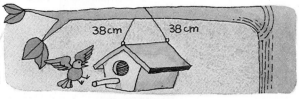

6. How much farther is it to go around the lake than to take the straight road?

7. *Try This* The lake is farther from home than the school, but not as far as the park. The school is farther from home than the store. Which is farthest from home? Hint: Draw a picture.

SKILLKEEPER

Add.

1.	**2.**	**3.**	**4.**	**5.**	**6.**
5	12	4	7	3	5
9	4	4	9	3	26
+ 13	+ 6	+ 4	14	3	37
			+ 2	+ 3	+ 14

Perimeter

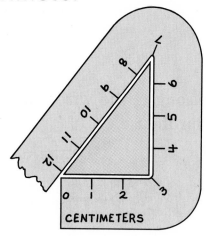

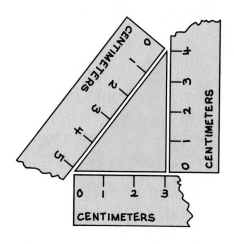

The distance around a figure is its **perimeter**. Look at the **triangle** within the bent ruler. Count the number of centimeters around the triangle. The perimeter is 12 cm.

Most rulers do not bend like the one above. So you may need to add to find the perimeter.

$$3 + 4 + 5 = 12$$
The perimeter is 12 cm.

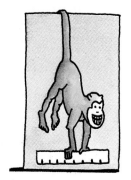

Warm Up   Find the perimeter for each figure.

1.
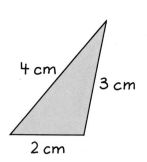
4 cm   3 cm   2 cm

2.
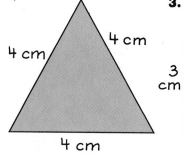
4 cm   4 cm   4 cm

3.
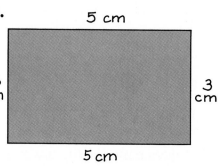
5 cm   3 cm   3 cm   5 cm

Use your centimeter ruler to measure the
sides. Then find the perimeter of each figure.

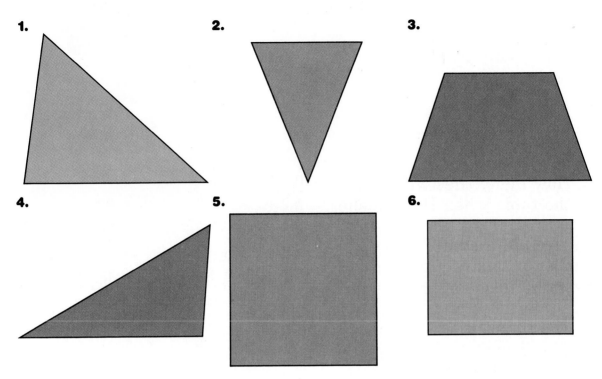

1.

2.

3.

4.

5.

6.

7. How many meters of fence
are needed for the yard?

8. How far is it around the
picture frame?

25 m

15 m   15 m

25 m

87 cm

58 cm

9. Find the perimeter of the
cover of your math book.

10. Find the perimeter of the top
of your desk.

11. A triangle has sides which
measure 5,876 m, 7,398 m,
and 8,597 m. Find the
perimeter of the triangle.

★ 12. The perimeter of a triangle is
24 cm. One side is 7 cm and
another side is 9 cm. What is
the length of the third side?

Area

Don is covering the top of his table with square tiles.

1. How many tiles are on the table now?

2. How many tiles does Don need to finish covering the table?

3. How many tiles will be on the table when Don finishes?

The **area** of a shape is the number of square units needed to cover the inside of the shape.

4. The blue tile is the unit of measurement. What is the area of Don's table top?

Warm Up This is a **square centimeter** unit. ⟶ Give the area of each shape in square centimeters.

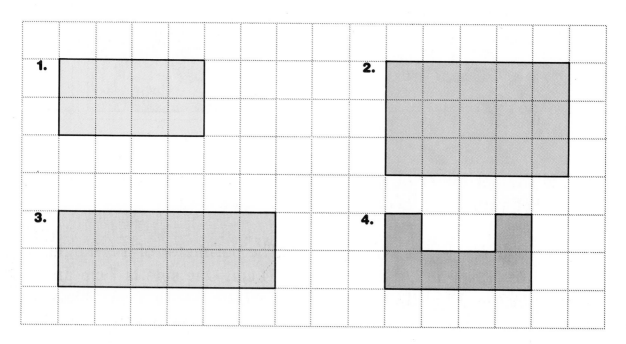

1.

2.

3.

4.

Find the area of each shape in square centimeters.

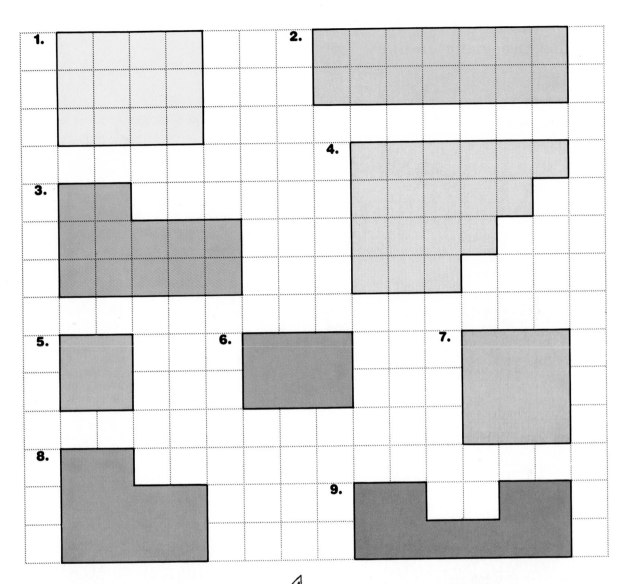

Use graph paper. Draw shapes with these areas.

10. 14 square units
11. 16 square units
12. 24 square units

Volume

A cube can be used as the unit for measuring **volume**.

The trailer holds 6 cubes. The volume of the trailer is 6 cubic units.

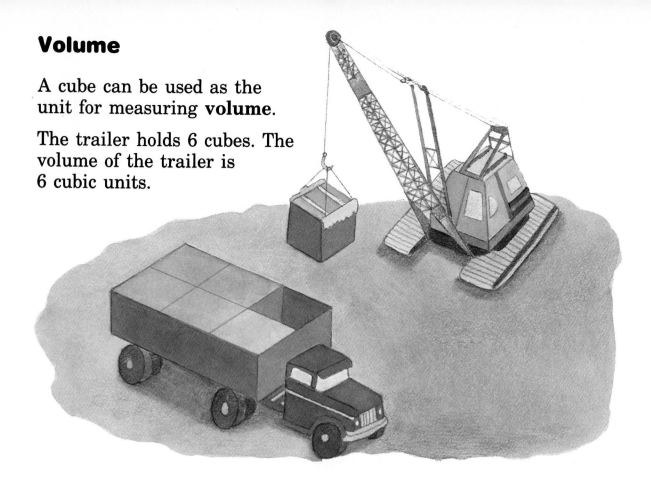

Warm Up Give the volume of each box in cubic units.

1.

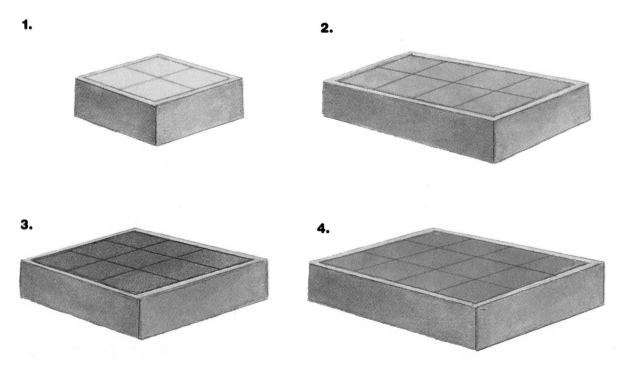

2.

3.

4.

This cubic centimeter is the unit of measurement for the figures below.

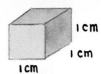
1 cm
1 cm
1 cm

Find the volume of each figure in cubic centimeters.

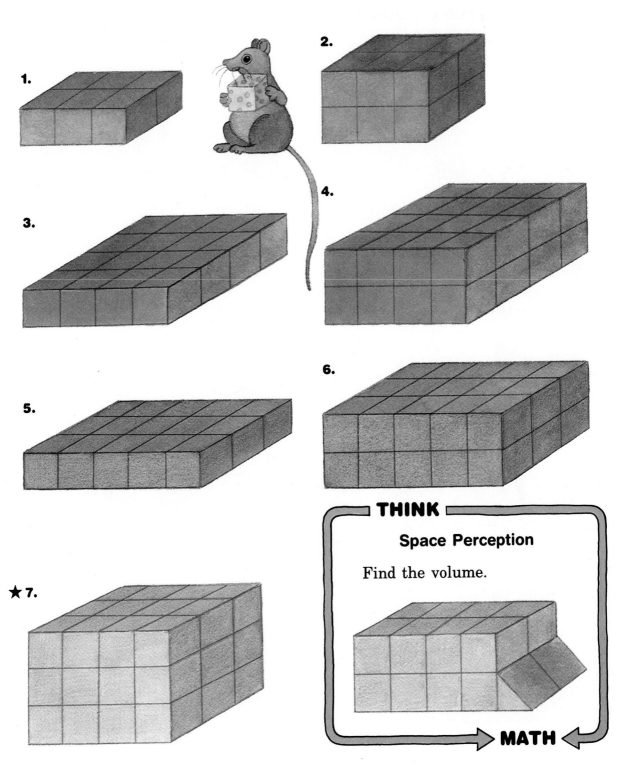

1.

2.

3.

4.

5.

6.

★7.

THINK

Space Perception

Find the volume.

MATH

Liquid Measure

This box holds 1,000 cubic centimeters.
It also holds 1 **liter** (L).

1 liter = 1,000 cubic centimeters

1 liter will fill 4 large glasses.

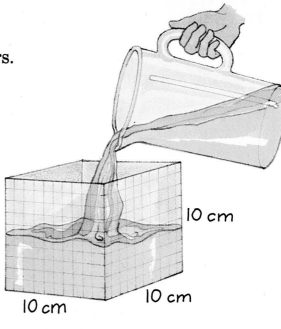

10 cm

10 cm

10 cm

Tell if the objects below hold
more than or less than a liter.

1. Water pail

2. Drinking glass

3. Paper cup

4. Aquarium

5. Roasting pan

6. Cereal bowl

Weight

The **gram** (g) and **kilogram** (kg) are units for measuring weight. A liter of water has a weight of one kilogram.

1 kilogram = 1,000 grams

A paper clip: about 1 gram

A large book: about 1 kilogram

Choose the better estimate for the weight.

1.

Baseball bat
A 1 g   **B** 1 kg

2.

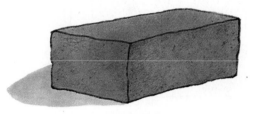

Brick
A 1 g   **B** 1 kg

3.

Apple
A 250 g   **B** 250 kg

4.

Small dog
A 10 g   **B** 10 kg

THINK

Guess and Check

The large block weighs 2 kg more than the small block. Together they weigh 8 kg. How much does the large block weigh?

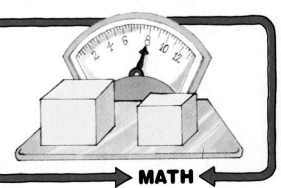

MATH

Temperature

A unit for measuring temperature is the **degree Celsius** (°C).

The thermometer at the right reads about 20°C (room temperature).

Give the reading for each thermometer below.

1. Boiling point of water

 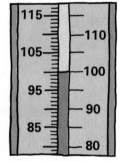

2. Drinking water

 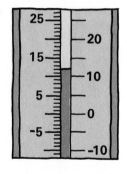

3. Freezing point of water

 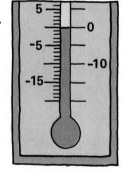

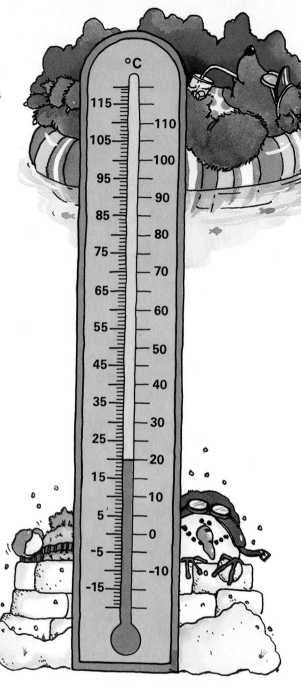

4. DATA HUNT Get a Celsius thermometer. Record the outside temperature. Record the room temperature. Find the difference between them.

PROBLEM SOLVING
Using Data from a Graph

1. The graph shows that Bill is 135 cm tall and Jim is 95 cm tall. How much taller is Bill than Jim?

2. How much taller is Ann than Jim?

3. Jim grew 7 cm a year after the graph was made. How tall was he then?

4. How much taller is Bill than Sue?

5. How much more does Kay weigh than Pam?

6. Joe and Tom both got on the scales. What do they weigh together?

7. How much do Pam and Kay weigh together?

8. **Try This** Peter weighs an odd number of kilograms. His weight is between Tom's and Kay's on the Our Weights graph. It is closer to Tom's. How much does Peter weigh?

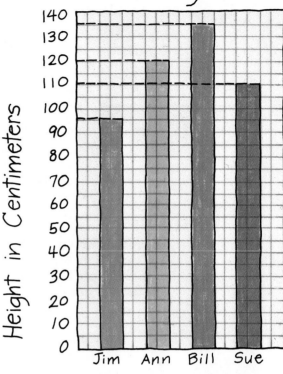

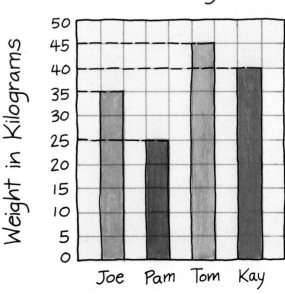

PROBLEM SOLVING
Make a List

QUESTION
DATA
PLAN
ANSWER
CHECK

To solve a problem like this, you may need to do more than just add or subtract. A strategy that can help you is given below.

Try This You can have one piece of fruit and one cracker. How many choices can you make?

MAKE A LIST

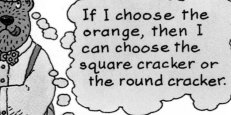

If I choose the apple, then I can choose the square cracker or the round cracker.

If I choose the orange, then I can choose the square cracker or the round cracker.

There are 4 different choices.

○ Apple-square cracker
Apple-round cracker
○

○ Orange-square cracker
Orange-round cracker
○

1. Apple-square cracker
○ 2. Apple-round cracker
3. Orange-square cracker
○ 4. Orange-round cracker

Solve.

1. Charles has a white shirt and a blue shirt. He has a pair of blue jeans and a pair of white jeans. How many outfits can he wear?

2. Amy makes sandwiches with either cheese, jam, or meat. She uses white bread or rye bread. How many different sandwiches can she make?

CHAPTER REVIEW/TEST

Write each time.

1.

2.

3.

4. Use your centimeter ruler. Give the length to the nearest centimeter.

Give the missing unit—cm, m, or km.

5. Tom lives 45 ___ from Reno.

6. The tree is 5 ___ tall.

7. Find the perimeter.

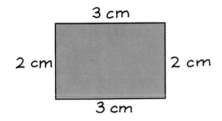

3 cm
2 cm   2 cm
3 cm

8. Find the area.

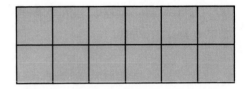

9. Find the volume.

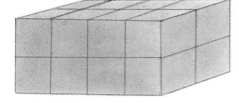

10. Does the bathtub hold more than or less than a liter?

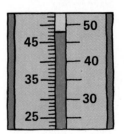

11. Choose the better estimate.

A 12 g   **B** 12 kg

12. Read the thermometer.

Solve.

13. Gym class starts at 2:30. It lasts 45 minutes. What time is gym class over?

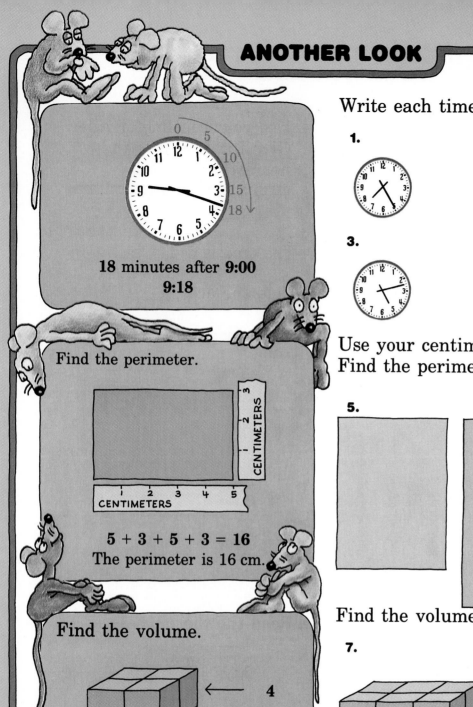

18 minutes after 9:00
9:18

Find the perimeter.

$5 + 3 + 5 + 3 = 16$
The perimeter is 16 cm.

Find the volume.

← 4
← + 4
―――
8

The volume is **8 cubic units.**

Write each time.

1.

2.

3.

4.

Use your centimeter ruler.
Find the perimeter.

5. **6.**

Find the volume.

7. **8.**
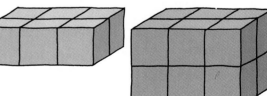

ENRICHMENT

Estimation in Measurement

1. If this length is 8 units,   estimate this length.

$\longleftarrow$ 8 units $\longrightarrow$ $\longleftarrow$? units $\longrightarrow$

2. If this area is 6 square units,   estimate this area.

6 square units      ? square units

3. If this volume is 2 cubic units,   estimate this volume.

2 cubic units      ? cubic units

4. If this perimeter is 20 units,   estimate this perimeter.

20 units   ? units

Flowcharts

Flowcharts show a step-by-step way of doing something.
Flowcharts are used to plan instructions for
computers. Special shapes are used to show each step.

(START) or (STOP) | Gives instructions |

How to Send a Letter

1. What is the first step in
sending a letter?

2. What is the next step after
sealing the envelope?

3. What is the last step after
sealing the envelope?

(START)

| Put letter in envelope. |

| Seal envelope. |

| Write address on envelope. |

| Put stamp on envelope. |

| Put letter in mailbox. |

(STOP)

Getting a Glass of Water

Give the missing instruction for the flowchart below.

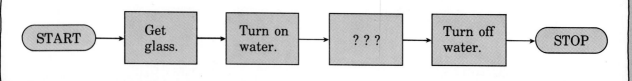

(START) → | Get glass. | → | Turn on water. | → | ? ? ? | → | Turn off water. | → (STOP)

The flowchart below uses the shape to ask a question.

You have to ask a question that has a YES or NO answer.

How to Make a Cheese Sandwich

1. What is the question in this flowchart?

2. If the answer to this question is NO, what is the next step?

3. If the answer to this question is YES, what is the next step?

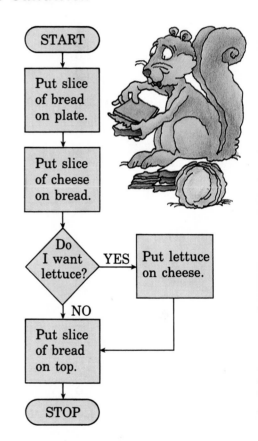

Putting on Your Shoes and Socks

Give the missing instruction for the flowchart below.

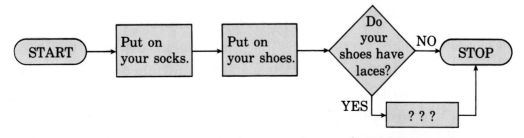

CUMULATIVE REVIEW

Give the letter for the correct answer.

1. 9
   + 9
   - A 0
   - B 18
   - C 10
   - D not given

2. 6
   + 7
   - A 1
   - B 15
   - C 13
   - D not given

3. 8
   + 5
   - A 3
   - B 13
   - C 12
   - D not given

4. 10
   + 0
   - A 0
   - B 1
   - C 10
   - D not given

5. 3
   + 8
   - A 12
   - B 10
   - C 5
   - D not given

6. 6
   + 8
   - A 16
   - B 2
   - C 14
   - D not given

7. 42
   + 86
   - A 128
   - B 148
   - C 138
   - D not given

8. 276
   + 54
   - A 220
   - B 320
   - C 330
   - D not given

9. 529
   + 683
   - A 1,212
   - B 1,202
   - C 1,102
   - D not given

10. 356 + 825
    - A 1,171
    - B 1,181
    - C 1,281
    - D not given

11. $9.86 + $6.02
    - A $16.88
    - B $15.16
    - C $15.88
    - D not given

12. $9.53 + $6.78
    - A $16.31
    - B $15.23
    - C $15.21
    - D not given

13. Marisa read 16 pages of a book. Then she read 19 more pages. How many pages did she read altogether?
    - A 25
    - B 36
    - C 35
    - D not given

14. Alex spent $7.98 for a gift. He spent $0.75 for a card. How much did he spend?
    - A $8.63
    - B $8.73
    - C $7.73
    - D not given

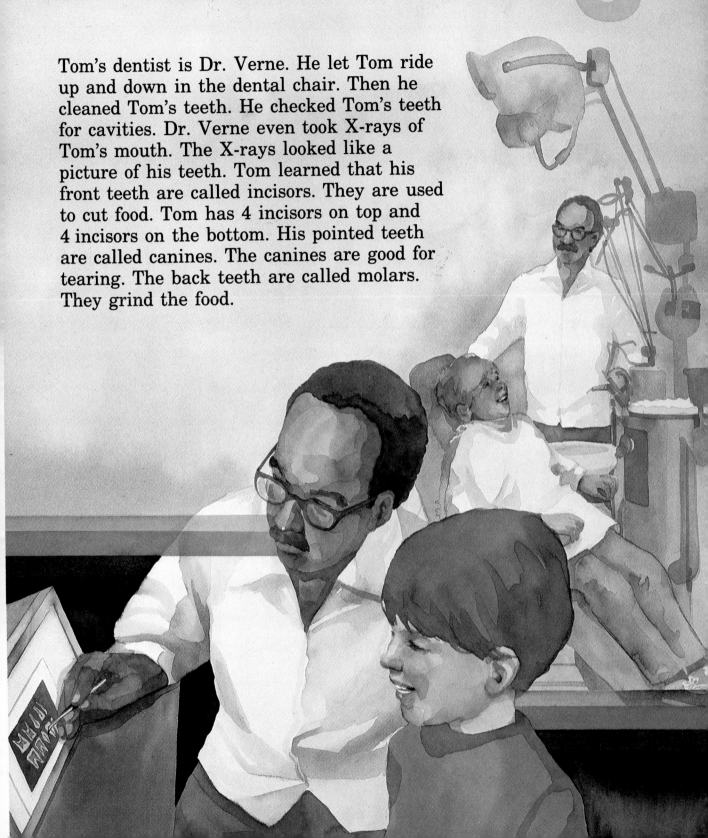

Tom's dentist is Dr. Verne. He let Tom ride up and down in the dental chair. Then he cleaned Tom's teeth. He checked Tom's teeth for cavities. Dr. Verne even took X-rays of Tom's mouth. The X-rays looked like a picture of his teeth. Tom learned that his front teeth are called incisors. They are used to cut food. Tom has 4 incisors on top and 4 incisors on the bottom. His pointed teeth are called canines. The canines are good for tearing. The back teeth are called molars. They grind the food.

Addition and Multiplication

How many tents are there?
You can find out by adding.

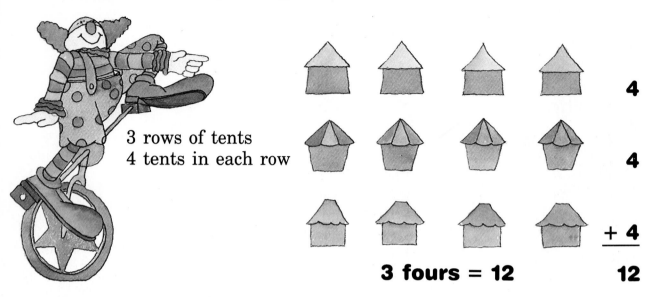

3 rows of tents
4 tents in each row

4

4

+ 4

3 fours = 12

12

Warm Up   How many are there?

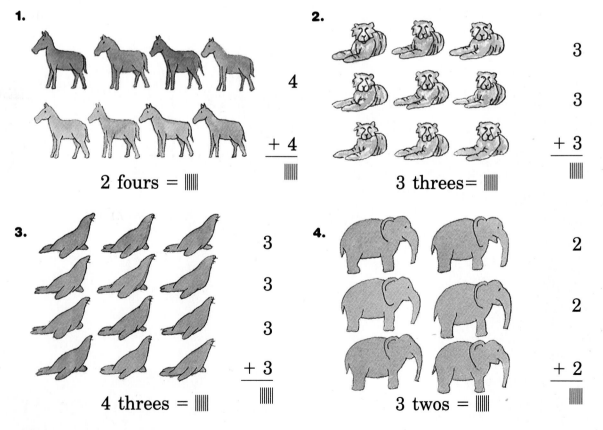

1.

4

+ 4

2 fours = ▯

2.

3

3

+ 3

3 threes= ▯

3.

3

3

3

+ 3

4 threes = ▯

4.

2

2

+ 2

3 twos = ▯

How many are there?

1.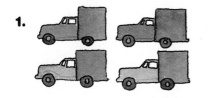

2 twos = ||||||

$$\begin{array}{r} 2 \\ + 2 \\ \hline \end{array}$$

2.

3 fives = ||||||

$$\begin{array}{r} 5 \\ 5 \\ + 5 \\ \hline \end{array}$$

3.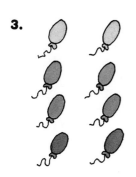

4 twos = ||||||

$$\begin{array}{r} 2 \\ 2 \\ 2 \\ + 2 \\ \hline \end{array}$$

4.

2 threes = ||||||

$$\begin{array}{r} 3 \\ + 3 \\ \hline \end{array}$$

5.

2 fives = ||||||

$$\begin{array}{r} 5 \\ + 5 \\ \hline \end{array}$$

6.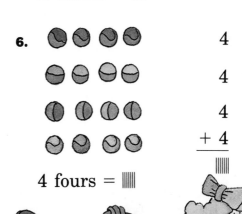

4 fours = ||||||

$$\begin{array}{r} 4 \\ 4 \\ 4 \\ + 4 \\ \hline \end{array}$$

How many cents are there?

7.

2 nickels equal ||||||¢

8.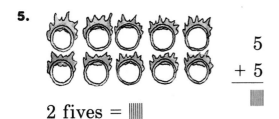

3 nickels equal ||||||¢

9.

4 nickels equal ||||||¢

THINK

Patterns

Give the next 3 numbers.

1. 2, 4, 6, 8, ||||||, ||||||, ||||||

2. 3, 6, 9, 12, ||||||, ||||||, ||||||

3. 8, 12, 16, 20, ||||||, ||||||, ||||||

4. 15, 20, 25, 30, ||||||, ||||||, ||||||

MATH

Understanding Multiplication

Heather has 3 pots of flowers. There are 2 flowers in each pot. How many flowers does Heather have?

The pots have the same number of flowers. You can **multiply** to find how many.

3 twos = 6
3 × 2 = 6

$$\begin{array}{r} 2 \\ \times\, 3 \\ \hline 6 \end{array}$$

We read the **equation** 3 × 2 = 6 as "**Three times two equal six.**" Heather has 6 flowers.

Warm Up Multiply.

1.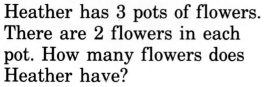

   2 fours
   2 × 4 = ___

2.

   4 threes
   4 × 3 = ___

3.

   2 fives

   $$\begin{array}{r} 5 \\ \times\, 2 \\ \hline \end{array}$$

4.

   3 threes

   $$\begin{array}{r} 3 \\ \times\, 3 \\ \hline \end{array}$$

Multiply.

1. $3 \times 4 = \underline{\hspace{1cm}}$

2. $4 \times 2 = \underline{\hspace{1cm}}$

3. $2 \times 5 = \underline{\hspace{1cm}}$

4. $3 \times 3 = \underline{\hspace{1cm}}$

5.
$$\begin{array}{r} 3 \\ \times 2 \\ \hline \end{array}$$

6.
$$\begin{array}{r} 4 \\ \times 2 \\ \hline \end{array}$$

7.
$$\begin{array}{r} 5 \\ \times 3 \\ \hline \end{array}$$

8.
$$\begin{array}{r} 2 \\ \times 2 \\ \hline \end{array}$$

THINK

Measurement

| 2 cm | 3 cm | 4 cm |

How long is each row?

1.

2.

3.

MATH

2 as a Factor

How many shoes are there in all?

3 twos = 6

$2 \leftarrow$ Factor
$\times 3 \leftarrow$ Factor
$\overline{6} \leftarrow$ Product

$$3 \times 2 = 6$$
Factor Factor Product

There are 6 shoes in all.

Find the products.

1. $2 \times 2 = $ ____   **2.** $4 \times 2 = $ ____   **3.** $5 \times 2 = $ ____

Use this picture if you need help.

4. 6 twos
$6 \times 2 = $ ____

5. 7 twos
$7 \times 2 = $ ____

6. 8 twos
$8 \times 2 = $ ____

7. 9 twos
$9 \times 2 = $ ____

Warm Up Read each number sentence aloud and give the product.

8. $4 \times 2 = $ ____   **9.** $2 \times 2 = $ ____   **10.** $7 \times 2 = $ ____   **11.** $5 \times 2 = $ ____

12. $6 \times 2 = $ ____   **13.** $8 \times 2 = $ ____   **14.** $3 \times 2 = $ ____   **15.** $9 \times 2 = $ ____

Give the product aloud.

16.
$\begin{array}{r} 2 \\ \times 8 \\ \hline \end{array}$
   17.
$\begin{array}{r} 2 \\ \times 4 \\ \hline \end{array}$
   18.
$\begin{array}{r} 2 \\ \times 6 \\ \hline \end{array}$
   19.
$\begin{array}{r} 2 \\ \times 9 \\ \hline \end{array}$
   20.
$\begin{array}{r} 2 \\ \times 3 \\ \hline \end{array}$
   21.
$\begin{array}{r} 2 \\ \times 2 \\ \hline \end{array}$
   22.
$\begin{array}{r} 2 \\ \times 7 \\ \hline \end{array}$

Multiply.

1. 2
    × 4

2. 2
    × 7

3. 2
    × 2

4. 2
    × 8

5. 2
    × 3

6. 2
    × 5

7. 2
    × 9

8. 2
    × 8

9. 2
    × 6

10. 2
     × 7

11. 2
     × 5

12. 2
     × 2

13. 2
     × 9

14. 2
     × 7

15. 2
     × 2

16. 2
     × 6

17. 2
     × 4

18. 2
     × 5

19. 2
     × 7

20. 2
     × 8

21. 2
     × 3

22. 9×2

23. 3×2

24. 6×2

25. 8×2

26. 5×2

27. 2×2

28. 9×2

29. 4×2

Each box has 2 shoes. How many shoes are there?

30.

31.

32.

SKILLKEEPER

Add or subtract.

1.   56
    − 35

2.   26
    + 73

3.   38
    + 59

4.   354
   − 108

5.   349
   + 685

6.   806
   − 687

7.   413
   + 377

8.   361
   − 220

More Practice, page 376, Set A

(one hundred fifty-nine) **159**

3 as a Factor

How many balls are there altogether?

$$4 \times 3 = 12$$

There are 12 tennis balls altogether.

4 threes = 12

Find the products.

1.
$2 \times 3 = \underline{\hspace{1cm}}$

2.
$3 \times 3 = \underline{\hspace{1cm}}$

3.
$5 \times 3 = \underline{\hspace{1cm}}$

Use this picture if you need help.

4. 6 threes
$6 \times 3 = \underline{\hspace{1cm}}$

5. 7 threes
$7 \times 3 = \underline{\hspace{1cm}}$

6. 8 threes
$8 \times 3 = \underline{\hspace{1cm}}$

7. 9 threes
$9 \times 3 = \underline{\hspace{1cm}}$

Warm Up Read each number sentence aloud and give the product.

8. $5 \times 3 = \underline{\hspace{1cm}}$ **9.** $3 \times 3 = \underline{\hspace{1cm}}$ **10.** $9 \times 3 = \underline{\hspace{1cm}}$ **11.** $2 \times 3 = \underline{\hspace{1cm}}$

12. $8 \times 3 = \underline{\hspace{1cm}}$ **13.** $4 \times 3 = \underline{\hspace{1cm}}$ **14.** $7 \times 3 = \underline{\hspace{1cm}}$ **15.** $6 \times 3 = \underline{\hspace{1cm}}$

Give the product aloud.

16. $\begin{array}{r} 3 \\ \times 9 \\ \hline \end{array}$ **17.** $\begin{array}{r} 3 \\ \times 7 \\ \hline \end{array}$ **18.** $\begin{array}{r} 3 \\ \times 2 \\ \hline \end{array}$ **19.** $\begin{array}{r} 3 \\ \times 5 \\ \hline \end{array}$ **20.** $\begin{array}{r} 3 \\ \times 3 \\ \hline \end{array}$ **21.** $\begin{array}{r} 3 \\ \times 6 \\ \hline \end{array}$ **22.** $\begin{array}{r} 3 \\ \times 8 \\ \hline \end{array}$

Multiply.

1. $\begin{array}{r} 3 \\ \times 4 \\ \hline \end{array}$
2. $\begin{array}{r} 3 \\ \times 9 \\ \hline \end{array}$
3. $\begin{array}{r} 3 \\ \times 2 \\ \hline \end{array}$
4. $\begin{array}{r} 3 \\ \times 8 \\ \hline \end{array}$
5. $\begin{array}{r} 2 \\ \times 6 \\ \hline \end{array}$
6. $\begin{array}{r} 3 \\ \times 7 \\ \hline \end{array}$
7. $\begin{array}{r} 3 \\ \times 5 \\ \hline \end{array}$

8. $\begin{array}{r} 3 \\ \times 3 \\ \hline \end{array}$
9. $\begin{array}{r} 3 \\ \times 6 \\ \hline \end{array}$
10. $\begin{array}{r} 2 \\ \times 9 \\ \hline \end{array}$
11. $\begin{array}{r} 3 \\ \times 4 \\ \hline \end{array}$
12. $\begin{array}{r} 3 \\ \times 2 \\ \hline \end{array}$
13. $\begin{array}{r} 3 \\ \times 5 \\ \hline \end{array}$
14. $\begin{array}{r} 3 \\ \times 9 \\ \hline \end{array}$

15. $\begin{array}{r} 3 \\ \times 8 \\ \hline \end{array}$
16. $\begin{array}{r} 3 \\ \times 4 \\ \hline \end{array}$
17. $\begin{array}{r} 3 \\ \times 2 \\ \hline \end{array}$
18. $\begin{array}{r} 2 \\ \times 3 \\ \hline \end{array}$
19. $\begin{array}{r} 2 \\ \times 4 \\ \hline \end{array}$
20. $\begin{array}{r} 2 \\ \times 8 \\ \hline \end{array}$
21. $\begin{array}{r} 2 \\ \times 2 \\ \hline \end{array}$

22. 7×2
23. 3×3
24. 9×3
25. 8×2

26. 5×3
27. 7×3
28. 8×3
29. 6×3

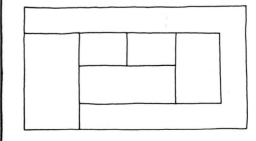

Each can has 3 tennis balls.
How many tennis balls are there?

30.

31.

32.

THINK

Shape Perception

Draw a figure like the one below. Color your map using just four colors. You must have different colors on each side of a line.

MATH

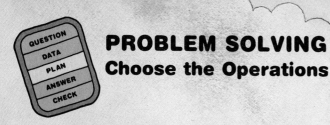

PROBLEM SOLVING
Choose the Operations

Now you have a new operation to think about when you make your **plan**.

Choose the operation and solve.

1. Mandy bought 4 boxes of golf balls. Each box had 3 golf balls. How many golf balls did Mandy buy?

2. There were 27 children who played softball in the morning. 35 played in the afternoon. How many children played that day?

3. Justin scored 23 points. Tod scored 16 points. How many more points did Justin score than Tod?

4. There were 45 children who played soccer. 18 of them left the game early. How many were still playing?

5. Becky scored 7 field goals in basketball. Each one was 2 points. How many points did Becky score?

6. Jim's team scored 39 points the first half and 27 points the second half. How many points did they score in all?

7. A field goal in football is 3 points. Gretchen scored 8 field goals. How many points did she score?

8. *Try This* Yolanda and Phil are pitchers. Barb and Luis are catchers. How many different pitcher-catcher pairs can they make? Hint: Make a list.

Practice the Facts

Give each product aloud.

1. 4×2 2. 7×3 3. 5×3 4. 6×2

5. 4×3 6. 8×2 7. 2×2 8. 2×3

9. 7×2 10. 9×3 11. 8×3 12. 5×2

13. 3×3 14. 3×2 15. 9×2 16. 6×3

Write each product.

17. $\begin{array}{r} 2 \\ \times 4 \\ \hline \end{array}$
18. $\begin{array}{r} 3 \\ \times 8 \\ \hline \end{array}$
19. $\begin{array}{r} 3 \\ \times 4 \\ \hline \end{array}$
20. $\begin{array}{r} 2 \\ \times 9 \\ \hline \end{array}$
21. $\begin{array}{r} 3 \\ \times 6 \\ \hline \end{array}$
22. $\begin{array}{r} 3 \\ \times 9 \\ \hline \end{array}$
23. $\begin{array}{r} 2 \\ \times 5 \\ \hline \end{array}$

24. $\begin{array}{r} 2 \\ \times 6 \\ \hline \end{array}$
25. $\begin{array}{r} 3 \\ \times 2 \\ \hline \end{array}$
26. $\begin{array}{r} 3 \\ \times 8 \\ \hline \end{array}$
27. $\begin{array}{r} 2 \\ \times 2 \\ \hline \end{array}$
28. $\begin{array}{r} 3 \\ \times 6 \\ \hline \end{array}$
29. $\begin{array}{r} 3 \\ \times 7 \\ \hline \end{array}$
30. $\begin{array}{r} 2 \\ \times 7 \\ \hline \end{array}$

Give the missing numbers.

× 2	
8	16
6	12
31. 4	
32. 9	
33. 3	
34. 5	
35. 7	

× 3	
5	15
9	27
36. 3	
37. 6	
38. 7	
39. 4	
40. 8	

THINK

Predictions

Pretend you closed your eyes and took a marble. Would it be red or blue? Now pretend you put it back. If you did this 50 times, would you get more red or blue marbles? How many blue marbles do you think you might get?

MATH

4 as a Factor

How many meatballs are there on all the plates?

3 × 4 = 12

There are 12 meatballs on all the plates.

3 fours = 12

Find the products.

1. 2 × 4 = ___   **2.** 4 × 4 = ___   **3.** 5 × 4 = ___

Use this picture if you need help.

4. 6 fours   **5.** 7 fours   **6.** 8 fours   **7.** 9 fours
　6 × 4 = ___   　7 × 4 = ___   　8 × 4 = ___   　9 × 4 = ___

Warm Up Give each product aloud.

8. 3 × 4 = ___   **9.** 7 × 4 = ___   **10.** 9 × 4 = ___   **11.** 4 × 4 = ___

12. 8 × 4 = ___   **13.** 5 × 4 = ___   **14.** 2 × 4 = ___   **15.** 6 × 4 = ___

16.	**17.**	**18.**	**19.**	**20.**	**21.**	**22.**
4	4	4	4	4	4	4
×9	×2	×4	×3	×8	×5	×7

Multiply.

1. 4 ×5
2. 4 ×8
3. 3 ×7
4. 4 ×4
5. 2 ×9
6. 3 ×4
7. 4 ×9

8. 4 ×7
9. 4 ×2
10. 3 ×6
11. 4 ×9
12. 4 ×6
13. 2 ×8
14. 4 ×3

15. 4 ×2
16. 4 ×5
17. 3 ×8
18. 4 ×7
19. 2 ×5
20. 3 ×5
21. 2 ×3

22. 6×2
23. 8×4
24. 3×4
25. 6×4

26. 9×4
27. 7×2
28. 4×4
29. 9×3

Each plate needs 4 meatballs.
How many meatballs are needed?

30.

31.

32.

THINK

Logical Reasoning

Solve these puzzle problems.

1. My digits are 7, 2, and 5.
   I'm between 500 and 550.
   Who am I?
2. My digits are 6, 0, and 3.
   I'm smaller than 350.
   Who am I?

MATH

5 as a Factor

How many letters are in these number names?

6 × 5 = 30

There are 30 letters in the 5-letter number names.

6 fives = 30

Find the products.

1. SMILE AGAIN.

$2 \times 5 = $ ____

2. BRUSH TEETH OFTEN.

$3 \times 5 = $ ____

3. DRINK CLEAR WATER TODAY.

$4 \times 5 = $ ____

Use these five-letter words if you need help.

4. 5 fives

$5 \times 5 = $ ____

5. 7 fives

$7 \times 5 = $ ____

6. 8 fives

$8 \times 5 = $ ____

7. 9 fives

$9 \times 5 = $ ____

Warm Up   Give each product aloud.

8. $3 \times 5 = $ ____

9. $5 \times 5 = $ ____

10. $2 \times 5 = $ ____

11. $7 \times 5 = $ ____

12. $6 \times 5 = $ ____

13. $8 \times 5 = $ ____

14. $4 \times 5 = $ ____

15. $9 \times 5 = $ ____

16.
$$\begin{array}{r} 5 \\ \times\,8 \\ \hline \end{array}$$

17.
$$\begin{array}{r} 5 \\ \times\,2 \\ \hline \end{array}$$

18.
$$\begin{array}{r} 5 \\ \times\,7 \\ \hline \end{array}$$

19.
$$\begin{array}{r} 5 \\ \times\,6 \\ \hline \end{array}$$

20.
$$\begin{array}{r} 5 \\ \times\,5 \\ \hline \end{array}$$

21.
$$\begin{array}{r} 5 \\ \times\,9 \\ \hline \end{array}$$

22.
$$\begin{array}{r} 5 \\ \times\,3 \\ \hline \end{array}$$

Multiply.

1. $\begin{array}{r} 5 \\ \times 4 \\ \hline \end{array}$ 2. $\begin{array}{r} 3 \\ \times 6 \\ \hline \end{array}$ 3. $\begin{array}{r} 5 \\ \times 9 \\ \hline \end{array}$ 4. $\begin{array}{r} 5 \\ \times 5 \\ \hline \end{array}$ 5. $\begin{array}{r} 3 \\ \times 9 \\ \hline \end{array}$ 6. $\begin{array}{r} 5 \\ \times 6 \\ \hline \end{array}$ 7. $\begin{array}{r} 2 \\ \times 8 \\ \hline \end{array}$

8. $\begin{array}{r} 4 \\ \times 7 \\ \hline \end{array}$ 9. $\begin{array}{r} 5 \\ \times 8 \\ \hline \end{array}$ 10. $\begin{array}{r} 4 \\ \times 9 \\ \hline \end{array}$ 11. $\begin{array}{r} 5 \\ \times 2 \\ \hline \end{array}$ 12. $\begin{array}{r} 5 \\ \times 7 \\ \hline \end{array}$ 13. $\begin{array}{r} 2 \\ \times 6 \\ \hline \end{array}$ 14. $\begin{array}{r} 5 \\ \times 3 \\ \hline \end{array}$

15. $\begin{array}{r} 3 \\ \times 5 \\ \hline \end{array}$ 16. $\begin{array}{r} 3 \\ \times 8 \\ \hline \end{array}$ 17. $\begin{array}{r} 5 \\ \times 7 \\ \hline \end{array}$ 18. $\begin{array}{r} 2 \\ \times 9 \\ \hline \end{array}$ 19. $\begin{array}{r} 4 \\ \times 4 \\ \hline \end{array}$ 20. $\begin{array}{r} 2 \\ \times 9 \\ \hline \end{array}$ 21. $\begin{array}{r} 4 \\ \times 8 \\ \hline \end{array}$

22. 6×5 23. 5×5 24. 7×3 25. 6×4

26. 8×5 27. 4×5 28. 7×2 29. 9×5

★ Here are some other number names that have five letters.

30. How many letters are there altogether in the number names first, fifth, and ninth?

31. How many letters are there altogether in the number names third, fifth, sixth, ninth, and tenth?

SKILLKEEPER

Give the value of each set of coins.

1.

2.

3.

4.

PROBLEM SOLVING
Using Data from an Advertisement

Use the advertisement to solve the following problems.

1. How much are E and D?

2. How much are 4 F?

3. How much more is D than B?

4. How much are 6 E?

5. How much are C, D, and E?

6. How much are 6 A?

7. How much more is A than E?

8. How much are 7 F?

★ 9. How much is one of each?

★ 10. How much are 3 E and 4 F?

11. **DATA HUNT** Look at some advertisements. Find something that costs 2, 3, 4, or 5 dollars. How much would it cost to get one for each member of your family?

12. *Try This* Lucia had $10. She spent more than $5. She spent an odd number of dollars. The number is closer to 5 than to 10. How much did Lucia spend?

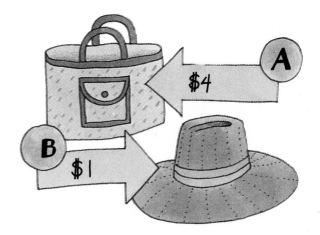

Practice the Facts

Multiply.

1. $\begin{array}{r} 3 \\ \times 5 \end{array}$	**2.** $\begin{array}{r} 2 \\ \times 8 \end{array}$	**3.** $\begin{array}{r} 4 \\ \times 4 \end{array}$	**4.** $\begin{array}{r} 5 \\ \times 3 \end{array}$	**5.** $\begin{array}{r} 2 \\ \times 6 \end{array}$	**6.** $\begin{array}{r} 3 \\ \times 3 \end{array}$	**7.** $\begin{array}{r} 4 \\ \times 9 \end{array}$

1. $\begin{array}{r} 3 \\ \times 5 \end{array}$ **2.** $\begin{array}{r} 2 \\ \times 8 \end{array}$ **3.** $\begin{array}{r} 4 \\ \times 4 \end{array}$ **4.** $\begin{array}{r} 5 \\ \times 3 \end{array}$ **5.** $\begin{array}{r} 2 \\ \times 6 \end{array}$ **6.** $\begin{array}{r} 3 \\ \times 3 \end{array}$ **7.** $\begin{array}{r} 4 \\ \times 9 \end{array}$

8. $\begin{array}{r} 2 \\ \times 5 \end{array}$ **9.** $\begin{array}{r} 4 \\ \times 7 \end{array}$ **10.** $\begin{array}{r} 2 \\ \times 2 \end{array}$ **11.** $\begin{array}{r} 5 \\ \times 5 \end{array}$ **12.** $\begin{array}{r} 2 \\ \times 7 \end{array}$ **13.** $\begin{array}{r} 5 \\ \times 8 \end{array}$ **14.** $\begin{array}{r} 3 \\ \times 8 \end{array}$

15. $\begin{array}{r} 5 \\ \times 7 \end{array}$ **16.** $\begin{array}{r} 2 \\ \times 9 \end{array}$ **17.** $\begin{array}{r} 3 \\ \times 7 \end{array}$ **18.** $\begin{array}{r} 2 \\ \times 5 \end{array}$ **19.** $\begin{array}{r} 4 \\ \times 6 \end{array}$ **20.** $\begin{array}{r} 5 \\ \times 6 \end{array}$ **21.** $\begin{array}{r} 5 \\ \times 7 \end{array}$

22. 4×5 　　　 **23.** 8×3 　　　 **24.** 4×3 　　　 **25.** 8×4

26. 7×2 　　　 **27.** 4×2 　　　 **28.** 9×5 　　　 **29.** 6×3

Give the missing numbers.

$\times 3$	
6	18
2	6
4	12
30. 3	▥

$\times 2$	
7	14
5	10
31. 8	▥
32. 4	▥

$\times 4$	
5	20
33. 7	▥
34. 9	▥
35. 8	▥

$\times 3$	
6	18
36. 8	▥
37. 5	▥
38. 9	▥

$\times 5$	
39. 6	▥
40. 3	▥
41. 5	▥
42. 4	▥

★ **43.**

$\times$ ▥	
4	12
7	21
★ **44.** 6	▥
★ **45.** ▥	6

0 and 1 as Factors

How many birds are there?

**4 cages
1 bird in each cage
4 × 1 = 4**

When 1 is a factor, the
product is the other factor.

How many birds are there?

**4 cages
0 birds in each cage
4 × 0 = 0**

When 0 is a factor, the
product is 0.

Give each product aloud.

1. $3 \times 0 =$ ____   2. $8 \times 1 =$ ____   3. $6 \times 1 =$ ____   4. $9 \times 0 =$ ____

5. $6 \times 1 =$ ____   6. $7 \times 0 =$ ____   7. $1 \times 1 =$ ____   8. $4 \times 0 =$ ____

9. $5 \times 0 =$ ____   10. $9 \times 1 =$ ____   11. $0 \times 0 =$ ____   12. $4 \times 1 =$ ____

13. $\begin{array}{r} 0 \\ \times 3 \\ \hline \end{array}$
14. $\begin{array}{r} 1 \\ \times 7 \\ \hline \end{array}$
15. $\begin{array}{r} 0 \\ \times 6 \\ \hline \end{array}$
16. $\begin{array}{r} 0 \\ \times 4 \\ \hline \end{array}$
17. $\begin{array}{r} 1 \\ \times 9 \\ \hline \end{array}$
18. $\begin{array}{r} 1 \\ \times 2 \\ \hline \end{array}$
19. $\begin{array}{r} 0 \\ \times 8 \\ \hline \end{array}$

20. $\begin{array}{r} 1 \\ \times 3 \\ \hline \end{array}$
21. $\begin{array}{r} 0 \\ \times 1 \\ \hline \end{array}$
22. $\begin{array}{r} 1 \\ \times 0 \\ \hline \end{array}$
23. $\begin{array}{r} 1 \\ \times 4 \\ \hline \end{array}$
24. $\begin{array}{r} 0 \\ \times 2 \\ \hline \end{array}$
25. $\begin{array}{r} 0 \\ \times 5 \\ \hline \end{array}$
26. $\begin{array}{r} 1 \\ \times 5 \\ \hline \end{array}$

More Practice, page 377, Set B

Practice the Facts

Multiply.

1. 4 ×3	2. 2 ×7	3. 5 ×7	4. 0 ×5	5. 3 ×5	6. 4 ×6	7. 1 ×5

8. 5 ×8	9. 0 ×6	10. 2 ×2	11. 4 ×4	12. 1 ×3	13. 3 ×8	14. 2 ×8

15. 3 ×6	16. 1 ×6	17. 2 ×4	18. 0 ×2	19. 3 ×3	20. 3 ×9	21. 4 ×8

22. 9×5 23. 4×3 24. 9×4 25. 6×5

26. 4×0 27. 7×3 28. 4×1 29. 5×5

Give the missing numbers.

× 5	
5	25
9	45
30. 7	||||
31. 8	||||
32. 6	||||
33. 4	||||
34. 3	||||

× 4	
6	24
3	12
35. 8	||||
36. 9	||||
37. 4	||||
38. 5	||||
39. 7	||||

THINK

Number Puzzle

Make a copy of this figure. Put the numbers 4, 5, 6, 7, 8, 9, and 10 in the circles so that the sum along each line is 21. Use each number only once.

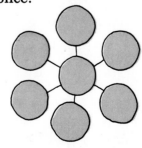

MATH

Order in Multiplication

How many cars are in the parking lot?

$$\begin{array}{r} 4 \\ \times\,3 \\ \hline 12 \end{array}$$

$$\begin{array}{r} 3 \\ \times\,4 \\ \hline 12 \end{array}$$

$$3 \times 4 = 12 \qquad\qquad 4 \times 3 = 12$$

You can change the order of the factors
and the product will be the same.

Give the products aloud.

If you know these facts,   then you know these facts.

| 2
×3
6 | 2
×4
8 | 2
×5
10 | 2
×6
12 | 2
×7
14 | 2
×8
16 | 2
×9
18 | ⇨ | 3
×2 | 4
×2 | 5
×2 | 6
×2 | 7
×2 | 8
×2 | 9
×2 |

| 3
×2
6 | 3
×4
12 | 3
×5
15 | 3
×6
18 | 3
×7
21 | 3
×8
24 | 3
×9
27 | ⇨ | 2
×3 | 4
×3 | 5
×3 | 6
×3 | 7
×3 | 8
×3 | 9
×3 |

| 4
×2
8 | 4
×3
12 | 4
×5
20 | 4
×6
24 | 4
×7
28 | 4
×8
32 | 4
×9
36 | ⇨ | 2
×4 | 3
×4 | 5
×4 | 6
×4 | 7
×4 | 8
×4 | 9
×4 |

| 5
×2
10 | 5
×3
15 | 5
×4
20 | 5
×6
30 | 5
×7
35 | 5
×8
40 | 5
×9
45 | ⇨ | 2
×5 | 3
×5 | 4
×5 | 6
×5 | 7
×5 | 8
×5 | 9
×5 |

Multiply.

1.	2.	3.	4.	5.
8 × 3 24	2 × 9 18	1 × 6 6	4 × 8	4 × 5

6.	7.	8.	9.	10.	11.	12.
5 × 7	5 × 5	6 × 3	5 × 2	7 × 0	3 × 4	2 × 7

13.	14.	15.	16.	17.	18.	19.
5 × 7	3 × 3	2 × 6	5 × 9	4 × 4	5 × 8	4 × 7

20. 3×9 **21.** 1×9 **22.** 4×6 **23.** 5×6

24. 8×0 **25.** 8×2 **26.** 2×4 **27.** 7×3

28. Find the product of 6 and 3.   **29.** Find the product of 4 and 9.

30. Find the product of 5 and 6.   **31.** Find the product of 8 and 2.

32. Find the product of 2 and 4.   **33.** Find the product of 7 and 5.

Four children tossed number cubes. Multiply to get each child's score.

Eva   Lee   Paco   Tara

34. Who had the lowest score?

35. Who had the highest score?

36. Who scored 35?

THINK

Logical Reasoning

Find the product of the two numbers that are

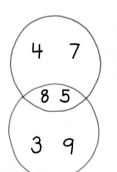

1. in the red ring but not the blue ring.

2. not in the red ring.

3. in both the red and the blue rings.

▶ **MATH** ◀

PROBLEM SOLVING ★★★★ Using the **5**-Point Checklist

To solve a problem

★ 1. Understand the Question
★ 2. Find the needed Data
★ 3. Plan what to do
★ 4. Find the Answer
★ 5. Check back

Use the 5-Point Checklist to help you solve the following problem.

There are 6 rows of plants in a box. Each row has 5 plants. How many plants are in the box?

1. Understand the QUESTION
What is the total number of plants?

2. Find the needed DATA
6 rows, 5 plants each

3. PLAN what to do
The sets of plants are equal. We can multiply.

4. Find the ANSWER
6 fives $6 \times 5 = 30$

5. CHECK back
Read the problem again. 30 plants seems about right.

Solve. Use the 5-Point Checklist.

1. There are 18 plants in a box and 24 in another. How many plants are in the two boxes?

2. There are 42 plants in the garden. 15 of them are cherry tomato plants. How many are not cherry tomatoes?

1. Donna picked 26 apples. She gave 9 to a friend. How many apples does she have left?

2. Ryan puts 5 drops of food on his plant 4 times each year. How many drops is this in one year?

3. Lisa's plant grew 27 cm in one year. It grew 19 cm during the next year. How much did her plant grow in the two years?

4. Casey planted 4 seeds of popcorn in each of 8 holes. How many seeds of popcorn did he plant?

5. Vida picked 42 lemons. Joyce picked 27. How many more lemons did Vida pick?

6. Dale's plants get 4 hours of sunlight each day. How many hours of sunlight do they get in 7 days?

7. Judi uses 8 liters of water to water her plants each week. How many liters of water does she use in 4 weeks?

8. James picked 27 plums and 36 peaches. How many pieces of fruit did he pick?

9. There are 27 rows of trees. Each row has 9 trees. How many trees are there?

10. **Try This** Jamie's plant is taller than Dale's. Nina's plant is shorter than Dale's. Jamie's plant is shorter than Brad's. Whose plant is tallest?

PROBLEM SOLVING
Make a Table

A problem like this can sometimes be solved by using a table. A strategy that can help you is given below.

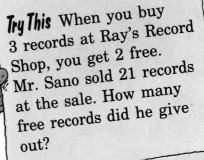

Try This When you buy 3 records at Ray's Record Shop, you get 2 free. Mr. Sano sold 21 records at the sale. How many free records did he give out?

Sell 3 more—3 + 3 = 6
Get 2 more—2 + 2 = 4

MAKE A TABLE

Number sold	3	6	9	12	15	18	21
Free records	2	4	6	8	10	12	14

When the number sold reaches 21, you will have the number of free records in your table.

Mr. Sano gave away 14 free records.
Copy and complete the tables to solve these problems.

1. Tod has the same number of pennies as nickels. He has 30 cents worth of nickels. How many pennies does he have?

Nickel value	5¢	10¢	15¢			
Penny value	1¢	2¢	3¢			

2. Lita sews 4 large buttons and 3 small buttons on each coat. When she has used 28 large buttons, how many small ones has she used?

Large buttons	4	8	12			
Small buttons	3	6	9			

Solve.

1. $5 \times 4 =$ ____ **2.** $7 \times 2 =$ ____

3. $6 \times 2 =$ ____ **4.** $6 \times 4 =$ ____ **5.** $4 \times 4 =$ ____ **6.** $4 \times 3 =$ ____

7. $3 \times 5 =$ ____ **8.** $7 \times 4 =$ ____ **9.** $3 \times 2 =$ ____ **10.** $5 \times 2 =$ ____

11. $9 \times 4 =$ ____ **12.** $9 \times 3 =$ ____ **13.** $5 \times 5 =$ ____ **14.** $8 \times 4 =$ ____

15. $\begin{array}{r} 4 \\ \times 7 \\ \hline \end{array}$
16. $\begin{array}{r} 0 \\ \times 8 \\ \hline \end{array}$
17. $\begin{array}{r} 5 \\ \times 2 \\ \hline \end{array}$
18. $\begin{array}{r} 3 \\ \times 6 \\ \hline \end{array}$
19. $\begin{array}{r} 1 \\ \times 9 \\ \hline \end{array}$
20. $\begin{array}{r} 2 \\ \times 2 \\ \hline \end{array}$
21. $\begin{array}{r} 3 \\ \times 8 \\ \hline \end{array}$

22. $\begin{array}{r} 5 \\ \times 8 \\ \hline \end{array}$
23. $\begin{array}{r} 3 \\ \times 3 \\ \hline \end{array}$
24. $\begin{array}{r} 4 \\ \times 2 \\ \hline \end{array}$
25. $\begin{array}{r} 0 \\ \times 6 \\ \hline \end{array}$
26. $\begin{array}{r} 5 \\ \times 6 \\ \hline \end{array}$
27. $\begin{array}{r} 2 \\ \times 0 \\ \hline \end{array}$
28. $\begin{array}{r} 1 \\ \times 6 \\ \hline \end{array}$

29. $\begin{array}{r} 7 \\ \times 1 \\ \hline \end{array}$
30. $\begin{array}{r} 6 \\ \times 4 \\ \hline \end{array}$
31. $\begin{array}{r} 0 \\ \times 5 \\ \hline \end{array}$
32. $\begin{array}{r} 8 \\ \times 5 \\ \hline \end{array}$
33. $\begin{array}{r} 5 \\ \times 4 \\ \hline \end{array}$
34. $\begin{array}{r} 3 \\ \times 5 \\ \hline \end{array}$
35. $\begin{array}{r} 9 \\ \times 4 \\ \hline \end{array}$

36. Curtis put 5 drops of plant food on each of his plants. He has 6 plants. How many drops of food did he use?

37. Sara scored 42 points. Bill scored 27 points. How many more points did Sara score than Bill?

0 and 1 as factors

$$\begin{array}{r} 1 \\ \times\,3 \\ \hline 3 \end{array}$$

3 ones = 3

$$\begin{array}{r} 0 \\ \times\,3 \\ \hline 0 \end{array}$$

3 zeros = 0

Multiply.

1. $\begin{array}{r} 0 \\ \times\,4 \\ \hline \end{array}$ **2.** $\begin{array}{r} 1 \\ \times\,6 \\ \hline \end{array}$ **3.** $\begin{array}{r} 0 \\ \times\,2 \\ \hline \end{array}$ **4.** $\begin{array}{r} 1 \\ \times\,8 \\ \hline \end{array}$

5. $\begin{array}{r} 1 \\ \times\,3 \\ \hline \end{array}$ **6.** $\begin{array}{r} 0 \\ \times\,7 \\ \hline \end{array}$ **7.** $\begin{array}{r} 0 \\ \times\,5 \\ \hline \end{array}$ **8.** $\begin{array}{r} 1 \\ \times\,9 \\ \hline \end{array}$

2 and 3 as factors

$$\begin{array}{r} 2 \\ \times\,4 \\ \hline 8 \end{array}$$

$$\begin{array}{r} 3 \\ \times\,4 \\ \hline 12 \end{array}$$

9. $\begin{array}{r} 3 \\ \times\,8 \\ \hline \end{array}$ **10.** $\begin{array}{r} 2 \\ \times\,6 \\ \hline \end{array}$ **11.** $\begin{array}{r} 2 \\ \times\,4 \\ \hline \end{array}$ **12.** $\begin{array}{r} 3 \\ \times\,6 \\ \hline \end{array}$

13. $\begin{array}{r} 2 \\ \times\,7 \\ \hline \end{array}$ **14.** $\begin{array}{r} 3 \\ \times\,2 \\ \hline \end{array}$ **15.** $\begin{array}{r} 2 \\ \times\,9 \\ \hline \end{array}$ **16.** $\begin{array}{r} 3 \\ \times\,5 \\ \hline \end{array}$

4 and 5 as factors

$$\begin{array}{r} 4 \\ \times\,4 \\ \hline 16 \end{array}$$

$$\begin{array}{r} 5 \\ \times\,2 \\ \hline 10 \end{array}$$

17. $\begin{array}{r} 4 \\ \times\,8 \\ \hline \end{array}$ **18.** $\begin{array}{r} 5 \\ \times\,9 \\ \hline \end{array}$ **19.** $\begin{array}{r} 4 \\ \times\,7 \\ \hline \end{array}$ **20.** $\begin{array}{r} 5 \\ \times\,5 \\ \hline \end{array}$

21. $\begin{array}{r} 5 \\ \times\,6 \\ \hline \end{array}$ **22.** $\begin{array}{r} 4 \\ \times\,4 \\ \hline \end{array}$ **23.** $\begin{array}{r} 4 \\ \times\,6 \\ \hline \end{array}$ **24.** $\begin{array}{r} 5 \\ \times\,2 \\ \hline \end{array}$

Finding Patterns

The examples below show the patterns
in some number sequences.

1 , 7 , 13 , 19 , ? , ? , ? , . . .

Rule: Add 6 each time.

2 , 4 , 8 , 16 , ? , ? , ? , . . .

Rule: Double the last number.

1 , 2 , 3 , 5 , 8 , ? , ? , ? , . . .

Rule: Add the last two numbers.

Give the next three numbers in each sequence.

1. 5, 10, 15, 20, . . .

2. 12, 23, 34, 45, . . .

3. 3, 6, 12, 24, . . .

4. 50, 42, 34, 26, . . .

5. 3, 0, 6, 0, 9, 0, . . .

6. 1, 3, 2, 4, 3, 5, 4, 6, . . .

7. 3, 2, 1, 6, 5, 4, 9, 8, 7, . . .

8. 2, 10, 8, 16, 14, 22, . . .

9. 1, 3, 6, 10, 15, 21, . . .

10. 4, 3, 2, 8, 7, 6, 12, 11, 10, . . .

CUMULATIVE REVIEW

Give the letter for the correct answer.

1. 35 rounded to the nearest ten

- **A** 30
- **B** 50
- **C** 40
- **D** not given

2. 21 rounded to the nearest ten

- **A** 30
- **B** 20
- **C** 25
- **D** not given

3. 429 rounded to the nearest hundred

- **A** 430
- **B** 500
- **C** 400
- **D** not given

4. 575 rounded to the nearest hundred

- **A** 600
- **B** 500
- **C** 1,000
- **D** not given

5. 9 tens and 5 ones

- **A** 95
- **B** 905
- **C** 59
- **D** not given

6. 2 hundreds, 6 tens, 3 ones

- **A** 623
- **B** 263
- **C** 236
- **D** not given

7.
$$\begin{array}{r} 91 \\ -\ 75 \\ \hline \end{array}$$
- **A** 16
- **B** 24
- **C** 26
- **D** not given

8.
$$\begin{array}{r} 843 \\ -\ 22 \\ \hline \end{array}$$
- **A** 21
- **B** 811
- **C** 821
- **D** not given

9.
$$\begin{array}{r} \$7.25 \\ -\ 3.19 \\ \hline \end{array}$$
- **A** $4.14
- **B** $4.06
- **C** $3.96
- **D** not given

10.
$$\begin{array}{r} \$6.00 \\ -\ 3.75 \\ \hline \end{array}$$
- **A** $2.25
- **B** $3.75
- **C** $3.25
- **D** not given

11. 623 − 27
- **A** 556
- **B** 646
- **C** 546
- **D** not given

12. 702 − 344
- **A** 358
- **B** 442
- **C** 368
- **D** not given

13. Jordan's mother gave him $5.00 to spend at the fair. He spent $3.50. How much money did Jordan have left?

- **A** $8.50
- **B** $1.50
- **C** $2.50
- **D** not given

14. Melissa bought a plant for $3.20. She bought a pot for $6.65. How much did she spend for both?

- **A** $3.45
- **B** $9.45
- **C** $9.85
- **D** not given

MORE MULTIPLICATION FACTS

7

Juanita and her grandfather are going to the hot-air balloon festival. It is in Albuquerque, New Mexico. Juanita's grandfather owns a hot-air balloon that will hold 3 people in its basket. At the festival hundreds of many-colored balloons will float up in the air together. Someday Juanita wants to get a private balloon pilot's license. Juanita is 8 years old now. When she is 2 times this age she can be the pilot of her grandfather's balloon.

6 as a Factor

How many bottles of orange juice were taken to the picnic?

$$3 \times 6 = 18$$

There were 18 bottles of orange juice taken to the picnic.

Find the products.

3 sixes = 18

1.

$$2 \times 6 = \underline{\hphantom{00}}$$

2.

$$4 \times 6 = \underline{\hphantom{00}}$$

Use this picture if you need help.

3. 6 sixes

$$6 \times 6 = \underline{\hphantom{00}}$$

4. 7 sixes

$$7 \times 6 = \underline{\hphantom{00}}$$

5. 8 sixes

$$8 \times 6 = \underline{\hphantom{00}}$$

6. 9 sixes

$$9 \times 6 = \underline{\hphantom{00}}$$

Warm Up   Read each number sentence aloud and give the product.

7. $9 \times 6 = \underline{\hphantom{00}}$ **8.** $4 \times 6 = \underline{\hphantom{00}}$ **9.** $7 \times 6 = \underline{\hphantom{00}}$ **10.** $5 \times 6 = \underline{\hphantom{00}}$

11. $8 \times 6 = \underline{\hphantom{00}}$ **12.** $6 \times 6 = \underline{\hphantom{00}}$ **13.** $0 \times 6 = \underline{\hphantom{00}}$ **14.** $7 \times 6 = \underline{\hphantom{00}}$

Give each product aloud.

15. $\begin{array}{r} 6 \\ \times\, 9 \\ \hline \end{array}$ **16.** $\begin{array}{r} 6 \\ \times\, 1 \\ \hline \end{array}$ **17.** $\begin{array}{r} 6 \\ \times\, 8 \\ \hline \end{array}$ **18.** $\begin{array}{r} 6 \\ \times\, 3 \\ \hline \end{array}$ **19.** $\begin{array}{r} 6 \\ \times\, 4 \\ \hline \end{array}$ **20.** $\begin{array}{r} 6 \\ \times\, 5 \\ \hline \end{array}$ **21.** $\begin{array}{r} 6 \\ \times\, 6 \\ \hline \end{array}$

Multiply.

1. 2 × 7	**2.** 6 × 8	**3.** 3 × 6	**4.** 5 × 6	**5.** 4 × 6
6. 1 × 6	**7.** 4 × 8	**8.** 6 × 2	**9.** 7 × 6	**10.** 8 × 5

11. 3 × 8	**12.** 4 × 6	**13.** 6 × 9	**14.** 4 × 7	**15.** 5 × 3	**16.** 2 × 7	**17.** 5 × 5

18. 7×6 **19.** 9×5 **20.** 6×5 **21.** 2×9

22. 3×6 **23.** 6×8 **24.** 5×7 **25.** 9×4

26. Multiply 6 by 4. **27.** Multiply 3 by 6.

28. Multiply 7 by 6. **29.** Multiply 6 by 9.

30. Multiply 6 by 6. **31.** Multiply 8 by 6.

If you forget a fact, sometimes you can figure it out.

Give each product.

32.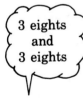
3 eights and 3 eights

6×8

33.
6 sixes and 1 six

7×6

34.
5 sixes and 4 sixes

9×6

35.
3 sixes and 3 sixes

6×6

THINK

Estimation

Estimate the area of the rug.

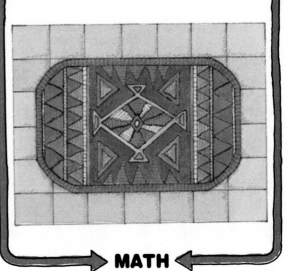

MATH

7 as a Factor

How many days are in 4 weeks?

4 × 7 = 28

There are 28 days in 4 weeks.

4 sevens = 28

Find the products.

1.

$3 \times 7 = \underline{\hspace{1cm}}$

2.

$5 \times 7 = \underline{\hspace{1cm}}$

Use this picture if you need help.

3. 6 sevens   **4.** 7 sevens   **5.** 8 sevens   **6.** 9 sevens

$6 \times 7 = \underline{\hspace{0.8cm}}$ $7 \times 7 = \underline{\hspace{0.8cm}}$ $8 \times 7 = \underline{\hspace{0.8cm}}$ $9 \times 7 = \underline{\hspace{0.8cm}}$

Warm Up   Give each product aloud.

7. $6 \times 7 = \underline{\hspace{0.8cm}}$ **8.** $9 \times 7 = \underline{\hspace{0.8cm}}$ **9.** $7 \times 7 = \underline{\hspace{0.8cm}}$ **10.** $5 \times 7 = \underline{\hspace{0.8cm}}$

11. $4 \times 7 = \underline{\hspace{0.8cm}}$ **12.** $1 \times 7 = \underline{\hspace{0.8cm}}$ **13.** $3 \times 7 = \underline{\hspace{0.8cm}}$ **14.** $8 \times 7 = \underline{\hspace{0.8cm}}$

15. $\begin{array}{r} 7 \\ \times\, 2 \\ \hline \end{array}$ **16.** $\begin{array}{r} 7 \\ \times\, 5 \\ \hline \end{array}$ **17.** $\begin{array}{r} 7 \\ \times\, 9 \\ \hline \end{array}$ **18.** $\begin{array}{r} 7 \\ \times\, 0 \\ \hline \end{array}$ **19.** $\begin{array}{r} 7 \\ \times\, 7 \\ \hline \end{array}$ **20.** $\begin{array}{r} 7 \\ \times\, 8 \\ \hline \end{array}$ **21.** $\begin{array}{r} 7 \\ \times\, 4 \\ \hline \end{array}$

Multiply.

1. $\begin{array}{r} 7 \\ \times 6 \\ \hline \end{array}$	**2.** $\begin{array}{r} 3 \\ \times 8 \\ \hline \end{array}$	**3.** $\begin{array}{r} 4 \\ \times 7 \\ \hline \end{array}$	**4.** $\begin{array}{r} 6 \\ \times 4 \\ \hline \end{array}$	**5.** $\begin{array}{r} 7 \\ \times 9 \\ \hline \end{array}$	**6.** $\begin{array}{r} 7 \\ \times 7 \\ \hline \end{array}$	**7.** $\begin{array}{r} 9 \\ \times 6 \\ \hline \end{array}$
8. $\begin{array}{r} 9 \\ \times 5 \\ \hline \end{array}$	**9.** $\begin{array}{r} 8 \\ \times 7 \\ \hline \end{array}$	**10.** $\begin{array}{r} 0 \\ \times 7 \\ \hline \end{array}$	**11.** $\begin{array}{r} 7 \\ \times 3 \\ \hline \end{array}$	**12.** $\begin{array}{r} 5 \\ \times 7 \\ \hline \end{array}$	**13.** $\begin{array}{r} 4 \\ \times 9 \\ \hline \end{array}$	**14.** $\begin{array}{r} 7 \\ \times 4 \\ \hline \end{array}$
15. $\begin{array}{r} 3 \\ \times 7 \\ \hline \end{array}$	**16.** $\begin{array}{r} 6 \\ \times 8 \\ \hline \end{array}$	**17.** $\begin{array}{r} 7 \\ \times 7 \\ \hline \end{array}$	**18.** $\begin{array}{r} 7 \\ \times 1 \\ \hline \end{array}$	**19.** $\begin{array}{r} 6 \\ \times 7 \\ \hline \end{array}$	**20.** $\begin{array}{r} 6 \\ \times 6 \\ \hline \end{array}$	**21.** $\begin{array}{r} 2 \\ \times 9 \\ \hline \end{array}$

22. 8×5 **23.** 7×9 **24.** 4×8 **25.** 6×5

26. 8×7 **27.** 3×9 **28.** 5×6 **29.** 5×7

30. Find the product of 7 and 6.

31. Find the product of 7 and 7.

32. Find the product of 5 and 7.

33. Find the product of 7 and 2.

34. Find the product of 7 and 8.

35. Find the product of 9 and 7.

36. It is 4 weeks until Juan's ninth birthday. How many days must Juan wait until he is nine?

★ **37.** Janet's vacation was 8 weeks and 3 days. How many days of vacation did Janet have?

★ **38.** Jim said, "It is 5 weeks and 5 days until summer." How many days is this?

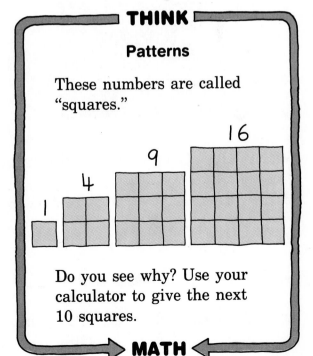

THINK

Patterns

These numbers are called "squares."

Do you see why? Use your calculator to give the next 10 squares.

MATH

More Practice, page 378, Set A

8 and 9 as Factors

The table shows all of the multiplication facts you have had so far. The pink squares are the "new" facts.

See if you can figure out the new facts. Some ways to think are given below.

×	0	1	2	3	4	5	6	7	8	9
0	0	0	0	0	0	0	0	0	0	0
1	0	1	2	3	4	5	6	7	8	9
2	0	2	4	6	8	10	12	14	16	18
3	0	3	6	9	12	15	18	21	24	27
4	0	4	8	12	16	20	24	28	32	36
5	0	5	10	15	20	25	30	35	40	45
6	0	6	12	18	24	30	36	42	48	54
7	0	7	14	21	28	35	42	49	56	63
8	0	8	16	24	32	40	48	56	8×8	8×9
9	0	9	18	27	36	45	54	63	9×8	9×9

8 × 8

That is the same as 4 eights and 4 eights.

$8 \times 8 =$ ___

8 × 9 and 9 × 8

That is the same as 4 nines and 4 nines.

$8 \times 9 =$ ___

9 × 9

That is the same as 5 nines and 4 nines.

$9 \times 9 =$ ___

Warm Up   Give each product aloud.

1. $7 \times 9 =$ ___   2. $9 \times 9 =$ ___   3. $9 \times 6 =$ ___   4. $8 \times 9 =$ ___

5. $9 \times 8 =$ ___   6. $7 \times 8 =$ ___   7. $8 \times 6 =$ ___   8. $8 \times 8 =$ ___

9. $6 \times 7 =$ ___   10. $5 \times 9 =$ ___   11. $9 \times 9 =$ ___   12. $7 \times 6 =$ ___

13. $\begin{array}{r} 9 \\ \times 8 \\ \hline \end{array}$ 14. $\begin{array}{r} 8 \\ \times 8 \\ \hline \end{array}$ 15. $\begin{array}{r} 8 \\ \times 6 \\ \hline \end{array}$ 16. $\begin{array}{r} 9 \\ \times 7 \\ \hline \end{array}$ 17. $\begin{array}{r} 9 \\ \times 6 \\ \hline \end{array}$ 18. $\begin{array}{r} 8 \\ \times 7 \\ \hline \end{array}$ 19. $\begin{array}{r} 9 \\ \times 8 \\ \hline \end{array}$

Multiply.

1. 9
× 8

2. 8
× 4

3. 6
× 9

4. 9
× 9

5. 7
× 7

6. 7
× 5

7. 8
× 9

8. 5
× 7

9. 9
× 9

10. 6
× 6

11. 8
× 8

12. 5
× 8

13. 9
× 5

14. 2
× 9

15. 8
× 6

16. 7
× 9

17. 7
× 6

18. 5
× 5

19. 8
× 3

20. 9
× 7

21. 3
× 9

22. 8
× 2

23. 4
× 9

24. 7
× 4

25. 6
× 5

26. 9
× 1

27. 8
× 0

28. 7
× 3

29. 9×8

30. 6×7

31. 7×8

32. 8×9

33. 7×4

34. 3×9

35. 9×9

36. 9×4

Copy and complete each table.

37.

×	5	9	8
4			
6			
3			

38.

×	7	6	8
9			
5			
6			

SKILLKEEPER

Write each time.

1.

2.

3.

4.

PROBLEM SOLVING
Practice

QUESTION
DATA
PLAN
ANSWER
CHECK

1. Sales Clerk:
T-shirts are $6 each.
Sold 9 shirts.
How much money did the
clerk receive?

2. Mail Carrier:
Delivered 376 letters. Then
delivered 295. How many
letters were delivered in all?

3. Office Worker:
Had 500 papers to file.
Filed 283 before lunch.
How many are left to file?

4. Waiter:
Served 2 rooms with 3 tables in
each room. How many tables
were served in all?
Each table had 4 people. How
many people were served?

5. Farmer:
Planted 9 rows of trees.
8 trees were in each row.
How many trees did the
farmer plant?

6. Painter:
Estimate for job was $185.
Actual cost was $208.
How much less was the
estimate?

7. *Try This* A worker uses 3 nails
for every 2 tacks. When she
has used 18 nails, how many
tacks has she used? Hint:
Make a table.

Nails	3	6	9
Tacks	2	4	6

Practice the Facts

Find the products.

Products: less than 35

1. 3
   × 6

2. 3
   × 5

3. 4
   × 7

4. 2
   × 2

5. 5
   × 5

6. 4
   × 4

7. 5
   × 4

8. 3
   × 8

9. 3
   × 4

10. 5
    × 1

11. 3
    × 7

12. 4
    × 2

13. 6
    × 5

14. 8
    × 3

15. 0
    × 4

16. 5
    × 2

17. 3
    × 2

18. 4
    × 1

19. 0
    × 5

20. 2
    × 1

21. 4
    × 3

22. 3
    × 5

23. 4
    × 6

24. 4
    × 5

25. 3
    × 9

26. 8
    × 4

27. 5
    × 6

28. 7
    × 3

Products: 35 and greater

29. 7
    × 5

30. 8
    × 6

31. 7
    × 7

32. 7
    × 8

33. 6
    × 6

34. 8
    × 9

35. 9
    × 7

36. 7
    × 6

37. 8
    × 8

38. 9
    × 5

39. 5
    × 7

40. 6
    × 7

41. 8
    × 5

42. 9
    × 6

43. 8
    × 7

44. 9
    × 8

45. 6
    × 8

46. 7
    × 9

47. 9
    × 9

48. 6
    × 9

49. 5
    × 9

50. 6
    × 7

51. 4
    × 9

52. 5
    × 8

53. 7
    × 8

54. 5
    × 9

55. 7
    × 7

56. 9
    × 4

Multiplying Three Numbers

There are 3 tennis balls in each can. There are 2 cans in each box. There are 4 boxes. How many tennis balls are in all?

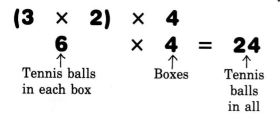

(3 × 2) × 4

6 × 4 = 24

↑ Tennis balls in each box   ↑ Boxes   ↑ Tennis balls in all

3 × (2 × 4)

3 × 8 = 24

↑ Tennis balls in each can   ↑ Cans   ↑ Tennis balls in all

These symbols ( ) tell which multiplication to do first.

Find these products.

1. $(2 × 4) × 1 =$ ____
2. $2 × (4 × 1) =$ ____
3. $(4 × 1) × 5 =$ ____
4. $4 × (1 × 5) =$ ____
5. $(4 × 2) × 4 =$ ____
6. $4 × (2 × 4) =$ ____

> When you multiply, you can change the grouping and get the same product.

Use the grouping shown. Find the product.

7. $(3 × 2) × 5 =$ ____
8. $8 × (4 × 2) =$ ____
9. $9 × (2 × 2) =$ ____
10. $(3 × 3) × 6 =$ ____
11. $7 × (2 × 3) =$ ____
12. $(2 × 4) × 6 =$ ____

Use any grouping you want. Find the product.

13. $4 × 2 × 1 =$ ____
14. $4 × 2 × 3 =$ ____
15. $6 × 1 × 3 =$ ____
16. $3 × 2 × 2 =$ ____
17. $2 × 4 × 2 =$ ____
18. $8 × 9 × 0 =$ ____
19. $4 × 1 × 5 =$ ____
20. $6 × 0 × 7 =$ ____
21. $3 × 3 × 2 =$ ____
22. $4 × 2 × 4 =$ ____
23. $3 × 1 × 3 =$ ____
24. $9 × 1 × 4 =$ ____

More Practice, page 378, Set C

Missing Factors

Can you tell what 1-digit factors Cathy's mittens are hiding? You cannot tell because

 ×  = **18**

2 × 9 = 18 and 3 × 6 = 18

Suppose only one factor is hidden. Can you tell now? The answer is 6.

3 ×  **= 18**

Find these factors.

1. 2 ×  = 6

2.  × 3 = 9

3. 4 ×  = 12

4.  × 5 = 15

5. 7 × 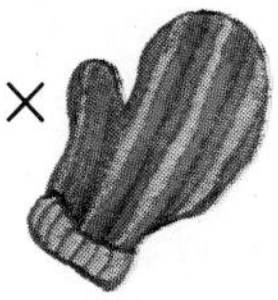 = 21

6.  × 5 = 30

7. 3 × ▯ = 15 **8.** ▯ × 2 = 14 **9.** 4 × ▯ = 32 **10.** ▯ × 8 = 40

11. 5 × ▯ = 20 **12.** ▯ × 7 = 28 **13.** 2 × ▯ = 18 **14.** ▯ × 4 = 24

15. 3 × ▯ = 21 **16.** ▯ × 6 = 36 **17.** 5 × ▯ = 30 **18.** ▯ × 9 = 27

19. 7 × ▯ = 35 **20.** ▯ × 3 = 24 **21.** 5 × ▯ = 25 **22.** ▯ × 3 = 12

SKILLKEEPER

Add or subtract.

1. 8 + 7 **2.** 13 − 4 **3.** 10 − 8 **4.** 5 + 9 **5.** 8 + 3 **6.** 17 − 9

7. 8 + 8 **8.** 12 − 5 **9.** 14 − 7 **10.** 16 − 9 **11.** 9 + 9 **12.** 7 + 6

PROBLEM SOLVING
Using Data from a Table

A dietitian plans meals for people. A dietitian needs to know how many **calories** are in different foods. Calories are the measure of energy supplied by our foods.

Calorie Table

Breakfast	Calories	Lunch	Calories	Dinner	Calories
juice	85	sandwich	395	chicken	283
cereal	95	salad	48	potatoes	197
banana	81	soup	147	peas	60
milk	166	apple	75	orange	64
		milk	166	milk	166

Use the table to solve the following problems.

1. How many calories are in the banana and cereal?

2. How many more calories are in the sandwich than the soup?

3. How many more calories are in the potatoes than the milk?

4. One piece of celery has 7 calories. How many calories are in 6 pieces?

★ 5. Find the total amount of calories for breakfast.

6. **DATA HUNT** Find the number of calories in a poached egg and a fried egg. What is the difference?

7. *Try This* Jack can have a pear, a banana, or an apple for a snack. He can have milk or juice with his snack. How many different ways can Jack choose his snack?

PROBLEM SOLVING
Identifying Needed Data

These problems need more data. Find the data on the Data Sheet. Then solve the problems.

1. Julie practices the piano 40 minutes a day. How much longer does she practice than Glen?

2. Glen has 5 minutes less for lunch than Julie. How long does Glen have for lunch?

3. Julie tries to keep her teeth clean and healthy. How many times does she brush a week (7 days)?

4. Julie's class has 29 children. How many children are in Julie's class and Glen's class?

5. Julie takes 15 minutes to walk home from school. What time does she get home?

6. It takes Glen 22 minutes to walk to school. How much longer does it take Glen than Julie?

Data Sheet

- Glen lives on the 6th floor.
- Julie has 40 minutes for lunch.
- Julie is out of school at 3:15.
- Glen sleeps 9 hours a night.
- Glen practices his music 25 minutes a day.
- Julie brushes her teeth 3 times a day.
- Glen eats 4 times a day.
- Julie walks to school in 15 minutes.
- Glen's class has 27 children
- Julie scored 16 points in the game.

7. Glen scored 14 points in the game. How many points did Julie and Glen score in all?

8. *Try This* Glen and Julie live in the same building. Julie lives on the 14th floor. How many floors of apartments are between them? Hint: Draw a picture.

PROBLEM SOLVING
Practice

People have given many names to the flag of the United States.

**THE STARS AND STRIPES
THE STAR-SPANGLED BANNER
OLD GLORY**

The flag stands for the land, the people, the government, and the ideals of the United States.

The U.S. Flag Today
50 stars
13 stripes

Solve.

1. The first flag of 1777 had 13 stars. How many fewer stars did the first flag have than today's flag?

2. There were 34 stars on the flag of 1861. How many more stars does today's flag have?

3. The flag of 1912 had 6 rows of stars. There were 8 stars in each row. How many stars did the flag have?

4. The flag of 1912 lasted for 47 years. The flag of 1777 lasted for 18 years. How many more years did the flag of 1912 last than that of 1777?

5. The flag of 1818 had 4 rows of stars with 5 in each row. How many stars did it have?

★ 6. One U.S. flag had 4 rows of stars with 7 in each row and 1 row with only 6 stars. How many stars did it have?

7. **DATA BANK** See page 362. How many more stars does today's flag have than the flag of 1795?

8. *Try This* Mary's flag is between 30 cm and 40 cm long. It is longer than 6 × 6. It is an even number of centimeters. How long is Mary's flag?

194 (one hundred ninety-four)

Practice the Facts

Multiply.

| 1. 6 $\times 8$ | 2. 9 $\times 9$ | 3. 8 $\times 8$ | 4. 3 $\times 8$ | 5. 5 $\times 9$ | 6. 7 $\times 6$ | 7. 9 $\times 4$ |

| 8. 8 $\times 9$ | 9. 7 $\times 9$ | 10. 8 $\times 7$ | 11. 9 $\times 8$ | 12. 9 $\times 6$ | 13. 7 $\times 3$ | 14. 5 $\times 6$ |

| 15. 4 $\times 7$ | 16. 7 $\times 7$ | 17. 8 $\times 6$ | 18. 7 $\times 2$ | 19. 6 $\times 3$ | 20. 4 $\times 8$ | 21. 2 $\times 9$ |

| 22. 6 $\times 2$ | 23. 7 $\times 4$ | 24. 9 $\times 5$ | 25. 8 $\times 2$ | 26. 9 $\times 1$ | 27. 8 $\times 0$ | 28. 5 $\times 3$ |

| 29. 8 $\times 4$ | 30. 5 $\times 7$ | 31. 8 $\times 5$ | 32. 7 $\times 0$ | 33. 9 $\times 7$ | 34. 8 $\times 3$ | 35. 8 $\times 1$ |

36. 7×5 37. 5×8 38. 9×3 39. 7×1 40. 4×5

41. 6×7 42. 9×9 43. 6×6 44. 9×6 45. 5×5

Write the products.

Multiply by 6	
46. 7	|||||
47. 9	|||||
48. 8	|||||
49. 6	|||||

Multiply by 7	
50. 5	|||||
51. 8	|||||
52. 7	|||||
53. 9	|||||

Multiply by 8	
54. 4	|||||
55. 8	|||||
56. 6	|||||
57. 9	|||||

Multiply by 9	
58. 7	|||||
59. 6	|||||
60. 9	|||||
61. 5	|||||

PROBLEM SOLVING
Choose the Operations

To solve this problem you need to use more than one operation. A strategy that can help you is given below.

Try This There were 7 cars and 1 bus to take people to the picnic. Each car took 4 children. The bus took 37. How many children went to the picnic?

CHOOSE THE OPERATIONS

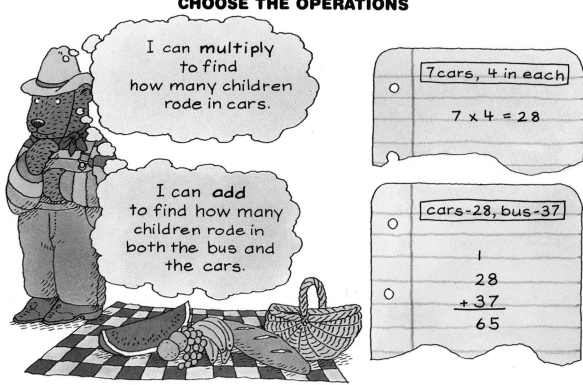

I can **multiply** to find how many children rode in cars.

I can **add** to find how many children rode in both the bus and the cars.

7 cars, 4 in each

$7 \times 4 = 28$

cars–28, bus–37

$$\begin{array}{r} 1 \\ 28 \\ + 37 \\ \hline 65 \end{array}$$

65 children went to the picnic.

Solve.

1. Diane has one book with 72 pictures in it. Another book has 8 pages with 6 pictures on each page. How many pictures are in both books?

2. At the book sale all $12-books were $5 off the regular price. Don bought 4 $12-books at the sale. How much did he pay for the books?

Multiply.

1. 8 × 4	**2.** 7 × 2	**3.** 8 × 3	**4.** 8 × 5	**5.** 9 × 4	**6.** 6 × 5	**7.** 7 × 3
8. 6 × 8	**9.** 6 × 7	**10.** 9 × 6	**11.** 6 × 6	**12.** 6 × 9	**13.** 7 × 6	**14.** 8 × 6
15. 8 × 7	**16.** 4 × 7	**17.** 7 × 7	**18.** 7 × 9	**19.** 7 × 8	**20.** 7 × 6	**21.** 9 × 7

22. 8×8 **23.** 7×9 **24.** 8×7 **25.** 8×9 **26.** 9×9

27. 6×8 **28.** 5×9 **29.** 7×6 **30.** 9×4 **31.** 3×8

Solve.

32. $2 \times 2 \times 2 =$ _____   **33.** $2 \times 4 \times 2 =$ _____   **34.** $3 \times 2 \times 3 =$ _____

Find the missing factor.

35. $6 \times$ _____ $= 18$ **36.** $5 \times$ _____ $= 25$ **37.** $7 \times$ _____ $= 21$

Solve.

38. Cook:
Baked 6 rows of biscuits.
8 biscuits are in each row.
How many are in all?

39. Plumber:
Had a 126-cm pipe.
Cut off 39-cm piece.
How long is the other piece?

ANOTHER LOOK

7 sixes

5 sixes and 2 sixes

30 + 12

7 × 6 = 42

8 sevens

7 sevens and 1 seven

49 + 7

8 × 7 = 56

9 eights

5 eights and 4 eights

40 + 32

9 × 8 = 72

Multiply.

1. $\begin{array}{r} 6 \\ \times\, 6 \\ \hline \end{array}$	**2.** $\begin{array}{r} 6 \\ \times\, 4 \\ \hline \end{array}$	**3.** $\begin{array}{r} 6 \\ \times\, 9 \\ \hline \end{array}$
4. $\begin{array}{r} 6 \\ \times\, 3 \\ \hline \end{array}$	**5.** $\begin{array}{r} 6 \\ \times\, 5 \\ \hline \end{array}$	**6.** $\begin{array}{r} 6 \\ \times\, 8 \\ \hline \end{array}$
7. $\begin{array}{r} 6 \\ \times\, 2 \\ \hline \end{array}$	**8.** $\begin{array}{r} 6 \\ \times\, 7 \\ \hline \end{array}$	**9.** $\begin{array}{r} 6 \\ \times\, 1 \\ \hline \end{array}$
10. $\begin{array}{r} 7 \\ \times\, 5 \\ \hline \end{array}$	**11.** $\begin{array}{r} 7 \\ \times\, 9 \\ \hline \end{array}$	**12.** $\begin{array}{r} 7 \\ \times\, 2 \\ \hline \end{array}$
13. $\begin{array}{r} 7 \\ \times\, 4 \\ \hline \end{array}$	**14.** $\begin{array}{r} 7 \\ \times\, 6 \\ \hline \end{array}$	**15.** $\begin{array}{r} 7 \\ \times\, 7 \\ \hline \end{array}$
16. $\begin{array}{r} 7 \\ \times\, 8 \\ \hline \end{array}$	**17.** $\begin{array}{r} 7 \\ \times\, 3 \\ \hline \end{array}$	**18.** $\begin{array}{r} 7 \\ \times\, 1 \\ \hline \end{array}$
19. $\begin{array}{r} 8 \\ \times\, 6 \\ \hline \end{array}$	**20.** $\begin{array}{r} 9 \\ \times\, 7 \\ \hline \end{array}$	**21.** $\begin{array}{r} 9 \\ \times\, 9 \\ \hline \end{array}$
22. $\begin{array}{r} 8 \\ \times\, 8 \\ \hline \end{array}$	**23.** $\begin{array}{r} 9 \\ \times\, 6 \\ \hline \end{array}$	**24.** $\begin{array}{r} 8 \\ \times\, 9 \\ \hline \end{array}$
25. $\begin{array}{r} 9 \\ \times\, 5 \\ \hline \end{array}$	**26.** $\begin{array}{r} 8 \\ \times\, 7 \\ \hline \end{array}$	**27.** $\begin{array}{r} 8 \\ \times\, 5 \\ \hline \end{array}$

Space Perception

Look at the piece of cardboard. If you could pick it up, how many flat surfaces could you touch?

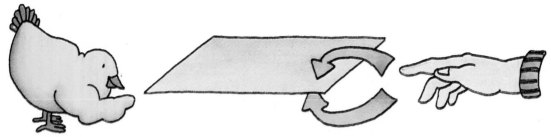

Cardboard

You could touch two flat surfaces—the two sides of the cardboard.

Look at the objects below.
How many different flat surfaces could you touch?

1.

Solid cube of wood

2.

Cut wooden cube

3.

Folded cardboard

4.

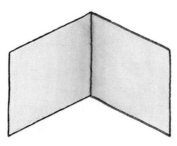

Open box

CUMULATIVE REVIEW

Give the letter for the correct answer.

1. 36
    + 54   **A** 90   **B** 80
             C 70   **D** not given

2. 185
    + 32   **A** 117   **B** 227
             C 217   **D** not given

3. 589
    + 176   **A** 765   **B** 655
             C 755   **D** not given

4. $3.50
    + 2.82   **A** $6.22 **B** $5.22
             C $5.32 **D** not given

5. 75
    + 76   **A** 151   **B** 141
             C 142   **D** not given

6. 76
    + 94   **A** 180   **B** 170
             C 160   **D** not given

What time does the clock show?

7.
    A 9:00
    B 9:15
    C 9:30
    D not given

8.
    A 11:50
    B 10:50
    C 10:55
    D not given

9. Use your centimeter ruler. What is the length?

    A 4 cm
    B 3 cm
    C 2 cm
    D not given

10. What is the perimeter?
    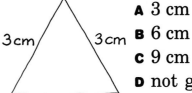
    A 3 cm
    B 6 cm
    C 9 cm
    D not given

11. What is the area?

    A 6 square units
    B 8 square units
    C 12 square units
    D not given

12. What is the volume?

    A 3 cubic units
    B 6 cubic units
    C 4 cubic units
    D not given

13. Rita rode her bike 12 km before lunch. After lunch she rode 9 km. How far did she ride?
    A 21 km   **B** 11 km
    C 3 km   **D** not given

14. Dean started hiking at 12:30 p.m. He stopped one hour later. What time did he stop?
    A 1:30 a.m. **B** 1:30 p.m.
    C 1:00 a.m. **D** not given

Tim was very happy when his baby sister was born. He helped design a card about the baby. The card was to be sent to friends of his family. Tim and his father took the design to a printer. At the printer's shop they picked the shape of the card. They also picked the size and color. The printer showed Tim many ways his sister's name could look on the front of the card. The finished card looked very nice.

Space Figures

Look at the objects below. Think of sorting them into the boxes so the shapes match. Give the name of the box for each object.

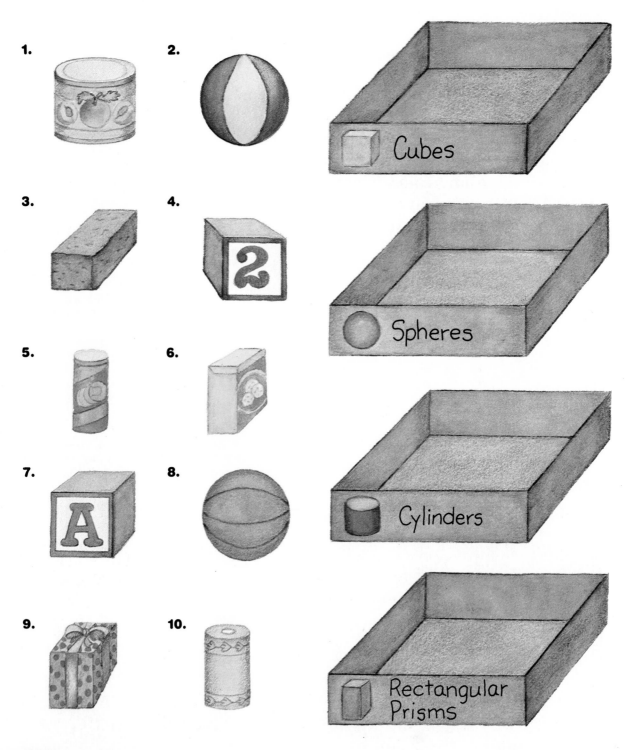

1.

2.

3.

4.

5.

6.

7.

8.

9.

10.

Cubes

Spheres

Cylinders

Rectangular Prisms

Write **cube**, **sphere**, **cylinder**, or
rectangular prism for each object.

1.

2.

3.

4.

5.

6.

7.

8.
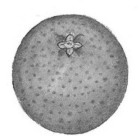

9.

◀ THINK ◀

Space Perception

A cube has 4 dots on each of its faces. You can
hold the cube any way you want.

1. What is the greatest number of dots you
   can see at one time?
2. What is the least number of dots you can
   see at one time?

MATH

Plane Figures

Plane figures lie on a "flat" surface.

A face of a cube has a **square** shape.

A face of a rectangular prism has a **rectangle** shape.

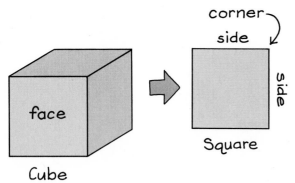

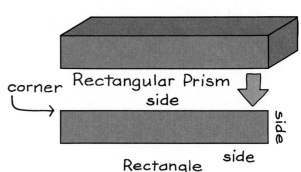

A face of a cylinder has a **circle** shape.

Cut off a corner of a cube to get a **triangle** shape.

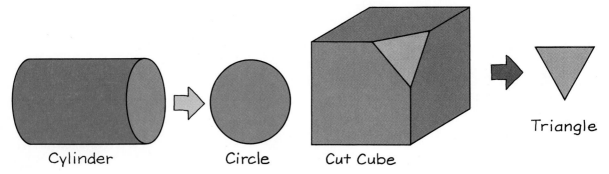

Warm Up Give the name of each figure—
square, **rectangle**, **circle**, or **triangle**.
Then give the number of sides and corners.

1.

2.

3.

4.

5.

6.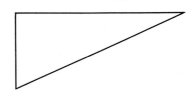

Tell whether the picture reminds you of a square, a rectangle, a circle, or a triangle.

1.

2.

3.

4.

5.

6.

Write **square**, **circle**, **rectangle**, or **triangle** for each figure.

7. 3 sides and 3 corners

8. 4 sides all the same length

9. No straight sides and no corners

10. 4 sides with two longer than the others

THINK

Shape Perception

How many can you find? There are more than you see at first.

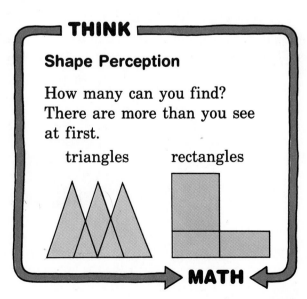

triangles   rectangles

MATH

Segments

Look at the cardboard strips.
You can put them together to
make different shapes.

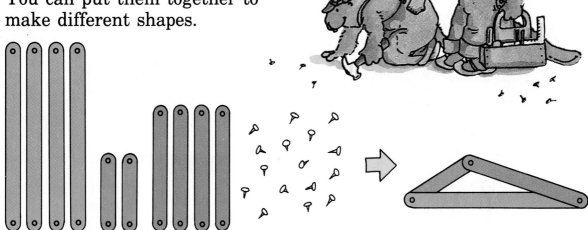

The sides of rectangles, squares, and triangles are **segments**.

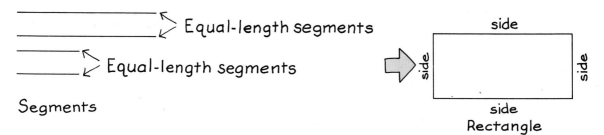

Equal-length segments

Equal-length segments

Segments

side
side
side
side
Rectangle

Warm Up Think of the strips as segments.

1. What shape has been made
with these strips?

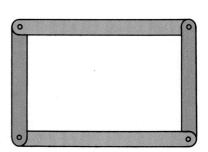

2. What shape could you make
with all these strips?

Tell who made each shape.

1. A triangle with all sides that are equal in length

2. A small square

3. A triangle with no sides that are equal in length

4. A rectangle

5. A triangle with just two sides that are equal in length

6. A large square

Ted's strips
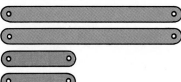

Patty's strips

Jorge's strips

Ann's strips
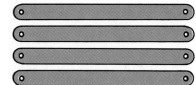

Ron's strips
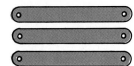

Lola's strips
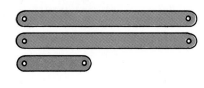

THINK

Geometry

Look at the cardboard strips below. How many different triangles can you make using just three strips at a time?

Example

MATH

Angles

Many things can remind you of an **angle**.

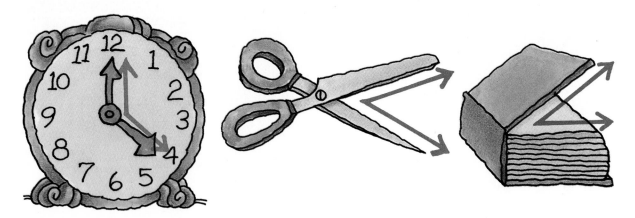

The corner of a triangle or rectangle can remind you of an angle.

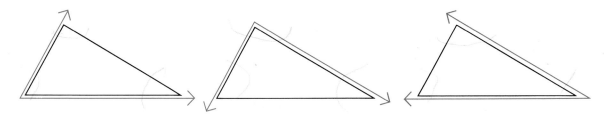

Each triangle has 3 angles.

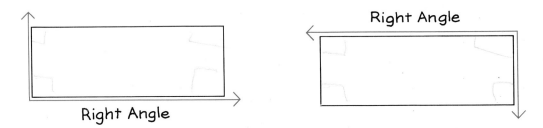

Right Angle

Right Angle

Each rectangle has 4 **right** angles.

Warm Up   Which of the angles below are right angles?

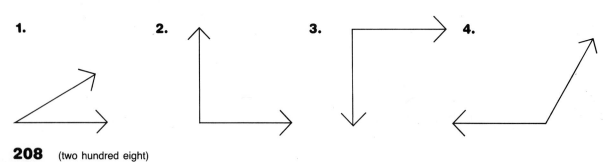

1.

2.

3.

4.

Which of the angles below are right angles?

1.

2.

3.

How many right angles does each figure have?

4.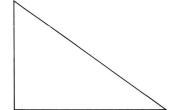

5.

6.

Give the number of segments and angles for each figure.

7.

8.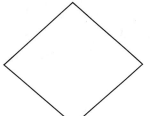

9.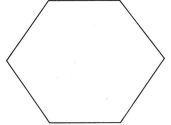

10. Name two different times when the clock hands form a right angle.

Congruent Figures

Carmen Reyes is making a
blouse. She must cut the
material exactly the same size
and shape as the pattern.

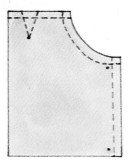

Pattern   Material

Figures that have the same size and shape
are **congruent** to each other. A copy of one
will fit exactly on the other.

These two triangles are
congruent.

These two triangles are not
congruent.

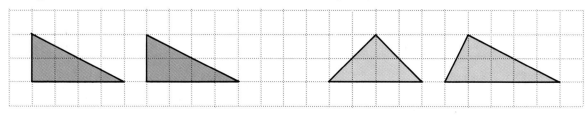

Warm Up   Which figure is congruent to the first?

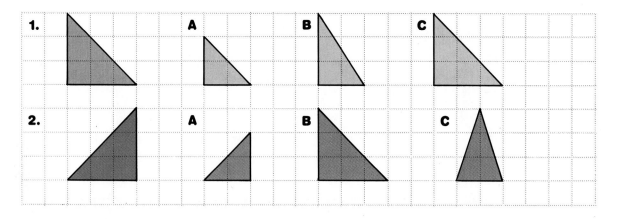

1.   A   B   C

2.   A   B   C

Which figure is congruent to the first?

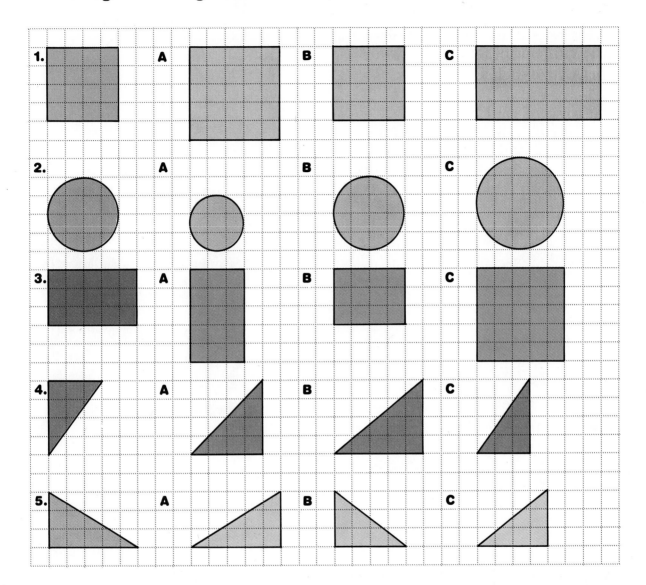

Lines of Symmetry

A figure has a line of **symmetry** if it can be folded so the two parts fit exactly.

Pictures of real objects sometimes appear to have a line of symmetry.

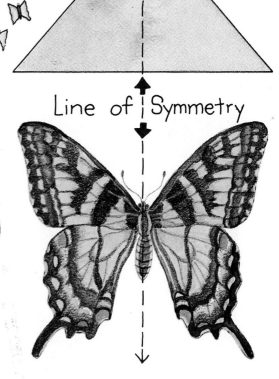

Line of Symmetry

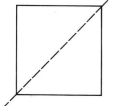

Warm Up Does the dashed line appear to be a line of symmetry? Answer yes or no.

Figures from geometry

1.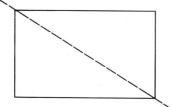

2.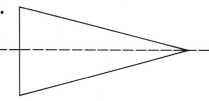

3.

Pictures from nature

4.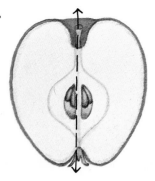

5.

6.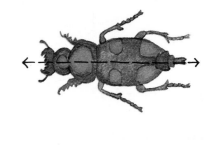

Which of these shapes can be folded to make a line of symmetry? Trace and fold if you cannot tell.

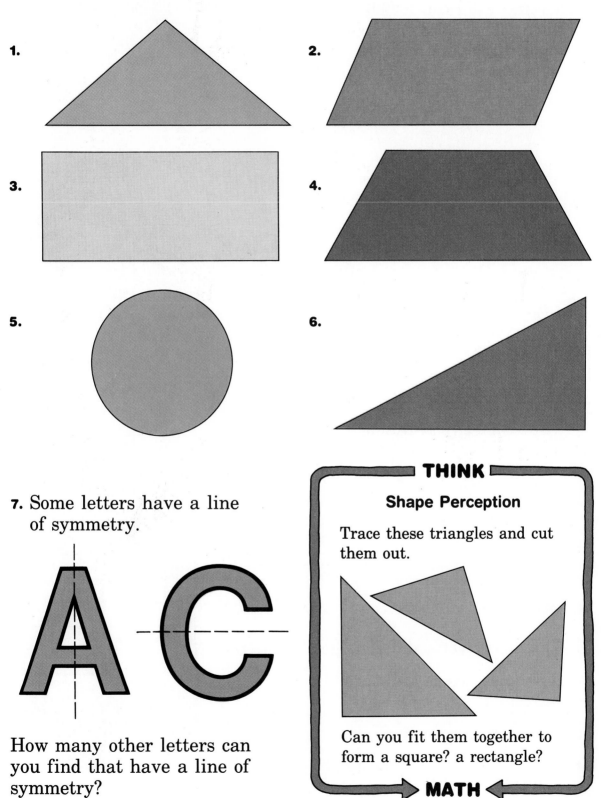

1.

2.

3.

4.

5.

6.

7. Some letters have a line of symmetry.

A C

How many other letters can you find that have a line of symmetry?

THINK

Shape Perception

Trace these triangles and cut them out.

Can you fit them together to form a square? a rectangle?

MATH

Tallies and Bar Graphs

Aaron and Tina ran for class president. These are the votes they got.

Niki made a **tally chart** to show the votes. He put one mark for each vote. Niki shows 5 votes as 卌 so the votes are easy to count.

Votes for Class President
Tina   卌 卌 ‖
Aaron   卌 ‖‖

Vera made a **bar graph** to show the votes.

Warm Up

1. How many votes did Tina get?

2. How many votes did Aaron get?

3. Who won the election?

4. Do the numbers on the tally chart agree with the graph?

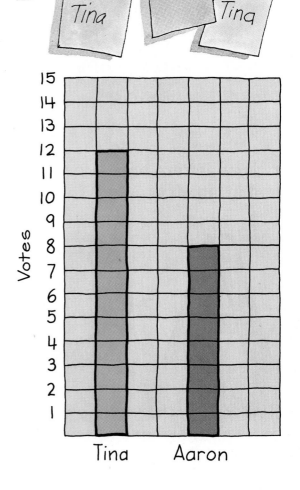

1. Liz and Ray ran for Vice-President. These are their votes. Count the votes for each person. Make a tally chart to show the votes.

FOR VICE-PRESIDENT
Liz

FOR VICE-PRESIDENT
Ray

2. Alicia and Tico ran for Secretary. This tally chart shows the votes. Make a graph to show Alicia's and Tico's votes.

Votes for Secretary

Alicia ||||| ||||| |
Tico ||||| ||||

3. Trudy and Ian ran for Treasurer. These are the votes they received. Make a tally chart and a bar graph to show their votes.

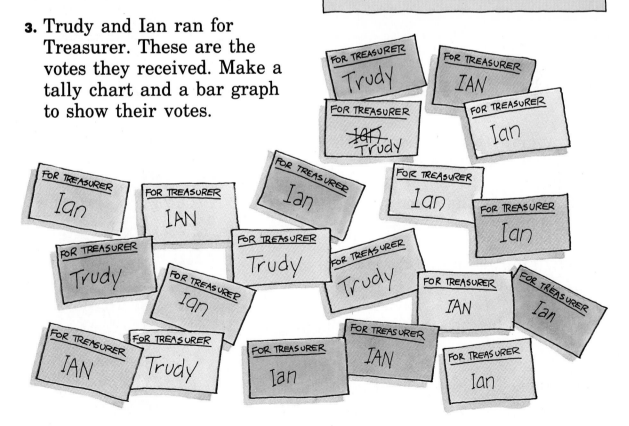

FOR TREASURER Trudy
FOR TREASURER IAN
FOR TREASURER Ian Trudy
FOR TREASURER Ian
FOR TREASURER Ian
FOR TREASURER Ian
FOR TREASURER Ian
FOR TREASURER Ian
FOR TREASURER IAN
FOR TREASURER Trudy
FOR TREASURER Trudy
FOR TREASURER Ian
FOR TREASURER Ian
FOR TREASURER IAN
FOR TREASURER IAN
FOR TREASURER Trudy
FOR TREASURER Ian
FOR TREASURER IAN
FOR TREASURER Ian

Picture Graphs

Ms. Hall runs her own business. The **picture graph** below shows the mail she got in one week. The graph shows 3 envelopes for Monday. Each envelope means 5 letters. So, Ms. Hall got **3 × 5**, or **15** letters, on Monday.

Ms. Hall's Mail

Each ⊠ means 5 letters.

Warm Up

1. How many letters did Ms. Hall get on Tuesday?

2. On what two days did Ms. Hall receive the same amount of mail?

3. How many letters did Ms. Hall get on Wednesday?

4. What is the most letters Ms. Hall got in one day?

5. What is the fewest letters Ms. Hall got in one day?

Use the magazine graph to answer questions 1–5.

1. How many magazines were delivered on Wednesday?

2. On which day were the fewest magazines delivered?

3. What is the most magazines delivered in one day?

4. How many magazines were delivered on Friday?

5. On which two days were the same number of magazines delivered?

Magazines Delivered

Monday

Tuesday

Wednesday

Thursday

Friday

Each ▢ means 5 magazines.

Use the new books graph to answer questions 6–10.

6. How many books were received on Friday?

7. What is the fewest number of books received in one day?

8. On what two days were the same number of books received?

9. What is the most books received in one day?

10. How many books were received on Thursday?

New Books Received

Monday

Tuesday

Wednesday

Thursday

Friday

Each 📕 means 4 books.

Number Pairs on a Graph

Number pairs give the location of a point on a graph. The number pair (3,4) gives you the location of the star (☆). The first number tells you to go 3 spaces to the right (⟶). The second number tells you to go 4 spaces up (↑).

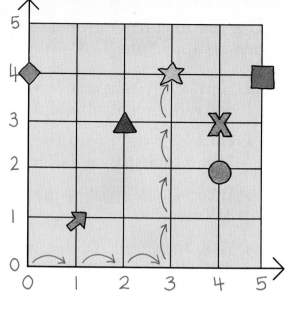

Other Examples

What is the number pair for the circle? The circle is over 4 and up 2. Its number pair is (4,2).

What figure has the number pair (2,3)? Start at (0,0) and go over 2 and up 3. The triangle has the number pair (2,3).

Warm Up   Use the graph to answer the questions.

1. What is the number pair for the times sign (✕)?

2. What figure has the number pair (5,4)?

3. What is the number pair for the diamond (◆)?

4. What figure has the number pair (1,1)?

Use the graph at the right to answer questions 1–4.

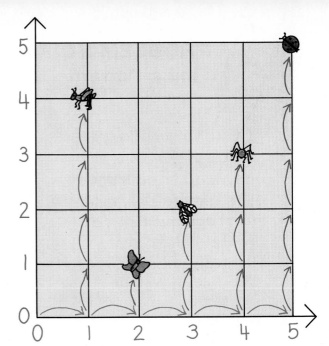

1. The fly is over 3 (↝) and up 2 (↑). What is the number pair for the fly?

2. What is the number pair for the grasshopper?

3. What is the number pair for the spider?

4. What is the number pair for the butterfly?

Use the graph at the right to answer questions 5–10.

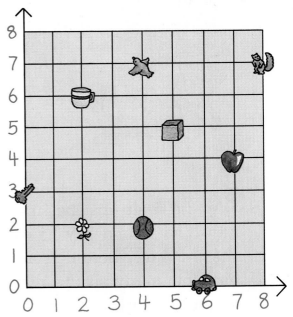

5. Go over 4 (↝) and up 2 (↑). What do you find?

6. What has the number pair (2,6)?

7. What has the number pair (7,4)?

8. What has the number pair (0,3)?

9. What has the number pair (4,7)?

10. What has the number pair (2,2)?

PROBLEM SOLVING
Find a Pattern

QUESTION
DATA
PLAN
ANSWER
CHECK

To solve a problem like this, you may need to do more than just quickly add, subtract, multiply, or divide. A strategy that can help you is given below.

Try This Guy started an exercise program. The first day he did 8 push-ups. The second day he did 10, the third day he did 12, and so on. How many push-ups did he do on the eighth day?

FIND A PATTERN

I will start a table and look for a pattern.

I see the pattern! Each day the number of push-ups is 2 more than the day before.

I'll complete the table using the pattern.

Day	1	2	3	
Push-ups	8	10	12	

Day	1	2	3	4
Push-ups	8	10	12	14

Day	1	2	3	4	5	6	7	8
Push-ups	8	10	12	14	16	18	20	22

Guy did 22 push-ups on the eighth day.

Solve.

1. Guy did 5 sit-ups the first day. The second day he did 6, the third day he did 7, and so on. How many sit-ups did he do on the 18th day?

2. Here is Guy's knee-bend list.

Day	1	2	3	4	5	6
Knee-bends	7	7	9	9	11	11

How many knee-bends did he do on the 14th day?

Name each figure.

1.

2.

3.

4.

5. Which figure matches these segments?

A    B   C

6. How many angles are in this figure?

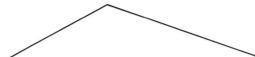

7. How many right angles are in this figure?

8. Which figure is congruent to the first?

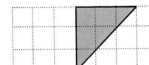   A 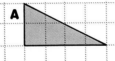   B   C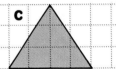

9. Which shape has a line of symmetry?

A    B   C

10. Use the graph below. How many votes did Tammy get?

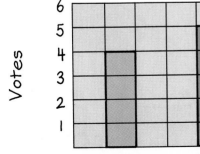

11. Use the graph below. What is the number pair for the bell?

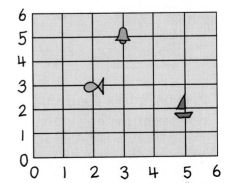

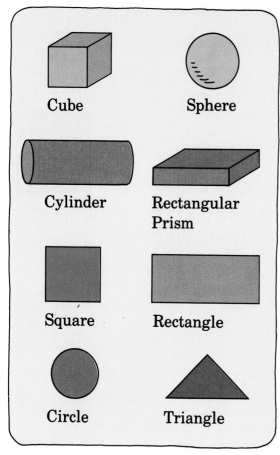

Cube   Sphere

Cylinder   Rectangular Prism

Square   Rectangle

Circle   Triangle

Name each shape.

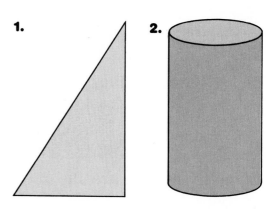

1.

2.

3.

4.

A tracing of a figure is congruent to the figure.

Which figure is congruent to the first?

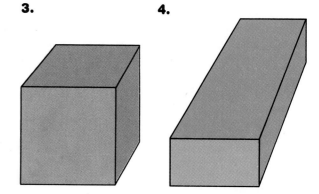

5.   A   B

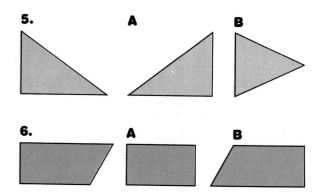

6.   A   B

Moving Figures on a Graph

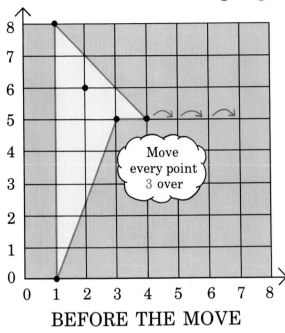

BEFORE THE MOVE

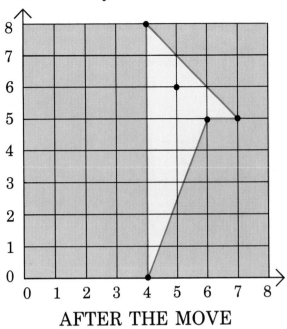

AFTER THE MOVE

Use graph paper. Put the numbers 0–10 on your graph paper as shown below. Show each figure AFTER THE MOVE.

1.

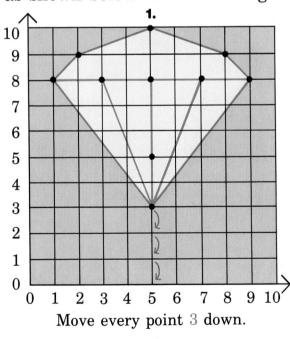

Move every point 3 down.

2.

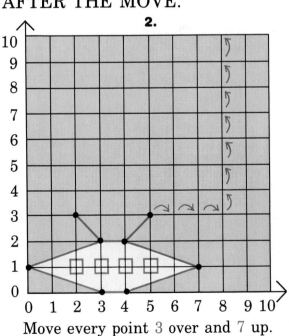

Move every point 3 over and 7 up.

Using Flowcharts

Copy this grid on your paper.

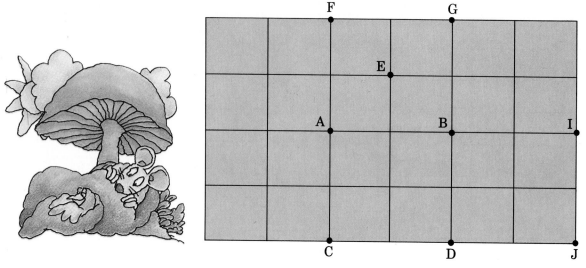

1. This flowchart will make a letter on the figure. What is it?

| START at F. | → | Draw segment FG. | → | Draw segment GA. | → | Draw segment AB. | → | STOP |

What shapes will you make if you follow these flowcharts?

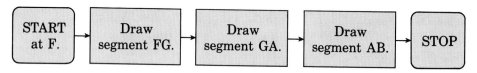

2. START at A. → Draw segment AB. → Draw segment BD. → Draw segment DC. → Draw segment CA. → STOP

3. START at D. → Draw segment DB. → Draw segment BI. → Draw segment ID. → STOP

4. Make your own flowchart for the letter L.

5. Make your own flowchart for a rectangle.

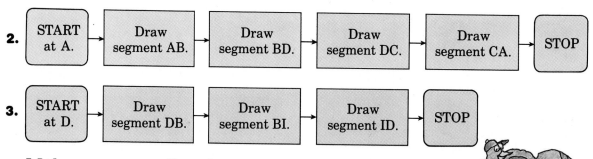

The flowcharts below give directions for the map.

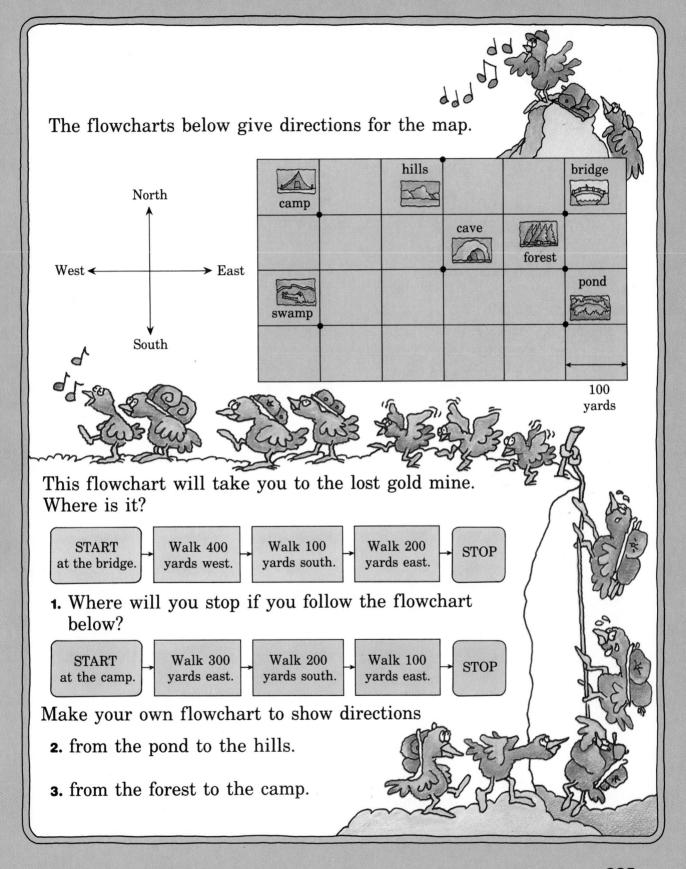

This flowchart will take you to the lost gold mine. Where is it?

| START at the bridge. | → | Walk 400 yards west. | → | Walk 100 yards south. | → | Walk 200 yards east. | → | STOP |

1. Where will you stop if you follow the flowchart below?

| START at the camp. | → | Walk 300 yards east. | → | Walk 200 yards south. | → | Walk 100 yards east. | → | STOP |

Make your own flowchart to show directions

2. from the pond to the hills.

3. from the forest to the camp.

CUMULATIVE REVIEW

Give the letter for the correct answer.

1. 38
   − 29
   - A 19
   - B 9
   - C 8
   - D not given

2. 186
   − 78
   - A 108
   - B 118
   - C 109
   - D not given

3. 582
   − 393
   - A 89
   - B 189
   - C 289
   - D not given

4. 736
   − 503
   - A 303
   - B 203
   - C 223
   - D not given

5. $7.25
   − 6.18
   - A $1.07
   - B $1.17
   - C $1.06
   - D not given

6. $5.00
   − 3.79
   - A $2.31
   - B $1.31
   - C $1.21
   - D not given

7. 2
   × 3
   - A 4
   - B 5
   - C 6
   - D not given

8. 4
   × 2
   - A 6
   - B 8
   - C 10
   - D not given

9. 5
   × 3
   - A 15
   - B 8
   - C 12
   - D not given

10. 1
    × 6
    - A 5
    - B 6
    - C 7
    - D not given

11. 4
    × 3
    - A 15
    - B 12
    - C 7
    - D not given

12. 0
    × 7
    - A 7
    - B 0
    - C 70
    - D not given

13. Manuel scored 3 field goals in the basketball game. Each field goal was worth 2 points. How many points did Manuel score?
    - A 3
    - B 6
    - C 5
    - D not given

14. Jenny is on a soccer team. Her team plays 3 games each week. How many games does Jenny's soccer team play in 5 weeks?
    - A 15
    - B 8
    - C 12
    - D not given

When Nina goes to the beach with her mother they find seashells. Nina has learned the names of many shells. Some animals live in shells. Nina knows that they like to stay on, under, and between rocks. On her last seashell hunt, Nina found some rocks covered with bluish-purple mussel shells. Nina also found 12 black shells called turban snail shells. She lined up the black shells on the sand with 4 in each row.

Understanding Division

Jay and Carmen are making cakes for the bake sale. Each cake takes 3 eggs. They have 12 eggs. How many cakes can they make?

Find how many threes are in 12.

1 three	2 threes	3 threes	4 threes

There are 4 threes in 12.

Jay and Carmen have enough eggs for 4 cakes.
We write 12 ÷ 3 = 4 ←Quotient
We read, "**Twelve divided by three equal four.**"

Answer the question. Then read the number sentence aloud and give the quotient.

1.

How many 2s are in 6?

6 ÷ 2 = ____

2.

How many 3s are in 9?

9 ÷ 3 = ____

3.

How many 2s are in 10?

10 ÷ 2 = ____

4.

How many 2s are in 4?

4 ÷ 2 = ____

Answer the question.

1.

How many 2s are in 8?

2.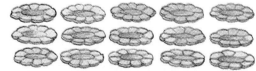

How many 3s are in 6?

3.

How many 2s are in 12?

4.

How many 3s are in 15?

Find the quotients.

5.

$8 \div 2 =$ ___

6.

$6 \div 3 =$ ___

7.

$12 \div 2 =$ ___

8.

$15 \div 3 =$ ___

Solve.

9. Dave and Helen made cakes. Each cake took 2 eggs. They had 10 eggs. How many cakes did they make?

10. Ben has 15 bananas. He uses 3 bananas for a loaf of banana bread. How many loaves does he make?

Dividing by 2 and 3

Divide by 2.

1. How many 2s are in 4?

$$4 \div 2 = \underline{}$$

2. How many 2s are in 6?

$$6 \div 2 = \underline{}$$

Use this picture if you need help.

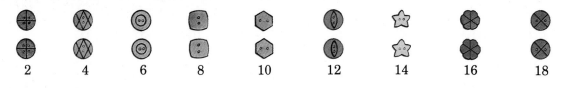

| 2 | 4 | 6 | 8 | 10 | 12 | 14 | 16 | 18 |

3. $8 \div 2 = \underline{}$ **4.** $10 \div 2 = \underline{}$ **5.** $12 \div 2 = \underline{}$

6. $14 \div 2 = \underline{}$ **7.** $16 \div 2 = \underline{}$ **8.** $18 \div 2 = \underline{}$

Divide by 3.

9. How many 3s are in 6?

$$6 \div 3 = \underline{}$$

10. How many 3s are in 9?

$$9 \div 3 = \underline{}$$

Use this picture if you need help.

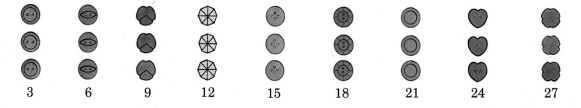

| 3 | 6 | 9 | 12 | 15 | 18 | 21 | 24 | 27 |

11. $12 \div 3 = \underline{}$ **12.** $15 \div 3 = \underline{}$ **13.** $18 \div 3 = \underline{}$

14. $21 \div 3 = \underline{}$ **15.** $24 \div 3 = \underline{}$ **16.** $27 \div 3 = \underline{}$

Warm Up Read each number sentence aloud and give the quotient.

17. $14 \div 2 = \underline{}$ **18.** $6 \div 3 = \underline{}$ **19.** $16 \div 2 = \underline{}$

20. $27 \div 3 = \underline{}$ **21.** $15 \div 3 = \underline{}$ **22.** $21 \div 3 = \underline{}$

Divide

1. $21 \div 3$ 2. $2 \div 2$ 3. $12 \div 2$ 4. $18 \div 3$

5. $14 \div 2$ 6. $3 \div 3$ 7. $8 \div 2$ 8. $9 \div 3$

9. $24 \div 3$ 10. $18 \div 2$ 11. $12 \div 3$ 12. $14 \div 2$

13. $10 \div 2$ 14. $6 \div 2$ 15. $27 \div 3$ 16. $6 \div 3$

17. $18 \div 3$ 18. $12 \div 2$ 19. $18 \div 2$ 20. $21 \div 3$

21. $16 \div 2$ 22. $24 \div 3$ 23. $15 \div 3$ 24. $4 \div 2$

25. $6 \div 2$ 26. $10 \div 2$ 27. $12 \div 3$ 28. $18 \div 2$

29. Divide 21 by 3.   30. Divide 8 by 2.   31. Divide 9 by 3.

32. Divide 27 by 3.   33. Divide 16 by 2.   34. Divide 12 by 2.

35. Divide 18 by 3.   36. Divide 24 by 3.   37. Divide 14 by 2.

Give the missing numbers.

÷ 2	
12	6
18	9
38. 10	▓
39. 8	▓
40. 14	▓
41. 16	▓

÷ 3	
24	8
15	5
42. 21	▓
43. 12	▓
44. 27	▓
45. 18	▓

THINK

Logical Reasoning

Find the sum of

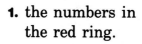
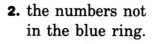

1. the numbers in the red ring.

2. the numbers not in the blue ring.

3. the numbers that are in the blue ring but not the red ring.

MATH

Multiplication and Division Are Related

$5 \times 3 = 15$

If you know this multiplication fact, you know another multiplication fact and two division facts.

Fact Family

$5 \times 3 = 15$

$3 \times 5 = 15$

$15 \div 3 = 5$

$15 \div 5 = 3$

Warm Up Solve each equation.

1. $8 \times 2 =$ ____   2. $7 \times 3 =$ ____   3. $9 \times 2 =$ ____   4. $6 \times 3 =$ ____

$2 \times 8 =$ ____ $3 \times 7 =$ ____ $2 \times 9 =$ ____ $3 \times 6 =$ ____

$16 \div 2 =$ ____ $21 \div 3 =$ ____ $18 \div 2 =$ ____ $18 \div 3 =$ ____

$16 \div 8 =$ ____ $21 \div 7 =$ ____ $18 \div 9 =$ ____ $18 \div 6 =$ ____

You can find quotients by thinking of missing factors.

5. THINK $? \times 3 = 12$

6. THINK $1 \times ? = 8$

7. THINK $? \times 3 = 24$

$12 \div 3 =$ ____

$8 \div 1 =$ ____

$24 \div 3 =$ ____

8. THINK $3 \times ? = 27$

9. THINK $? \times 1 = 5$

10. THINK $3 \times ? = 9$

$27 \div 3 =$ ____

$5 \div 1 =$ ____

$9 \div 3 =$ ____

Divide. Think about missing factors.

1. $21 \div 3$ 2. $15 \div 3$ 3. $16 \div 2$ 4. $27 \div 3$

5. $9 \div 3$ 6. $10 \div 2$ 7. $6 \div 3$ 8. $14 \div 2$

9. $8 \div 2$ 10. $2 \div 1$ 11. $24 \div 3$ 12. $16 \div 2$

13. $27 \div 3$ 14. $3 \div 3$ 15. $4 \div 2$ 16. $18 \div 3$

17. $6 \div 2$ 18. $14 \div 2$ 19. $7 \div 1$ 20. $2 \div 2$

21. $9 \div 1$ 22. $12 \div 3$ 23. $12 \div 2$ 24. $3 \div 1$

Write a multiplication and a division equation for each picture.
Example

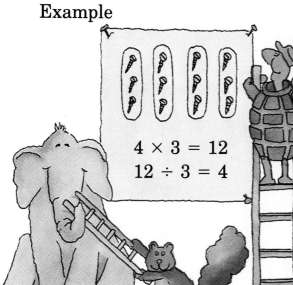

$$4 \times 3 = 12$$
$$12 \div 3 = 4$$

25.

26.

27.

28.

Multiply.

1. $\begin{array}{r} 7 \\ \times 2 \\ \hline \end{array}$	2. $\begin{array}{r} 3 \\ \times 5 \\ \hline \end{array}$	3. $\begin{array}{r} 4 \\ \times 1 \\ \hline \end{array}$	4. $\begin{array}{r} 2 \\ \times 6 \\ \hline \end{array}$	5. $\begin{array}{r} 8 \\ \times 0 \\ \hline \end{array}$	6. $\begin{array}{r} 2 \\ \times 3 \\ \hline \end{array}$
7. $\begin{array}{r} 3 \\ \times 9 \\ \hline \end{array}$	8. $\begin{array}{r} 6 \\ \times 2 \\ \hline \end{array}$	9. $\begin{array}{r} 2 \\ \times 4 \\ \hline \end{array}$	10. $\begin{array}{r} 5 \\ \times 3 \\ \hline \end{array}$	11. $\begin{array}{r} 9 \\ \times 2 \\ \hline \end{array}$	12. $\begin{array}{r} 2 \\ \times 2 \\ \hline \end{array}$

Dividing by 4

Divide by 4.

1. How many 4s are in 20?

$$20 \div 4 = \underline{}$$

2. How many 4s are in 8?

$$8 \div 4 = \underline{}$$

3. How many 4s are in 12?

$$12 \div 4 = \underline{}$$

4. How many 4s are in 16?

$$16 \div 4 = \underline{}$$

Use these pictures if you need help.

| 4 | 8 | 12 | 16 | 20 | 24 | 28 | 32 | 36 |

5. $28 \div 4 = \underline{}$ **6.** $4 \div 4 = \underline{}$ **7.** $36 \div 4 = \underline{}$

8. $20 \div 4 = \underline{}$ **9.** $32 \div 4 = \underline{}$ **10.** $24 \div 4 = \underline{}$

Warm Up   Give each quotient aloud.

11. $28 \div 4 = \underline{}$ **12.** $12 \div 4 = \underline{}$ **13.** $18 \div 3 = \underline{}$

14. $36 \div 4 = \underline{}$ **15.** $12 \div 2 = \underline{}$ **16.** $32 \div 4 = \underline{}$

17. $14 \div 2 = \underline{}$ **18.** $20 \div 4 = \underline{}$ **19.** $24 \div 4 = \underline{}$

20. $24 \div 3 = \underline{}$ **21.** $4 \div 4 = \underline{}$ **22.** $18 \div 2 = \underline{}$

23. $16 \div 2 = \underline{}$ **24.** $27 \div 3 = \underline{}$ **25.** $16 \div 4 = \underline{}$

26. $8 \div 4 = \underline{}$ **27.** $21 \div 3 = \underline{}$ **28.** $15 \div 3 = \underline{}$

Divide.

1. $16 \div 4$ 2. $21 \div 3$ 3. $32 \div 4$ 4. $18 \div 2$

5. $20 \div 4$ 6. $8 \div 4$ 7. $10 \div 2$ 8. $24 \div 4$

9. $14 \div 2$ 10. $36 \div 4$ 11. $9 \div 1$ 12. $24 \div 3$

13. $28 \div 4$ 14. $18 \div 3$ 15. $12 \div 2$ 16. $36 \div 4$

17. $16 \div 2$ 18. $28 \div 4$ 19. $24 \div 4$ 20. $32 \div 4$

21. How many 4s are in 16?   22. How many 4s are in 24?

23. How many 4s are in 32?   24. How many 4s are in 12?

25. How many 4s are in 8?   26. How many 4s are in 36?

27.

How many boxes of 4 can you fill?

28.

How many boxes of 3 can you fill?

Find the missing numbers.

X3	
4	12
6	18
29. ▥	6
30. ▥	15
31. ▥	9
32. ▥	24

X4	
5	20
7	28
33. ▥	24
34. ▥	36
35. ▥	12
36. ▥	32

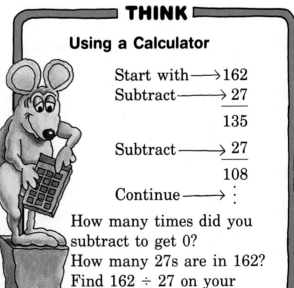

THINK

Using a Calculator

Start with ⟶ 162
Subtract ⟶ 27
———
135

Subtract ⟶ 27
———
108

Continue ⟶ ⋮

How many times did you subtract to get 0?
How many 27s are in 162?
Find $162 \div 27$ on your calculator.

MATH

Dividing by 5

Divide by 5.

1. How many 5s are in 20?

20 ÷ 5 = ___

2. How many 5s are in 15?

15 ÷ 5 = ___

3. How many 5s are in 10?

10 ÷ 5 = ___

4. How many 5s are in 25?

25 ÷ 5 = ___

Use this picture if you need help.

| 5 | 10 | 15 | 20 | 25 | 30 | 35 | 40 | 45 |

5. $40 \div 5 =$ ___   **6.** $5 \div 5 =$ ___   **7.** $30 \div 5 =$ ___

8. $25 \div 5 =$ ___   **9.** $45 \div 5 =$ ___   **10.** $35 \div 5 =$ ___

Warm Up   Give each quotient aloud.

11. $15 \div 5 =$ ___   **12.** $32 \div 4 =$ ___   **13.** $35 \div 5 =$ ___

14. $18 \div 2 =$ ___   **15.** $27 \div 3 =$ ___   **16.** $25 \div 5 =$ ___

17. $10 \div 5 =$ ___   **18.** $20 \div 4 =$ ___   **19.** $45 \div 5 =$ ___

20. $21 \div 3 =$ ___   **21.** $40 \div 5 =$ ___   **22.** $16 \div 2 =$ ___

23. $30 \div 5 =$ ___   **24.** $24 \div 4 =$ ___   **25.** $5 \div 5 =$ ___

26. $20 \div 5 =$ ___   **27.** $12 \div 2 =$ ___   **28.** $28 \div 4 =$ ___

Divide.

1. $10 \div 5$ 2. $24 \div 4$ 3. $30 \div 5$ 4. $10 \div 2$

5. $21 \div 3$ 6. $5 \div 5$ 7. $40 \div 5$ 8. $12 \div 4$

9. $20 \div 5$ 10. $35 \div 5$ 11. $18 \div 3$ 12. $45 \div 5$

13. $12 \div 2$ 14. $15 \div 5$ 15. $16 \div 4$ 16. $40 \div 5$

17. $30 \div 5$ 18. $16 \div 2$ 19. $35 \div 5$ 20. $20 \div 5$

21. $20 \div 4$ 22. $25 \div 5$ 23. $45 \div 5$ 24. $27 \div 3$

25. What is 35 divided by 5?   26. What is 20 divided by 5?

27. What is 40 divided by 5?   28. What is 30 divided by 5?

How many nickels could you get for these pennies?

29.

20 pennies

30.

15 pennies

How many nickels will it take to buy each toy?

31.

32.

═══ **SKILLKEEPER** ═══

Multiply.

1. $\begin{array}{r} 9 \\ \times 5 \\ \hline \end{array}$ 2. $\begin{array}{r} 7 \\ \times 6 \\ \hline \end{array}$ 3. $\begin{array}{r} 9 \\ \times 9 \\ \hline \end{array}$ 4. $\begin{array}{r} 6 \\ \times 8 \\ \hline \end{array}$ 5. $\begin{array}{r} 8 \\ \times 8 \\ \hline \end{array}$ 6. $\begin{array}{r} 5 \\ \times 6 \\ \hline \end{array}$

7. $\begin{array}{r} 3 \\ \times 8 \\ \hline \end{array}$ 8. $\begin{array}{r} 8 \\ \times 7 \\ \hline \end{array}$ 9. $\begin{array}{r} 7 \\ \times 9 \\ \hline \end{array}$ 10. $\begin{array}{r} 6 \\ \times 9 \\ \hline \end{array}$ 11. $\begin{array}{r} 2 \\ \times 8 \\ \hline \end{array}$ 12. $\begin{array}{r} 5 \\ \times 4 \\ \hline \end{array}$

PROBLEM SOLVING
Understanding the Operation

There are 5 boxes of apples.
4 apples are in each box.
There are 20 apples in all.

You can use division two different ways.

Division Problem		Division Problem

Suppose you know:
20 apples, 4 for each box
You can **divide** to find
how many boxes.

20 ÷ 4 = 5

There are 5 boxes.

Division tells
how many sets.

Suppose you know:
20 apples, put in 5 boxes
You can **divide** to find
how many in each box.

20 ÷ 5 = 4

There are 4 apples in each box.

Division tells
how many in each set.

Solve.

1. There are 12 berries. The berries are shared equally by 4 children. How many berries does each child get?

2. There are 12 berries. Each child gets 3 berries. How many children will get berries?

3. Adam bought 5 tickets. He spent 35 dollars. How much did he pay for each ticket?

4. Rana spent 21 dollars for tickets. Each ticket cost 3 dollars. How many tickets did she buy?

5. *Try This* Rosa had 12 red apples and 8 yellow apples. She divided the apples equally into 5 baskets. How many apples are in each basket? Hint: Choose the operations.

A New Sign for Division

There are 32 marbles.
Each bag holds 4 marbles.
How many bags are there?

32 MARBLES  ?

Two ways to write it

$$32 \div 4 = 8 \qquad 4\overline{)32}$$

Quotient → **8**

Divisor

There are 8 bags of marbles.

Find the quotients.

1. $4\overline{)24}$ 2. $3\overline{)18}$ 3. $5\overline{)10}$ 4. $1\overline{)8}$ 5. $5\overline{)30}$

6. $4\overline{)32}$ 7. $3\overline{)24}$ 8. $5\overline{)45}$ 9. $4\overline{)16}$ 10. $2\overline{)14}$

11. $3\overline{)21}$ 12. $5\overline{)25}$ 13. $4\overline{)36}$ 14. $5\overline{)15}$ 15. $4\overline{)12}$

16. $8 \div 2$ 17. $40 \div 5$ 18. $20 \div 4$ 19. $27 \div 3$

20. $15 \div 3$ 21. $35 \div 5$ 22. $28 \div 4$ 23. $20 \div 5$

How many bags of marbles are there?

24. 28 MARBLES

25. 30 MARBLES

PROBLEM SOLVING
Identifying Unneeded Data

Each of these problems has more data than you need. Use only the numbers you need.

Tell what data you do not need. Then solve.

1. There are 15 columns on the first story and 30 columns on the next 6 stories. It takes an hour to clean 5 columns. How long will it take to clean the first story columns?

2. The Tower leans 6 meters. It is 54 meters tall and 16 meters wide. How much taller is it than it is wide?

3. One day 3 workers climbed the 294 steps to the top of the Tower. They cleaned the 12 columns. How many columns did each worker clean if they each cleaned an equal number of columns?

4. A worker sweeps 8 steps a minute for 7 minutes. Then he rests for 15 minutes. How many steps did he sweep?

★ 5. Workers started building the Leaning Tower of Pisa in the year 1173. It began to lean after 3 stories were built. The Tower was finished 199 years after it was started. What year was it finished?

6. *Try This* One day, 30 people went into the Tower the first hour, 35 in the second hour, and 40 in the third hour. At this rate, how many people would go into the Tower in the sixth hour? Hint: Find a pattern.

Practice the Facts

Find the products.

1. $\begin{array}{r}4\\ \times 8\\ \hline\end{array}$	**2.** $\begin{array}{r}2\\ \times 7\\ \hline\end{array}$	**3.** $\begin{array}{r}3\\ \times 6\\ \hline\end{array}$	**4.** $\begin{array}{r}5\\ \times 7\\ \hline\end{array}$	**5.** $\begin{array}{r}2\\ \times 9\\ \hline\end{array}$	**6.** $\begin{array}{r}3\\ \times 8\\ \hline\end{array}$	**7.** $\begin{array}{r}2\\ \times 5\\ \hline\end{array}$
8. $\begin{array}{r}5\\ \times 8\\ \hline\end{array}$	**9.** $\begin{array}{r}4\\ \times 9\\ \hline\end{array}$	**10.** $\begin{array}{r}2\\ \times 3\\ \hline\end{array}$	**11.** $\begin{array}{r}3\\ \times 3\\ \hline\end{array}$	**12.** $\begin{array}{r}4\\ \times 4\\ \hline\end{array}$	**13.** $\begin{array}{r}5\\ \times 5\\ \hline\end{array}$	**14.** $\begin{array}{r}4\\ \times 7\\ \hline\end{array}$
15. $\begin{array}{r}5\\ \times 3\\ \hline\end{array}$	**16.** $\begin{array}{r}4\\ \times 5\\ \hline\end{array}$	**17.** $\begin{array}{r}5\\ \times 4\\ \hline\end{array}$	**18.** $\begin{array}{r}3\\ \times 4\\ \hline\end{array}$	**19.** $\begin{array}{r}2\\ \times 4\\ \hline\end{array}$	**20.** $\begin{array}{r}3\\ \times 3\\ \hline\end{array}$	**21.** $\begin{array}{r}4\\ \times 6\\ \hline\end{array}$

22. 9×5 **23.** 4×2 **24.** 4×3 **25.** 6×2

26. 7×3 **27.** 6×5 **28.** 8×2 **29.** 9×3

Find the quotients.

30. $3\overline{)21}$ **31.** $5\overline{)40}$ **32.** $2\overline{)16}$ **33.** $5\overline{)25}$ **34.** $4\overline{)32}$

35. $2\overline{)12}$ **36.** $4\overline{)24}$ **37.** $5\overline{)10}$ **38.** $4\overline{)16}$ **39.** $3\overline{)24}$

40. $5\overline{)20}$ **41.** $4\overline{)36}$ **42.** $3\overline{)27}$ **43.** $5\overline{)35}$ **44.** $2\overline{)18}$

45. $20 \div 4$ **46.** $10 \div 2$ **47.** $45 \div 5$ **48.** $12 \div 4$

49. $15 \div 3$ **50.** $18 \div 3$ **51.** $14 \div 2$ **52.** $28 \div 4$

53. $8 \div 2$ **54.** $32 \div 4$ **55.** $18 \div 2$ **56.** $18 \div 3$

PROBLEM SOLVING
Estimation

QUESTION
DATA
PLAN
ANSWER
CHECK

Use estimation or the basic facts to choose the correct answer.

1. The coach divided 45 players into 5 equal teams. Each team had how many players?
   A 50   B 40   C 9

2. A team scored 48 points the first half and 53 the second. How many points were scored?
   A 101   B 5   C 51

3. The Jets scored 35 points. The Giants scored 17. The Jets won by how much?
   A 52   B 26   C 18

4. The Rams scored 52 points. They made 19 points more than the Eagles. How many did the Eagles make?
   A 33   B 71   C 47

5. There are 9 tennis courts. 4 players are on each court. How many players are there?
   A 13   B 5   C 36

6. There were 24 teams at the track meet. They were in 4 equal groups. How many teams were in each group?
   A 4   B 6   C 20

7. Laura's bowling score was 102. Tod's was 85. How much higher was Laura's score?
   A 17   B 23   C 94

8. *Try This*   There were 4 teams A, B, C, and D in the school. Each team played every other team once. How many games were played? Hint: Make a list.

PROBLEM SOLVING
Practice

Solve. You may need to use the fact sheet.

1. One night only 87 rooms were rented. How many rooms were empty?

2. A family rented a double room and a single room. How much did they pay for both rooms?

3. A housekeeper used 16 sheets. He put 2 on each bed. How many beds did he make?

4. The kitchen workers are divided into 4 equal groups. How many workers are in each group?

5. A group of 32 people checked in. 4 of them stayed in each room. How many rooms were needed?

6. How many people work in the kitchen, the coffee shop, and the dining room of the hotel altogether?

Some Hotel Facts

Number of rooms	205
Cost of rooms	
single	$ 55
double	$ 65
Number of employees	
kitchen	28
coffee shop	19
dining room	18
front desk	12
housekeeping	32
other	43

7. **DATA BANK** See page 361. Suppose everyone on a full DC-10 wanted their own room in the hotel. If the hotel were empty, how many could still not have a room?

8. *Try This* Mr. Brown and Mr. Davis check in. There are 3 rooms, 701, 308, and 512. How many different ways could they be given 2 rooms? Hint: Make a list.

PROBLEM SOLVING
Using the Strategies

Use one or more of the strategies listed to solve each problem below.

PROBLEM-SOLVING STRATEGIES

Guess and Check
Use Logical Reasoning
Draw a Picture
Make a List
Make a Table
Choose the Operations
Find a Pattern

Name	Height
Amy	137 cm
Lee	129 cm
Sam	155 cm
Mary	118 cm
Juan	146 cm

1. Look at the table. Which two children have heights that differ by 17 cm?

2. Maya bought 3 rolls of film. She can take 24 pictures with each roll. The first day Maya took 17 pictures. How many pictures can she still take?

3. Jeff said, "My weight is between 25 kg and 40 kg. It is an even number. The sum of the two digits is 9." How much does Jeff weigh?

4. Sandy had 3 pairs of socks—white, blue, and yellow. The socks were mixed up in her drawer. One morning, without looking, she picked out 2 socks to wear. How many different ways could this "pair" of socks look?

Answer the questions.

1.

How many 2s are in 12?

2.

How many 3s are in 18?

Find the quotients.

3. 21 ÷ 3	**4.** 25 ÷ 5	**5.** 12 ÷ 4	**6.** 18 ÷ 2
7. 35 ÷ 5	**8.** 32 ÷ 4	**9.** 15 ÷ 3	**10.** 8 ÷ 2
11. 2 ÷ 2	**12.** 9 ÷ 3	**13.** 45 ÷ 5	**14.** 24 ÷ 4
15. 14 ÷ 2	**16.** 20 ÷ 4	**17.** 27 ÷ 3	**18.** 15 ÷ 5

19. $4\overline{)8}$ **20.** $5\overline{)10}$ **21.** $2\overline{)12}$ **22.** $5\overline{)40}$ **23.** $3\overline{)12}$

24. $4\overline{)16}$ **25.** $2\overline{)16}$ **26.** $1\overline{)6}$ **27.** $4\overline{)36}$ **28.** $3\overline{)18}$

29. $5\overline{)30}$ **30.** $3\overline{)24}$ **31.** $5\overline{)20}$ **32.** $2\overline{)10}$ **33.** $4\overline{)28}$

Solve.

34. Luis bought 5 tickets. He spent 30 dollars. How much was each ticket?

35. Trudy bought 8 tickets. Each ticket cost 4 dollars. How much did she spend for the tickets?

36. There were 40 clean towels. Each room needs 5 towels. How many rooms can get clean towels?

37. Jack spent 40 cents for 8 pencils. How much did each pencil cost?

Dividing by 2 and 3

1	2	3	4	5	6	7	8	9
X X	X X	X X	X X	X X	X X	X X	X X	X X
2	4	6	8	10	12	14	16	18

1	2	3	4	5	6	7	8	9
O O O	O O O	O O O	O O O	O O O	O O O	O O O	O O O	O O O
3	6	9	12	15	18	21	24	27

$12 \div 2 = 6$ $15 \div 3 = 5$
$16 \div 2 = 8$ $27 \div 3 = 9$

Using multiplication to find quotients.

$3 \times 4 = 12$ $4 \times 5 = 20$

$12 \div 4 = 3$ $20 \div 5 = 4$
$12 \div 3 = 4$ $20 \div 4 = 5$

$5 \times \boxed{8} = 40$ $4 \times \boxed{7} = 28$

$5)\overline{40}$ $4)\overline{28}$

$3 \times \boxed{9} = 27$ $2 \times \boxed{6} = 12$

$3)\overline{27}$ $2)\overline{12}$

Divide.

1. $12 \div 2$ 2. $21 \div 3$

3. $12 \div 3$ 4. $10 \div 2$

5. $16 \div 2$ 6. $27 \div 3$

7. $18 \div 3$ 8. $18 \div 2$

9. $8 \div 2$ 10. $14 \div 2$

11. $15 \div 3$ 12. $9 \div 3$

13. $32 \div 4$ 14. $25 \div 5$

15. $35 \div 5$ 16. $24 \div 4$

17. $16 \div 4$ 18. $40 \div 5$

19. $15 \div 5$ 20. $20 \div 4$

21. $5)\overline{35}$ 22. $3)\overline{18}$ 23. $2)\overline{18}$

24. $4)\overline{32}$ 25. $3)\overline{24}$ 26. $5)\overline{45}$

27. $4)\overline{16}$ 28. $4)\overline{28}$ 29. $2)\overline{14}$

Probability Zoo Game

Use a spinner like the one shown at the right.

Game Rules

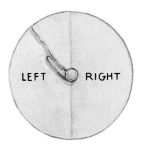

1. Start at Enter. Follow the zoo path until it splits into two paths.
2. Spin to find out which way to turn.
3. Follow the new path.
4. Spin again every time the path splits into two paths.

1. How many spins do you think it takes to visit each animal?
2. Do you have an even chance of turning left or right at each spin?
3. Play the game 24 times. Use tally marks to make a record of the animals you visit. Do you visit them all about the same number of times or do you visit some animals more?

NUMBER OF VISITS
TO EACH ANIMAL

LIONS
TIGERS
MONKEYS
BEARS
GIRAFFES
ELEPHANTS
SEALS
PENGUINS

CUMULATIVE REVIEW

Give the letter for the correct answer.

1. 9
   × 7
   - A 56
   - B 54
   - C 63
   - D not given

2. 7
   × 7
   - A 46
   - B 49
   - C 56
   - D not given

3. 9
   × 8
   - A 72
   - B 56
   - C 64
   - D not given

4. 8
   × 6
   - A 48
   - B 56
   - C 63
   - D not given

5. 7
   × 8
   - A 63
   - B 64
   - C 56
   - D not given

6. 9
   × 9
   - A 49
   - B 89
   - C 84
   - D not given

7. What time is shown?

   - A 10:05
   - B 1:52
   - C 10:52
   - D not given

8. Give the perimeter.

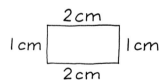

   - A 2 cm
   - B 4 cm
   - C 6 cm
   - D not given

9. A kitchen counter is about 1 ____ high.
   - A centimeter
   - B meter
   - C kilometer
   - D not given

10. Choose the best estimate.

    A cup
    - A more than a liter
    - B less than a liter
    - C a liter
    - D not given

11. Choose the best estimate.

    A banana
    - A more than a gram
    - B less than a gram
    - C a gram
    - D not given

12. Read the thermometer.

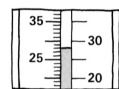

    - A 32°C
    - B 28°C
    - C 23°C
    - D not given

13. Timothy gets on the bus at 8:10 a.m. The ride to school takes 25 minutes. What time does he get to school?
    - A 8:25 a.m.
    - B 8:35 a.m.
    - C 8:45 a.m.
    - D not given

14. Jessica's ride home from school takes 45 minutes. She gets home at 4:00 p.m. What time does she leave school?
    - A 4:45 p.m.
    - B 3:45 p.m.
    - C 3:15 p.m.
    - D not given

Diane is the mail carrier who delivers mail on Steve's block. One summer day Diane asked Steve if he wanted to come with her for a few hours. First he watched as she opened her truck and filled her mailbag. There is so much mail that Diane often fills her bag 12 times in one day. Her arms must be strong because she carries about 9 kg of mail at a time. Diane works 5 days a week. Each week she walks more than 45 km.

Dividing by 6

Scott bought 30 cans of juice. There were 6 cans in each box. How many boxes of juice did Scott buy?

Betsy bought 42 cans of juice. There were 6 cans in each box. How many boxes of juice did Betsy buy?

THINK
? × 6 = 30

30 ÷ 6 = 5

Scott bought 5 boxes of juice.

THINK
? × 6 = 42

42 ÷ 6 = 7

Betsy bought 7 boxes of juice.

Solve. Think about missing factors.

1. (? × 6 = 36)

36 ÷ 6 = ___

2. (? × 6 = 48)

48 ÷ 6 = ___

3. (? × 6 = 54)

54 ÷ 6 = ___

Warm Up   Read each number sentence aloud and give the quotient.

4. 12 ÷ 6 = ___   5. 24 ÷ 3 = ___   6. 18 ÷ 6 = ___   7. 54 ÷ 6 = ___

8. 24 ÷ 6 = ___   9. 48 ÷ 6 = ___   10. 30 ÷ 5 = ___   11. 45 ÷ 5 = ___

Give each quotient aloud.

12. $4\overline{)32}$ 13. $6\overline{)30}$ 14. $4\overline{)28}$ 15. $5\overline{)40}$

16. $6\overline{)54}$ 17. $3\overline{)27}$ 18. $6\overline{)24}$ 19. $2\overline{)16}$

Divide.

1. $6\overline{)12}$ 2. $6\overline{)30}$ 3. $4\overline{)36}$ 4. $6\overline{)24}$ 5. $6\overline{)36}$

6. $6\overline{)18}$ 7. $6\overline{)48}$ 8. $1\overline{)8}$ 9. $5\overline{)25}$ 10. $6\overline{)42}$

11. $27 \div 3$ 12. $24 \div 6$ 13. $18 \div 2$ 14. $30 \div 6$

15. $42 \div 6$ 16. $30 \div 5$ 17. $36 \div 6$ 18. $6 \div 6$

19. How many 6s are in 24?   20. How many 6s are in 42?

21. How many 6s are in 12?   22. How many 6s are in 30?

23. How many 6s are in 48?   24. How many 6s are in 54?

25. How many 6s are in 36?   26. How many 6s are in 18?

Solve.

27. Pam bought 36 muffins. There were 6 muffins in each package. How many packages did she buy?

28. Ms. Chan bought 9 packages of rolls. There were 6 rolls in each package. How many rolls did she buy?

29. There are 6 boxes of juice bars in the freezer. The same number are in each box. There are 48 juice bars in all. How many are in each box?

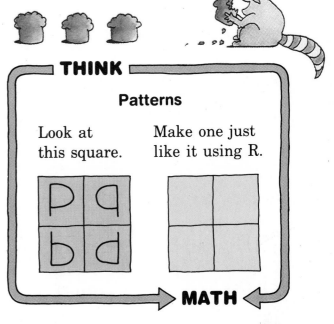

THINK

Patterns

Look at this square.

Make one just like it using R.

MATH

More Practice, page 380, Set B

Dividing by 7

Peg's puppy is 42 days old. There are 7 days in a week. How many weeks old is the puppy?

Eric's kitten is only 28 days old. There are 7 days in a week. How many weeks old is Eric's kitten?

THINK
? × 7 = 42

42 ÷ 7 = 6

Peg's puppy is 6 weeks old.

THINK
? × 7 = 28

28 ÷ 7 = 4

Eric's kitten is 4 weeks old.

Solve. Think about missing factors.

1. (? × 7 = 49)

49 ÷ 7 = ____

2. (? × 7 = 63)

63 ÷ 7 = ____

3. (? × 7 = 56)

56 ÷ 7 = ____

Warm Up Give each quotient aloud.

4. 35 ÷ 7 = ____   5. 14 ÷ 7 = ____   6. 30 ÷ 5 = ____   7. 28 ÷ 7 = ____

8. 28 ÷ 4 = ____   9. 63 ÷ 7 = ____   10. 42 ÷ 7 = ____   11. 36 ÷ 4 = ____

12. $1\overline{)7}$ 13. $2\overline{)14}$ 14. $7\overline{)7}$ 15. $3\overline{)24}$

16. $7\overline{)63}$ 17. $7\overline{)21}$ 18. $7\overline{)49}$ 19. $7\overline{)28}$

Divide.

1. $6\overline{)42}$ 2. $7\overline{)35}$ 3. $7\overline{)49}$ 4. $4\overline{)24}$ 5. $7\overline{)21}$

6. $7\overline{)56}$ 7. $7\overline{)28}$ 8. $7\overline{)7}$ 9. $7\overline{)42}$ 10. $5\overline{)25}$

11. $6\overline{)48}$ 12. $3\overline{)27}$ 13. $7\overline{)56}$ 14. $6\overline{)54}$ 15. $7\overline{)63}$

16. $7\overline{)35}$ 17. $7\overline{)14}$ 18. $5\overline{)40}$ 19. $6\overline{)36}$ 20. $7\overline{)49}$

21. $10 \div 2$ 22. $42 \div 7$ 23. $63 \div 7$ 24. $28 \div 7$

25. Divide 49 by 7.   26. Divide 21 by 7.

27. Divide 56 by 7.   28. Divide 35 by 7.

29. Divide 7 by 7.   30. Divide 63 by 7.

31. Divide 42 by 7.   32. Divide 28 by 7.

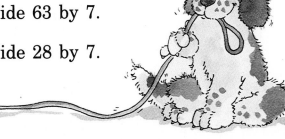

Solve.

33. Stephen's rabbit is 56 days old. There are 7 days in a week. How many weeks old is Stephen's rabbit?

34. Dora's puppy is 7 weeks old. How many days old is Dora's puppy?

SKILLKEEPER

Add.

1. $\begin{array}{r} \$1.58 \\ + 1.21 \\ \hline \end{array}$ 2. $\begin{array}{r} \$7.50 \\ + 3.60 \\ \hline \end{array}$ 3. $\begin{array}{r} \$8.95 \\ + 7.23 \\ \hline \end{array}$ 4. $\begin{array}{r} \$5.39 \\ + 6.56 \\ \hline \end{array}$ 5. $\begin{array}{r} \$1.06 \\ + 2.78 \\ \hline \end{array}$

6. $\begin{array}{r} \$6.05 \\ + 8.98 \\ \hline \end{array}$ 7. $\begin{array}{r} \$5.50 \\ + 2.25 \\ \hline \end{array}$ 8. $\begin{array}{r} \$3.80 \\ + 7.52 \\ \hline \end{array}$ 9. $\begin{array}{r} \$6.98 \\ + 3.23 \\ \hline \end{array}$ 10. $\begin{array}{r} \$6.86 \\ + 7.54 \\ \hline \end{array}$

Practice the Facts

Division Fact Helpers

Fact-Family Numbers	Missing Factor	Thinking About Sets
4 7 28	What number times 5 gives 35?	How many 4s are in 24?
$28 \div 7 = \underline{}$	$35 \div 5 = \underline{}$	$24 \div 4 = \underline{}$

Find the quotients.

1. $36 \div 4$ **2.** $7 \div 7$ **3.** $35 \div 5$ **4.** $54 \div 6$

5. $35 \div 7$ **6.** $16 \div 2$ **7.** $18 \div 3$ **8.** $9 \div 3$

9. $8 \div 4$ **10.** $48 \div 6$ **11.** $10 \div 5$ **12.** $12 \div 6$

13. $56 \div 7$ **14.** $6 \div 3$ **15.** $20 \div 4$ **16.** $4 \div 4$

17. $21 \div 3$ **18.** $14 \div 7$ **19.** $12 \div 2$ **20.** $40 \div 5$

21. $6\overline{)24}$ **22.** $4\overline{)12}$ **23.** $5\overline{)5}$ **24.** $7\overline{)28}$ **25.** $2\overline{)14}$

26. $7\overline{)63}$ **27.** $3\overline{)3}$ **28.** $4\overline{)16}$ **29.** $3\overline{)12}$ **30.** $5\overline{)25}$

31. $6\overline{)18}$ **32.** $5\overline{)20}$ **33.** $2\overline{)18}$ **34.** $7\overline{)49}$ **35.** $6\overline{)42}$

36. $3\overline{)24}$ **37.** $7\overline{)21}$ **38.** $5\overline{)45}$ **39.** $4\overline{)24}$ **40.** $3\overline{)15}$

PROBLEM SOLVING
Choose the Operations

Tell which equation you would use to solve the problem. Then solve the problem.

1. Dee bought some buttons for 32¢. Each one cost 4¢. How many buttons did Dee buy?

  A $32 - 4 =$ ___

  B $32 + 4 =$ ___

  C $32 \div 4 =$ ___

2. Paco has $12. He spends $4 for a gift for his sister. How much does he have left?

  A $12 + 4 =$ ___

  B $12 - 4 =$ ___

  C $12 \div 4 =$ ___

3. Rita bought 6 cans of paint. Each one cost $3. What was the total cost?

  A $6 + 3 =$ ___

  B $6 \times 3 =$ ___

  C $6 \div 3 =$ ___

4. Lee saved $24. He earned another $8 for cutting grass. How much does he have now?

  A $24 - 8 =$ ___

  B $24 + 8 =$ ___

  C $24 \div 8 =$ ___

5. Luke paid $30 for 5 tickets. How much did Luke pay for each ticket?

  A $30 + 5 =$ ___

  B $30 - 5 =$ ___

  C $30 \div 5 =$ ___

6. *Try This* Gail had $43. She bought a gift for $28. She spent the rest of her money on books for $3 each. How many books did she buy?

Dividing by 8

There are 40 arms in all. Each octopus has 8 arms. How many octopuses are there?

There are 64 arms in all. Each octopus has 8 arms. How many octopuses are there?

THINK
? × 8 = 40

40 ÷ 8 = 5

There are 5 octopuses.

THINK
? × 8 = 64

64 ÷ 8 = 8

There are 8 octopuses.

Solve. Think about missing factors.

1. ? × 8 = 48

   48 ÷ 8 = ___

2. ? × 8 = 72

   72 ÷ 8 = ___

3. ? × 8 = 56

   56 ÷ 8 = ___

Warm Up Give each quotient aloud.

4. 24 ÷ 8 = ___   5. 56 ÷ 7 = ___   6. 56 ÷ 8 = ___   7. 32 ÷ 8 = ___

8. 72 ÷ 8 = ___   9. 40 ÷ 8 = ___   10. 48 ÷ 6 = ___   11. 64 ÷ 8 = ___

12. 8)‾32‾   13. 4)‾32‾   14. 6)‾54‾   15. 8)‾24‾

16. 7)‾49‾   17. 8)‾8‾   18. 8)‾64‾   19. 8)‾56‾

Divide.

1. $7\overline{)42}$ 2. $8\overline{)48}$ 3. $6\overline{)30}$ 4. $8\overline{)16}$ 5. $8\overline{)64}$

6. $8\overline{)32}$ 7. $8\overline{)72}$ 8. $8\overline{)40}$ 9. $8\overline{)56}$ 10. $4\overline{)36}$

11. $5\overline{)35}$ 12. $6\overline{)54}$ 13. $7\overline{)35}$ 14. $6\overline{)36}$ 15. $8\overline{)24}$

16. $4\overline{)32}$ 17. $8\overline{)64}$ 18. $8\overline{)8}$ 19. $8\overline{)72}$ 20. $8\overline{)48}$

21. $40 \div 8$ 22. $42 \div 6$ 23. $56 \div 8$ 24. $56 \div 7$

25. What is 32 divided by 8?

26. What is 48 divided by 8?

27. What is 64 divided by 8?

28. What is 24 divided by 8?

29. What is 16 divided by 8?

30. What is 72 divided by 8?

Solve.

31. There are 32 arms in all. Each octopus has 8 arms. How many octopuses are there?

32. There are 56 legs in all. Each spider has 8 legs. How many spiders are there?

33. There are 48 legs in all. Each bug has 6 legs. How many bugs are there?

THINK

Clock Puzzle

How many minutes will it be until the hands form a straight line?

How many minutes will it be until the hands form a right angle?

MATH

Dividing by 9

36 children wanted to play baseball. There are 9 players on each team. How many teams can be made?

There were 45 orange slices for the team. The 9 players shared them equally. How many orange slices did each player get?

THINK
? × 9 = 36

36 ÷ 9 = 4

4 teams can be made.

THINK
? × 9 = 45

45 ÷ 9 = 5

Each player gets 5 orange slices.

Solve. Think about missing factors.

1.   ? × 9 = 63

63 ÷ 9 = ____

2.   ? × 9 = 72

72 ÷ 9 = ____

3.   ? × 9 = 81

81 ÷ 9 = ____

Warm Up   Give each quotient aloud.

4. 36 ÷ 9 = ____   5. 54 ÷ 6 = ____   6. 63 ÷ 9 = ____   7. 64 ÷ 8 = ____

8. 72 ÷ 9 = ____   9. 63 ÷ 7 = ____   10. 45 ÷ 9 = ____   11. 18 ÷ 9 = ____

12. $8\overline{)40}$ 13. $9\overline{)9}$ 14. $8\overline{)72}$ 15. $9\overline{)63}$

16. $9\overline{)45}$ 17. $8\overline{)56}$ 18. $7\overline{)49}$ 19. $9\overline{)27}$

Divide.

1. $9\overline{)54}$ 2. $8\overline{)56}$ 3. $9\overline{)63}$

4. $9\overline{)36}$ 5. $9\overline{)72}$ 6. $8\overline{)72}$

7. $6\overline{)48}$ 8. $7\overline{)56}$ 9. $9\overline{)9}$ 10. $8\overline{)48}$ 11. $9\overline{)81}$

12. $9\overline{)27}$ 13. $9\overline{)63}$ 14. $6\overline{)54}$ 15. $9\overline{)72}$ 16. $9\overline{)54}$

17. $42 \div 6$ 18. $64 \div 8$ 19. $81 \div 9$ 20. $45 \div 9$

21. How many 9s are in 63?   22. How many 9s are in 54?

23. How many 9s are in 72?   24. How many 9s are in 18?

25. How many 9s are in 45?   26. How many 9s are in 81?

Solve.

27. There are 9 players on each baseball team. How many teams can be made from 54 players?

28. There were 7 teams with 9 players on each team. How many players were there altogether?

SKILLKEEPER

Find the missing factors.

1. $7 \times \text{\rule{0.5em}{0.8em}} = 49$ 2. $\text{\rule{0.5em}{0.8em}} \times 3 = 24$ 3. $8 \times \text{\rule{0.5em}{0.8em}} = 72$

4. $7 \times \text{\rule{0.5em}{0.8em}} = 56$ 5. $9 \times \text{\rule{0.5em}{0.8em}} = 54$ 6. $\text{\rule{0.5em}{0.8em}} \times 5 = 40$

7. $\text{\rule{0.5em}{0.8em}} \times 4 = 28$ 8. $9 \times \text{\rule{0.5em}{0.8em}} = 81$ 9. $8 \times \text{\rule{0.5em}{0.8em}} = 48$

More about Division

Kirk planned to give all the fish he caught to 2 friends. But Kirk did not catch any fish. How many fish did his friends get?

Joni caught 6 fish. She gave 0 fish to each of her friends. How many friends could she give 0 fish to?

THINK
$? \times 2 = 0$

THINK
$? \times 0 = 6$

0 ÷ 2 = 0

6 ÷ 0 = ___

His friends got 0 fish.

This does not make sense!

Zero divided by any number (not 0) is zero.	Never divide by zero.

Divide.

1. $5\overline{)45}$ **2.** $6\overline{)36}$ **3.** $1\overline{)9}$ **4.** $5\overline{)0}$ **5.** $7\overline{)49}$

6. $3\overline{)27}$ **7.** $9\overline{)72}$ **8.** $2\overline{)18}$ **9.** $4\overline{)12}$ **10.** $6\overline{)54}$

11. $8\overline{)64}$ **12.** $5\overline{)40}$ **13.** $9\overline{)0}$ **14.** $8\overline{)48}$ **15.** $5\overline{)30}$

16. $6\overline{)42}$ **17.** $4\overline{)16}$ **18.** $9\overline{)81}$ **19.** $4\overline{)0}$ **20.** $1\overline{)3}$

21. $42 \div 6$ **22.** $16 \div 4$ **23.** $81 \div 9$ **24.** $0 \div 4$

25. $3 \div 1$ **26.** $16 \div 2$ **27.** $28 \div 7$ **28.** $35 \div 7$

29. $56 \div 8$ **30.** $0 \div 7$ **31.** $63 \div 9$ **32.** $12 \div 2$

PROBLEM SOLVING
Practice

Solve.

1. Jamie paid $1.95 for a pen and $0.98 for paper. How much did she pay for both?

2. Mike bought a package of 6 file folders. He paid 54¢ for the package. How much did each file folder cost?

3. Ron bought 4 books. He paid $3 for each book. How much did he pay for all the books?

4. Lori bought 6 pencils for 36 cents. How much did each pencil cost?

5. Dick bought 8 envelopes. Each envelope cost 5 cents. How much did Dick spend?

6. Terry bought 32 colored pencils. There were 4 of each color. How many different colors did she get?

7. Jim had a 5-dollar bill. He spent $3.95. How much did he get back in change?

8. Vicki bought an eraser for $0.39. She also bought a box of crayons for $1.29 and a pad of paper for $0.79. How much did she spend?

9. **Try This** Lois saw some books on sale. The prices were $3, $5, $6, and $7. She bought two books for $9. What were the prices of her books?

PROBLEM SOLVING
Using Data from a Table

Supermarket Jobs	
Jobs	Number of People
Manager	5
Check-out	32
Baggers	15
Stock	11
Produce	5
Meat	7
Other	9
TOTAL	84

Many people are needed to run a supermarket. The table shows the different jobs and the number of people in each job.

Decide whether you need to use the data from the table. Then solve the problems.

1. Mr. Thomas is the head manager. How many other managers are there?

2. How many more check-out people are there than baggers?

3. A produce worker counted 32 kinds of vegetables and 14 kinds of fruit. How many more kinds of vegetables were there?

4. The meat workers worked a total of 56 hours on Friday. Each person worked the same number of hours. How many hours did each person work?

5. A worker put 56 packages of ground meat into 7 equal stacks. How many packages were in each stack?

6. Each person in meats worked 6 hours on Friday. What was the total amount of hours they worked?

7. How many people work at the supermarket other than the managers?

8. Oranges are sacked 8 to a bag. How many bags can be filled with 72 oranges?

9. The baggers are divided into 3 equal groups. How many are in each group?

10. Mrs. Clark bought 6 bunches of carrots. Each bunch had 7 carrots. How many carrots did she buy?

11. In July, 7 check-out people went on vacation. How many check-out people were left?

12. A produce worker opened a box of apples. She put 8 apples in each of 9 bags. There were 19 apples left in the box. How many were in the box when she opened it?

13. On Monday, all the baggers, stock, produce, and meat people worked in the stock room. How many people worked in the stock room?

14. **DATA BANK** Look at page 360. What is the total number of stores for the first three supermarkets?

15. **DATA HUNT** Go to a supermarket. Count the different kinds of fresh vegetables and fresh fruits. What is the difference in the number of vegetables and fruits?

16. *Try This* Linda and Steve are checkers. Joshua, Meg, and Nate are baggers. How many different checker-bagger pairs can they make? Hint: Make a list.

PROBLEM SOLVING
Using the Strategies

Use one or more of the strategies listed to solve each problem below.

PROBLEM-SOLVING STRATEGIES

Guess and Check
Use Logical Reasoning
Draw a Picture
Make a List
Make a Table
Choose the Operations
Find a Pattern

1. Chuy can ride his bicycle 6 miles in 1 hour. Ross can ride 5 miles in 1 hour. They start riding at the same time. How far has Ross gone when Chuy has ridden 36 miles?

Chuy	6	12	18
Ross	5	10	15

2. Celia's grandmother lives farther from her than her uncle. Her aunt lives between her grandmother and her uncle. Her best friend lives closer than her uncle. Who lives farthest from Celia?

3. Mr. Abrams drove from home to the park one way. He drove back home another way. He traveled 23 km. What two roads did he take?

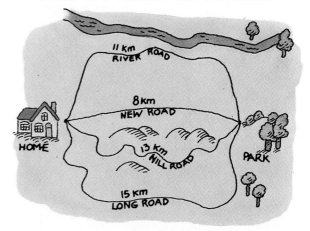

4. There are 17 girls and 19 boys going to the park. Each car can hold 4 children. How many cars are needed?

Find the quotients.

1. $6\overline{)36}$ 2. $7\overline{)56}$ 3. $6\overline{)42}$ 4. $6\overline{)30}$ 5. $7\overline{)49}$

6. $6\overline{)48}$ 7. $7\overline{)63}$ 8. $7\overline{)42}$ 9. $6\overline{)54}$ 10. $7\overline{)35}$

11. $8\overline{)64}$ 12. $9\overline{)63}$ 13. $8\overline{)40}$ 14. $8\overline{)72}$ 15. $9\overline{)36}$

16. $8\overline{)56}$ 17. $9\overline{)81}$ 18. $9\overline{)27}$ 19. $7\overline{)49}$ 20. $9\overline{)54}$

21. $8\overline{)72}$ 22. $6\overline{)42}$ 23. $7\overline{)14}$ 24. $8\overline{)40}$ 25. $6\overline{)18}$

26. $9\overline{)27}$ 27. $9\overline{)72}$ 28. $8\overline{)24}$ 29. $7\overline{)0}$ 30. $9\overline{)45}$

31. $8\overline{)48}$ 32. $6\overline{)24}$ 33. $9\overline{)63}$ 34. $7\overline{)56}$ 35. $8\overline{)48}$

Solve.

36. There were 36 check-out people. 19 baggers were helping them. How many workers were there in all?

37. There were 8 bunches of bananas. Each bunch had 7 bananas. How many bananas were there?

38. Ted spent 48 cents for 6 plums. How much did each plum cost?

39. Laura had $9.00. She spent a total of $6.95 on school supplies. How much was left?

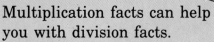

ANOTHER LOOK

Multiplication facts can help
you with division facts.

$$\begin{array}{r}6\\\times 6\\\hline 36\end{array} \quad \begin{array}{r}6\\\times 7\\\hline 42\end{array} \quad \begin{array}{r}6\\\times 8\\\hline 48\end{array} \quad \begin{array}{r}6\\\times 9\\\hline 54\end{array}$$

$$\overset{7}{6)42} \qquad \overset{9}{6)54}$$

$$\begin{array}{r}7\\\times 6\\\hline 42\end{array} \quad \begin{array}{r}7\\\times 7\\\hline 49\end{array} \quad \begin{array}{r}7\\\times 8\\\hline 56\end{array} \quad \begin{array}{r}7\\\times 9\\\hline 63\end{array}$$

$$\overset{6}{7)42} \qquad \overset{8}{7)56}$$

$$\begin{array}{r}8\\\times 6\\\hline 48\end{array} \quad \begin{array}{r}8\\\times 7\\\hline 56\end{array} \quad \begin{array}{r}8\\\times 8\\\hline 64\end{array} \quad \begin{array}{r}8\\\times 9\\\hline 72\end{array}$$

$$\overset{7}{8)56} \qquad \overset{8}{8)64}$$

$$\begin{array}{r}9\\\times 6\\\hline 54\end{array} \quad \begin{array}{r}9\\\times 7\\\hline 63\end{array} \quad \begin{array}{r}9\\\times 8\\\hline 72\end{array} \quad \begin{array}{r}9\\\times 9\\\hline 81\end{array}$$

$$\overset{6}{9)54} \qquad \overset{9}{9)81}$$

Divide.

1. $6)\overline{36}$ 2. $6)\overline{30}$ 3. $6)\overline{48}$

4. $6)\overline{24}$ 5. $6)\overline{54}$ 6. $6)\overline{42}$

7. $7)\overline{63}$ 8. $7)\overline{35}$ 9. $7)\overline{49}$

10. $7)\overline{28}$ 11. $7)\overline{56}$ 12. $7)\overline{42}$

13. $8)\overline{48}$ 14. $8)\overline{72}$ 15. $8)\overline{56}$

16. $8)\overline{64}$ 17. $8)\overline{40}$ 18. $8)\overline{32}$

19. $9)\overline{63}$ 20. $9)\overline{45}$ 21. $9)\overline{81}$

22. $9)\overline{72}$ 23. $9)\overline{54}$ 24. $9)\overline{36}$

Negative Numbers

Elena made this graph to show the temperature from 1:00 a.m. to 8:00 a.m. She used **negative numbers** to show temperatures **below** zero.

Read negative numbers as:

negative one
negative two
negative three
.
.
.

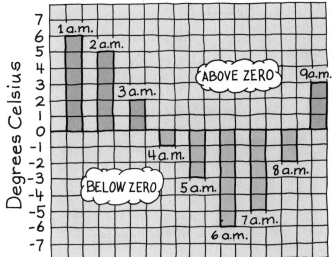

The temperature at 2:00 a.m. was 5 degrees.
The temperature at 5:00 a.m. was ⁻3 degrees.

Use the graph to answer the questions.

1. What was the temperature at 1:00 a.m.?

2. What was the temperature at 7:00 a.m.?

3. At what time was the temperature ⁻2 degrees?

4. At what time was the temperature 2 degrees?

5. At what time was it coldest?

6. What was the difference in temperature between 2:00 a.m. and 3:00 a.m.?

7. What was the difference in temperature between 4:00 a.m. and 5:00 a.m.?

CUMULATIVE REVIEW

Give the letter for the correct answer.

1. Name the figure.

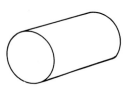

    A sphere
    B circle
    C cylinder
    D not given

2. Name the figure.

    A cube
    B rectangle
    C square
    D not given

3. Name the figure.

    A triangle
    B cube
    C rectangular prism
    D not given

4. Which shape is congruent to this shape?

    A   **B**

    C   **D** not given

5. Which shape is congruent to this shape?

    A   **B**

    C   **D** not given

6. Which is a line of symmetry?

    A 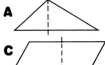   **B**

    C    **D** not given

7.
$$\begin{array}{r} 2 \\ \times\ 8 \\ \hline \end{array}$$
  A 10   **B** 16
  C 21   **D** not given

8.
$$\begin{array}{r} 3 \\ \times\ 7 \\ \hline \end{array}$$
  A 24   **B** 28
  C 21   **D** not given

9.
$$\begin{array}{r} 4 \\ \times\ 9 \\ \hline \end{array}$$
  A 34   **B** 36
  C 38   **D** not given

10.
$$\begin{array}{r} 5 \\ \times\ 8 \\ \hline \end{array}$$
  A 40   **B** 45
  C 48   **D** not given

11.
$$\begin{array}{r} 6 \\ \times\ 9 \\ \hline \end{array}$$
  A 63   **B** 48
  C 54   **D** not given

12.
$$\begin{array}{r} 5 \\ \times\ 7 \\ \hline \end{array}$$
  A 45   **B** 35
  C 30   **D** not given

13. Dana made 4 field goals. Each one was 2 points. How many points did Dana make?
  A 6   **B** 8
  C 2   **D** not given

14. Wendy baked 2 cakes. Each cake took 3 eggs. How many eggs did she use?
  A 6   **B** 5
  C 8   **D** not given

MULTIPLICATION

When Tania turned 11 she took over her brother's paper route. Tania must get up at 5:30 every morning. First she counts the papers to make sure she has enough. It takes her about 10 minutes to fold the papers. Then she delivers the papers to the houses. Once a month Tania collects for the paper from the people on her route.

Special Products: Mental Math

Leo bought 6 packages of pencils and 3 cards of tacks. How many pencils and how many tacks did he buy?

Since we want totals for equal sets, we multiply.

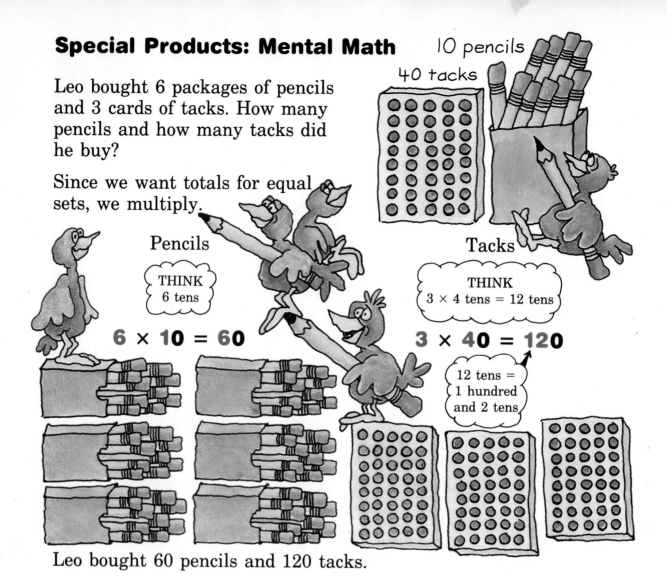

10 pencils
40 tacks

Pencils

THINK
6 tens

$6 \times 10 = 60$

Tacks

THINK
3×4 tens = 12 tens

$3 \times 40 = 120$

12 tens =
1 hundred
and 2 tens

Leo bought 60 pencils and 120 tacks.

Other Examples

$3 \times 10 = 30$ $4 \times 20 = 80$ $5 \times 40 = 200$

20 tens = 2 hundred

Warm Up   Give each product aloud.

1. 4×10 2. 6×10 3. 8×10 4. 7×10

5. 3×20 6. 4×30 7. 6×40 8. 5×30

9. 2×10 10. 2×80 11. 5×10 12. 4×40

13. 5×80 14. 1×10 15. 2×50 16. 9×10

Find the products.

1. 3×10 2. 6×10 3. 4×10 4. 7×10

5. 8×10 6. 2×10 7. 5×10 8. 9×10

9. 2×40 10. 4×30 11. 6×40 12. 2×90

13. 7×20 14. 5×70 15. 8×30 16. 4×50

17. 7×10 18. 2×30 19. 1×10 20. 6×30

21. 8×20 22. 5×10 23. 3×70 24. 4×90

25. Give the product of 3 and 10.   26. Give the product of 9 and 40.

27. Give the product of 7 and 50.   28. Give the product of 3 and 90.

★ 29. $2 \times 3 \times 10$ ★ 30. $4 \times 2 \times 10$ ★ 31. $3 \times 3 \times 10$

★ 32. $2 \times 4 \times 20$ ★ 33. $3 \times 3 \times 30$ ★ 34. $3 \times 2 \times 40$

Solve.

35. There are 50 rubberbands in a bag. How many rubberbands are in 6 bags?

36. **DATA HUNT** How many crayons come in a box? How many crayons are in 10 boxes?

Mental Math

CAT is worth 12 points.

C   A   T
2 + 2 + 8

1. Find the points for these words.
   DOG   SUN   TWO
   ONE   SIX   TEN

2. Find the points for your name.
3. Find a 10-point word.

Multiplication and Addition

Mike mailed three packages. He bought a 5¢ stamp and a 40¢ stamp for each package. Here is how the clerk figured out how much Mike had to pay.

THINK 3 fives   **3 × 5 =   15**

THINK 3 forties   **3 × 40 = 120**

Add   **135**

The clerk asked Mike to pay 135¢ ($1.35).

Find the cost.

1. 5 packages

Think (5 fours)

Think (5 thirties)

Then add.

2. 7 packages

Think (7 threes)

Think (7 forties)

Then add.

3. 4 packages

Think (4 × 8¢)

Think (4 × 20¢)

Then add.

How much to mail

4. 2 blue packages?

5. 4 blue packages?

6. 5 yellow packages?

7. 3 yellow packages?

8. 4 brown packages?

9. 5 brown packages?

Solve.

★ **10.** Doris mailed 6 small packages to her friends. The clerk put stamps worth 32¢ on each package. How much did Doris have to pay?

11. DATA BANK See page 359. How much will it cost to mail 5 packages if each package has a First Man on the Moon stamp and a Circus stamp?

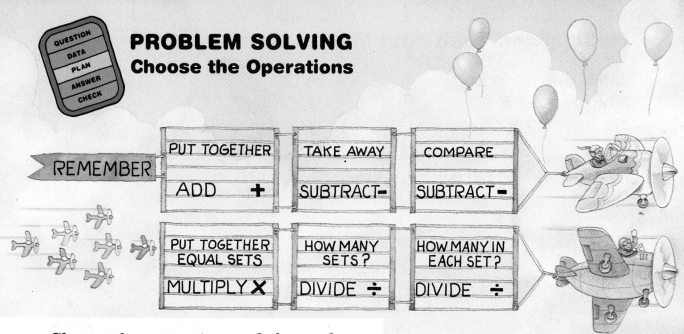

PROBLEM SOLVING
Choose the Operations

REMEMBER

PUT TOGETHER	TAKE AWAY	COMPARE
ADD +	SUBTRACT −	SUBTRACT −

PUT TOGETHER EQUAL SETS	HOW MANY SETS?	HOW MANY IN EACH SET?
MULTIPLY ✕	DIVIDE ÷	DIVIDE ÷

Choose the operation and then solve.

1. Miguel Gonzales bought 7 40¢-stamps and 7 5¢-stamps. How much did he pay in all?

2. On Tuesday Bill paid $1.76 to mail a package. On Friday he paid $2.35 to mail another package. How much less did he pay on Tuesday?

3. A clerk sold 8 books of stamps. There are 30 stamps in each book. How many stamps were sold?

4. Don put the same number of stamps on 5 packages. He used 15 stamps. How many stamps are on each package?

5. Matt mailed 3 packages. One cost $2.85 to mail. The second cost $0.95. The third cost $1.33. How much did Matt pay?

6. Liz bought 5 20¢-stamps. How much did she pay? She gave the clerk $5. How much money did she get back?

7. *Try This* Cindy collects flag stamps and animal stamps. Every time she buys 5 flag stamps, she buys 3 animal stamps. She has 18 animal stamps. How many flag stamps does she have? Hint: Complete the table.

Flag Stamps	5	10	15	
Animal Stamps	3	6	9	

Multiply and Then Add: Mental Math

Sandy and Jerry are playing a multiply and add game. What are their scores?

To find the scores, multiply the numbers on the red cubes and then add the number on the blue cube.

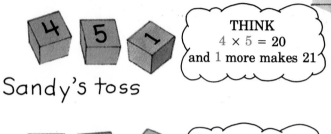

Sandy's toss

> THINK
> $4 \times 5 = 20$
> and 1 more makes 21

> THINK
> $6 \times 3 = 18$
> and 2 more make 20

Jerry's toss

Sandy scored 21 points and Jerry scored 20 points.

Warm Up   Give each score aloud.

1.

> THINK
> 4×3
> and 1 more

2.

> THINK
> 4×4
> and 2 more

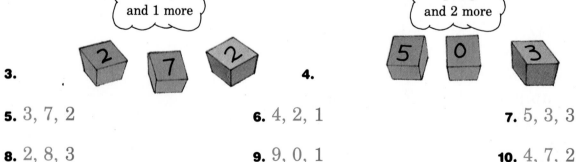

3.

4.

5. 3, 7, 2   **6.** 4, 2, 1   **7.** 5, 3, 3

8. 2, 8, 3   **9.** 9, 0, 1   **10.** 4, 7, 2

11. 2, 4, 3   **12.** 3, 6, 3   **13.** 2, 9, 2

Multiply and then add 1. Write answers only.

1. 2×3 **2.** 7×5 **3.** 4×9 **4.** 8×0

5. 6×2 **6.** 4×1 **7.** 3×8 **8.** 4×2

Multiply and then add 2. Write answers only.

9. 5×2 **10.** 6×1 **11.** 4×5 **12.** 3×3

13. 4×7 **14.** 9×0 **15.** 2×9 **16.** 5×6

Multiply and then add 3. Write answers only.

17. 3×4 **18.** 2×2 **19.** 4×0 **20.** 8×1

21. 3×9 **22.** 9×5 **23.** 7×4 **24.** 4×2

Multiply and then add 4. Write answers only.

25. 3×5 **26.** 4×8 **27.** 8×5 **28.** 2×3

29. 7×0 **30.** 1×7 **31.** 6×3 **32.** 9×4

Find the score for each toss. Write answers only. The first one is done for you.

★ **37.** Pamela scored 28. The blue cube was 3. What numbers showed on the red cubes?

Red Cube	Red Cube	Blue Cube	Score
3	7	2	23
33. 4	6	1	||||
34. 5	3	3	||||
35. 8	4	2	||||
36. 9	3	3	||||

THINK

Logical Reasoning

Find the missing numbers.

1. $3 \times \boxed{} = 120$

2. $8 \times \boxed{} = 240$

3. $\boxed{} \times 50 = 450$

MATH

Multiplying: Trading Ones

Joanne collects coins. How many quarters does the coin folder hold?

Since there are the same number on each of 4 pages, we multiply.

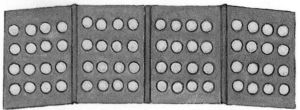

16 quarters on each page

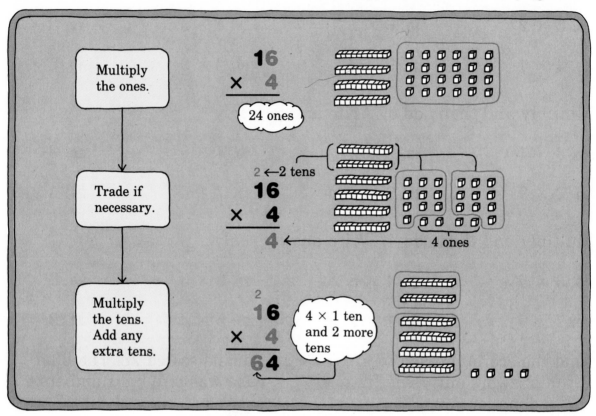

Multiply the ones.	$\begin{array}{r} 16 \\ \times\ 4 \\ \hline \end{array}$ 24 ones	
Trade if necessary.	$2 \leftarrow$ 2 tens $\begin{array}{r} 16 \\ \times\ 4 \\ \hline 4 \end{array}$ 4 ones	
Multiply the tens. Add any extra tens.	$\begin{array}{r} 2 \\ 16 \\ \times\ 4 \\ \hline 64 \end{array}$	4 × 1 ten and 2 more tens

There are 64 quarters in the coin folder.

Other Examples

$\begin{array}{r} 1 \\ 25 \\ \times\ 3 \\ \hline 75 \end{array}$
$\begin{array}{r} 3 \\ 18 \\ \times\ 4 \\ \hline 72 \end{array}$
$\begin{array}{r} 13 \\ \times\ 2 \\ \hline 26 \end{array}$ NO TRADE NECESSARY
$\begin{array}{r} 1 \\ 35 \\ \times\ 2 \\ \hline 70 \end{array}$
$\begin{array}{r} 20 \\ \times\ 4 \\ \hline 80 \end{array}$ NO TRADE NECESSARY

Warm Up Multiply

1. $\begin{array}{r} 24 \\ \times\ 2 \\ \hline \end{array}$
2. $\begin{array}{r} 26 \\ \times\ 3 \\ \hline \end{array}$
3. $\begin{array}{r} 12 \\ \times\ 4 \\ \hline \end{array}$
4. $\begin{array}{r} 29 \\ \times\ 3 \\ \hline \end{array}$
5. $\begin{array}{r} 19 \\ \times\ 5 \\ \hline \end{array}$
6. $\begin{array}{r} 15 \\ \times\ 6 \\ \hline \end{array}$

Find the products.

1. 14
× 2

2. 34
× 2

3. 16
× 3

4. 21
× 4

5. 32
× 3

6. 12
× 8

7. 17
× 3

8. 20
× 4

9. 19
× 4

10. 16
× 5

11. 43
× 2

12. 12
× 7

13. 15
× 6

14. 19
× 5

15. 13
× 5

16. 11
× 9

17. 46
× 2

18. 28
× 2

19. 33
× 3

20. 15
× 4

21. 4 × 22

22. 2 × 18

23. 5 × 12

24. 3 × 30

25. Multiply 15 by 5.

26. Multiply 42 by 2.

Solve.

27. Carlos has a coin folder for nickels. It has spaces for 21 nickels on each page. There are 3 pages. How many nickels does the folder hold?

28. Janet put her silver dollars in a picture frame. She has 4 rows with 13 dollars in each row. How many dollars are in the frame?

SKILLKEEPER

Divide.

1. 16 ÷ 8

2. 25 ÷ 5

3. 48 ÷ 6

4. 45 ÷ 9

5. 28 ÷ 4

6. 36 ÷ 9

7. 24 ÷ 6

8. 10 ÷ 5

9. 18 ÷ 2

10. 54 ÷ 9

11. 16 ÷ 2

12. 36 ÷ 6

13. 20 ÷ 5

14. 24 ÷ 8

15. 12 ÷ 6

16. 49 ÷ 7

Multiplying: Trading Ones and Tens

Geri David is putting new tile down.
There will be 4 rows of tile with
32 tiles in each row. How
many tiles does she need?

Since we want the total and each
row has the same number of
tiles, we multiply.

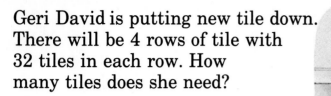

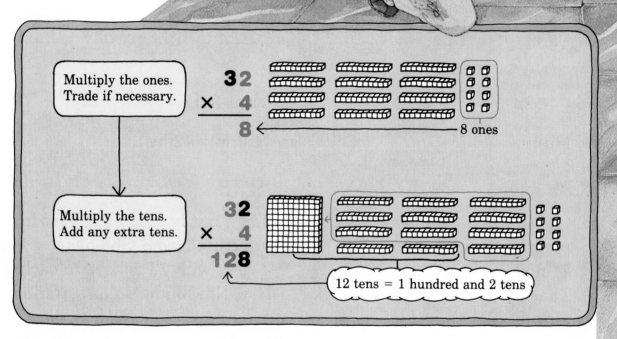

Multiply the ones.
Trade if necessary.

$$\begin{array}{r} 32 \\ \times\ 4 \\ \hline 8 \end{array}$$

8 ones

Multiply the tens.
Add any extra tens.

$$\begin{array}{r} 32 \\ \times\ 4 \\ \hline 128 \end{array}$$

12 tens = 1 hundred and 2 tens

Ms. David needs 128 tiles.

Other Examples

$$\begin{array}{r} 21 \\ \times\ 6 \\ \hline 126 \end{array} \qquad \begin{array}{r} {\scriptstyle 1} \\ 46 \\ \times\ 3 \\ \hline 138 \end{array} \qquad \begin{array}{r} {\scriptstyle 4} \\ 35 \\ \times\ 8 \\ \hline 280 \end{array} \qquad \begin{array}{r} {\scriptstyle 2} \\ 25 \\ \times\ 4 \\ \hline 100 \end{array}$$

Warm Up Multiply.

1. $\begin{array}{r} 42 \\ \times\ 3 \\ \hline \end{array}$
2. $\begin{array}{r} 41 \\ \times\ 7 \\ \hline \end{array}$
3. $\begin{array}{r} 24 \\ \times\ 6 \\ \hline \end{array}$
4. $\begin{array}{r} 36 \\ \times\ 5 \\ \hline \end{array}$
5. $\begin{array}{r} 75 \\ \times\ 4 \\ \hline \end{array}$
6. $\begin{array}{r} 68 \\ \times\ 3 \\ \hline \end{array}$

Find the products.

1. 32
× 4

2. 63
× 2

3. 58
× 3

4. 43
× 5

5. 42
× 6

6. 23
× 3

7. 45
× 8

8. 67
× 5

9. 23
× 7

10. 94
× 2

11. 13
× 7

12. 35
× 6

13. 25
× 7

14. 66
× 3

15. 52
× 6

16. 19
× 4

17. 36
× 5

18. 42
× 8

19. 4 × 49

20. 3 × 83

21. 8 × 25

22. 9 × 23

23. 6 × 14

24. 2 × 52

25. 3 × 29

26. 9 × 15

27. Give the product of 2 and 75.

28. Give the product of 5 and 25.

29. Give the product of 4 and 62.

30. Give the product of 6 and 53.

Solve.

31. Mr. Allen tiled an office floor with 9 rows of tile. There were 35 tiles in each row. How many tiles did he use?

32. How many tiles would be needed for a hallway with 9 rows of tile and 99 tiles in each row?

More Practice, page 382, Set B

THINK

Guess and Check

Find the largest score possible by multiplying two of the numbers and adding the third number.

3   4   7

MATH

(two hundred seventy-nine) **279**

Multiplying with Money

Sean needs to buy 6 AA batteries for his radio. How much will they cost?

Since we want the total amounts, we multiply.

Multiply. $\longrightarrow$ Show cents or dollars and cents.

$$\begin{array}{r} \overset{1}{4}3¢ \\ \times\ 6 \\ \hline 258 \end{array}$$

$$\begin{array}{r} 43¢ \\ \times\ 6 \\ \hline 258¢ \end{array} \text{ or } \$2.58$$

The cost of 6 batteries is $2.58.

Other Examples

1.
$$\begin{array}{r} 14¢ \\ \times\ 4 \\ \hline 56¢ \\ \$0.56 \end{array}$$

2.
$$\begin{array}{r} 65¢ \\ \times\ 4 \\ \hline 260¢ \\ \$2.60 \end{array}$$

3.
$$\begin{array}{r} 34¢ \\ \times\ 9 \\ \hline 306¢ \\ \$3.06 \end{array}$$

4.
$$\begin{array}{r} 25¢ \\ \times\ 8 \\ \hline 200¢ \\ \$2.00 \end{array}$$

Warm Up Find the amounts.
Write the answers with dollars and cents.

1.
$$\begin{array}{r} 82¢ \\ \times\ 2 \\ \hline \end{array}$$

2.
$$\begin{array}{r} 54¢ \\ \times\ 5 \\ \hline \end{array}$$

3.
$$\begin{array}{r} 12¢ \\ \times\ 8 \\ \hline \end{array}$$

4.
$$\begin{array}{r} 34¢ \\ \times\ 3 \\ \hline \end{array}$$

5.
$$\begin{array}{r} 75¢ \\ \times\ 4 \\ \hline \end{array}$$

Find the amounts.
Write the amounts with dollars and cents.

1. 41¢
× 6

2. 23¢
× 3

3. 45¢
× 7

4. 68¢
× 2

5. 56¢
× 4

6. 36¢
× 5

7. 54¢
× 8

8. 81¢
× 5

9. 42¢
× 9

10. 95¢
× 3

11. 15¢
× 6

12. 48¢
× 7

13. 98¢
× 4

14. 34¢
× 7

15. 26¢
× 4

16. 55¢
× 9

17. 77¢
× 3

18. 57¢
× 5

19. 3 × 38¢

20. 4 × 49¢

21. 9 × 13¢

22. 2 × 52¢

23. 5 × 78¢

24. 8 × 25¢

25. 3 at 45¢ each

26. 6 at 53¢ each

27. 8 at 19¢ each

28. 5 at 92¢ each

29. 7 at 32¢ each

30. 4 at 67¢ each

Solve. Look at page 280.

31. Juanita needs to buy 4 of the AA batteries. How much will they cost?

32. The AAA batteries are on sale. You save 12¢ on each package. How much do you save if you buy 6 packages?

33. What is the cost of 7 AA batteries? 43¢ is the same as 0.43.

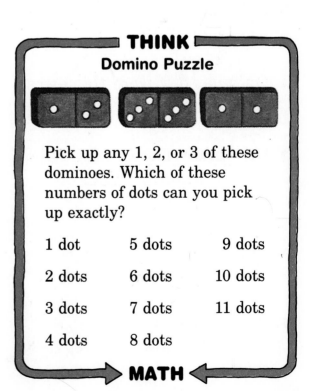

THINK
Domino Puzzle

Pick up any 1, 2, or 3 of these dominoes. Which of these numbers of dots can you pick up exactly?

1 dot	5 dots	9 dots
2 dots	6 dots	10 dots
3 dots	7 dots	11 dots
4 dots	8 dots	

MATH

PROBLEM SOLVING
Using Data from a Picture Graph

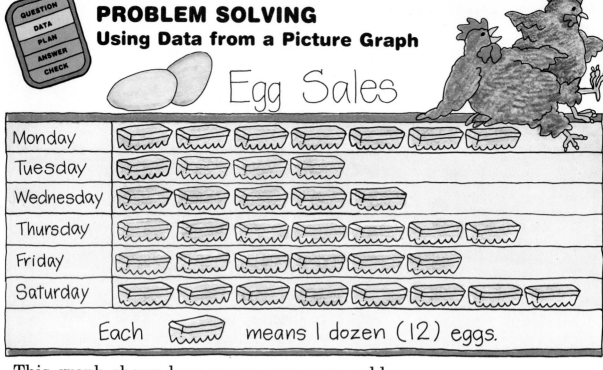

Egg Sales

Monday	🥚🥚🥚🥚🥚🥚🥚
Tuesday	🥚🥚🥚🥚
Wednesday	🥚🥚🥚🥚🥚
Thursday	🥚🥚🥚🥚🥚🥚🥚🥚
Friday	🥚🥚🥚🥚🥚🥚🥚🥚🥚
Saturday	🥚🥚🥚🥚🥚🥚🥚🥚🥚🥚

Each 🥚 means 1 dozen (12) eggs.

This graph shows how many eggs were sold on the Sanders' farm in one week.

Use the graph to answer the questions.

1. On what day were the most eggs sold?

2. On what day were the fewest eggs sold?

3. How many more dozen were sold on Saturday than on Wednesday?

4. How many dozen were sold in the first 3 days?

5. On Tuesday 4 dozen eggs were sold. How many eggs are there in 4 dozen?

6. How much money did the Sanders make on Wednesday if they sold the eggs at 93¢ a dozen?

★ 7. How much more money would they have made on Wednesday if they had raised the price to 99¢ a dozen?

8. *Try This* The Sanders had 4 hens named Lulu, Peck, Red, and Queen. Peck is larger than Red. Lulu is smaller than Red. Peck is smaller than Queen. Which hen is largest?

Multiplication Practice

Find the products.

1. 31 × 3	**2.** 35 × 2	**3.** 11 × 9	**4.** 24 × 4	**5.** 13 × 5	**6.** 23 × 3
7. 33 × 8	**8.** 68 × 4	**9.** 60 × 3	**10.** 75 × 4	**11.** 14 × 2	**12.** 29 × 3
13. 34¢ × 6	**14.** 19¢ × 4	**15.** 52¢ × 7	**16.** 62¢ × 2	**17.** 55¢ × 3	**18.** 29¢ × 5
19. 12¢ × 5	**20.** 20¢ × 5	**21.** 75¢ × 2	**22.** 49¢ × 4	**23.** 53¢ × 5	**24.** 63¢ × 5

25. 8 × 24   **26.** 5 × 37   **27.** 2 × 76

28. 3 × 47¢   **29.** 4 × 52¢   **30.** 6 × 13¢

SKILLKEEPER

Subtract.

1. 95 − 73	**2.** 82 − 79	**3.** 30 − 16	**4.** 67 − 48
5. $2.05 − 1.69	**6.** $3.52 − 0.71	**7.** $5.13 − 4.07	**8.** $8.21 − 7.89

Estimating Products with Money: Mental Math

About how many dollars do 3 rolls of film cost?

Since you want an answer that is only **close** to the exact answer, you **estimate** by rounding to the nearest dollar and multiplying in your head.

3 × $2.12

THINK
3 × $2 = $6

Film costs about $6 for 3 rolls.

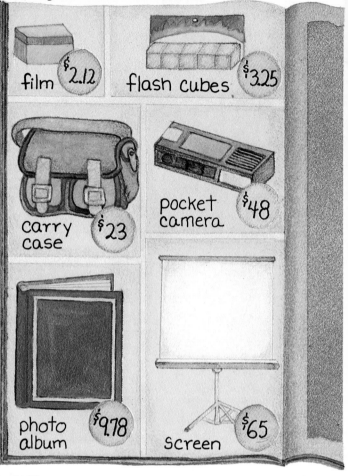

film $2.12   flash cubes $3.25

carry case $23   pocket camera $48

photo album $9.78   Screen $65

Other Examples

nearest dollar
8 × $3.78

8 × $4 = $32

nearest ten
4 × $73

4 × $70 = $280

Estimate by rounding to the nearest dollar.
Write answers only.

1. 4 × $4.34

2. 3 × $6.92

3. 7 × $3.50

4. 5 × $8.07

5. 8 × $2.03

6. 3 × $5.82

7. 5 × $3.26

8. 2 × $9.15

9. 4 × $3.50

Estimate by rounding to the nearest ten.
Write answers only.

10. 3 × $27

11. 8 × $33

12. 4 × $85

13. 2 × $66

14. 4 × $21

15. 3 × $68

16. 6 × $53

17. 7 × $25

18. 9 × $36

PROBLEM SOLVING
Estimating to Check Answers

Jean and Dan used estimation to check the totals on their sales slips.

Jean's sales slip

3 photo albums
TOTAL $29.34

3 × $10 = $30

The total should be about $30. It is. The sales slip seems to be right.

Dan's sales slip

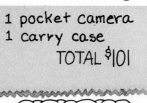

1 pocket camera
1 carry case
TOTAL $101

$50 + $20 = $70

The total should be about $70. It is not. The sales slip seems to be wrong. The total should be $71.

Use the pictures on page 284.
Write an estimate for each purchase. If a sales slip seems to be wrong, find the actual total and write it next to your estimate.

1.
1 roll of film
1 photo album
TOTAL $11.90

2.
4 pocket cameras
TOTAL $38.40

3.
1 package of flash cubes
1 roll of film
TOTAL $4.37

4.
8 rolls of film
TOTAL $6.96

5.
5 screens
TOTAL $385

★ 6.
1 screen
2 carry cases
1 pocket camera
TOTAL $250

7. *Try This* Dan wants to take a picture of his friends, Alex, Bess, and Connie. How many different ways can he line them up?

PROBLEM SOLVING
Practice

Penny Patterson studies how gorillas think. She has been teaching Koko and Michael to talk using sign language.

Solve. You may need to use the table on page 287.

1. In one year, Koko learned 5 signs each month. There are 12 months in a year. How many signs did Koko learn that year?

2. Michael learned 24 signs in 6 months. He learned the same number of signs each month. How many did he learn each month?

3. Koko knows 210 more signs than Michael. Michael knows 190 signs. How many signs does Koko know?

4. When Koko becomes an adult gorilla, she will weigh about 110 kg. How much weight does she have to gain?

5. How much weight will Michael have to gain to weigh 110 kg?

6. How much taller is Michael than Koko?

	Koko	Michael
Weight	93 kg	86 kg
Height	145 cm	152 cm
Wrist	25 cm	27 cm
Hand	24 cm	26 cm
Foot	28 cm	30 cm
Eats	4 kg of food each day	5 kg of food each day

7. How many kilograms of food does Koko eat in 2 weeks (14 days)?

8. How many kilograms of food does Michael eat in one month (31 days)?

9. Koko's chest measurement is 30 cm less than her height. What is Koko's chest measurement?

10. Michael's chest measurement is 73 cm greater than his wrist measurement. What is Michael's chest measurement?

11. Michael's neck measurement is 2 times the measurement of his foot. What is his neck measurement?

★ **12.** Koko's neck measurement is 2 cm more than twice her foot measurement. What is her neck measurement?

13. DATA HUNT Each gorilla has the same number of teeth as an adult human. How many teeth do Koko and Michael have together?

14. *Try This* Koko is 13 years old. Michael is 15 years younger than twice Koko's age. How old is Michael?

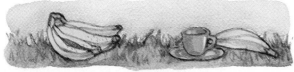

APPLIED PROBLEM SOLVING

You are going shopping to buy gifts for Tyler, Monica, and Trisha. You have $20. You want to choose from these gifts:

Some Things to Consider

- You do not want to spend all of your money.
- Trisha is your best friend.

- You do not want to hurt anyone's feelings by spending too much or too little.

Some Questions to Answer

1. If you bought A, C, and F, how much would you spend?
2. Should you buy all 3 friends a C? How much money would you have left over?
3. Should you buy all 3 friends the same gift?
4. If you bought a B and a D, how much would you have left for the other gift?

What Is Your Decision?

What did you buy for Tyler, Monica, and Trisha?
Do you have any money left over?

CHAPTER REVIEW/TEST

Multiply.

1. 3×30 **2.** 4×60 **3.** 2×30 **4.** 8×40 **5.** 5×70

6. $\begin{array}{r} 28 \\ \times\ 3 \\ \hline \end{array}$ **7.** $\begin{array}{r} 46 \\ \times\ 2 \\ \hline \end{array}$ **8.** $\begin{array}{r} 21 \\ \times\ 4 \\ \hline \end{array}$ **9.** $\begin{array}{r} 16 \\ \times\ 3 \\ \hline \end{array}$ **10.** $\begin{array}{r} 35 \\ \times\ 2 \\ \hline \end{array}$

11. $\begin{array}{r} 61 \\ \times\ 5 \\ \hline \end{array}$ **12.** $\begin{array}{r} 43 \\ \times\ 7 \\ \hline \end{array}$ **13.** $\begin{array}{r} 82 \\ \times\ 4 \\ \hline \end{array}$ **14.** $\begin{array}{r} 78 \\ \times\ 5 \\ \hline \end{array}$ **15.** $\begin{array}{r} 34 \\ \times\ 9 \\ \hline \end{array}$

16. $\begin{array}{r} 32¢ \\ \times\ 6 \\ \hline \end{array}$ **17.** $\begin{array}{r} 12¢ \\ \times\ 8 \\ \hline \end{array}$ **18.** $\begin{array}{r} 62¢ \\ \times\ 3 \\ \hline \end{array}$ **19.** $\begin{array}{r} 74¢ \\ \times\ 2 \\ \hline \end{array}$ **20.** $\begin{array}{r} 50¢ \\ \times\ 6 \\ \hline \end{array}$

Estimate the product by rounding to the nearest dollar or ten.

21. $4 \times \$2.75$ **22.** $8 \times \$4.02$ **23.** $5 \times \$3.50$

24. $2 \times \$53$ **25.** $6 \times \$35$ **26.** $3 \times \$62$

Solve. Use the graph for problems 27–29.

27. How much more film was used in June than in July?

28. How many pictures were taken in June?

29. How many pictures were taken in July?

30. How much for 9 A?

31. How much for 4 B?

Month	Number of Pictures
June	▭ ▭ ▭ ▭ ▭ ▭
July	▭ ▭ ▭
August	▭ ▭ ▭

Each ▭ means 24 pictures.

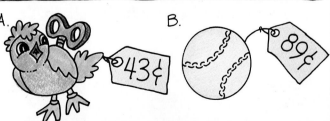

A. 43¢   B. 89¢

ANOTHER LOOK

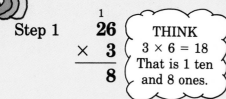

Step 1 $\overset{1}{26}$ $\times\ 3$ ——— 8

THINK
3 × 6 = 18
That is 1 ten
and 8 ones.

Step 2 $\overset{1}{26}$ $\times\ 3$ ——— 78

THINK
2 × 3 = 6
and 1 more
makes 7.

Step 1 $\overset{2}{37}$ $\times\ 4$ ——— 8

THINK
4 × 7 = 28
That is 2 tens
and 8 ones.

Step 2 $\overset{2}{37}$ $\times\ 4$ ——— 148

THINK
4 × 3 = 12
and 2 more
make 14.

$\overset{3}{54}$¢
$\times\ 8$
————
$4\ 32$¢
$\$4.32$

Multiply.

1. 24×3	**2.** 16×4	**3.** 45×2
4. 12×4	**5.** 19×5	**6.** 17×3
7. 15×5	**8.** 13×5	**9.** 25×3
10. 76×2	**11.** 25×7	**12.** 43×7
13. 63×3	**14.** 57×5	**15.** 34×6
16. 64×5	**17.** 43×4	**18.** 35×5
19. $82¢ \times 2$	**20.** $23¢ \times 9$	**21.** $79¢ \times 4$
22. $83¢ \times 5$	**23.** $25¢ \times 8$	**24.** $15¢ \times 6$

290 (two hundred ninety)

Estimation and Mental Math

Many states charge a sales tax on some of the things you buy. For example, one state charges 5¢ on each dollar you spend. You can use estimation and mental math to help you decide if your total bill is about right.

Hammer	Tax	Estimated total
THINK about $7.00	THINK $7 × 5¢ 35¢	THINK $7.00 + 0.35 $7.35

The total $7.30 on the bill seems about right.

Sandy's Hardware Store

ITEM	AMOUNT
1 hammer	$6.95
Tax	0.35
Total	$7.30

Thank You

Use 5¢ for the sales tax. Estimate the total bill for each of the items below. Write answers only.

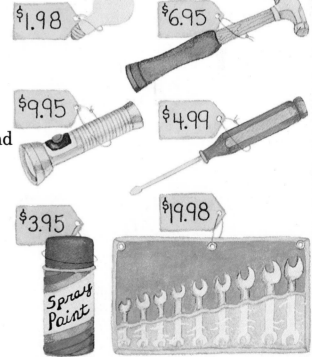

1. light bulb

2. flashlight

3. screwdriver

4. wrench set

5. paint

6. screwdriver and paint

7. light bulb and wrench set

8. hammer and screwdriver

$1.98

$6.95

$9.95

$4.99

$3.95 Spray Paint

$19.98

Using a Computer

To give instructions to a computer you must use words and symbols the computer understands. The first word we will use with the computer is PRINT. You know the symbols for addition (+) and subtraction (−). Other important symbols are quotation marks (" ") and semicolons (;).

Instruction to be typed into the computer	What you will see come on the screen when you press RETURN or ENTER
| ```
PRINT 19 + 72
PRINT "19 + 72"
PRINT "19 + 72 = "; 19 + 72
``` | ```
91
19 + 72
19 + 72 = 91
``` |

What do the quotation marks do?

Tell what you would see come on the screen after you type these lines and press return after each.

```
PRINT 84 - 61
PRINT "84 - 61"
PRINT "84 - 61 = "; 84 - 61
```

1. ?
2. ?
3. ?

The computer does not understand a symbol that has more than one meaning. We cannot use × for multiplication so we use an asterisk (∗). We use the slash (/) symbol for division. The key next to the 9 key is zero. When we press it, it looks like this Ø.

Example

Instruction	Screen

`PRINT "13 * 12 = "; 13 * 12`
`PRINT "124/4 = "; 124/4`
`PRINT "300 - 29 = ";`
`300 - 29`
	`13 * 12 = 156`
	`124/4 = 31`
	`300 - 29 = 271`

Tell what you will see come on the screen after typing and entering these instructions.

1. `PRINT "74 - 39"`
2. `PRINT 74 - 39`
3. `PRINT "74 - 39 = ";`
   `74 - 39`
4. `PRINT "21 + 34 = "; 21 + 34`
5. `PRINT 19 * 9`
6. `PRINT "19 * 9"`
7. `PRINT "19 * 9 = "; 19 * 9`
8. `PRINT "70 * 20 = ";`
   `70 * 20`
9. `PRINT 93/3`
10. `PRINT "93/3 = "; 93/3`

CUMULATIVE REVIEW

Give the letter for the correct answer.

1.
$$6 \times 7$$
A 48
B 42
C 49
D not given

2.
$$8 \times 8$$
A 48
B 64
C 56
D not given

3.
$$9 \times 6$$
A 56
B 64
C 53
D not given

4.
$$9 \times 0$$
A 9
B 0
C 8
D not given

5.
$$6 \times 6$$
A 32
B 30
C 36
D not given

6.
$$8 \times 5$$
A 40
B 48
C 45
D not given

7. $9 \div 3$
A 2
B 3
C 4
D not given

8. $18 \div 2$
A 6
B 8
C 9
D not given

9. $35 \div 5$
A 6
B 7
C 5
D not given

10. $8)\overline{48}$
A 6
B 5
C 4
D not given

11. $9)\overline{63}$
A 8
B 6
C 7
D not given

12. $6)\overline{54}$
A 9
B 8
C 7
D not given

13. Paul needs 9 buttons. Each card has 3 buttons. How many cards of buttons must Paul buy?

A 2
B 3
C 27
D not given

14. Alice needs 3 bananas to make a loaf of banana bread. How many bananas will Alice need to make 4 loaves?

A 3
B 12
C 8
D not given

John started piano lessons when he was 9 years old. The first year he learned how to read music. He also learned about rhythm. Rhythm is the beat of the music. Here is one of the first pieces John learned to play:

Hey did-dle, did-dle, the cat and the fid-dle the

This part of the song has 12 notes divided into 4 groups. Now John plays music written by famous composers. He plays one piece written by Mozart at the age of five.

Showing Remainders

There are 7 paint brushes and 6 tubes of paint for 3 children to share equally. How many does each child get? How many are left?

Since we want to find the number in each set, we divide.

7 brushes   6 tubes of paint

7 paint brushes divided into 3 equal groups

6 tubes of paint divided into 3 equal groups

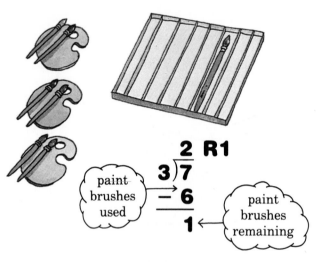

paint brushes used

$$\begin{array}{r} 2\ \textbf{R1} \\ 3\overline{)7} \\ -\ 6 \\ \hline 1 \end{array}$$

paint brushes remaining

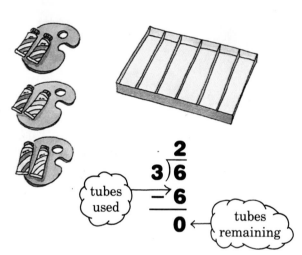

tubes used

$$\begin{array}{r} 2 \\ 3\overline{)6} \\ -\ 6 \\ \hline 0 \end{array}$$

tubes remaining

Each child gets 2 paint brushes. There is 1 brush left.

Each child gets 2 tubes of paint. There are no tubes left.

Other Examples

$$\begin{array}{r} 2\ \textbf{R2} \\ 3\overline{)8} \\ -\ 6 \\ \hline 2 \end{array} \qquad \begin{array}{r} 3\ \textbf{R1} \\ 2\overline{)7} \\ -\ 6 \\ \hline 1 \end{array} \qquad \begin{array}{r} 2 \\ 4\overline{)8} \\ -\ 8 \\ \hline 0 \end{array} \qquad \begin{array}{r} 0\ \textbf{R3} \\ 5\overline{)3} \\ -\ 0 \\ \hline 3 \end{array} \qquad \begin{array}{r} 0 \\ 4\overline{)0} \\ -\ 0 \\ \hline 0 \end{array}$$

Warm Up   Divide by finding the quotients and remainders.

1. $2\overline{)5}$ 2. $5\overline{)6}$ 3. $3\overline{)6}$ 4. $4\overline{)2}$ 5. $2\overline{)0}$

6. $4\overline{)7}$ 7. $2\overline{)4}$ 8. $3\overline{)0}$ 9. $5\overline{)9}$ 10. $4\overline{)1}$

Divide. Find the quotients and remainders.

1. $4\overline{)6}$ 2. $2\overline{)8}$ 3. $2\overline{)9}$ 4. $5\overline{)4}$ 5. $5\overline{)0}$

6. $4\overline{)2}$ 7. $4\overline{)3}$ 8. $4\overline{)4}$ 9. $4\overline{)5}$ 10. $4\overline{)6}$

11. $4\overline{)7}$ 12. $2\overline{)3}$ 13. $3\overline{)0}$ 14. $5\overline{)9}$ 15. $3\overline{)4}$

16. $3\overline{)2}$ 17. $4\overline{)8}$ 18. $3\overline{)7}$ 19. $5\overline{)8}$ 20. $3\overline{)9}$

21. $3 \div 5$ 22. $4 \div 2$ 23. $0 \div 3$

24. $7 \div 5$ 25. $7 \div 4$ 26. $2 \div 4$

27. Divide 9 by 4. 28. Divide 6 by 2.

Solve.

29. There are 7 crayons for 2 children to share equally. How many does each child get? How many are left?

30. There are 9 pieces of clay for 4 children to divide equally. How many does each child get? How many are left?

THINK

Remainder Game

1. Make these cards from green paper.

2. Make these cards from yellow paper.

3. Mix and give each player one card of each color.

4. Make a division problem. Yellow cards are divisors.

5. Largest remainder wins.

Example

$$\overset{2\ R1}{3\overline{)7}}$$ $$\overset{0\ R3}{5\overline{)3}}$$

Winner

MATH

Finding Quotients and Remainders

Some children picked 34 apples. They wanted to divide the apples equally into 4 bags. How many apples will they put in each bag? How many will be left?

Since we want to find the number in each set, we divide.

These children guessed the number in each bag.

I guess 7 apples in each bag.

I guess 9 apples in each bag.

I guess 8 apples in each bag.

Sandy's guess is too small.

Sam's guess is too large.

Laura's guess is just right.

$$
\begin{array}{r}
\textcircled{7} \\
4\overline{)34} \\
-28 \\
\hline
6
\end{array}
$$
This remainder is too large.

$$
\begin{array}{r}
\textcircled{9} \\
4\overline{)34} \\
-36 \\
\hline
\end{array}
$$
36 is too many. There are only 34 apples.

$$
\begin{array}{r}
8\ \textbf{R2} \\
4\overline{)34} \\
-32 \\
\hline
2
\end{array}
$$
This remainder is not too large.

There will be 8 apples in each bag.
There will be 2 apples left.

Other Examples

$$
\begin{array}{r}
4\ \textbf{R3} \\
5\overline{)23} \\
-20 \\
\hline
3
\end{array}
\qquad
\begin{array}{r}
9\ \textbf{R1} \\
2\overline{)19} \\
-18 \\
\hline
1
\end{array}
\qquad
\begin{array}{r}
8 \\
3\overline{)24} \\
-24 \\
\hline
0
\end{array}
$$

Warm Up Find the quotients and remainders.

1. $2\overline{)13}$ 2. $4\overline{)18}$ 3. $5\overline{)26}$ 4. $4\overline{)20}$ 5. $3\overline{)17}$

6. $2\overline{)10}$ 7. $5\overline{)49}$ 8. $3\overline{)27}$ 9. $3\overline{)26}$ 10. $5\overline{)38}$

Divide. Find the quotients and the remainders.

1. $2\overline{)17}$
2. $3\overline{)16}$
3. $4\overline{)26}$
4. $5\overline{)13}$
5. $3\overline{)14}$

6. $5\overline{)34}$
7. $4\overline{)20}$
8. $4\overline{)35}$
9. $3\overline{)25}$
10. $4\overline{)3}$

11. $2\overline{)15}$
12. $5\overline{)29}$
13. $5\overline{)12}$
14. $4\overline{)27}$
15. $3\overline{)0}$

16. $5\overline{)37}$
17. $3\overline{)8}$
18. $4\overline{)29}$
19. $5\overline{)27}$
20. $3\overline{)12}$

21. $19 \div 5$
22. $31 \div 4$
23. $45 \div 5$

24. $11 \div 2$
25. $10 \div 3$
26. $39 \div 4$

27. What is 19 divided by 2?
28. What is 36 divided by 5?

29. What is 23 divided by 3?
30. What is 11 divided by 4?

Solve.

31. Blair picked 44 peaches. He wanted to divide the peaches equally into 5 bags. How many peaches will go into each bag? How many will be left?

32. Marcie picked 38 plums. How many cartons like this can she fill? How many plums will be left?

4 plums

PROBLEM SOLVING
Understanding the Answer

Sometimes division does not give you the answer you want. You have to understand how to use the remainder.

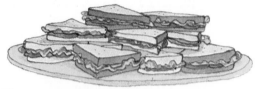

Examples

Sandwiches

Dan makes sandwiches using 2 pieces of bread. How many sandwiches can he make with 19 pieces of bread?

$$
\begin{array}{r}
9 \text{ R1} \\
2{\overline{\smash{)}19}} \\
-18 \\
\hline
1
\end{array}
$$

Answer
9 sandwiches can be made.

> The 1 remaining piece is not enough to make another sandwich.

Cars

There are 33 children going on a picnic. Each car can hold 5 children. How many cars are needed?

$$
\begin{array}{r}
6 \text{ R3} \\
5{\overline{\smash{)}33}} \\
-30 \\
\hline
3
\end{array}
$$

Answer
7 cars are needed.

> There will be 6 full cars, but another car is needed for the 3 remaining children.

Warm Up Answer these problems carefully.

1. Jason is making cookies for the picnic. A batch of cookies takes 3 eggs. How many batches will 11 eggs make?

2. There will be 39 people sitting at picnic tables. Only 4 people can sit at each table. How many tables are needed?

300 (three hundred)

Answer these problems carefully.

1. Jill has 18 oranges for the picnic. She can only fit 5 oranges into a bag. How many bags does she need?

2. Mark is making ribbon prizes for the picnic races. He has 29 pieces of ribbon and needs 3 pieces for each prize. How many prizes can he make?

3. Bradley is making triple-deck sandwiches with 3 pieces of bread. How many sandwiches can he make from a loaf of bread that has 25 slices?

4. Jim is putting 26 cans of juice into boxes. Each box will hold 4 cans. How many boxes does he need?

9. *Try This* There were 2 players on each team. The table shows each player's score. The winning team made 30 points. Which 2 players were on that team?

5. There are 24 children who want to run relay races. Each relay team has 3 children. How many teams can be made?

6. Susan is making apple pies. She needs 5 apples for each pie. How many pies can she make with 37 apples?

7. There are 18 children who want a boat ride. Each boat holds 4 children. How many boats are needed?

8. There are 33 children who want to play soccer. Each soccer team has 11 players. How many teams can be made?

Name	Points
Brian	11
Joan	17
Lori	12
Pablo	14
Beth	15
Dave	18

Checking Division

You can check a
division problem by
multiplying the
quotient by the
divisor and then
adding the **remainder**.

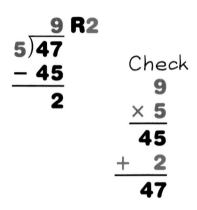

Barry missed two
division problems on
his paper. Check his
problems. Which ones
did he miss?

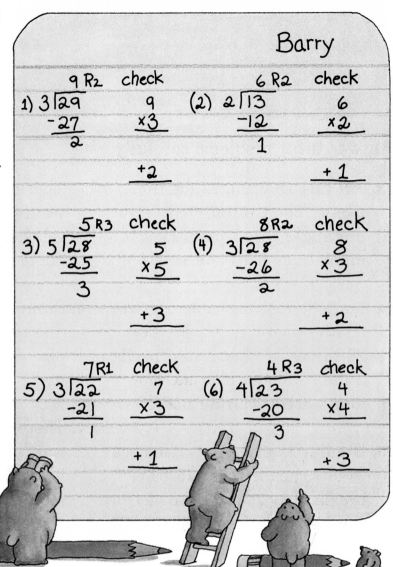

Find the quotients. Use Barry's method to check each answer.

1. $2\overline{)11}$ 2. $5\overline{)14}$ 3. $3\overline{)26}$ 4. $2\overline{)15}$ 5. $4\overline{)25}$

6. $3\overline{)20}$ 7. $2\overline{)19}$ 8. $3\overline{)13}$ 9. $5\overline{)18}$ 10. $4\overline{)22}$

11. $5\overline{)48}$ 12. $4\overline{)19}$ 13. $2\overline{)17}$ 14. $5\overline{)45}$ 15. $5\overline{)33}$

16. Check this problem by multiplying
and then adding. Is it correct?
$4\overline{)3853}$ with quotient 964 R1

PROBLEM SOLVING
Practice

Solve.

1. The roller rink charges $3 a ticket. Brian has $25 for skating. How many tickets can he buy? How much money would be left?

2. The roller rink rents skates for 75¢. How much do Kristi, Roberto, and Daryl have to pay in all to rent skates?

3. The roller rink sold 583 tickets on Friday, 716 on Saturday, and 398 on Sunday. How many tickets were sold in all?

4. Knee pads cost $32 for 4 pads. How much does each pad cost?

5. Janet has $25 in the bank. She will get $6 more today. How much money will she have in all?
   How much more will she need to buy skates that cost $44?

★ 6. Tom has $8 in the bank. He will get $3 more today. How much more will he need to buy a skate helmet that costs $17?

7. DATA BANK See page 362. How many more skaters does the Jellibeans skating rink hold than the Happy Wheels skating rink?

8. *Try This* The Yellow Rink is larger than the Blue Rink. The Red Rink is the largest. The Green Rink is larger than the Yellow Rink. Give the order of these four rinks, starting with the largest.

2-Digit Quotients

A card game has 36 cards. There are 2 children playing. Each child gets the same number of cards. How many does each child get?

Since we want to know how many in each set, we divide.

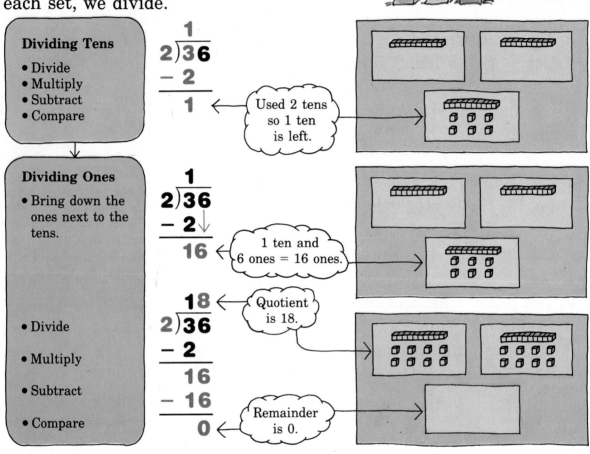

Dividing Tens
- Divide
- Multiply
- Subtract
- Compare

$$\begin{array}{r} 1 \\ 2\overline{)36} \\ -\,2 \\ \hline 1 \end{array}$$

Used 2 tens so 1 ten is left.

Dividing Ones
- Bring down the ones next to the tens.

$$\begin{array}{r} 1 \\ 2\overline{)36} \\ -\,2\downarrow \\ \hline 16 \end{array}$$

1 ten and 6 ones = 16 ones.

- Divide
- Multiply
- Subtract
- Compare

$$\begin{array}{r} 18 \\ 2\overline{)36} \\ -\,2 \\ \hline 16 \\ -\,16 \\ \hline 0 \end{array}$$

Quotient is 18.

Remainder is 0.

Each child gets 18 cards.

Other Examples

$$\begin{array}{r} 19 \\ 4\overline{)76} \\ -\,4 \\ \hline 36 \\ -\,36 \\ \hline 0 \end{array} \qquad \begin{array}{r} 45 \\ 2\overline{)90} \\ -\,8 \\ \hline 10 \\ -\,10 \\ \hline 0 \end{array} \qquad \begin{array}{r} 31 \\ 3\overline{)93} \\ -\,9 \\ \hline 03 \\ -\,3 \\ \hline 0 \end{array} \qquad \begin{array}{r} 10 \\ 5\overline{)50} \\ -\,5 \\ \hline 00 \\ -\,0 \\ \hline 0 \end{array}$$

Warm Up   Find the quotients. Check your answers.

1. $3\overline{)42}$ **2.** $5\overline{)60}$ **3.** $4\overline{)64}$ **4.** $3\overline{)69}$ **5.** $2\overline{)80}$

Find the quotients.

1. $2\overline{)32}$ 2. $5\overline{)80}$ 3. $4\overline{)96}$

4. $5\overline{)65}$ 5. $2\overline{)86}$ 6. $3\overline{)84}$

7. $4\overline{)84}$ 8. $3\overline{)78}$ 9. $2\overline{)50}$ 10. $2\overline{)40}$ 11. $3\overline{)51}$

12. $3\overline{)27}$ 13. $2\overline{)44}$ 14. $3\overline{)63}$ 15. $3\overline{)60}$ 16. $4\overline{)72}$

17. $3\overline{)63}$ 18. $2\overline{)72}$ 19. $2\overline{)38}$ 20. $4\overline{)32}$ 21. $4\overline{)44}$

22. $76 \div 2$ 23. $60 \div 4$ 24. $85 \div 5$ 25. $96 \div 6$

26. $56 \div 4$ 27. $72 \div 3$ 28. $46 \div 2$ 29. $52 \div 4$

30. What is 70 divided by 5?   31. What is 86 divided by 2?

32. What is 60 divided by 3?   33. What is 68 divided by 4?

Solve.

34. Four children are playing a card game with 52 cards. Each person gets the same number of cards. How many cards does each person get?

35. Eric, Lucy, and Larry are playing cards. They deal out all of the 45 cards. How many does each person get?

SKILLKEEPER

Add or subtract.

1. $\begin{array}{r} 8 \\ + 5 \\ \hline \end{array}$ 2. $\begin{array}{r} 9 \\ - 3 \\ \hline \end{array}$ 3. $\begin{array}{r} 9 \\ + 8 \\ \hline \end{array}$ 4. $\begin{array}{r} 4 \\ + 7 \\ \hline \end{array}$ 5. $\begin{array}{r} 11 \\ - 6 \\ \hline \end{array}$ 6. $\begin{array}{r} 8 \\ + 8 \\ \hline \end{array}$

7. $\begin{array}{r} 13 \\ - 6 \\ \hline \end{array}$ 8. $\begin{array}{r} 12 \\ - 4 \\ \hline \end{array}$ 9. $\begin{array}{r} 5 \\ + 9 \\ \hline \end{array}$ 10. $\begin{array}{r} 15 \\ - 8 \\ \hline \end{array}$ 11. $\begin{array}{r} 6 \\ + 4 \\ \hline \end{array}$ 12. $\begin{array}{r} 9 \\ + 6 \\ \hline \end{array}$

2-Digit Quotients and Remainders

Sharon has 67¢. How many Pony Express stamps can she buy? How much money would she have left?

Pony Express
4¢

Johnny Appleseed
5¢

Since we want to know how many fours are in 67, we divide.

Dividing Tens	Dividing Ones	Write the remainder next to the quotient.
• Divide • Multiply • Subtract • Compare	• Bring down • Divide • Multiply • Subtract • Compare	

```
    1            16          16 R3
4)67         4)67         4)67
 - 4          - 4↓         - 4
----         ----         ----
    2            27           27
             - 24         - 24
             ----         ----
                 3            3
```

Sharon can buy 16 Pony Express stamps. She would have 3¢ left.

Other Examples

```
  23 R1       21 R2       10 R4         45
4)93        3)65        5)54        2)90
 - 8         - 6         - 5         - 8
----        ----        ----        ----
  13          05          04          10
- 12         - 3         - 0        - 10
----        ----        ----        ----
   1           2           4           0
```

Warm Up Find the quotients and remainders.

1. 3)43   2. 5)62   3. 2)21   4. 3)54   5. 4)55

Find the quotients and remainders.

1. $2\overline{)71}$ **2.** $4\overline{)62}$ **3.** $3\overline{)85}$ **4.** $2\overline{)58}$ **5.** $3\overline{)74}$

6. $4\overline{)76}$ **7.** $5\overline{)91}$ **8.** $2\overline{)34}$ **9.** $4\overline{)92}$ **10.** $3\overline{)92}$

11. $5\overline{)82}$ **12.** $4\overline{)35}$ **13.** $3\overline{)50}$ **14.** $4\overline{)83}$ **15.** $5\overline{)60}$

16. $38 \div 3$ **17.** $70 \div 4$ **18.** $53 \div 2$

19. $59 \div 5$ **20.** $75 \div 5$ **21.** $88 \div 3$

22. Divide 83 by 4.

23. Divide 78 by 2.

Solve.

24. Look at the picture on page 306. How many Johnny Appleseed stamps can Gina buy with 91¢? How much money would she have left?

25. Jake has 58 stamps. He needs 4 stamps on each package. How many packages could get 4 stamps? How many stamps would be left?

26. **DATA BANK** See page 359. How many Crane stamps can you buy with 53¢? How much money would be left?

More Practice, page 384, Set A

THINK

Patterns

Jack's birthday is October 15.

❧ ❧ ❧ OCTOBER ❧ ❧ ❧						
SUN	MON	TUES	WED	THURS	FRI	SAT
				1	2	3
4	5	6	7	8	9	10
11	12	13	14	(15)	16	17
18	19	20	21	22	23	24
25	26	27	28	29	30	31

1. Add the numbers on each side of his birthday (14 + 16). Divide the sum by 2.

2. Add the numbers above and below his birthday. Divide the sum by 2.

What is special about Jack's birthday?

Find out what is special about Mindy's and Karl's birthdays by doing the same. Mindy's birthday is October 9. Karl's birthday is October 20.

→ **MATH** ←

Estimating Quotients with Money: Mental Math

About how many dollars does 1 package of marking pens cost?

Since you want an answer that is only close to the exact answer, you **estimate** by rounding and dividing in your head.

$5.96 ÷ 3
↓

THINK
$6 ÷ 3 = $2

Marking Pens   3 for $5.96

The cost of 1 package of pens is about $2.

Other Examples

$8.10 ÷ 2
↓

$8 ÷ 2 = $4

$35.95 ÷ 4
↓

$36 ÷ 4 = $9

Estimate the quotients. Give answers aloud.

Round to the nearest dollar and divide.

1. $3.12 ÷ 3   **2.** $3.96 ÷ 4   **3.** $7.95 ÷ 2   **4.** $1.88 ÷ 2

5. $5.25 ÷ 5   **6.** $8.30 ÷ 4   **7.** $5.90 ÷ 3   **8.** $8.88 ÷ 3

9. $10.05 ÷ 2   **10.** $14.95 ÷ 3   **11.** $20.25 ÷ 4   **12.** $17.75 ÷ 3

Estimate the quotients. Write answers only.

13. $6.30 ÷ 2   **14.** $7.96 ÷ 4   **15.** $5.70 ÷ 3   **16.** $4.05 ÷ 4

17. $23.95 ÷ 3   **18.** $16.10 ÷ 4   **19.** $9.95 ÷ 2   **20.** $34.95 ÷ 5

21. $27.15 ÷ 3   **22.** $4.10 ÷ 2   **23.** $27.95 ÷ 4   **24.** $4.95 ÷ 5

PROBLEM SOLVING
Using Data from an Advertisement

Use the advertisement for 1–9. **Estimate** your answer. Write estimated answers only.

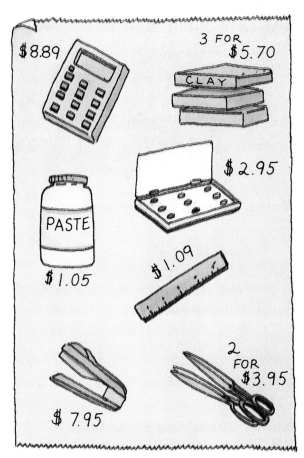

$8.89

3 FOR $5.70
CLAY

$2.95

PASTE
$1.05

$1.09

2 FOR $3.95

$7.95

1. About how many dollars does it cost to buy a calculator and a ruler?

2. About how many dollars does it cost to buy 1 pair of scissors?

3. About how many more dollars does a calculator cost than a stapler?

4. About how much do 4 jars of paste cost?

5. How many paint sets can you buy with $9?

6. About how many dollars less is a paint set than a calculator?

7. About how many dollars does it cost to buy 1 box of clay? About how many dollars does it cost to buy 1 box of clay and 1 ruler?

8. DATA HUNT Find a newspaper advertisement for three things that you would like to have. Estimate the cost for all three.

9. *Try This* Anthony wanted to buy the calculator, the ruler, the paint set, and the stapler. He bought only two of them and spent $9.04. Which two things did he buy?

APPLIED PROBLEM SOLVING

QUESTION
DATA
PLAN
ANSWER
CHECK

You live in Green Hill, and you want to spend the day at the park. You can walk or ride a bicycle. There are 3 roads to the park. Plan your trip.

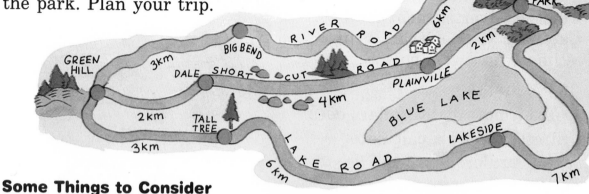

Some Things to Consider

- River Road has steep hills. The shortcut is not good for bikes. Lake Road is smooth and even.
- You can ride twice as fast on level ground as you can walk. Lake Road is twice as long as the shortcut.

- River Road is the most scenic.
- You want to get to the park quickly, but also see some scenery.
- The morning is supposed to be sunny. There is a chance of rain in the afternoon.

Some Questions to Answer

1. How many kilometers is the River Road trip? Would you walk it or ride it? Why?
2. How many kilometers is the shortcut trip? Would you walk it or ride it? Why?
3. How many kilometers is the Lake Road trip? Would you walk it or ride it? Why?
4. Could you take one road to get to the park and a different one back?

What Is Your Decision?

Would you walk or ride?
Would you take River Road, shortcut, or Lake Road? A combination?

Divide.

1. $3\overline{)7}$ 2. $2\overline{)9}$ 3. $5\overline{)3}$ 4. $4\overline{)7}$ 5. $4\overline{)2}$

6. $4\overline{)30}$ 7. $3\overline{)19}$ 8. $5\overline{)24}$ 9. $2\overline{)19}$ 10. $4\overline{)14}$

11. $2\overline{)42}$ 12. $3\overline{)96}$ 13. $4\overline{)80}$ 14. $3\overline{)39}$ 15. $2\overline{)68}$

16. $2\overline{)56}$ 17. $4\overline{)92}$ 18. $5\overline{)90}$ 19. $2\overline{)74}$ 20. $3\overline{)48}$

21. $4\overline{)78}$ 22. $3\overline{)46}$ 23. $2\overline{)85}$ 24. $4\overline{)67}$ 25. $5\overline{)53}$

Estimate the quotient by rounding to the nearest dollar.

26. $4.23 \div 2$ 27. $9.50 \div 5$ 28. $14.82 \div 3$

Solve. Use the newspaper ad for problems 29–32.

29. How much does it cost to buy 2 kg of bananas?

30. How much does 1 pineapple and 1 kg of grapes cost in all?

31. How much does a 4-kg watermelon cost?

32. How many boxes of oranges can you buy with $35?

59¢ for 1kg

83¢ for 1 kg

65¢ for 1 kg

$4.00 a box

99¢

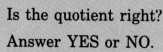

Is the quotient right?

Answer YES or NO.

$$\begin{array}{r} 8 \\ 3\overline{)28} \\ -24 \\ \hline 4 \end{array} \qquad \begin{array}{r} 4 \\ 5\overline{)17} \\ 20 \\ \hline \end{array} \qquad \begin{array}{r} 9 \\ 4\overline{)37} \\ -36 \\ \hline 1 \end{array}$$

No.
8 is too
small

No.
4 is too
large

Yes.

Find the right quotient.

$$4\overline{)27}$$

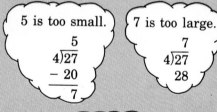

5 is too small.
$$\begin{array}{r} 5 \\ 4\overline{)27} \\ -20 \\ \hline 7 \end{array}$$

7 is too large.
$$\begin{array}{r} 7 \\ 4\overline{)27} \\ 28 \end{array}$$

6 is just right.
$$\begin{array}{r} 6 \\ 4\overline{)27} \\ -24 \\ \hline 3 \end{array}$$

Is the quotient right? Answer YES or NO.

1. $\begin{array}{r} 3 \\ 4\overline{)10} \\ 12 \\ \hline \end{array}$ **2.** $\begin{array}{r} 6 \\ 3\overline{)22} \\ -18 \\ \hline 4 \end{array}$ **3.** $\begin{array}{r} 7 \\ 5\overline{)39} \\ -35 \\ \hline 4 \end{array}$

4. $\begin{array}{r} 4 \\ 4\overline{)17} \\ -16 \\ \hline 1 \end{array}$ **5.** $\begin{array}{r} 7 \\ 3\overline{)25} \\ -21 \\ \hline 4 \end{array}$ **6.** $\begin{array}{r} 9 \\ 5\overline{)42} \\ 45 \\ \hline \end{array}$

Find the quotients and remainders.

7. $4\overline{)15}$ **8.** $3\overline{)23}$ **9.** $4\overline{)33}$

10. $5\overline{)28}$ **11.** $2\overline{)13}$ **12.** $3\overline{)14}$

13. $4\overline{)34}$ **14.** $3\overline{)28}$ **15.** $5\overline{)49}$

Logical Reasoning

Make these pieces.
There are 2 colors, 2 sizes, and 3 shapes.

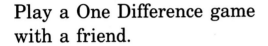

Play a One Difference game with a friend.

1. Pass out six pieces to each player.

2. The first player puts down a piece to start.

3. Take turns placing the pieces next to each other in a row.

   To play a piece, it must be different from the one next to it in one and only one way. It can be different in color, or shape, or size.

   If you cannot play a piece, skip your turn.

4. The first player to use up all six pieces wins.

Winner

Now play a Two Difference game. Each piece played must have exactly two differences from the one next to it.

Give the letter for the correct answer.

1. Name the figure.

A square
B rectangular prism
C rectangle
D not given

2. Name the figure.

A sphere
B circle
C cylinder
D not given

3. Name the figure.

A rectangle
B square
C circle
D not given

4. Which figure is congruent to this figure?

A
B
C
D not given

5. Which figure is congruent to this figure?

A
B
C
D not given

6. Which shape has a line of symmetry?

A
B
C
D not given

7. 30
× 5

A 15   B 150
C 1,500   D not given

8. 34
× 2

A 14   B 86
C 68   D not given

9. 27
× 3

A 81   B 61
C 621   D not given

10. 74
× 5

A 370   B 350
C 3,520   D not given

11. 68
× 4

A 274   B 242
C 272   D not given

12. 56¢
× 7

A $3.92   B $35.2
C $35.42   D not given

13. Martin wants to buy 4 rolls of film. A roll of film costs $2.12. Estimate the cost of 4 rolls of film to the nearest dollar.

A $12   B $6
C $8   D not given

14. Loni's vacation lasted 12 days. She took 4 pictures each day. How many pictures did she take?

A 3   B 46
C 48   D not given

FRACTIONS AND DECIMALS
13

One day Moriko showed Tina how to do "origami." Origami is the Japanese art of folding colored paper. Tina picked a red paper. Moriko told Tina to fold the paper into 2 equal parts. In three more steps Tina had made a red sailboat. Tina also learned how to make a bird. She started by folding a blue paper into 4 equal parts. When Tina was finished she had a beautiful blue crane.

Naming Parts of a Whole

Give the missing word.

Halves
Each piece is one half
of the whole.

1. Ned and Philip shared the
sandwich equally. Each boy
had one _____ of it.

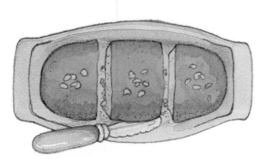

Thirds
Each piece is one third
of the whole.

2. Patty, Marianne, and Nora
shared the nut bread equally.
Each girl had one _____ of it.

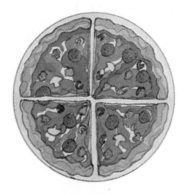

Fourths
Each piece is one fourth
of the whole.

3. Rodney, Kris, Tomas, and
Janice shared the pizza
equally. Each child had one
_____ of the pizza.

Here are some other names of parts of a whole.

5 Equal Parts	6 Equal Parts	8 Equal Parts	10 Equal Parts	100 Equal Parts
Fifths	Sixths	Eighths	Tenths	Hundredths

Choose the correct letter.

1.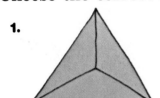
   A halves
   B thirds
   C fourths
   D not given

2.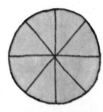
   A fourths
   B sixths
   C eighths
   D not given

3.
   A halves
   B thirds
   C fourths
   D not given

4.
   A sixths
   B eighths
   C tenths
   D not given

5.
   A fifths
   B sixths
   C eighths
   D not given

6.
   A eighths
   B tenths
   C hundredths
   D not given

7. Kenneth cut a pizza into 2 equal pieces. Then he cut each of those pieces into 2 equal pieces. How was the pizza divided?

THINK

Space Perception

Read the problem all the way through. First guess the answer. Then do the folding to check your guess.

1. Start with a paper strip.

2. Fold it once.

3. Fold it again.

4. Fold it once more. How do the folds divide the paper?

MATH

Finding Fractions of a Whole

Diane cut a pizza into **fourths**. She and two friends ate 3 of the pieces. What part of the pizza did they eat?

Three pieces were eaten. → $\dfrac{3}{4}$
Each piece was a fourth. →

We use the **fraction** $\dfrac{3}{4}$ (three fourths) to answer the question.

The children ate $\dfrac{3}{4}$ of the pizza.

Fourths

Warm Up Choose the fraction that tells how much pizza is left on the tray.

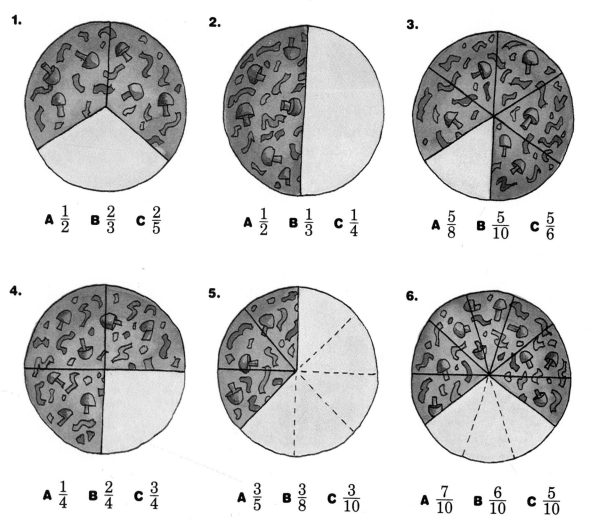

1.

A $\dfrac{1}{2}$ B $\dfrac{2}{3}$ C $\dfrac{2}{5}$

2.

A $\dfrac{1}{2}$ B $\dfrac{1}{3}$ C $\dfrac{1}{4}$

3.

A $\dfrac{5}{8}$ B $\dfrac{5}{10}$ C $\dfrac{5}{6}$

4.

A $\dfrac{1}{4}$ B $\dfrac{2}{4}$ C $\dfrac{3}{4}$

5.

A $\dfrac{3}{5}$ B $\dfrac{3}{8}$ C $\dfrac{3}{10}$

6.

A $\dfrac{7}{10}$ B $\dfrac{6}{10}$ C $\dfrac{5}{10}$

318 (three hundred eighteen)

Write the fraction that tells what part is yellow.

1.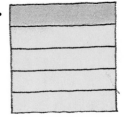

2.

3.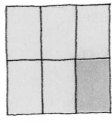

4.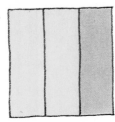

5.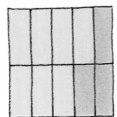

6.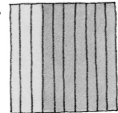

7.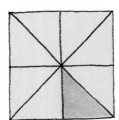

8.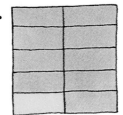

9.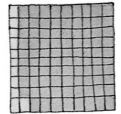

10. This is how William cut his pizza. 7 pieces of the pizza were eaten. What fraction of the pizza was left?

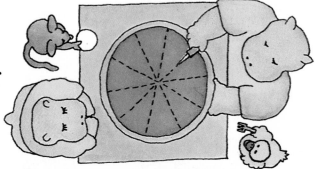

SKILLKEEPER

Find the quotients and remainders.

1. $3\overline{)7}$ **2.** $4\overline{)9}$ **3.** $4\overline{)14}$ **4.** $2\overline{)17}$

5. $3\overline{)13}$ **6.** $5\overline{)17}$ **7.** $4\overline{)11}$ **8.** $3\overline{)14}$

Finding Fractional Parts of a Set

There are 8 stamps in the strip. Kent used 3 of them to mail some letters. What fraction of the strip did Kent use?

Three stamps were used. $\longrightarrow$ **3**

Each stamp was an eighth. $\rightarrow$ **8**

Kent used $\frac{3}{8}$ of the strip.

Warm Up Tell what fraction of each strip of stamps is used.

1. 5 stamps in the strip

2. 4 stamps in the strip

3. 6 stamps in the strip

4. 3 stamps in the strip

What fractions of the stamps are used?

1.

Answer $\frac{4}{5}$

2.
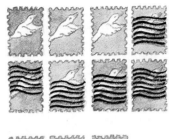

3.
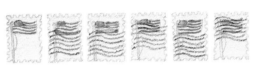

4.

5.

6.

7.

8.

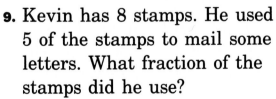

9. Kevin has 8 stamps. He used 5 of the stamps to mail some letters. What fraction of the stamps did he use?

★ **10.** Cindy has 10 stamps. She used 7 of the stamps on a package. What fraction of the stamps does she have left?

THINK

Shape Perception

How many different ways can you tear 3 stamps from a large sheet of stamps?

Example

Draw pictures on a sheet of paper to show your answers.

MATH

Fractions of a Set

Jack had 8 toy boats.   He painted $\frac{1}{2}$ of them blue.

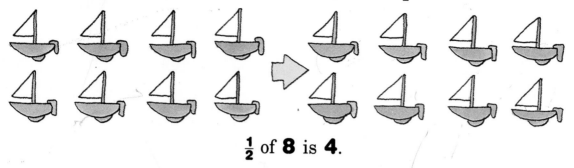

$\frac{1}{2}$ of **8** is **4**.

To find $\frac{1}{2}$ of a number, divide by 2.

Other Examples

Marcia painted $\frac{1}{3}$ of the cars red.

Brad painted $\frac{1}{4}$ of the trucks green.

$\frac{1}{3}$ of **6** is **2**.

$\frac{1}{4}$ of **12** is **3**.

To find $\frac{1}{3}$ of a number, divide by 3.

To find $\frac{1}{4}$ of a number, divide by 4.

Solve.

1. Sara had 10 toy boats. She painted $\frac{1}{2}$ of them yellow. How many did she paint yellow?

2. Tony had 6 toy airplanes. He painted $\frac{1}{3}$ of them blue. How many did he paint blue?

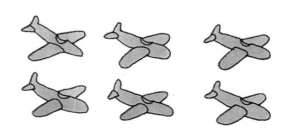

PROBLEM SOLVING
Practice

Solve.

1. Dick has 8 toy cars. Each car has 4 wheels. How many wheels are there?

2. Larry has 12 balloons. He popped $\frac{1}{3}$ of them. How many balloons did Larry pop?

3. Peggy had 24 marbles. She gave away 9 of them. How many marbles does Peggy have left?

4. June has 6 toy horses. She painted $\frac{1}{2}$ of them brown. How many of June's horses are brown?

5. Isabel had 10 pennies. She spent $\frac{1}{2}$ of them. How many pennies did Isabel spend?

6. Marie saw a toy train pulling 18 cars. $\frac{1}{3}$ of the cars were boxcars. How many of the cars were boxcars?

7. Rick has 16 fish in his tank. $\frac{1}{2}$ of the fish are goldfish. How many goldfish does Rick have in his tank?

8. Ron has 16 red balloons and 17 yellow balloons. How many balloons does Ron have?

9. Dave had 15 pennies. He spent $\frac{1}{3}$ of them. How many pennies did Dave spend?

★ 10. Javier had 32 baseball cards. He gave away $\frac{1}{4}$ of them. How many baseball cards did Javier keep?

11. *Try This* Corey sold between 15 and 20 toy trains on Saturday. He sold an even number of trains. Corey has never sold 18 trains in one day. How many toy trains did Corey sell?

Equivalent Fractions

Brenda and Tim each colored part of a paper strip.

I colored $\frac{1}{2}$ of my strip.

I colored $\frac{2}{4}$ of my strip.

The children colored the **same amount** of the strips. Fractions that name the same amount are **equivalent fractions**.

$$\text{We write } \frac{1}{2} = \frac{2}{4}$$

Many fractions are equivalent to $\frac{1}{2}$.

Warm Up Give the missing fractions.

1.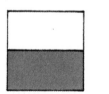

$$\frac{1}{2} = \frac{\text{\rule{1cm}{0pt}}}{\text{\rule{1cm}{0pt}}}$$

2.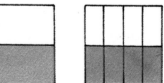

$$\frac{1}{2} = \frac{\text{\rule{1cm}{0pt}}}{\text{\rule{1cm}{0pt}}}$$

3.

$$\frac{1}{2} = \frac{\text{\rule{1cm}{0pt}}}{\text{\rule{1cm}{0pt}}}$$

4.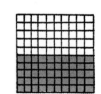

$$\frac{1}{2} = \frac{\text{\rule{1cm}{0pt}}}{\text{\rule{1cm}{0pt}}}$$

Write the missing fractions.

1.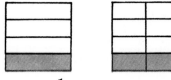

$$\frac{1}{4} = \underline{\quad}$$

2.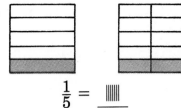

$$\frac{1}{5} = \underline{\quad}$$

3.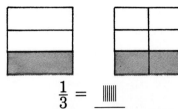

$$\frac{1}{3} = \underline{\quad}$$

4.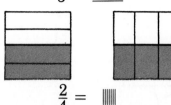

$$\frac{2}{4} = \underline{\quad}$$

5.

$$\frac{1}{10} = \underline{\quad}$$

6.

$$\frac{4}{8} = \underline{\quad}$$

7.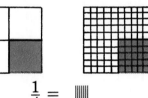

$$\frac{1}{4} = \underline{\quad}$$

8.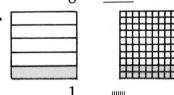

$$\frac{1}{5} = \underline{\quad}$$

9. Janet's sandwich was cut into fourths. She ate half of it. How many pieces did she eat?

THINK

Estimation

Give a fraction to tell how much gasoline is in the tank.

Example   1.   2.   3.

Answer $\frac{1}{4}$

MATH

Comparing Fractions

The colored strips will help you compare fractions.

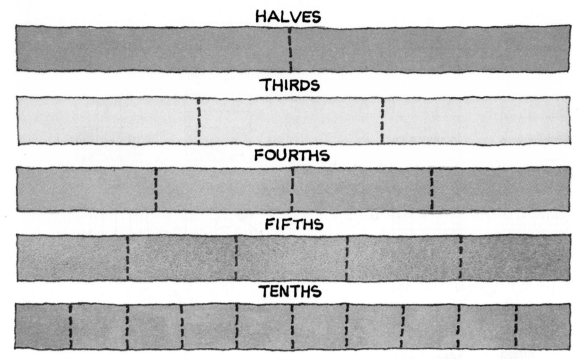

Examples

$\frac{1}{3}$ is greater than $\frac{1}{4} \rightarrow \frac{1}{3} > \frac{1}{4}$

$\frac{1}{4}$ is less than $\frac{2}{5} \rightarrow \frac{1}{4} < \frac{2}{5}$

$\frac{1}{2}$ is equal to $\frac{2}{4} \rightarrow \frac{1}{2} = \frac{2}{4}$

Write the sign >, <, or = for each ◍.

1. $\frac{1}{2}$ ◍ $\frac{1}{3}$ **2.** $\frac{1}{5}$ ◍ $\frac{1}{3}$ **3.** $\frac{1}{10}$ ◍ $\frac{1}{5}$ **4.** $\frac{1}{4}$ ◍ $\frac{1}{5}$ **5.** $\frac{2}{4}$ ◍ $\frac{5}{10}$

6. $\frac{1}{3}$ ◍ $\frac{1}{10}$ **7.** $\frac{2}{5}$ ◍ $\frac{1}{2}$ **8.** $\frac{1}{5}$ ◍ $\frac{3}{10}$ **9.** $\frac{1}{5}$ ◍ $\frac{2}{10}$ **10.** $\frac{3}{4}$ ◍ $\frac{2}{3}$

11. $\frac{3}{5}$ ◍ $\frac{6}{10}$ **12.** $\frac{7}{10}$ ◍ $\frac{4}{5}$ **13.** $\frac{5}{10}$ ◍ $\frac{4}{5}$ **14.** $\frac{8}{10}$ ◍ $\frac{4}{5}$ **15.** $\frac{1}{2}$ ◍ $\frac{2}{3}$

16. $\frac{2}{3}$ ◍ $\frac{2}{5}$ **17.** $\frac{4}{10}$ ◍ $\frac{3}{5}$ **18.** $\frac{2}{5}$ ◍ $\frac{1}{4}$ **19.** $\frac{1}{5}$ ◍ $\frac{1}{4}$ **20.** $\frac{9}{10}$ ◍ $\frac{4}{5}$

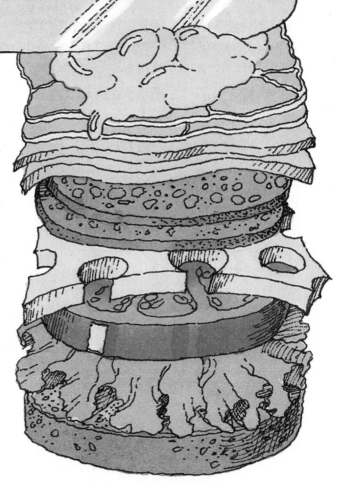

PROBLEM SOLVING
Practice

QUESTION
DATA
PLAN
ANSWER
CHECK

Solve.

1. Marie ate $\frac{1}{2}$ of her sandwich. Tod ate $\frac{1}{4}$ of his sandwich. Who ate more, Marie or Tod?

2. Sheri bought 4 packages of lunch meat. Each package weighed 14 ounces. How many ounces of lunch meat did Sheri buy?

3. Salvador ran $\frac{3}{4}$ of a mile. Drew ran $\frac{1}{2}$ of a mile. Who ran farther?

4. Karl practiced the piano for $\frac{1}{2}$ of an hour. Brandon practiced for $\frac{1}{3}$ of an hour. Who practiced longer?

5. Tess ate 42 raisins. Joyce ate 19 raisins. How many more raisins did Tess eat?

6. Lana had 24 grapes. Lana ate $\frac{1}{3}$ of her grapes. How many grapes did Lana eat?

7. Alex and Jon each had 20 raisins. Alex ate 6 of his raisins. Jon ate $\frac{1}{4}$ of his raisins. Who ate more raisins?

8. *Try This* Keiko and Robert each got a pizza. Keiko's was cut into sixths. Robert's was cut into eighths. They both ate half of their pizzas. How many more pieces did Robert eat?

Fractions and Decimals

There are 10 books on the shelf. **3** of the **10** books are red. Three tenths of the books are red. For three tenths, you can write a fraction or a **decimal**.

Fraction	Decimal
$\dfrac{3}{10}$	**0.3**
	↑ Decimal point

We read, "**three tenths**."

Other Examples

$\dfrac{6}{10}$ **0.6** $\dfrac{7}{10}$ **0.7**

Warm Up   Read each decimal.

1. 0.4   **2.** 0.9   **3.** 0.2   **4.** 0.5   **5.** 0.4   **6.** 0.8

Write a fraction in tenths and a decimal for the red part of each set or figure.

7.   **8.**   **9.**

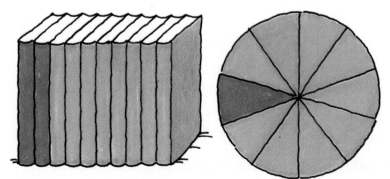

Write a decimal for the red part of each set or figure.

1. **2.**

3. **4.**

5. **6.**

7. **8.**

Multiply.

1. $\begin{array}{r} 17 \\ \times\ 3 \\ \hline \end{array}$ **2.** $\begin{array}{r} 22 \\ \times\ 4 \\ \hline \end{array}$ **3.** $\begin{array}{r} 26 \\ \times\ 3 \\ \hline \end{array}$ **4.** $\begin{array}{r} 12 \\ \times\ 4 \\ \hline \end{array}$ **5.** $\begin{array}{r} 35 \\ \times\ 2 \\ \hline \end{array}$

6. $\begin{array}{r} 32¢ \\ \times\ 4 \\ \hline \end{array}$ **7.** $\begin{array}{r} 58¢ \\ \times\ 2 \\ \hline \end{array}$ **8.** $\begin{array}{r} 43¢ \\ \times\ 3 \\ \hline \end{array}$ **9.** $\begin{array}{r} 38¢ \\ \times\ 5 \\ \hline \end{array}$ **10.** $\begin{array}{r} 76¢ \\ \times\ 4 \\ \hline \end{array}$

Larger Decimals

The class had enough art papers to fill 1 whole bulletin board and 0.7 of another. For one and seven tenths, you can write a **mixed number** or a decimal.

1

0.7

Mixed Number	Decimal
$1\frac{7}{10}$	**1.7**

We read, "**one and seven tenths.**"

Other Examples

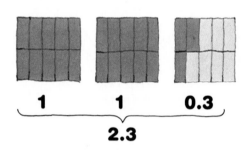

1   1   0.3

2.3

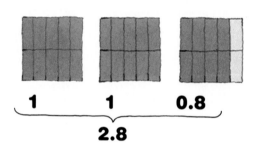

1   1   0.8

2.8

Warm Up Read each decimal.

1. 6.8 **2.** 4.5 **3.** 23.6 **4.** 75.2 **5.** 38.1 **6.** 49.7

Write a decimal for each part.

7.

8.

Write a decimal for each part.

1.

2.

3.

4.

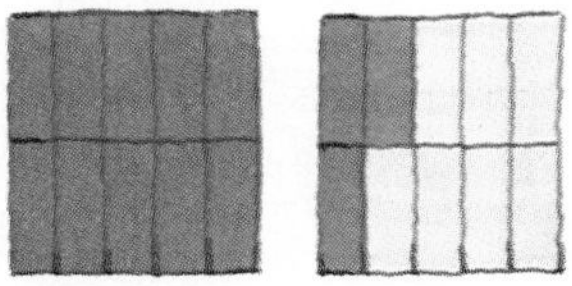

5.

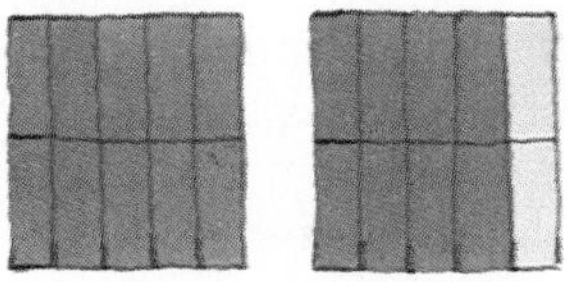

6.

7.

8.

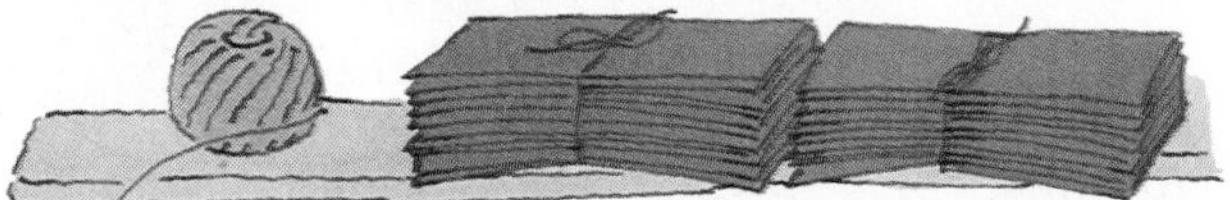

9.

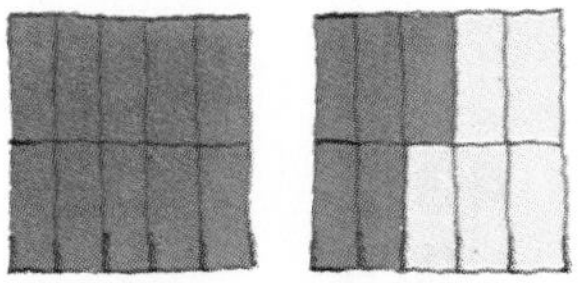

THINK

Patterns

What comes next?

1. 3.4, 3.5, 3.6, 3.7, ▓▓▓

2. 2.8, 2.9, 3.0, 3.1, ▓▓▓

3. 4.6, 4.7, 4.8, 4.9, ▓▓▓

4. 0.6, 0.7, 0.8, 0.9, ▓▓▓

MATH

10.

Adding Decimals

How much juice is used in the recipe?

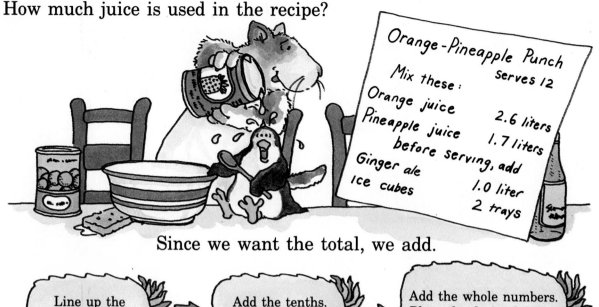

Orange-Pineapple Punch serves 12

Mix these:
Orange juice — 2.6 liters
Pineapple juice — 1.7 liters
before serving, add
Ginger ale — 1.0 liter
Ice cubes — 2 trays

Since we want the total, we add.

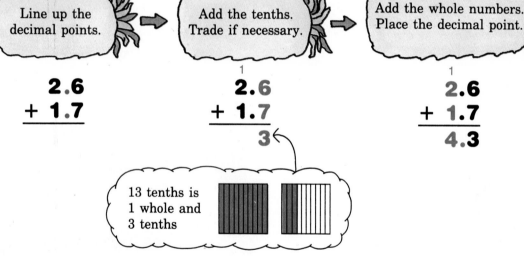

Line up the decimal points.

$$
\begin{array}{r}
2.6 \\
+\ 1.7 \\
\end{array}
$$

Add the tenths. Trade if necessary.

$$
\begin{array}{r}
\overset{1}{2}.6 \\
+\ 1.7 \\
\hline
3 \\
\end{array}
$$

Add the whole numbers. Place the decimal point.

$$
\begin{array}{r}
\overset{1}{2}.6 \\
+\ 1.7 \\
\hline
4.3 \\
\end{array}
$$

13 tenths is 1 whole and 3 tenths

There are 4.3 liters of juice.

Other Examples

$$
\begin{array}{r}
\overset{1}{8}.4 \\
+\ 6.9 \\
\hline
15.3 \\
\end{array}
\qquad
\begin{array}{r}
\overset{1}{2}\overset{1}{7}.6 \\
+\ 39.8 \\
\hline
67.4 \\
\end{array}
\qquad
\begin{array}{r}
\overset{1}{4}3.2 \\
+\ \ 9.5 \\
\hline
52.7 \\
\end{array}
$$

Warm Up Add.

1. $\begin{array}{r} 3.6 \\ +\ 1.9 \end{array}$ 2. $\begin{array}{r} 8.7 \\ +\ 9.6 \end{array}$ 3. $\begin{array}{r} 6.2 \\ +\ 7.3 \end{array}$ 4. $\begin{array}{r} 35.4 \\ +\ 27.8 \end{array}$ 5. $\begin{array}{r} 56.7 \\ +\ 9.8 \end{array}$

Find the sums.

1. 2.8 + 1.3	**2.** 5.6 + 1.8	**3.** 7.9 + 6.7	**4.** 25.8 + 7.6	**5.** 32.0 + 7.6
6. 32.8 + 6.5	**7.** 54.7 + 12.9	**8.** 65.3 + 18.2	**9.** 76.7 + 14.8	**10.** 85.3 + 12.9
11. 46.3 + 8.9	**12.** 75.4 + 6.8	**13.** 80.6 + 18.7	**14.** 16.2 + 75.3	**15.** 38.7 + 19.6

16. 4.7 + 2.8

17. 6.9 + 3.5

18. 7.3 + 2.6

19. 37.2 + 46.5

20. 37.4 + 28.9

21. 64.7 + 9.8

22. Add 5.6 to 1.8.

23. Add 32.8 + 14.9.

24. Find the sum of 16.7 and 17.8.

25. Find the sum of 39.3 and 8.9.

Use the recipe to solve 26–27.

26. How much lemonade and limeade is there altogether?

★ **27.** Each ice cube tray had 0.5 liters of water. How much Lemon-Lime Cooler will there be when the ice melts?

Lemon - Lime Cooler

Lemonade	2.5 liters
Limeade	1.8 liters
Ginger ale	1.0 liter
Ice	2 trays

THINK

Patterns

Give a decimal between the two numbers.

1. 0.5 and 0.7   **2.** 6.8 and 7.0   **3.** 27.4 and 27.6   **4.** 39.9 and 40.1

MATH

Subtracting Decimals

When Jill had the flu, her temperature was 40.1°C. After taking medicine for one day, her temperature dropped to 37.3°C. How much did it drop?

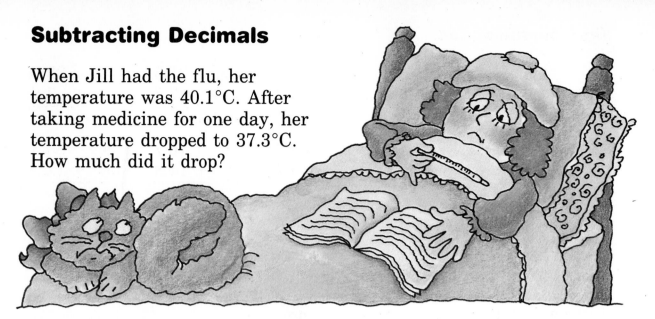

Since we want to find how much less, we subtract.

Line up the decimal points.	Subtract the tenths. Trade if necessary.	Subtract the whole numbers. Place the decimal point.

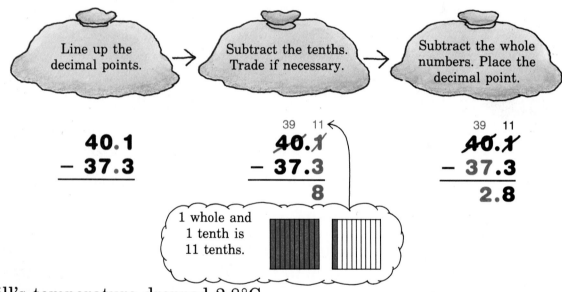

$$
\begin{array}{r}
40.1 \\
-\ 37.3 \\
\end{array}
$$

$$
\begin{array}{r}
^{39}\ ^{11} \\
4\cancel{0}.\cancel{1} \\
-\ 37.3 \\
\hline
8 \\
\end{array}
$$

1 whole and 1 tenth is 11 tenths.

$$
\begin{array}{r}
^{39}\ ^{11} \\
\cancel{40}.\cancel{1} \\
-\ 37.3 \\
\hline
2.8 \\
\end{array}
$$

Jill's temperature dropped 2.8°C.

Other Examples

$$
\begin{array}{r}
^{7}\ ^{13} \\
\cancel{8}.\cancel{3} \\
-\ 2.7 \\
\hline
5.6 \\
\end{array}
\qquad
\begin{array}{r}
^{1}\ ^{13} \\
1\cancel{2}.\cancel{3} \\
-\ 11.9 \\
\hline
0.4 \\
\end{array}
\qquad
\begin{array}{r}
^{4}\ ^{12} \\
\cancel{5}\cancel{2}.6 \\
-\ 17.2 \\
\hline
35.4 \\
\end{array}
\qquad
\begin{array}{r}
^{4}\ ^{10} \\
7\cancel{5}.\cancel{0} \\
-\ 21.3 \\
\hline
53.7 \\
\end{array}
$$

Warm Up Subtract.

1.
$$
\begin{array}{r}
7.4 \\
-\ 2.6 \\
\hline
\end{array}
$$

2.
$$
\begin{array}{r}
59.5 \\
-\ 21.8 \\
\hline
\end{array}
$$

3.
$$
\begin{array}{r}
30.2 \\
-\ 17.9 \\
\hline
\end{array}
$$

4.
$$
\begin{array}{r}
78.0 \\
-\ 35.6 \\
\hline
\end{array}
$$

5.
$$
\begin{array}{r}
54.3 \\
-\ 53.6 \\
\hline
\end{array}
$$

Find the differences.

1. 9.2 – 1.6	**2.** 3.1 – 1.7	**3.** 6.4 – 2.9	**4.** 7.3 – 3.8	**5.** 8.4 – 2.1
6. 57.3 – 14.6	**7.** 65.4 – 38.1	**8.** 56.0 – 10.4	**9.** 16.2 – 15.9	**10.** 32.7 – 6.9
11. 52.1 – 24.3	**12.** 34.6 – 16.0	**13.** 45.2 – 17.8	**14.** 57.1 – 56.9	**15.** 62.0 – 30.4

16. 17.3 − 9.6   **17.** 5.0 − 2.7   **18.** 6.8 − 3.5

19. Subtract 7.8 from 9.3.   **20.** Subtract 54.6 from 92.3.

Solve.

21. Lou's temperature was 39.6°C when he was sick. When he took medicine it dropped to 37.9°C. How much did it drop?

★ **22.** Pia had a temperature of 40.2°C when she was sick. It dropped 1.7°C the first day and 1.5°C the second. What was it then?

THINK

Decimal Puzzle

What grows down instead of up, lives in the winter, and dies in the summer?

5.6	5.4	6.3	7.2
C	I	L	E

Copy the problems in order. Work each problem. Put the code letter under each answer.

2.8 + 2.6	9.1 – 3.5	12.0 – 6.6	1.9 + 3.7	35.2 – 28.9	4.8 + 2.4

➤ **MATH** ◀

PROBLEM SOLVING
Using Data from a Map

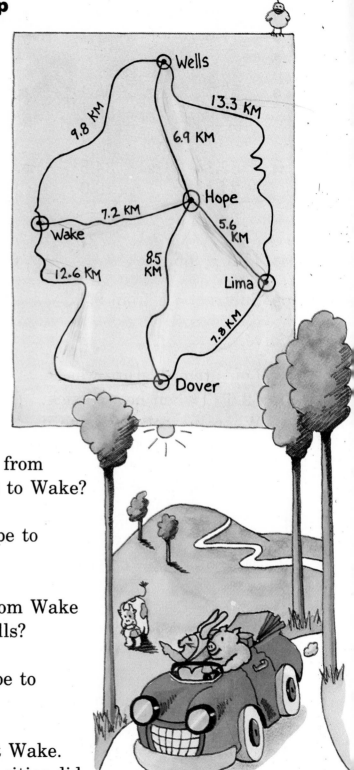

Use the map to answer the
following questions.

1. How far is it from Lima to
   Hope to Wells?

2. How much farther is it from
   Dover to Hope than from
   Dover to Lima?

3. How much closer is Wake to
   Hope than Dover to Hope?

4. How far is it from Dover to
   Wake to Wells?

5. How much shorter is the drive from
   Wells to Hope than from Wells to Wake?

6. How long is the drive from Hope to
   Wake to Wells?

7. How much longer is the trip from Wake
   to Hope than from Hope to Wells?

★ 8. How far is it from Lima to Hope to
   Dover to Wake?

9. *Try This* Jenny and Jay started at Wake.
   They drove 16.7 km. What two cities did
   they visit? Hint: Guess and check.

PROBLEM SOLVING
Using a Calculator

Try these calculator activities.

To enter 372.4 on your calculator, press [3][7][2][·][4]

To enter $48.65 on your calculator, press [4][8][·][6][5]

To divide 230.4 by 4, press [2][3][0][·][4][÷][4][=]

Use your calculator to solve these problems.

1. Ben bought 4 sacks of flour. Each sack weighed 2.3 kg. How many kilograms of flour did Ben buy?
Hint: Press [2][·][3][X][4][=]

2. Debra has 4.8 kg of peanuts. She divides them equally into 3 bags. How many kilograms of peanuts are in each bag?
Hint: Press [4][·][8][÷][3][=]

3. The total cost of one car was $8,275.56. Another car was $9,049.79. What was the difference in price?

4. Mona bought 5 pairs of socks. Each pair cost $1.79. How much did she pay for the socks?

5. Ms. Moore paid $7,875.45 for a new car. Taxes and license were $767.75 more. How much did she spend?

6. There is a total of 11.4 L in 6 cans of juice. How much juice is in each can?

7. *Try This* These are the prices of four TV sets. Mr. Wu bought two of them for $624.20. Which two did he buy?

Set A $287.95
Set B $349.55
Set C $298.75
Set D $325.45

APPLIED PROBLEM SOLVING

You want to have a dog. Your parents will let you have it if you take care of it. Can you afford it?

Some Things to Consider

- Your dog must be fed twice a day, and it needs fresh water every day.
- The dog needs about 650 grams of food each day.
- A large can of dog food (666 grams) costs 73¢.
- You must buy the food.

- Your parents will pay for the dog's shots and veterinary care.
- A leash, collar, and 2 dog bowls cost about $16.00.
- You earn $7.00 a week working around the house.
- You like to buy a record album every month or two. An album costs about $7.00 or $8.00.

Some Questions to Answer

1. How many cans of food will the dog eat in 1 week?   How much money is this each week?

2. About how many weeks must you save to buy the leash, collar, and 2 dog bowls?

3. How much will you have left from $7.00 if you buy food for one week?

What Is Your Decision?

Can you afford the dog? Can you still buy an album every month or two?

Give the correct letter.

1. How is the square divided?

- **A** sixths
- **B** eighths
- **C** tenths
- **D** hundredths

2. What fraction is shaded?

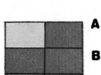

- **A** $\frac{2}{3}$
- **B** $\frac{3}{4}$
- **C** $\frac{5}{6}$
- **D** $\frac{7}{8}$

3. What fraction is used?

- **A** $\frac{2}{3}$
- **B** $\frac{1}{2}$
- **C** $\frac{3}{4}$
- **D** $\frac{1}{4}$

4. Jean had 6 balloons. She popped $\frac{1}{2}$ of them. How many balloons did Jean pop?

5. Write the missing fraction.

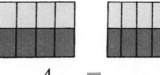

$$\frac{4}{8} = \frac{|||||}{\underline{\quad}}$$

8. Write a decimal for the picture.

Write the sign > or < for each .

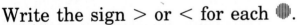
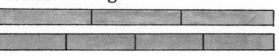

6. $\frac{1}{3}$ ◖ $\frac{1}{4}$

7. $\frac{2}{3}$ ◖ $\frac{3}{4}$

Add or subtract.

9.
$$\begin{array}{r} 3.7 \\ + 2.8 \\ \hline \end{array}$$

10.
$$\begin{array}{r} 14.6 \\ + 18.9 \\ \hline \end{array}$$

11.
$$\begin{array}{r} 7.2 \\ - 3.5 \\ \hline \end{array}$$

12.
$$\begin{array}{r} 24.3 \\ - 11.6 \\ \hline \end{array}$$

Solve.

13. Geri drove 7.8 km. Then she drove 6.9 km. How far did she drive in all?

14. Al drove 9.4 km Sunday and 5.8 km Monday. How much farther did he drive Sunday?

ANOTHER LOOK

3 parts shaded

8 parts in all

$\frac{3}{8}$ of the strip is shaded.

Write a fraction for the shaded parts.

1. 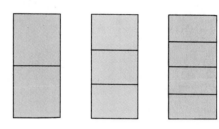   **2.**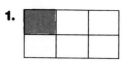

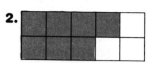

3. 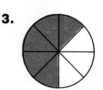   **4.**

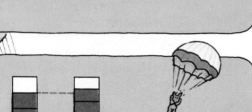

$\frac{2}{3}$ < $\frac{3}{4}$ $\frac{2}{3}$ is less than $\frac{3}{4}$.

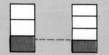

$\frac{1}{3}$ > $\frac{1}{4}$ $\frac{1}{3}$ is greater than $\frac{1}{4}$.

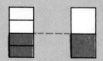

$\frac{2}{4}$ = $\frac{1}{2}$ $\frac{2}{4}$ is equal to $\frac{1}{2}$.

Give the sign >, <, or = for each ◗.

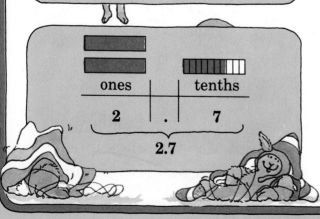

5. $\frac{1}{2}$ ◗ $\frac{1}{3}$ **6.** $\frac{1}{4}$ ◗ $\frac{2}{3}$

7. $\frac{1}{4}$ ◗ $\frac{1}{2}$ **8.** $\frac{3}{4}$ ◗ $\frac{1}{2}$

9. $\frac{2}{3}$ ◗ $\frac{1}{2}$ **10.** $\frac{1}{2}$ ◗ $\frac{2}{4}$

Write a decimal for the shaded parts.

11.    **12.**

13.    **14.**

ones		tenths
2	.	7

2.7

Magic Squares with Your Calculator

Look at the square at the right.
It is a **magic square**.

The sum along each

ROW →

COLUMN ↓

DIAGONAL ↗↘

is the same.

In the square, the **magic sum** is
15. Check it.

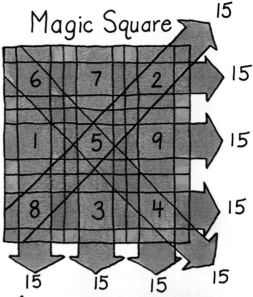

Magic Square

6	7	2	15
1	5	9	15
8	3	4	15

15   15   15   15

15

Copy this square. Fill in the
missing numbers so it is a
magic square.

Hint 1: Add the numbers in the top row to
find the **magic sum**.

Hint 2: Then find the number in the middle
box. The sum for the middle column
should be 18.

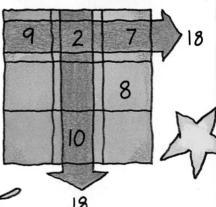

9	2	7	18
	8	
	10	

18

Use your **calculator** to make
this a magic square.

Now try this one.

160	105	116
		171
	149	

7.3	15.0	
12.8		
11.7		13.9

TECHNOLOGY

More About Computers

A **line number** tells the computer the order in which you want it to follow your instructions. A set of instructions is called a **program**.

```
10 PRINT "20 * 15"        10 PRINT "HELLO"
20 PRINT 20 * 15          20 PRINT "GOODBYE"
30 END                    30 END
```

If you press return for these programs, nothing will happen. We must tell the computer to **RUN** the program.

```
10 PRINT "39/13"
20 PRINT 39/13
30 END
RUN
```

```
39/13
3
```

```
40 PRINT "I'M GOOD AT MATH"
50 PRINT "I KNOW 25 * 17"
60 END
RUN
```

```
39/13
3
```

Look at the second RUN. Notice that 39/13 and 3 were printed again. The computer remembered the first program. We need to use the command **NEW** if we want the computer to erase the last set of instructions.

Write the RUN for each program.

1. NEW
```
10 PRINT "FIND 27 - 19"
20 PRINT 27 - 19
30 END
```

2. NEW
```
10 PRINT "FIND 175
     DIVIDED BY 25"
20 PRINT 175/25
30 END
```

3. NEW
```
10 PRINT "THE ANSWER
   TO"
20 PRINT "29 TIMES
   14 IS";
30 PRINT 29 * 14
40 END
```

4.
```
50 PRINT "42 MINUS
     25 IS"
60 PRINT 42 - 25
70 END
```

5. NEW
```
10 PRINT "HELLO"
20 PRINT "(your name)"
30 PRINT "THIS IS FUN"
40 END
```

6. NEW
```
10 PRINT "COMPUTERS
   CAN'T THINK"
20 PRINT "THEY ONLY
   FOLLOW OUR
   INSTRUCTIONS"
30 PRINT "10 * 15 = ";
   10 * 10
40 END
```

7. What did the semicolon do in number 3?

8. Why did the computer "make a mistake" in number 6?

9. How many lines did you see on the screen when you ran number 4?

★ Make a program for each of these RUNS.

10.
```
21 * 9 = ?
21 * 9 = 189
```

11.
```
HELLO
I KNOW THAT
183/3 = 61
```

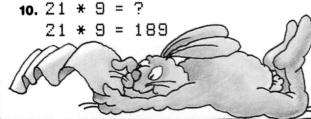

Give the letter for the correct answer.

1. $1\overline{)3}$
 A 1
 B 3
 C 0
 D not given

2. $4\overline{)28}$
 A 8
 B 7
 C 6
 D not given

3. $3\overline{)24}$
 A 8
 B 9
 C 7
 D not given

4. $9\overline{)54}$
 A 4
 B 5
 C 6
 D not given

5. $7\overline{)35}$
 A 5
 B 6
 C 7
 D not given

6. $8\overline{)40}$
 A 4
 B 5
 C 6
 D not given

7. $3\overline{)8}$
 A 1 R5
 B 2 R2
 C 3 R1
 D not given

8. $5\overline{)36}$
 A 7 R2
 B 6 R6
 C 8 R4
 D not given

9. $26 \div 4$
 A 6 R2   B 6 R1
 C 6   D not given

10. $17 \div 5$
 A 3 R1   B 3 R2
 C 2 R4   D not given

11. $29 \div 3$
 A 9 R2   B 9 R3
 C 9   D not given

12. $27 \div 4$
 A 6 R8   B 6
 C 6 R3   D not given

13. One pie is enough for 6 people. How many pies are needed for 12 people?
 A 72   B 18
 C 2   D not given

14. Paul needs 4 apples to make a pie. He picked 38 apples. How many pies can he make?
 A 8 pies
 B 9 pies, 2 apples left over
 C 5 pies, 3 apples left over
 D not given

MEASUREMENT: Customary Units

14

One day Jamie found a baby raccoon in the woods behind her house. Its eyes were closed and it was no bigger than her mother's fist. Jamie named her new pet "Bandit." At first Jamie fed Bandit from a baby bottle. After a few months Bandit was drinking milk and mashed bread from a bowl. After about nine months the raccoon was almost full-grown. Its tail alone was as long as this math book. Jamie had lots of fun taking care of Bandit.

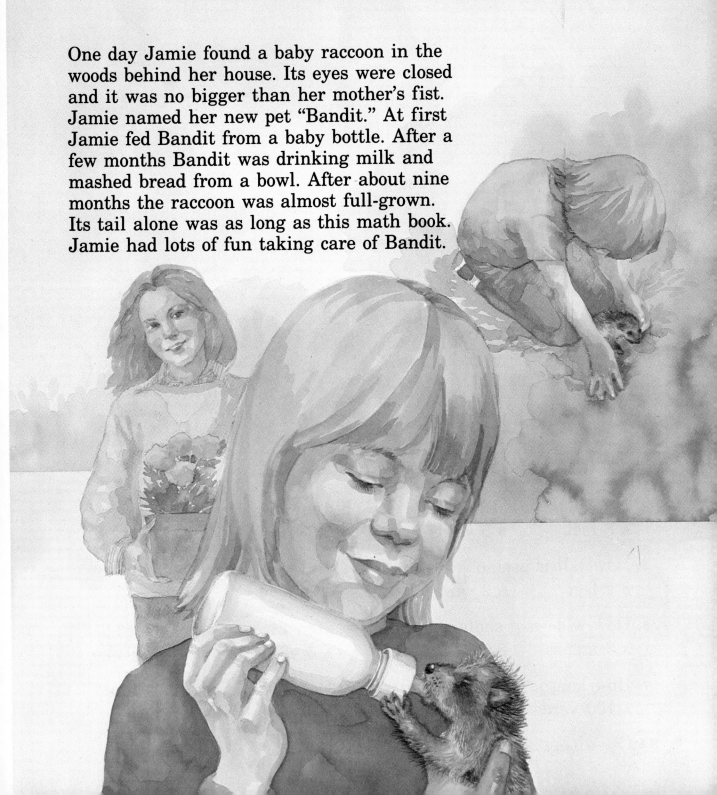

Customary Units for Length

The pictures below help you think about different **customary** units for measuring length.

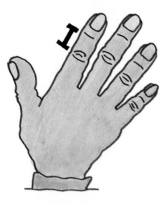

1 inch

1 foot
12 inches

1 yard
3 feet or 36 inches

1 mile = 1,760 yards.
1 mile = 5,280 feet.

Warm Up   Choose the better estimate.

1. How high is a door?
   A 8 feet   B 8 yards

2. How long is a train?
   A 1 yard   B 1 mile

3. How tall is a man?
   A 2 feet   B 2 yards

4. How long is a pencil?
   A 7 inches   B 7 feet

5. How wide is a chalkboard?
   A 8 inches   B 8 feet

6. How high is an airplane?
   A 5 yards   B 5 miles

7. How long is a football field?
   A 100 yards   B 100 miles

8. How far is it across a lake?
   A 3 yards   B 3 miles

Choose the better estimate.

1. How wide is a classroom door?
   A 1 yard   **B** 1 foot

2. How far can a car go in an hour?
   A 50 yards   **B** 50 miles

3. How long is a room?
   A 35 inches   **B** 35 feet

4. How high is a ceiling?
   A 3 yards   **B** 3 feet

5. How far did the batter hit a ball?
   A 100 yards   **B** 100 miles

6. How wide is a person's hand?
   A 3 feet   **B** 3 inches

7. How high is your desk top?
   A 1 foot   **B** 1 yard

8. How long is a car?
   A 10 feet   **B** 10 yards

9. The length of a pencil is
   A less than 1 foot.
   B more than 1 foot.

10. The height of an adult is
    A less than 1 yard.
    B more than 1 yard.

11. An hour bike ride is
    A less than 1 mile.
    B more than 1 mile.

12. The width of a fingernail is
    A less than an inch.
    B more than an inch.

THINK

Estimation

The map shows two distances. Estimate each of these distances.

1. Jackson to Union City
2. Kent to Lake
3. Lake to Kane
4. Union City to Kane

JACKSON   12 MILES   KENT

20 MILES

UNION CITY   LAKE   KANE

MATH

Measuring with Inch Units

The piece of ribbon is 5 inches (in.) long.

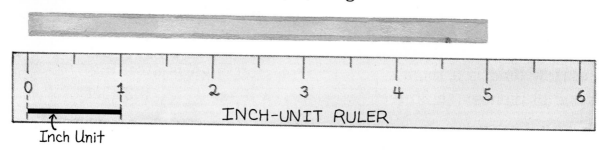

Inch Unit

Other Examples

Fractions may be used when you measure with inch units.

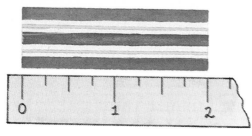

This ribbon is 2 inches long.

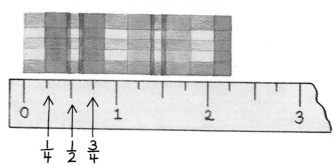

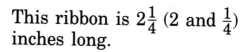

This ribbon is $2\frac{1}{4}$ (2 and $\frac{1}{4}$) inches long.

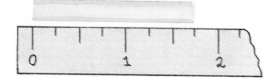

This ribbon is $1\frac{3}{4}$ inches long.

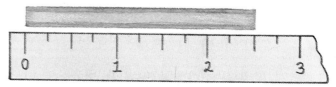

This ribbon is $2\frac{1}{2}$ inches long.

Warm Up Use your inch ruler. Give each length.

1.

2.

3.

4.

Use your inch ruler. Find each length.

1.

2.

3.

4.

Choose the best estimate.

5.

The length is about   **A** 3 inches.   **B** $3\frac{1}{4}$ inches.   **C** $3\frac{1}{2}$ inches.

6.

The length is about   **A** $2\frac{1}{4}$ inches.   **B** $2\frac{1}{2}$ inches.   **C** $2\frac{3}{4}$ inches.

7.

The length is about   **A** $4\frac{3}{4}$ inches.   **B** 5 inches.   **C** $5\frac{1}{4}$ inches.

SKILLKEEPER

Write a fraction to tell what part is shaded.

1.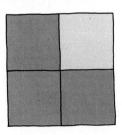

2.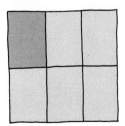

3.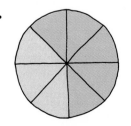

Cups, Pints, Quarts, and Gallons

You can pour 4 glasses of juice from a **quart** container. Each glass is about 1 **cup**.

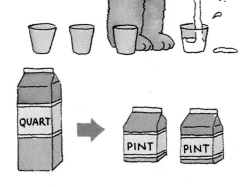

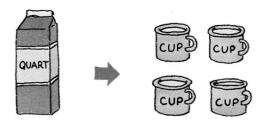

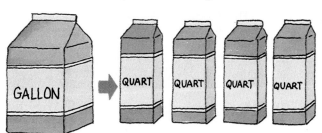

1 quart = 4 cups

1 quart = 2 pints

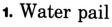

1 pint = 2 cups

1 gallon = 4 quarts

Warm Up Choose the better measure.

1. Water pail

A 2 pints   **B** 2 gallons

2. Soup bowl

A 2 cups   **B** 2 quarts

3. Bathtub

A 10 pints   **B** 10 gallons

4. Aquarium

A 8 pints   **B** 8 gallons

Choose the better measure.

1. Coffee pot

  A 10 cups   **B** 10 quarts

2. Vase

  A 1 pint   **B** 1 gallon

3. Wading pool

  A 12 pints   **B** 12 gallons

4. Cooking pot

  A 2 cups   **B** 2 quarts

5. Birdbath

  A 1 pint   **B** 1 gallon

6. Fishbowl

  A 2 cups   **B** 2 quarts

Copy and complete the tables.

7.

Quarts	1	2	3	4	5
Pints	2	4			

8.

Gallons	1	2	3	4	5
Quarts	4	8			

THINK

Logical Reasoning

You have these empty jars.

How can you go to a faucet and return with exactly 3 pints of water?

MATH

Weight: Ounces and Pounds

The **ounce** (oz) and **pound** (lb) are units for measuring weight.

1 pound = 16 ounces

9 pennies
about 1 ounce

Package of butter
about 1 pound

Choose the better estimate for the weight.

1. Large book

A 3 pounds   **B** 3 ounces

2. Strawberry

A 1 pound   **B** 1 ounce

3. Chalkboard eraser

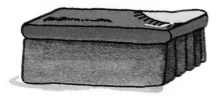

A 3 pounds   **B** 3 ounces

4. Television

A 30 pounds   **B** 30 ounces

5. Quart of milk

A 32 pounds   **B** 32 ounces

6. Bicycle

A 25 pounds   **B** 25 ounces

Temperature

A unit for measuring temperature is the **degree Fahrenheit** (°F). The thermometer at the right reads about 85°F (warm summer day).

Give the reading for each thermometer below.

1.

Ice

2.

Your body temperature

3.

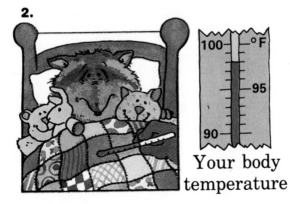

Cool fall day

°F

110 — 105
100 — 95
90 — 85
80 — 75
70 — 65
60 — 55
50 — 45
40 — 35
30 — 25
20 — 15
10 — 5
0
— -5
-10

THINK

Negative Numbers

On a cold winter night the temperature fell to ⁻12°F. The next day the temperature rose to only 5°F. How many degrees did the temperature rise?

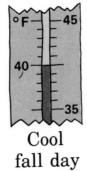

MATH

APPLIED PROBLEM SOLVING

You and a friend want to open a lemonade stand. You want to make a profit. You need to decide how much to charge for each cup of lemonade.

Some Things to Consider

- Your parents will give you all of the ice, water, and pitchers you need for free.
- Paper cups cost 2¢ each.
- Lemons cost 13¢ each, and a cup of sugar costs about 20¢.
- You need 4 lemons and 1 cup of sugar to make one pitcher of lemonade.
- One pitcher can hold 8 cups of lemonade.
- You want to make a profit.

Some Questions to Answer

1. What does it cost to make one pitcher of lemonade?
2. How much does it cost for 8 paper cups?
3. How much is this altogether?
4. How much does each cup of lemonade cost?

What Is Your Decision?

How much are you going to charge for each cup of lemonade?

Choose the better estimate.

1. How high is the bookshelf?
  A 3 feet   **B** 3 yards

2. How wide is the desk?
  A 1 foot   **B** 1 yard

3. How long was the bus ride?
  A 10 yards   **B** 10 miles

4. How long is the shoe?
  A 7 inches   **B** 7 feet

Use your inch ruler. Give each length.

5.

6.

Use your inch ruler. Choose the better estimate.

7.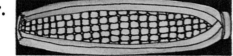

  A $2\frac{1}{4}$ inches   **B** $2\frac{1}{2}$ inches

8.

  A $1\frac{1}{2}$ inches   **B** $1\frac{3}{4}$ inches

Choose the better estimate.

9. How much milk is on your cereal?
  A 1 cup
  B 1 quart

10. How much water is in the sink?
  A 1 pint
  B 1 gallon

11. Tube of toothpaste
  A 12 ounces
  B 12 pounds

12. Turkey
  A 12 ounces
  B 12 pounds

13. Give the temperature reading.

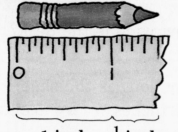

1 inch $\frac{1}{2}$ inch

The pencil is $1\frac{1}{2}$ inches long.

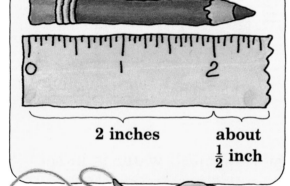

2 inches   about $\frac{1}{2}$ inch

1 foot = 12 inches
1 yard = 3 feet
1 yard = 36 inches
1 mile = 5,280 feet
1 mile = 1,760 yards

Use your inch ruler. Give each length.

1.

2.

3.

Use your inch ruler. Choose the better estimate.

4.

   A $1\frac{1}{2}$ inches   **B** $1\frac{3}{4}$ inches

5.

   A $1\frac{3}{4}$ inches   **B** $1\frac{1}{4}$ inches

6. How far does Ramona live from school?
   A 3 yards   **B** 3 miles

7. How far did Ira swim today?
   A 100 yards   **B** 100 miles

8. How high is the basketball rim?
   A 10 feet   **B** 10 yards

Area Using Half Units

Find the area of each figure.

Example

Figure	Cut apart.	How many unit squares?

The area is 2 square units.

1.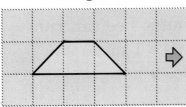

2.

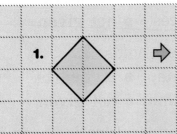 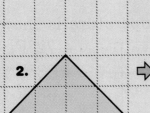

3.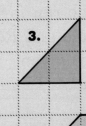

4.

5.

6.

7.

CUMULATIVE REVIEW

Give the letter for the correct answer.

1.   **A** halves **B** thirds **C** fourths **D** not given

2.   **A** thirds **B** sixths **C** eighths **D** not given

What part is shaded?

3.   **A** $\frac{1}{2}$ **B** $\frac{1}{3}$ **C** $\frac{2}{3}$ **D** not given

4.   **A** $\frac{1}{5}$ **B** $\frac{3}{8}$ **C** $\frac{1}{8}$ **D** not given

5. Which statement is correct?

A $\frac{2}{3} < \frac{3}{4}$ **B** $\frac{1}{4} > \frac{2}{3}$
C $\frac{1}{3} < \frac{1}{4}$ **D** not given

Which decimal is shown?

6.
A 5.1   **B** 1.5
C 10.5   **D** not given

7.
A 10.3   **B** 3.1
C 1.3   **D** not given

Choose the best estimate.

8. How long is the bicycle?
   A 5 inches **B** 5 yards
   C 5 feet   **D** not given

9. In 8 minutes Lee can run
   A 10 yards **B** 1 mile
   C 10 miles **D** not given

10. A bicycle weighs
   A 25 ounces **B** 25 pounds
   C 5 ounces   **D** not given

11. A bathtub holds
   A 10 pints   **B** 10 quarts
   C 10 gallons **D** not given

12. What temperature is shown?
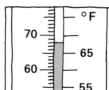
   A 72°F
   B 73°F
   C 68°F
   D not given

13. Ron ran $\frac{1}{2}$ of a mile. Cole ran $\frac{1}{3}$ of a mile. Who ran farther?
   A Ron   **B** Cole and Ron
   C Cole **D** not given

14. Kim ran $\frac{2}{3}$ of a mile. Dee ran $\frac{1}{2}$ of a mile. Who ran farther?
   A Kim   **B** Dee
   C Kim and Dee **D** not given

Appendix

Fred's Famous Zoo

Average Weights of Animals

Animal	Weight
Buffalo	804 kg
Camel	561 kg
Deer	125 kg
Elk	676 kg
Rhinoceros	2,290 kg
Lion	158 kg
Tiger	182 kg
Hippopotamus	3,563 kg
Bear	376 kg
Elephant	4,093 kg

Some U.S. Stamps

Stamps	Price
Buffalo	6¢
Polar Bears	8¢
First Man on the Moon	10¢
Butterfly	13¢
Owl	15¢
Crane	3¢
Circus	5¢
Windmill	15¢

DAILY DRY DOG FOOD NEEDS

Dog	Daily Need
Chihuahua	45 grams
Yorkshire terrier	100 grams
Dachshund	156 grams
Poodle	198 grams
Beagle	255 grams
Cocker spaniel	355 grams
Bulldog	481 grams
Collie	596 grams
German shepherd	719 grams

LEADING U.S. SUPERMARKETS IN A RECENT YEAR

Supermarkets	Number of Stores
Safeway	2,416
Kroger	1,245
A&P	1,542
Lucky	530
Winn-Dixie	1,192
American	749
Jewel	345
Southland	6,895
Food Fair	203
Albertson's	396

TALL BUILDINGS

BUILDING	CITY	ROOF HEIGHT (IN METERS)	STORIES
SEARS TOWER	CHICAGO, IL	443	110
WORLD TRADE CENTER	NEW YORK CITY, NY	411	110
EMPIRE STATE	NEW YORK CITY, NY	381	102
STANDARD OIL	CHICAGO, IL	346	80
JOHN HANCOCK	CHICAGO, IL	337	100
FIRST BANK TOWER	TORONTO, ON	285	70
CHRYSLER	NEW YORK CITY, NY	264	77
FIRST INTERSTATE TOWER	LOS ANGELES, CA	262	62
40 WALL STREET	NEW YORK CITY, NY	259	71
RCA	NEW YORK CITY, NY	259	70

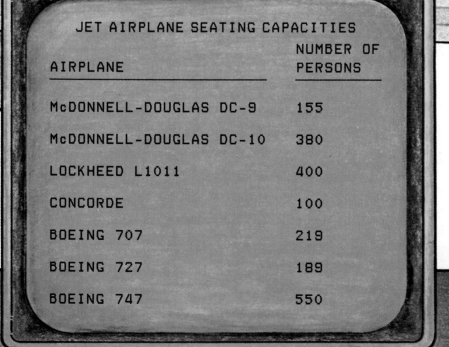

JET AIRPLANE SEATING CAPACITIES

AIRPLANE	NUMBER OF PERSONS
McDONNELL-DOUGLAS DC-9	155
McDONNELL-DOUGLAS DC-10	380
LOCKHEED L1011	400
CONCORDE	100
BOEING 707	219
BOEING 727	189
BOEING 747	550

· SKATERS' QUARTERLY ·

SKATING RINK CAPACITIES

NAME OF RINK	NUMBER OF SKATERS RINK CAN HOLD
Circle K State Ranch, Fresno, CA	500
Happy Wheels, Portland, ME	750
Jellibeans, Atlanta, GA	1,200
Red Wing Rollerway, Columbia, SC	2,500
Roll-on-America, Groton, CT	800
Roller City, Cheyenne, WY	400
Roller Dome South, Ft. Wayne, IN	1,435
Riverdale Roller World, Warwick, RI	1,650
Spinning Wheels, Concordville, PA	2,500
Stars Roller Rink, Bronx, NY	1,500

FLAGS of the UNITED STATES

Date	Stars	Stripes
1777	13	13
1795	15	15
1818	20	13
1861	34	13
1912	48	13
1959	49	13
1960	50	13

HIGHWAY DISTANCES

More Practice

Add.

1. $\begin{array}{r} 3 \\ +\ 1 \\ \hline \end{array}$	**2.** $\begin{array}{r} 2 \\ +\ 5 \\ \hline \end{array}$	**3.** $\begin{array}{r} 3 \\ +\ 6 \\ \hline \end{array}$	**4.** $\begin{array}{r} 1 \\ +\ 7 \\ \hline \end{array}$	**5.** $\begin{array}{r} 2 \\ +\ 1 \\ \hline \end{array}$	**6.** $\begin{array}{r} 5 \\ +\ 5 \\ \hline \end{array}$	**7.** $\begin{array}{r} 9 \\ +\ 0 \\ \hline \end{array}$
8. $\begin{array}{r} 2 \\ +\ 6 \\ \hline \end{array}$	**9.** $\begin{array}{r} 4 \\ +\ 5 \\ \hline \end{array}$	**10.** $\begin{array}{r} 3 \\ +\ 7 \\ \hline \end{array}$	**11.** $\begin{array}{r} 5 \\ +\ 2 \\ \hline \end{array}$	**12.** $\begin{array}{r} 1 \\ +\ 8 \\ \hline \end{array}$	**13.** $\begin{array}{r} 0 \\ +\ 4 \\ \hline \end{array}$	**14.** $\begin{array}{r} 5 \\ +\ 3 \\ \hline \end{array}$
15. $\begin{array}{r} 7 \\ +\ 2 \\ \hline \end{array}$	**16.** $\begin{array}{r} 3 \\ +\ 5 \\ \hline \end{array}$	**17.** $\begin{array}{r} 7 \\ +\ 3 \\ \hline \end{array}$	**18.** $\begin{array}{r} 3 \\ +\ 5 \\ \hline \end{array}$	**19.** $\begin{array}{r} 6 \\ +\ 1 \\ \hline \end{array}$	**20.** $\begin{array}{r} 4 \\ +\ 2 \\ \hline \end{array}$	**21.** $\begin{array}{r} 8 \\ +\ 1 \\ \hline \end{array}$
22. $\begin{array}{r} 4 \\ +\ 6 \\ \hline \end{array}$	**23.** $\begin{array}{r} 6 \\ +\ 2 \\ \hline \end{array}$	**24.** $\begin{array}{r} 4 \\ +\ 1 \\ \hline \end{array}$	**25.** $\begin{array}{r} 6 \\ +\ 3 \\ \hline \end{array}$	**26.** $\begin{array}{r} 2 \\ +\ 7 \\ \hline \end{array}$	**27.** $\begin{array}{r} 3 \\ +\ 4 \\ \hline \end{array}$	**28.** $\begin{array}{r} 4 \\ +\ 4 \\ \hline \end{array}$

Subtract.

1. $\begin{array}{r} 8 \\ -\ 5 \\ \hline \end{array}$	**2.** $\begin{array}{r} 8 \\ -\ 4 \\ \hline \end{array}$	**3.** $\begin{array}{r} 10 \\ -\ 3 \\ \hline \end{array}$	**4.** $\begin{array}{r} 3 \\ -\ 1 \\ \hline \end{array}$	**5.** $\begin{array}{r} 7 \\ -\ 6 \\ \hline \end{array}$	**6.** $\begin{array}{r} 5 \\ -\ 1 \\ \hline \end{array}$	**7.** $\begin{array}{r} 10 \\ -\ 4 \\ \hline \end{array}$
8. $\begin{array}{r} 7 \\ -\ 3 \\ \hline \end{array}$	**9.** $\begin{array}{r} 8 \\ -\ 6 \\ \hline \end{array}$	**10.** $\begin{array}{r} 5 \\ -\ 2 \\ \hline \end{array}$	**11.** $\begin{array}{r} 9 \\ -\ 4 \\ \hline \end{array}$	**12.** $\begin{array}{r} 4 \\ -\ 4 \\ \hline \end{array}$	**13.** $\begin{array}{r} 9 \\ -\ 6 \\ \hline \end{array}$	**14.** $\begin{array}{r} 6 \\ -\ 2 \\ \hline \end{array}$
15. $\begin{array}{r} 9 \\ -\ 3 \\ \hline \end{array}$	**16.** $\begin{array}{r} 7 \\ -\ 4 \\ \hline \end{array}$	**17.** $\begin{array}{r} 10 \\ -\ 8 \\ \hline \end{array}$	**18.** $\begin{array}{r} 6 \\ -\ 1 \\ \hline \end{array}$	**19.** $\begin{array}{r} 8 \\ -\ 7 \\ \hline \end{array}$	**20.** $\begin{array}{r} 10 \\ -\ 5 \\ \hline \end{array}$	**21.** $\begin{array}{r} 7 \\ -\ 5 \\ \hline \end{array}$
22. $\begin{array}{r} 10 \\ -\ 2 \\ \hline \end{array}$	**23.** $\begin{array}{r} 9 \\ -\ 8 \\ \hline \end{array}$	**24.** $\begin{array}{r} 5 \\ -\ 0 \\ \hline \end{array}$	**25.** $\begin{array}{r} 8 \\ -\ 2 \\ \hline \end{array}$	**26.** $\begin{array}{r} 9 \\ -\ 0 \\ \hline \end{array}$	**27.** $\begin{array}{r} 8 \\ -\ 1 \\ \hline \end{array}$	**28.** $\begin{array}{r} 9 \\ -\ 2 \\ \hline \end{array}$

Add.

1. $\begin{array}{r} 7 \\ +\ 4 \\ \hline \end{array}$	**2.** $\begin{array}{r} 8 \\ +\ 7 \\ \hline \end{array}$	**3.** $\begin{array}{r} 5 \\ +\ 9 \\ \hline \end{array}$	**4.** $\begin{array}{r} 9 \\ +\ 8 \\ \hline \end{array}$	**5.** $\begin{array}{r} 8 \\ +\ 5 \\ \hline \end{array}$	**6.** $\begin{array}{r} 4 \\ +\ 7 \\ \hline \end{array}$	**7.** $\begin{array}{r} 9 \\ +\ 9 \\ \hline \end{array}$
8. $\begin{array}{r} 7 \\ +\ 6 \\ \hline \end{array}$	**9.** $\begin{array}{r} 8 \\ +\ 3 \\ \hline \end{array}$	**10.** $\begin{array}{r} 5 \\ +\ 7 \\ \hline \end{array}$	**11.** $\begin{array}{r} 6 \\ +\ 8 \\ \hline \end{array}$	**12.** $\begin{array}{r} 4 \\ +\ 9 \\ \hline \end{array}$	**13.** $\begin{array}{r} 7 \\ +\ 5 \\ \hline \end{array}$	**14.** $\begin{array}{r} 3 \\ +\ 9 \\ \hline \end{array}$
15. $\begin{array}{r} 8 \\ +\ 9 \\ \hline \end{array}$	**16.** $\begin{array}{r} 6 \\ +\ 6 \\ \hline \end{array}$	**17.** $\begin{array}{r} 9 \\ +\ 4 \\ \hline \end{array}$	**18.** $\begin{array}{r} 7 \\ +\ 8 \\ \hline \end{array}$	**19.** $\begin{array}{r} 2 \\ +\ 9 \\ \hline \end{array}$	**20.** $\begin{array}{r} 5 \\ +\ 8 \\ \hline \end{array}$	**21.** $\begin{array}{r} 9 \\ +\ 7 \\ \hline \end{array}$
22. $\begin{array}{r} 6 \\ +\ 5 \\ \hline \end{array}$	**23.** $\begin{array}{r} 7 \\ +\ 7 \\ \hline \end{array}$	**24.** $\begin{array}{r} 9 \\ +\ 2 \\ \hline \end{array}$	**25.** $\begin{array}{r} 8 \\ +\ 8 \\ \hline \end{array}$	**26.** $\begin{array}{r} 9 \\ +\ 5 \\ \hline \end{array}$	**27.** $\begin{array}{r} 7 \\ +\ 9 \\ \hline \end{array}$	**28.** $\begin{array}{r} 4 \\ +\ 8 \\ \hline \end{array}$

Subtract.

1. $\begin{array}{r} 12 \\ -\ 9 \\ \hline \end{array}$	**2.** $\begin{array}{r} 14 \\ -\ 8 \\ \hline \end{array}$	**3.** $\begin{array}{r} 12 \\ -\ 7 \\ \hline \end{array}$	**4.** $\begin{array}{r} 11 \\ -\ 6 \\ \hline \end{array}$	**5.** $\begin{array}{r} 15 \\ -\ 9 \\ \hline \end{array}$	**6.** $\begin{array}{r} 12 \\ -\ 3 \\ \hline \end{array}$	**7.** $\begin{array}{r} 17 \\ -\ 9 \\ \hline \end{array}$
8. $\begin{array}{r} 16 \\ -\ 9 \\ \hline \end{array}$	**9.** $\begin{array}{r} 14 \\ -\ 6 \\ \hline \end{array}$	**10.** $\begin{array}{r} 12 \\ -\ 5 \\ \hline \end{array}$	**11.** $\begin{array}{r} 16 \\ -\ 8 \\ \hline \end{array}$	**12.** $\begin{array}{r} 13 \\ -\ 5 \\ \hline \end{array}$	**13.** $\begin{array}{r} 13 \\ -\ 4 \\ \hline \end{array}$	**14.** $\begin{array}{r} 11 \\ -\ 7 \\ \hline \end{array}$
15. $\begin{array}{r} 13 \\ -\ 8 \\ \hline \end{array}$	**16.** $\begin{array}{r} 14 \\ -\ 9 \\ \hline \end{array}$	**17.** $\begin{array}{r} 17 \\ -\ 8 \\ \hline \end{array}$	**18.** $\begin{array}{r} 11 \\ -\ 3 \\ \hline \end{array}$	**19.** $\begin{array}{r} 14 \\ -\ 7 \\ \hline \end{array}$	**20.** $\begin{array}{r} 14 \\ -\ 5 \\ \hline \end{array}$	**21.** $\begin{array}{r} 13 \\ -\ 7 \\ \hline \end{array}$
22. $\begin{array}{r} 11 \\ -\ 2 \\ \hline \end{array}$	**23.** $\begin{array}{r} 12 \\ -\ 8 \\ \hline \end{array}$	**24.** $\begin{array}{r} 13 \\ -\ 9 \\ \hline \end{array}$	**25.** $\begin{array}{r} 13 \\ -\ 6 \\ \hline \end{array}$	**26.** $\begin{array}{r} 11 \\ -\ 5 \\ \hline \end{array}$	**27.** $\begin{array}{r} 11 \\ -\ 9 \\ \hline \end{array}$	**28.** $\begin{array}{r} 16 \\ -\ 7 \\ \hline \end{array}$

Add.

1.	2	2.	4	3.	8	4.	3	5.	6	6.	7	7.	2
	4		2		2		1		1		1		5
	+ 5		+ 3		+ 5		+ 6		+ 2		+ 6		+ 3

8.	5	9.	4	10.	5	11.	3	12.	1	13.	3	14.	4
	3		1		4		3		5		5		1
	+ 6		+ 5		+ 6		+ 4		+ 2		+ 3		+ 7

Set B   **For use after page 31**

Give the number that comes after.

1. 108   2. 60   3. 111   4. 69   5. 18   6. 633

Give the number that comes before.

7. 181   8. 222   9. 100   10. 812   11. 600   12. 88

Give the number that is between.

13. 543 and 545   14. 229 and 231   15. 699 and 701

Set C   **For use after page 32**

Count by twos. Give the next four numbers.

1. 10, 12, 14, 16, ▥, ▥, ▥, ▥   2. 25, 27, 29, 31, ▥, ▥, ▥, ▥

Count by fives. Give the next four numbers.

3. 20, 25, 30, 35, ▥, ▥, ▥, ▥   4. 110, 115, 120, 125, ▥, ▥, ▥, ▥

Count by tens. Give the next four numbers.

5. 120, 130, 140, ▥, ▥, ▥, ▥   6. 340, 350, 360, ▥, ▥, ▥, ▥

Set A **For use after page 37**

Write each amount.

1. 4 dollars, 3 dimes

2. 6 dollars, 2 dimes, 2 pennies

3. 8 dollars

4. 9 dollars and 56 cents

5. 2 dollars, 1 dime, 3 pennies

6. 7 dollars and 98 cents

7. 5 dollars, 5 dimes

8. 3 dollars and 4 cents

Set B **For use after page 39**

Round to the nearest ten.

1. $24 \rightarrow$ ▓

2. $37 \rightarrow$ ▓

3. $83 \rightarrow$ ▓

4. $64 \rightarrow$ ▓

5. $17 \rightarrow$ ▓

6. $35 \rightarrow$ ▓

7. $89 \rightarrow$ ▓

8. $42 \rightarrow$ ▓

9. $14 \rightarrow$ ▓

10. $84 \rightarrow$ ▓

11. $57 \rightarrow$ ▓

12. $62 \rightarrow$ ▓

Set C **For use after page 41**

Round to the nearest hundred.

1. $538 \rightarrow$ ▓

2. $281 \rightarrow$ ▓

3. $108 \rightarrow$ ▓

4. $152 \rightarrow$ ▓

5. $198 \rightarrow$ ▓

6. $663 \rightarrow$ ▓

7. $948 \rightarrow$ ▓

8. $328 \rightarrow$ ▓

Round to the nearest dollar.

9. $\$3.48 \rightarrow$ ▓

10. $\$8.88 \rightarrow$ ▓

11. $\$7.23 \rightarrow$ ▓

12. $\$8.69 \rightarrow$ ▓

13. $\$8.05 \rightarrow$ ▓

14. $\$7.53 \rightarrow$ ▓

15. $\$6.85 \rightarrow$ ▓

16. $\$8.91 \rightarrow$ ▓

Write > or < for each 💠 .

1. 90 💠 60   2. 200 💠 400   3. 1,000 💠 6,000

4. 28 💠 30   5. 847 💠 837   6. 8,064 💠 8,062

7. 40 💠 60   8. 265 💠 295   9. 5,232 💠 5,832

Set B   **For use after page 47**

Write the number. Use a comma to separate thousands.

1. twenty-six thousand

2. nine hundred twenty-seven thousand

3. eighty-one thousand, two hundred twenty-six

4. thirty-three thousand, eight hundred eight

Set C   **For use after page 61**

Find the sums.

1. 12 + 29	2. 37 + 43	3. 12 + 27	4. 80 + 16	5. 58 + 24	6. 44 + 29
7. 15 + 25	8. 34 + 27	9. 55 + 12	10. 26 + 57	11. 49 + 49	12. 36 + 9
13. 75 + 19	14. 22 + 48	15. 13 + 43	16. 2 + 69	17. 12 + 46	18. 46 + 17

Set A   **For use after page 63**

Find the sums.

1. 49 + 61	2. 84 + 62	3. 98 + 17	4. 63 + 27	5. 88 + 28	6. 37 + 75
7. 85 + 79	8. 58 + 83	9. 27 + 95	10. 66 + 67	11. 80 + 52	12. 45 + 39
13. 66 + 89	14. 73 + 41	15. 36 + 96	16. 87 + 43	17. 22 + 98	18. 48 + 73
19. 33 + 73	20. 85 + 65	21. 20 + 68	22. 27 + 96	23. 77 + 75	24. 82 + 91

Set B   **For use after page 67**

Find the sums.

1. 648 + 104	2. 291 + 464	3. 260 + 917	4. 418 + 750	5. 386 + 452	6. 605 + 327
7. 123 + 94	8. 685 + 812	9. 228 + 517	10. 625 + 962	11. 38 + 180	12. 285 + 483
13. 329 + 480	14. 605 + 821	15. 243 + 747	16. 802 + 993	17. 208 + 67	18. 473 + 518
19. 230 + 589	20. 266 + 451	21. 805 + 621	22. 632 + 241	23. 200 + 947	24. 628 + 54

Set A   **For use after page 69**

Find the sums.

1. 652
   + 189

2. 805
   + 929

3. 472
   + 687

4. 226
   + 98

5. 753
   + 685

6. 764
   + 187

7. 375
   + 687

8. 457
   + 382

9. 607
   + 798

10. 263
    + 88

11. 486
    + 978

12. 362
    + 805

13. 288
    + 554

14. 702
    + 859

15. 729
    + 928

16. 447
    + 285

17. 221
    + 918

18. 605
    + 98

19. 685
    + 873

20. 843
    + 97

21. 782
    + 507

22. 485
    + 608

23. 212
    + 484

24. 375
    + 829

Set B   **For use after page 70**

Add.

1. $3.46
   + 0.75

2. $2.57
   + 8.26

3. $5.04
   + 2.57

4. $9.52
   + 3.75

5. $7.39
   + 2.26

6. $0.87
   + 3.34

7. $6.20
   + 8.99

8. $4.65
   + 6.35

9. $8.16
   + 0.55

10. $1.32
    + 7.87

11. $9.05
    + 0.36

12. $5.25
    + 3.83

13. $2.17
    + 6.84

14. $3.42
    + 2.95

15. $8.20
    + 0.98

16. $5.56
    + 8.67

17. $2.65
    + 4.92

18. $3.12
    + 0.94

19. $4.85
    + 2.62

20. $2.82
    + 8.54

Find the sums. Write answers only.

1. 60 + 80   2. 70 + 30   3. 90 + 40   4. 30 + 30

5. 900 + 200   6. 500 + 400   7. 300 + 500   8. 900 + 800

9.   20   10.   70   11.   60   12.   80   13.   90   14.   20
    + 80   + 70   + 30   + 50   + 10   + 50

15.   500   16.   400   17.   800   18.   600   19.   100   20.   700
    + 800   + 300   + 200   + 600   + 500   + 800

21.   200   22.   300   23.   200   24.   700   25.   600   26.   800
    + 500   + 800   + 200   + 500   + 800   + 100

Estimate by rounding to the nearest ten.

1.   32   2.   86   3.   25   4.   66   5.   82
   + 49   + 43   + 28   + 47   + 34

Estimate by rounding to the nearest hundred.

6.   480   7.   638   8.   476   9.   880
   + 520   + 402   + 154   + 321

Estimate by rounding to the nearest dollar.

10. $6.11   11. $4.00   12. $2.95
   + 4.95   + 9.00   + 6.12

Find the sums.

1.	23 46 + 17	**2.**	28 42 + 23	**3.**	66 43 + 40	**4.**	57 83 + 8	**5.**	16 74 + 37	**6.**	53 4 + 69
7.	25 43 18 + 77	**8.**	45 62 19 + 33	**9.**	28 48 31 + 84	**10.**	54 29 71 + 15	**11.**	62 85 47 + 41	**12.**	35 49 20 + 74
13.	315 416 + 207	**14.**	151 74 + 607	**15.**	423 185 + 359	**16.**	512 372 + 429	**17.**	114 183 + 620	**18.**	641 88 + 745

Find the sums.

1.	3,059 + 2,717	**2.**	2,964 + 5,682	**3.**	1,429 + 6,507	**4.**	6,781 + 2,657	**5.**	4,812 + 3,968
6.	7,811 + 1,829	**7.**	1,854 + 643	**8.**	5,584 + 3,145	**9.**	3,808 + 6,137	**10.**	4,125 + 4,992
11.	6,815 + 2,376	**12.**	2,964 + 3,071	**13.**	4,615 + 4,607	**14.**	2,976 + 4,192	**15.**	3,804 + 1,562
16.	1,247 + 5,086	**17.**	3,358 + 3,692	**18.**	4,532 + 1,607	**19.**	7,729 + 1,805	**20.**	3,643 + 5,818

Set A   For use after page 93

Find the differences.

1. 64 − 27	**2.** 81 − 14	**3.** 66 − 59	**4.** 44 − 23	**5.** 30 − 19	**6.** 64 − 38
7. 85 − 37	**8.** 42 − 8	**9.** 61 − 54	**10.** 99 − 66	**11.** 34 − 18	**12.** 50 − 36
13. 62 − 48	**14.** 45 − 19	**15.** 63 − 58	**16.** 44 − 27	**17.** 39 − 25	**18.** 82 − 46
19. 65 − 29	**20.** 45 − 6	**21.** 34 − 17	**22.** 68 − 34	**23.** 73 − 15	**24.** 67 − 48

Set B   For use after page 97

Find the differences.

1. 408 − 297	**2.** 364 − 182	**3.** 512 − 190	**4.** 648 − 294	**5.** 355 − 72	**6.** 411 − 270
7. 353 − 181	**8.** 859 − 284	**9.** 314 − 181	**10.** 487 − 391	**11.** 405 − 124	**12.** 687 − 196
13. 559 − 167	**14.** 348 − 295	**15.** 442 − 180	**16.** 312 − 91	**17.** 559 − 168	**18.** 607 − 234
19. 344 − 161	**20.** 581 − 390	**21.** 650 − 460	**22.** 327 − 84	**23.** 659 − 167	**24.** 526 − 375

Set A   For use after page 99

Find the differences.

1. $423 - 187$	**2.** $154 - 89$	**3.** $865 - 467$	**4.** $312 - 140$	**5.** $568 - 179$	**6.** $205 - 97$
7. $439 - 281$	**8.** $644 - 356$	**9.** $212 - 144$	**10.** $761 - 395$	**11.** $366 - 287$	**12.** $391 - 105$
13. $604 - 196$	**14.** $227 - 154$	**15.** $364 - 185$	**16.** $228 - 149$	**17.** $361 - 184$	**18.** $641 - 397$
19. $322 - 195$	**20.** $612 - 184$	**21.** $351 - 267$	**22.** $885 - 693$	**23.** $904 - 689$	**24.** $326 - 148$

Set B   For use after page 105

Find the differences.

1. $307 - 158$	**2.** $511 - 299$	**3.** $305 - 166$	**4.** $200 - 96$	**5.** $405 - 168$	**6.** $508 - 145$
7. $805 - 467$	**8.** $500 - 186$	**9.** $805 - 298$	**10.** $601 - 486$	**11.** $305 - 297$	**12.** $400 - 161$
13. $201 - 84$	**14.** $308 - 169$	**15.** $702 - 246$	**16.** $805 - 361$	**17.** $100 - 67$	**18.** $203 - 186$
19. $208 - 159$	**20.** $804 - 366$	**21.** $201 - 89$	**22.** $607 - 358$	**23.** $405 - 269$	**24.** $307 - 148$

Find the differences in the amounts.

1. $7.00 − 0.98	**2.** $8.25 − 4.00	**3.** $4.00 − 1.98	**4.** $7.50 − 0.75	**5.** $6.95 − 4.50
6. $3.25 − 1.40	**7.** $8.00 − 0.79	**8.** $2.50 − 0.75	**9.** $6.65 − 4.80	**10.** $9.00 − 7.25
11. $6.00 − 5.25	**12.** $4.00 − 1.98	**13.** $6.25 − 2.75	**14.** $4.50 − 1.75	**15.** $6.60 − 1.75
16. $8.25 − 1.50	**17.** $9.75 − 4.25	**18.** $8.35 − 4.50	**19.** $7.25 − 3.98	**20.** $6.75 − 3.00

Find the differences. Write answers only.

1. $60 − 40$ **2.** $800 − 300$ **3.** $40 − 10$ **4.** $1,300 − 600$

5. $1,800 − 900$ **6.** $90 − 70$ **7.** $600 − 500$ **8.** $130 − 80$

9. 1,000 − 300	**10.** 170 − 60	**11.** 300 − 100	**12.** 1,300 − 800	**13.** 80 − 70	**14.** 600 − 100
15. 1,400 − 600	**16.** 50 − 10	**17.** 600 − 300	**18.** 90 − 20	**19.** 400 − 300	**20.** 1,200 − 800
21. 1,100 − 100	**22.** 180 − 90	**23.** 600 − 400	**24.** 120 − 70	**25.** 1,000 − 200	**26.** 150 − 70

Estimate by rounding to the nearest ten.

1.   36
    − 19

2.   84
    − 26

3.   22
    − 14

4.   69
    − 28

5.   42
    − 33

Estimate by rounding to the nearest hundred.

6.   418
    − 297

7.   630
    − 149

8.   850
    − 429

9.   645
    − 168

Estimate by rounding to the nearest dollar.

10. $6.84
    − 3.20

11. $5.50
    − 3.50

12. $8.71
    − 2.56

13. $6.89
    − 1.35

Find the differences.

1.   4,077
    − 2,165

2.   9,624
    − 4,312

3.   1,026
    − 647

4.   3,855
    − 1,862

5.   6,338
    − 4,290

6.   7,529
    − 6,188

7.   4,036
    − 2,154

8.   3,624
    − 1,518

9.   9,165
    − 2,618

10. 3,277
    − 1,484

11. 8,826
    − 5,471

12. 3,061
    − 1,890

13. 6,429
    − 5,161

14. 2,436
    − 1,085

15. 6,009
    − 2,324

16. 6,514
    − 91

17. 7,268
    − 4,517

18. 3,664
    − 836

19. 9,258
    − 5,064

20. 7,228
    − 1,416

Multiply.

1. 2
×6

2. 2
×4

3. 2
×7

4. 2
×3

5. 2
×5

6. 2
×2

7. 2
×8

8. 2
×9

9. 2
×6

10. 2
×2

11. 2
×4

12. 2
×8

13. 2
×5

14. 2
×9

15. 2
×3

16. 2
×7

17. 2
×4

18. 2
×9

19. 2
×6

20. 2
×3

21. 2
×5

Set B **For use after page 161**

Multiply.

1. 3
×5

2. 3
×3

3. 2
×5

4. 3
×6

5. 3
×2

6. 3
×7

7. 3
×4

8. 3
×9

9. 3
×6

10. 3
×4

11. 3
×7

12. 3
×8

13. 3
×7

14. 3
×5

Set C **For use after page 165**

Multiply.

1. 4
×7

2. 4
×4

3. 4
×9

4. 4
×5

5. 2
×7

6. 4
×2

7. 4
×8

8. 3
×4

9. 4
×6

10. 2
×9

11. 4
×3

12. 3
×5

13. 4
×7

14. 4
×5

Set A   For use after page 167

Multiply.

1. $\begin{array}{r} 5 \\ \times\,2 \\ \hline \end{array}$	2. $\begin{array}{r} 5 \\ \times\,5 \\ \hline \end{array}$	3. $\begin{array}{r} 4 \\ \times\,6 \\ \hline \end{array}$	4. $\begin{array}{r} 5 \\ \times\,6 \\ \hline \end{array}$	5. $\begin{array}{r} 5 \\ \times\,8 \\ \hline \end{array}$	6. $\begin{array}{r} 4 \\ \times\,4 \\ \hline \end{array}$	7. $\begin{array}{r} 3 \\ \times\,5 \\ \hline \end{array}$
8. $\begin{array}{r} 5 \\ \times\,9 \\ \hline \end{array}$	9. $\begin{array}{r} 5 \\ \times\,4 \\ \hline \end{array}$	10. $\begin{array}{r} 3 \\ \times\,3 \\ \hline \end{array}$	11. $\begin{array}{r} 5 \\ \times\,3 \\ \hline \end{array}$	12. $\begin{array}{r} 4 \\ \times\,5 \\ \hline \end{array}$	13. $\begin{array}{r} 3 \\ \times\,9 \\ \hline \end{array}$	14. $\begin{array}{r} 5 \\ \times\,7 \\ \hline \end{array}$
15. $\begin{array}{r} 5 \\ \times\,6 \\ \hline \end{array}$	16. $\begin{array}{r} 2 \\ \times\,5 \\ \hline \end{array}$	17. $\begin{array}{r} 3 \\ \times\,8 \\ \hline \end{array}$	18. $\begin{array}{r} 4 \\ \times\,6 \\ \hline \end{array}$	19. $\begin{array}{r} 5 \\ \times\,7 \\ \hline \end{array}$	20. $\begin{array}{r} 5 \\ \times\,4 \\ \hline \end{array}$	21. $\begin{array}{r} 2 \\ \times\,6 \\ \hline \end{array}$

Set B   For use after page 170

Multiply.

1. $\begin{array}{r} 1 \\ \times\,7 \\ \hline \end{array}$	2. $\begin{array}{r} 0 \\ \times\,1 \\ \hline \end{array}$	3. $\begin{array}{r} 1 \\ \times\,0 \\ \hline \end{array}$	4. $\begin{array}{r} 0 \\ \times\,4 \\ \hline \end{array}$	5. $\begin{array}{r} 1 \\ \times\,3 \\ \hline \end{array}$	6. $\begin{array}{r} 0 \\ \times\,9 \\ \hline \end{array}$	7. $\begin{array}{r} 1 \\ \times\,9 \\ \hline \end{array}$
8. $\begin{array}{r} 1 \\ \times\,8 \\ \hline \end{array}$	9. $\begin{array}{r} 0 \\ \times\,8 \\ \hline \end{array}$	10. $\begin{array}{r} 1 \\ \times\,6 \\ \hline \end{array}$	11. $\begin{array}{r} 0 \\ \times\,2 \\ \hline \end{array}$	12. $\begin{array}{r} 1 \\ \times\,4 \\ \hline \end{array}$	13. $\begin{array}{r} 0 \\ \times\,5 \\ \hline \end{array}$	14. $\begin{array}{r} 0 \\ \times\,6 \\ \hline \end{array}$

Set C   For use after page 183

Multiply.

1. $\begin{array}{r} 6 \\ \times\,5 \\ \hline \end{array}$	2. $\begin{array}{r} 2 \\ \times\,8 \\ \hline \end{array}$	3. $\begin{array}{r} 6 \\ \times\,7 \\ \hline \end{array}$	4. $\begin{array}{r} 5 \\ \times\,7 \\ \hline \end{array}$	5. $\begin{array}{r} 4 \\ \times\,6 \\ \hline \end{array}$	6. $\begin{array}{r} 6 \\ \times\,2 \\ \hline \end{array}$	7. $\begin{array}{r} 6 \\ \times\,0 \\ \hline \end{array}$
8. $\begin{array}{r} 4 \\ \times\,5 \\ \hline \end{array}$	9. $\begin{array}{r} 6 \\ \times\,1 \\ \hline \end{array}$	10. $\begin{array}{r} 1 \\ \times\,5 \\ \hline \end{array}$	11. $\begin{array}{r} 6 \\ \times\,9 \\ \hline \end{array}$	12. $\begin{array}{r} 3 \\ \times\,6 \\ \hline \end{array}$	13. $\begin{array}{r} 6 \\ \times\,6 \\ \hline \end{array}$	14. $\begin{array}{r} 5 \\ \times\,6 \\ \hline \end{array}$

Set A   **For use after page 185**

Multiply.

1. $\begin{array}{r} 7 \\ \times\ 5 \\ \hline \end{array}$	2. $\begin{array}{r} 6 \\ \times\ 9 \\ \hline \end{array}$	3. $\begin{array}{r} 7 \\ \times\ 7 \\ \hline \end{array}$	4. $\begin{array}{r} 2 \\ \times\ 7 \\ \hline \end{array}$	5. $\begin{array}{r} 3 \\ \times\ 3 \\ \hline \end{array}$	6. $\begin{array}{r} 7 \\ \times\ 1 \\ \hline \end{array}$	7. $\begin{array}{r} 4 \\ \times\ 7 \\ \hline \end{array}$

8. $\begin{array}{r} 7 \\ \times\ 3 \\ \hline \end{array}$	9. $\begin{array}{r} 3 \\ \times\ 7 \\ \hline \end{array}$	10. $\begin{array}{r} 6 \\ \times\ 5 \\ \hline \end{array}$	11. $\begin{array}{r} 0 \\ \times\ 7 \\ \hline \end{array}$	12. $\begin{array}{r} 1 \\ \times\ 4 \\ \hline \end{array}$	13. $\begin{array}{r} 7 \\ \times\ 6 \\ \hline \end{array}$	14. $\begin{array}{r} 3 \\ \times\ 6 \\ \hline \end{array}$

Set B   **For use after page 187**

Multiply.

1. $\begin{array}{r} 9 \\ \times\ 9 \\ \hline \end{array}$	2. $\begin{array}{r} 8 \\ \times\ 5 \\ \hline \end{array}$	3. $\begin{array}{r} 9 \\ \times\ 6 \\ \hline \end{array}$	4. $\begin{array}{r} 5 \\ \times\ 7 \\ \hline \end{array}$	5. $\begin{array}{r} 9 \\ \times\ 2 \\ \hline \end{array}$	6. $\begin{array}{r} 4 \\ \times\ 8 \\ \hline \end{array}$	7. $\begin{array}{r} 5 \\ \times\ 9 \\ \hline \end{array}$

8. $\begin{array}{r} 4 \\ \times\ 7 \\ \hline \end{array}$	9. $\begin{array}{r} 3 \\ \times\ 9 \\ \hline \end{array}$	10. $\begin{array}{r} 6 \\ \times\ 8 \\ \hline \end{array}$	11. $\begin{array}{r} 2 \\ \times\ 8 \\ \hline \end{array}$	12. $\begin{array}{r} 6 \\ \times\ 4 \\ \hline \end{array}$	13. $\begin{array}{r} 8 \\ \times\ 7 \\ \hline \end{array}$	14. $\begin{array}{r} 9 \\ \times\ 8 \\ \hline \end{array}$

Set C   **For use after page 190**

Use the grouping shown. Find the products.

1. $(3 \times 1) \times 5 =$ ____   2. $(2 \times 3) \times 3 =$ ____   3. $2 \times (1 \times 4) =$ ____

4. $5 \times (2 \times 3) =$ ____   5. $4 \times (2 \times 4) =$ ____   6. $5 \times (4 \times 2) =$ ____

Use any grouping you want. Find the products.

7. $7 \times 1 \times 5 =$ ____   8. $8 \times 0 \times 6 =$ ____   9. $4 \times 2 \times 2 =$ ____

10. $3 \times 2 \times 4 =$ ____   11. $5 \times 1 \times 9 =$ ____   12. $3 \times 3 \times 2 =$ ____

Set A   For use after page 191

Find these factors.

1. $6 \times \square = 42$ 2. $\square \times 2 = 16$ 3. $7 \times \square = 56$ 4. $\square \times 7 = 63$

5. $9 \times \square = 45$ 6. $\square \times 8 = 64$ 7. $4 \times \square = 16$ 8. $\square \times 9 = 36$

9. $8 \times \square = 72$ 10. $\square \times 7 = 21$ 11. $8 \times \square = 32$ 12. $2 \times \square = 18$

13. $\square \times 8 = 48$ 14. $6 \times \square = 54$ 15. $\square \times 9 = 81$ 16. $3 \times \square = 21$

Set B   For use after page 231

Divide.

1. $12 \div 3 =$ 2. $10 \div 2 =$ 3. $6 \div 3 =$ 4. $14 \div 2 =$

5. $16 \div 2 =$ 6. $6 \div 2 =$ 7. $18 \div 3 =$ 8. $6 \div 2 =$

9. $27 \div 3 =$ 10. $2 \div 2 =$ 11. $18 \div 2 =$ 12. $9 \div 3 =$

13. $8 \div 2 =$ 14. $6 \div 3 =$ 15. $24 \div 3 =$ 16. $12 \div 2 =$

17. $15 \div 3 =$ 18. $3 \div 3 =$ 19. $18 \div 2 =$ 20. $21 \div 3 =$

Set C   For use after page 235

Divide.

1. $16 \div 4 =$ 2. $6 \div 3 =$ 3. $32 \div 4 =$ 4. $12 \div 4 =$

5. $18 \div 2 =$ 6. $4 \div 4 =$ 7. $14 \div 2 =$ 8. $24 \div 3 =$

9. $8 \div 2 =$ 10. $28 \div 4 =$ 11. $18 \div 3 =$ 12. $20 \div 4 =$

13. $24 \div 4 =$ 14. $15 \div 3 =$ 15. $8 \div 4 =$ 16. $36 \div 4 =$

17. $12 \div 3 =$ 18. $6 \div 2 =$ 19. $21 \div 3 =$ 20. $4 \div 2 =$

Set A   For use after page 237

Divide.

1. $15 \div 5 =$ 	2. $35 \div 5 =$ 	3. $16 \div 4 =$ 	4. $20 \div 5 =$

5. $45 \div 5 =$ 	6. $9 \div 3 =$ 	7. $5 \div 5 =$ 	8. $8 \div 2 =$

9. $27 \div 3 =$ 	10. $10 \div 2 =$ 	11. $30 \div 5 =$ 	12. $36 \div 4 =$

13. $10 \div 5 =$ 	14. $40 \div 5 =$ 	15. $20 \div 4 =$ 	16. $25 \div 5 =$

17. $12 \div 4 =$ 	18. $16 \div 2 =$ 	19. $18 \div 3 =$ 	20. $32 \div 4 =$

Set B   For use after page 251

Divide.

1. $6\overline{)12}$ 	2. $4\overline{)20}$ 	3. $6\overline{)54}$ 	4. $6\overline{)36}$ 	5. $3\overline{)18}$

6. $2\overline{)18}$ 	7. $6\overline{)42}$ 	8. $6\overline{)6}$ 	9. $2\overline{)16}$ 	10. $3\overline{)21}$

11. $5\overline{)25}$ 	12. $3\overline{)6}$ 	13. $3\overline{)27}$ 	14. $4\overline{)24}$ 	15. $6\overline{)24}$

16. $6\overline{)18}$ 	17. $5\overline{)30}$ 	18. $4\overline{)16}$ 	19. $6\overline{)30}$ 	20. $7\overline{)56}$

Set C   For use after page 253

Divide.

1. $7\overline{)28}$ 	2. $2\overline{)10}$ 	3. $7\overline{)49}$ 	4. $3\overline{)6}$ 	5. $7\overline{)63}$

6. $5\overline{)40}$ 	7. $7\overline{)7}$ 	8. $6\overline{)42}$ 	9. $7\overline{)21}$ 	10. $7\overline{)42}$

11. $5\overline{)30}$ 	12. $3\overline{)21}$ 	13. $7\overline{)14}$ 	14. $3\overline{)27}$ 	15. $7\overline{)21}$

16. $7\overline{)35}$ 	17. $6\overline{)24}$ 	18. $7\overline{)56}$ 	19. $4\overline{)36}$ 	20. $5\overline{)35}$

Divide.

1. $8\overline{)24}$ 2. $4\overline{)32}$ 3. $8\overline{)72}$ 4. $8\overline{)8}$ 5. $7\overline{)49}$

6. $6\overline{)36}$ 7. $8\overline{)56}$ 8. $3\overline{)21}$ 9. $6\overline{)12}$ 10. $8\overline{)40}$

11. $8\overline{)16}$ 12. $5\overline{)40}$ 13. $8\overline{)64}$ 14. $7\overline{)28}$ 15. $3\overline{)24}$

16. $5\overline{)35}$ 17. $8\overline{)32}$ 18. $7\overline{)49}$ 19. $5\overline{)45}$ 20. $8\overline{)48}$

21. $8\overline{)48}$ 22. $7\overline{)63}$ 23. $8\overline{)16}$ 24. $5\overline{)45}$ 25. $8\overline{)40}$

26. $3\overline{)24}$ 27. $8\overline{)56}$ 28. $4\overline{)36}$ 29. $6\overline{)18}$ 30. $8\overline{)72}$

31. $6\overline{)42}$ 32. $6\overline{)18}$ 33. $2\overline{)12}$ 34. $6\overline{)6}$ 35. $3\overline{)27}$

Divide.

1. $9\overline{)18}$ 2. $9\overline{)81}$ 3. $3\overline{)24}$ 4. $9\overline{)54}$ 5. $4\overline{)36}$

6. $8\overline{)72}$ 7. $9\overline{)27}$ 8. $4\overline{)20}$ 9. $5\overline{)30}$ 10. $9\overline{)72}$

11. $6\overline{)36}$ 12. $7\overline{)56}$ 13. $9\overline{)45}$ 14. $9\overline{)9}$ 15. $2\overline{)18}$

16. $9\overline{)36}$ 17. $3\overline{)18}$ 18. $8\overline{)24}$ 19. $9\overline{)63}$ 20. $6\overline{)54}$

21. $9\overline{)63}$ 22. $3\overline{)12}$ 23. $9\overline{)18}$ 24. $3\overline{)27}$ 25. $9\overline{)45}$

26. $5\overline{)45}$ 27. $9\overline{)9}$ 28. $4\overline{)24}$ 29. $9\overline{)72}$ 30. $5\overline{)40}$

31. $8\overline{)8}$ 32. $7\overline{)21}$ 33. $6\overline{)42}$ 34. $3\overline{)15}$ 35. $2\overline{)16}$

36. $8\overline{)48}$ 37. $6\overline{)24}$ 38. $5\overline{)25}$ 39. $7\overline{)63}$ 40. $4\overline{)16}$

Set A   For use after page 277

Find the products.

1. 14
    × 5

2. 32
    × 3

3. 25
    × 3

4. 18
    × 5

5. 14
    × 2

6. 12
    × 7

7. 46
    × 2

8. 24
    × 3

9. 12
    × 8

10. 14
    × 4

11. 17
    × 5

12. 21
    × 4

Set B   For use after page 279

Find the products.

1. 42
    × 4

2. 34
    × 5

3. 61
    × 3

4. 12
    × 9

5. 44
    × 6

6. 38
    × 3

7. 22
    × 3

8. 17
    × 8

9. 44
    × 5

10. 39
    × 2

11. 63
    × 3

12. 24
    × 4

Set C   For use after page 281

Write the amounts with dollars and cents.

1. 48¢
    × 3

2. 65¢
    × 4

3. 36¢
    × 7

4. 87¢
    × 5

5. 22¢
    × 8

6. 39¢
    × 5

7. 18¢
    × 8

8. 62¢
    × 4

9. 33¢
    × 6

10. 25¢
    × 2

11. 36¢
    × 3

12. 42¢
    × 8

13. 63¢
    × 3

14. 24¢
    × 9

15. 35¢
    × 4

Divide. Find the quotients and remainders.

1. $3\overline{)5}$ 2. $2\overline{)9}$ 3. $3\overline{)6}$ 4. $5\overline{)5}$ 5. $4\overline{)0}$

6. $4\overline{)3}$ 7. $4\overline{)9}$ 8. $3\overline{)7}$ 9. $5\overline{)4}$ 10. $5\overline{)7}$

11. $3\overline{)9}$ 12. $2\overline{)3}$ 13. $3\overline{)2}$ 14. $4\overline{)7}$ 15. $5\overline{)6}$

16. $3\overline{)4}$ 17. $2\overline{)4}$ 18. $2\overline{)0}$ 19. $4\overline{)4}$ 20. $3\overline{)8}$

Divide. Find the quotients and remainders.

1. $5\overline{)14}$ 2. $3\overline{)26}$ 3. $5\overline{)18}$ 4. $5\overline{)34}$ 5. $4\overline{)21}$

6. $6\overline{)0}$ 7. $6\overline{)30}$ 8. $3\overline{)22}$ 9. $4\overline{)18}$ 10. $6\overline{)29}$

11. $3\overline{)16}$ 12. $5\overline{)36}$ 13. $4\overline{)22}$ 14. $2\overline{)19}$ 15. $4\overline{)30}$

16. $4\overline{)0}$ 17. $5\overline{)18}$ 18. $3\overline{)23}$ 19. $3\overline{)11}$ 20. $2\overline{)18}$

Find the quotients.

1. $2\overline{)46}$ 2. $4\overline{)56}$ 3. $5\overline{)55}$ 4. $2\overline{)82}$ 5. $4\overline{)36}$

6. $2\overline{)74}$ 7. $3\overline{)66}$ 8. $2\overline{)36}$ 9. $3\overline{)39}$ 10. $4\overline{)64}$

11. $4\overline{)76}$ 12. $5\overline{)40}$ 13. $3\overline{)72}$ 14. $2\overline{)52}$ 15. $4\overline{)80}$

16. $5\overline{)70}$ 17. $2\overline{)54}$ 18. $3\overline{)24}$ 19. $5\overline{)95}$ 20. $3\overline{)96}$

Set A   **For use after page 307**

Find the quotients and remainders.

1. $5\overline{)62}$ 2. $4\overline{)65}$ 3. $3\overline{)35}$ 4. $3\overline{)64}$ 5. $4\overline{)48}$

6. $2\overline{)17}$ 7. $2\overline{)29}$ 8. $4\overline{)45}$ 9. $5\overline{)68}$ 10. $4\overline{)79}$

11. $2\overline{)91}$ 12. $5\overline{)64}$ 13. $2\overline{)69}$ 14. $4\overline{)88}$ 15. $3\overline{)55}$

16. $3\overline{)47}$ 17. $5\overline{)86}$ 18. $4\overline{)66}$ 19. $2\overline{)36}$ 20. $5\overline{)48}$

Set B   **For use after page 333**

Find the sums.

	1.	2.	3.	4.	5.
	2.4	4.7	82.6	27.4	64.5
	+ 3.5	+ 2.8	+ 11.3	+ 36.8	+ 27.5

	6.	7.	8.	9.	10.
	7.2	65.3	73.6	26.2	30.8
	+ 1.8	+ 26.1	+ 21.8	+ 45.9	+ 9.5

	11.	12.	13.	14.	15.
	4.8	16.3	65.2	16.8	59.4
	+ 7.6	+ 42.9	+ 28.8	+ 14.2	+ 27.7

Set C   **For use after page 335**

Find the differences.

	1.	2.	3.	4.	5.
	8.6	6.0	25.2	64.1	40.6
	− 5.1	− 4.7	− 1.9	− 29.4	− 28.4

	6.	7.	8.	9.	10.
	26.2	8.0	11.1	98.4	41.2
	− 14.1	− 7.4	− 5.6	− 39.3	− 26.5

Table of Measures

Metric System		Customary System	

———— Length ————

1 centimeter (cm)	10 millimeters (mm)	1 foot (ft)	12 inches (in.)
1 decimeter (dm)	$\begin{cases}100 \text{ millimeters (mm)} \\ 10 \text{ centimeters (cm)}\end{cases}$	1 yard (yd)	$\begin{cases}36 \text{ inches (in.)} \\ 3 \text{ feet (ft)}\end{cases}$
1 meter (m)	$\begin{cases}1{,}000 \text{ millimeters (mm)} \\ 100 \text{ centimeters (cm)} \\ 10 \text{ decimeters (dm)}\end{cases}$	1 mile (m)	$\begin{cases}5{,}280 \text{ feet (ft)} \\ 1{,}760 \text{ yards (yd)}\end{cases}$
1 kilometer (km)	1,000 meters (m)		

———— Area ————

| 1 square meter (m^2) | $\begin{cases}100 \text{ square decimeters } (dm^2) \\ 10{,}000 \text{ square centimeters } (cm^2)\end{cases}$ | 1 square foot (ft^2) | $\begin{cases}144 \text{ square inches } (in.^2)\end{cases}$ |

———— Volume ————

| 1 cubic decimeter (dm^3) | $\begin{cases}1{,}000 \text{ cubic centimeters } (cm^3) \\ 1 \text{ liter (L)}\end{cases}$ | 1 cubic foot (ft^3) | $\begin{cases}1{,}728 \text{ cubic inches } (in.^3)\end{cases}$ |

———— Capacity ————

		1 cup (c)	8 fluid ounces (fl oz)
		1 pint (pt)	$\begin{cases}16 \text{ fluid ounces (fl oz)} \\ 2 \text{ cups (c)}\end{cases}$
1 teaspoon	5 milliliters (mL)	1 quart (qt)	$\begin{cases}32 \text{ fluid ounces (fl oz)} \\ 4 \text{ cups (c)} \\ 2 \text{ pints (pt)}\end{cases}$
1 tablespoon	12.5 milliliters (mL)		
1 liter (L)	$\begin{cases}1{,}000 \text{ milliliters (mL)} \\ 1{,}000 \text{ cubic centimeters } (cm^3) \\ 1 \text{ cubic decimeter } (dm^3) \\ 4 \text{ metric cups}\end{cases}$	1 gallon (gal)	$\begin{cases}128 \text{ fluid ounces (fl oz)} \\ 16 \text{ cups (c)} \\ 8 \text{ pints (pt)} \\ 4 \text{ quarts (qt)}\end{cases}$

———— Weight ————

| 1 gram (g) | 1,000 milligrams (mg) | 1 pound (lb) | 16 ounces (oz) |
| 1 kilogram (kg) | 1,000 grams (g) | | |

———— Time ————

1 minute (min)	60 seconds (s)	1 year (yr)	$\begin{cases}365 \text{ days} \\ 52 \text{ weeks} \\ 12 \text{ months}\end{cases}$
1 hour (h)	60 minutes (min)		
1 day (d)	24 hours (h)		
1 week (w)	7 days (d)	1 decade	10 years
1 month (mo)	about 4 weeks	1 century	100 years

Glossary

a.m. A way to indicate the times from 12:00 midnight to 12:00 noon.

addend One of the numbers to be added.

Example: addends

addition An operation that gives the total number when you put together two or more numbers.

angle Two rays from a single point.

area The measure of a region, expressed in square units.

associative (grouping) principle When adding (or multiplying) three or more numbers, the grouping of the addends (or factors) can be changed and the sum (or product) is the same.

Examples: $2 + (8 + 6) = (2 + 8) + 6$
$3 \times (4 \times 2) = (3 \times 4) \times 2$

calendar A chart that shows months, days, and dates.

centimeter (cm) A unit of length in the metric system. 100 centimeters equal 1 meter.

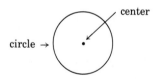

1 centimeter

circle A plane figure in which all the points are the same distance from a point called the center.

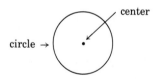

commutative (order) principle When adding (or multiplying) two or more numbers, the order of the addends (or factors) can be changed and the sum (or product) is the same.

Examples: $4 \times 5 = 5 + 4$
$2 \times 3 = 3 \times 2$

congruent figures Figures that have the same size and shape.

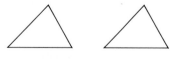

congruent triangles

coordinates Number pairs used in graphing.

cube A space figure that has squares for all of its faces.

cup (c) A unit for measuring liquids. 1 quart equals 4 cups.

cylinder A space figure that has a circle for a face.

cylinder

decimal A number that shows tenths by using a decimal point.

3.2 ← decimal
↑
decimal point

degree Celsius (°C) A unit for measuring temperature in the metric system.

degree Fahrenheit (°F) A unit for measuring temperature in the customary system of measurement.

difference The number obtained by subtracting one number from another.

digits The symbols used to write numerals: 0, 1, 2, 3, 4, 5, 6, 7, 8, and 9.

dividend A number to be divided.

$$\frac{4}{7 \overline{)28}} \leftarrow \text{dividend}$$

division An operation that tells how many sets or how many in each set.

divisor The number by which a dividend is divided.

$$\text{divisor} \rightarrow 7 \overline{)28}^{\,4}$$

END An instruction in a computer program that tells the computer to stop.

equation A number sentence involving the use of the equality symbol.

Examples: $9 + 2 = 11$
$8 - 4 = 4$

equivalent fractions Fractions that name the same amount.

Example: $\frac{1}{2}$ and $\frac{2}{4}$

estimate To find an answer that is close to the exact answer.

even number   A whole number that has 0, 2, 4, 6, or 8 in the ones' place.

factors   Numbers that are multiplied together to form a product.

Example: 6 × 7 = 42
                  ↑   ↑
                  factors

flowchart   A chart that shows a step-by-step way of doing something.

foot (ft)   A unit for measuring length. 1 foot equals 12 inches.

fraction   A number that expresses parts of a whole or a set.

Example: $\frac{3}{4}$

gallon (gal)   A unit of liquid measure. 1 gallon equals 4 quarts.

gram (g)   The basic unit for measuring weight in the metric system. A paper clip weighs about 1 gram.

graph   A picture that shows information in an organized way.

greater than   The relationship of one number being larger than another number.

Example: 6 > 5, read "6 is greater than 5"

inch (in.)   A unit for measuring length. 12 inches equal 1 foot.

1 inch

kilogram (kg)   A unit of weight in the metric system. 1 kilogram is 1,000 grams.

kilometer (km)   A unit of length in the metric system. 1 kilometer is 1,000 meters.

length   The measure of distance from one end to the other end of an object.

less than   The relationship of being smaller than another number.

Example: 5 < 6, read "5 is less than 6"

line   A straight path that is endless in both directions.

line of symmetry   A line on which a figure can be folded so that the two parts fit exactly.

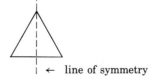

i ← line of symmetry

LIST   A copy of the set of instructions that tells a computer what to do.

liter (L)   A metric unit used to measure liquids. 1 liter equals 1,000 cubic centimeters.

measure   A number indicating the relation between a given object and a suitable unit.

meter (m)   A unit of length in the metric system. 1 meter is 100 centimeters.

mile (mi)   A unit for measuring length. 1 mile equals 5,280 feet.

minus (−)   Used to indicate the subtraction operation, as in 7 − 3 = 4, read, "7 minus 3 equal 4."

mixed number   A number that has a whole number part and a fractional part, such as $2\frac{3}{4}$.

multiplication   An operation that combines two numbers, called factors, to give one number, called the product.

negative number   A number that is less than zero.

number line   A line that shows numbers in order.

Example: ←•—•—•—•→
                  7   8   9   10

number pair   Two numbers that are used to give the location of a point on a graph.

Example: (3,2)

number sentence   A way to express a relationship between numbers.

Examples: 3 + 5 = 8
                    6 ÷ 2 = 3

numeral   A symbol for a number.

odd number   A whole number that has 1, 3, 5, 7, or 9 in the ones' place.

ordinal number   A number that is used to tell order.

Example: first, fifth

ounce (oz)   A unit for measuring weight. 16 ounces equal 1 pound.

p.m.   A way to indicate the times from 12:00 noon to 12:00 midnight.

perimeter   The distance around a figure.

pint (pt)   A unit for measuring liquid. 2 pints equal 1 quart.

place value   The value given to the place a digit occupies in a number.

Example: 3 5 6
              hundreds' place ⌐↑ ↑
                  tens' place ⌐⌐↑
                  ones' place ⌐⌐⌐

plane figures   Figures that lie on a flat surface.

Examples: □   △   ○
            square   triangle   circle

plus (+) Used to indicate the addition operation, as in 4 + 3 = 7, read, "4 plus 3 equal 7."

pound (lb) A unit for measuring weight. 1 pound equals 16 ounces.

PRINT An instruction in a computer program that tells the computer to print something.

product The result of the multiplication operation.

Example: 6 × 7 = 42
↑
product

program The set of instructions that tells a computer what to do.

quart (qt) A unit for measuring liquids. 1 quart equals 4 cups.

quotient The number (other than the remainder) that is the result of the division operation.

Examples: 45 ÷ 9 = 5   6 ← quotient
↑   7)45
quotient   − 42
            3

rectangle A plane figure with 4 sides and 4 right angles.

rectangular prism A space figure with six faces. It has the shape of a box.

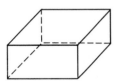

remainder The number less than the divisor that remains after the division process is completed.

Example: 6
         7)47
         − 42
            5 ← remainder

right angle An angle that has the same shape as the corner of a square.

Roman numerals Numerals used by the Romans.

Examples: I = 1
            V = 5
            VI = 6

rounding Replacing a number with a number that tells about how many.

Example: 23 rounded to the nearest 10 is 20.

RUN What appears on the video screen when a computer program is used.

segment A straight path from one point to another.

skip counting Counting by a number other than 1.

Example: 0 , 5 , 10 , 15
          Skip counting by fives

space figure A figure that is not flat but that has volume.

Examples:

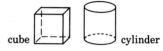

cube   cylinder

sphere A space figure that has the shape of a round ball.

square A plane figure that has four equal sides and four equal corners.

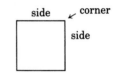

side   ↙ corner
       side

subtraction An operation that tells the difference between two numbers, or how many are left when some are taken away.

sum The number obtained by adding numbers.

Example: 3
        + 2
          5 ← sum

times (×) Used to indicate the multiplication operation, as in 3 × 4 = 12, read, "3 times 4 equal 12."

trading To make a group of ten from one of the next highest place value, or one from ten of the next lowest place value.

Examples: one hundred can be traded for ten tens; ten ones can be traded for one ten.

triangle A plane figure with three segments as sides.

unit An amount or quantity used as a standard of measurement.

volume The number of units of space that a space figure holds.

yard (yd) A unit for measuring length. 1 yard equals 3 feet.

Index

A

Addend, 2
Addition
  associative property of, 16–17
  column, sums through 18, 16–17
  column, 2- and 3-digit numbers, 78–79
  commutative property of, 10–11
  of decimals, 332–333
  estimating sums by rounding, 74–75
  fact families, 10–11
  facts, through 10, 2–3
  facts, through 18, 6–7
  of 4-digit numbers, 80–81
  grouping property of, 16–17
  with money, 70–71
  with more than two addends, with trading, 78–79
  and multiplication, 154–155
  order in, 10–11
  problem-solving applications, 14–15, 18, 19, 64, 65, 70, 82–83, 94, 102, 103, 114, 115, 135, 145, 174–175, 188, 192, 262–263, 286–287, 336
  with three addends, mentally, 76–77
  with three addends, sums through 18, 16–17
  of 3-digit numbers, one trade, 66–67
  of 3-digit numbers, two or more trades, 68–69
  of 2-digit numbers, one trade, 60–61
  of 2-digit numbers, two trades, 62–63
Angles, 208–209
Applied Problem-Solving pages, 288, 310, 338, 354
Area, 138–139, 357
Associative Property
  of addition, 16–17
  of multiplication, 190

B

Bar graph
  making a, 214–215
  reading a, 64, 78, 145, 267
Basic facts
  see Facts

C

Calculator, using a, 54–55
Calculator activities, 54–55, 69, 97, 99, 185, 235, 237, 341
Calendar, 128–129
Capacity
  in customary units, 350–351
  in metric units, 142

Careers
  dentist, 83, 153
  dietician, 192
  factory worker, 188
  farmer, 188, 282
  hotel employees, 243
  mail carrier, 188, 249
  office worker, 188
  painter, 188
  post office employee, 272
  printer, 201
  psychologist, 286
  roller rink clerk, 303
  sales clerk, 188
  supermarket employees, 262–263
  tile layer, 278
  waiter, 188
Celsius scale, 144
Centimeter
  cubic, 140–141
  measurement to nearest, 132–133
  square, 138–139
  unit, 131
Checking
  division, 302
  subtraction, 100–101
Circle, 204–205
Clock, 122–125
Coins
  see Money
Column addition
  with sums through 18, 16–17
  of 2- and 3-digit numbers with trading, 78–79
Commutative property
  of addition, 10–11
  of multiplication, 172–173
Comparison
  of fractions, 326
  of whole numbers, 44–45
Computer literacy
  END, 292–293, 342–343
  flow charts, 150–151, 224–225
  multiplication (*) and division (/) signs, 293
  PRINT, 292–293, 342–343
  programs, 292–293, 342–343
  quotation marks in programs, 292–293, 342–343
  RUN, 292–293, 342–343
Congruent figures, 210–211
Consumer applications
  adding money, 70–71
  applied problem solving, 288, 338, 354
  counting change, 34–35
  counting money, 33

dollars and cents, 36
  estimating products with money, 284
  estimating to check sales slip total, 285
  estimating totals with sales tax, 291
  multiplication with money, 280–281
  obtaining information from a catalog, 114
  obtaining information from an advertisement,
    70–71, 168, 309
  price, 37
  rounding to the nearest dollar, 40–41
  rounding to the nearest ten cents, 38–39
  sales tax, 291
  subtracting money, 106, 107
  using a calculator with money, 337
Coordinate graphing, 218–219
Counting and order
  even and odd numbers, 32
  number line used to illustrate, 30
  skip counting, 32
  whole numbers, 30–31
Counting money
  change, 34–35
  coins, 33
  coins and currency, 36–37
  using skip counting, 33
Cube, 202–203
Cubic
  centimeters, 141
  units, 140
Cup, 350–351
Currency
  see Money
Customary units of measurement, 346–353
  see also Pound, Quart, *etc.*
Cylinder, 202–203

D

Data banks, 359–362
Decimals
  addition of, 332–333
  and fractions, 328–329
  and mixed numbers, 330–331
  problem-solving applications, 336, 337
  subtraction of, 334–335
  tenths, 328–329
Difference, 4
Division
  and missing factors, 232–233
  by 0, discussed, 260
  by 2 and 3, 230–231
  by 4, 234–235
  by 5, 236–237

by 6, 250–251
by 7, 252–253
by 8, 256–257
by 9, 258–259
checking by multiplying, 302
concept of, 228–229
estimating quotients with money, 308
facts through 5, 230–237
facts through 9, 250–259
1-digit quotients with remainders, 296–299
problem-solving applications, 238, 240, 242, 243,
    254, 261, 262–263, 300–301, 303
quotients and missing factors, 232–233
as related to multiplication, 232–233
with remainders, 296–299, 306–307
as repeated subtraction, 235
signs (symbols), 239
2-digit quotients with remainders, 306–307
2-digit quotients without remainders, 304–305
with zero as dividend, 260
Divisor, 239
Dollars and cents
  see Money

E

Equations
  addition, 2
  division, 228
  multiplication, 156
  subtraction, 4
Equivalent fractions, 324–325
Estimating
  area, 183
  to check sums and products, 285
  differences, 107, 110–111
  fractions, 325
  map distance, 347
  in measurement, 149
  problem-solving applications, 114, 242, 285, 309
  products involving money, 284
  quotients involving money, 308
  sales totals involving tax, 291
  sums, 74–75, 81
Even and odd numbers, 32

F

Fact families
  addition and subtraction, 10–11
  multiplication and division, 232–233
Factor, 158

Facts
    addition, through 10, 2–3
    addition, through 18, 6–7
    division, through 5, 230–237
    division, through 9, 250–259
    multiplication, through 5, 158–171
    multiplication, through 9, 182–189
    subtraction, through 10, 4–5
    subtraction, through 18, 8–9
Fahrenheit scale, 353
5-Point Checklist for problem solving, 14,
    82–83, 174–175
Flowcharts, 150–151, 224–225
Foot, 346–347
Fractions
    comparing, 326
    and decimals, 328–329
    equivalent, 324–325
    and mixed numbers, 330
    parts of a set, 320–323
    parts of a whole, 316–319
    problem-solving applications, 323, 327

G

Gallon, 350–351
Games
    Largest Remainder, 297
    Logical Reasoning, 313
    Nim, 23
    One Difference, 313
    Place Value, 37
    Probability, 247
    Smallest Difference, 105
    A Strategy Game, 9
Geometry
    angles, 208–209
    congruent figures, 210–211
    lines of symmetry, 212–213
    plane figures, 204–205
    right angles, 208–209
    segments, 206–207
    space figures, 202–203
    symmetry, 212–213
Glossary, 386–388
Gram, 143
Graphs
    bar, 64, 78, 145, 214–215, 267
    coordinate, 218–219, 223
    bar graph, making a, 214–215
    picture, 216–217, 282
    problem-solving applications, 64, 145, 282

Grouping
    property of addition, 16–17
    property of multiplication, 16–17
    by hundreds, 28–29
    by tens, 26–27
    by thousands, 42–43

H

Hundreds, 28–29

I

Inch, 346–349
Inequalities
    fractional, 326
    whole number, 44–45

K

Kilogram, 143
Kilometer, 134

L

Length
    customary units, 346–349
    metric units, 131–134
    nonstandard units, 130
Lines of symmetry, 212–213
Liquid measurement
    customary units, 350–351
    liter, 142
Liter, 142
Logical reasoning, 5, 11, 23, 35, 59, 67, 84, 113,
    231, 275, 313

M

Magic Squares, 341
Map
    estimating distance, 347
    problem-solving applications, 102, 336
Measurement
    customary units
        capacity, 350–351
        length, 346–349
        liquid, 350–351
        temperature, 353
        weight, 352
    metric units
        area, 138–139

capacity, 142
length, 131–134
liquid, 142
perimeter, 136–137
volume, 140–141
weight, 143
nonstandard units, 130
Table of Measures, 385
temperature, 144, 353
time, 122–129
Mental Math
differences, 108–109
estimating products with money, 284
estimating quotients with money, 308
estimating totals involving sales tax, 291
products, 270–271
sums, 72–73, 76–77, 271
2-step problems, 274–275
Meter, 134
Metric units of measurement, 130–144
see also Gram, Meter, *etc.*
Mile, 346–347
Missing factors
and division, 232–233
in multiplication, 191
Mixed numbers, 330
Money
adding, 70–71
checking totals by estimation, 285
coin values, 33
counting change, 34–35
counting coins, 33–35
dollars and cents, 36–37
estimating differences by rounding, 110–111
estimating products, 284
estimating quotients, 308
estimating sums by rounding, 74–75
estimating totals with sales tax, 291
multiplication with, 280–281
problem-solving applications, 71, 114, 273, 285,
288, 309, 338, 354
rounding to nearest dollar, 40–41
rounding to nearest ten cents, 38–39
subtracting, 106–107
More practice, 363–384
Multiplication
0 and 1 as factors, 170
2 as a factor, 158–159
3 as a factor, 160–161
4 as a factor, 164–165
5 as a factor, 166–167
6 as a factor, 182–183
7 as a factor, 184–185

8 and 9 as factors, 186–187
and addition, 154–155
associative property of, 190
commutative property of, 172–173
concept of, 154–157
estimating products with money, 284
facts through 5, 158–172
facts through 9, 182–187
grouping property of, 190
missing factors, 191
with money, 280–281
multiples of 10 as factors, 270–271
order in, 172–173
parentheses in, 190
problem-solving applications, 162, 168, 174–175,
188, 194, 262–263, 273
properties of zero and one, 170
as related to division, 232–233
as repeated addition, 154–155
table, 186
three factors, 190
2-digit times 1-digit, trading ones, 276–277
2-digit times 1-digit, trading ones and tens,
278–279

N

Negative numbers, 267
Nim, 23
Nonstandard units of measurement, 130
Number line
to illustrate rounding, 38, 40
and whole numbers, 30
Number pairs, 218–219
Number sentences
addition, 2
division, 228
multiplication, 156
subtraction, 4
Number sequences, 179

O

Odd and even numbers, 32
Order
in addition, 10–11
in multiplication, 172–173
of whole numbers, 30–31
Ordered pairs, 218–219
Ordinal numbers, 48–49, 128–129
Ounce, 352

P

Parentheses in multiplication, 190
Patterns, 3, 13, 29, 47, 73, 79, 87, 93, 109, 139, 155, 179, 185, 207, 229, 251, 307, 331, 333
Perimeter, 136–137
Picture graph
  problem-solving applications, 282
  reading a, 216–217
Pint, 350–351
Place value
  2-digit, 26–27
  3-digit, 28–29
  4-digit, 42–43
  5- and 6-digit, 46–47
  game, 37
  grouping by hundreds, 28–29
  grouping by tens, 26–27
  grouping by thousands, 42–43
Plane figures, 204–205
Pound, 352
Powers of two, 87
Predictions, 119, 163
Probability, 119, 163, 247
Problem solving
  See also Applied problem solving, Problem-solving applications, Problem-solving strategies
  choosing correct operation, 20, 65, 162, 196, 254, 273
  5-Point Checklist, 14–15, 82–83, 174–175
  identifying needed data, 193
  identifying unneeded data, 240
  insufficient data, 113, 193
  practice, 115, 127, 188, 194, 243, 261, 286–287, 303, 323, 327
  too much data, 240
  understanding the operation, 238
  understanding the question, 18, 94
  using a calculator, 337
  using data from an advertisement, 71, 168, 309
  using data from a catalog, 114
  using data from a graph, 64, 145, 282
  using data from a map, 102, 310, 336
  using data from a picture, 19, 115, 135
  using data from a picture graph, 282
  using data from a table, 83, 103, 192, 243, 262–263
  using the strategies, 244, 264
Problem-solving applications
  addition, 14–15, 18, 19, 64, 65, 71, 82–83, 94, 102, 103, 114, 115, 135, 145, 174–175, 188, 262–263, 286–287, 336

decimals, 244, 336
division, 238, 240, 242, 243, 254, 261, 262–263, 300–301, 303
estimation, 114, 242, 285, 309
fractions, 323, 327
graphs, 62, 145, 282
money, 71, 114, 273, 285, 288, 301, 338, 354
multiplication, 162, 168, 174–175, 188, 194, 262–263, 273
subtraction, 14–15, 18, 19, 65, 82–83, 94, 102, 103, 114, 115, 135, 145, 174–175, 188, 192, 240, 242, 243, 262–263, 286–287, 336
time, 127
Problem-solving strategies
  Choose the Operations, 196, 254
  Draw a Picture, 116
  Find a Pattern, 220
  Guess and Check, 50
  Logical Reasoning, 84
  Make a List, 146
  Make a Table, 176
Product, 158

Q

Quart, 350–351
Quotient, 228
Quotients and missing factors, 232–233

R

Rectangle, 204–205
Rectangular prism, 202–203
Remainders, 296–297, 300–301, 306–307
Repeated addition, and multiplication, 154–155
Repeated subtraction, and division, 235
Right angles, 208–209
Roman numerals, 53
Rounding
  to estimate differences, 110–111
  to estimate sums, 74–75
  to nearest dollar, 40–41
  to nearest hundred, 40–41
  to nearest ten, 38–39
  to nearest ten cents, 38–39
  using a number line, 38, 40
Ruler
  centimeter, 131–133
  inch, 348–349

S

Sales tax, 291

Segments and space figures, 206–207
Shape perception, 205, 209, 213, 321
Skip counting
   to count money, 33
   by twos, fives, and tens, 32
Space figures, 202–203
Space perception, 141, 199, 203, 317
Special differences, multiples of 10 and 100, 108–109
Special products, multiples of 10 as factors, 270–271
Special sums, multiples of 10 and 100, 72–73
Sphere, 202–203
Square
   centimeter, 138–139
   of a number, 185
   as a plane figure, 204–205
   units, 138–139
Subtraction
   checking, 100–101
   with decimals, 334–335
   estimating differences by rounding, 110–111
   fact families, 10–11
   facts through 10, 4–5
   facts through 18, 8–9
   of 4-digit numbers, 112–113
   with money, 106–107
   with multiples of 10 and 100, 108–109
   problem-solving applications, 14–15, 18, 19, 65, 82–83, 94, 102, 103, 114, 115, 135, 145, 174–175, 188, 194, 240, 242, 243, 262–263, 286–287, 336
   of 3-digit numbers, trading hundreds, 96–97
   of 3-digit numbers, two trades, 98–99
   of 2-digit numbers, trading tens, 92–93
   zeros in, 104–105
Sum, 2
Symmetry, 212–213

T

Table of Measures, 385
Tallies, 214–215
Temperature
   Celsius, 144
   Fahrenheit, 353
Tens
   and ones, 26–27
   trading 1 ten for 10 ones, 90–91
   trading 10 ones for 1 ten, 58–59
   trading 10 tens for 1 hundred, 61–63
Tenths, 328–329

Thermometer
   Celsius, 144
   Fahrenheit, 353
Thousands, 42–43
Time
   a.m. and p.m., 126
   calendar, 128–129
   digital, 122–125
   half hour, 122–123
   hour, 122–123
   minutes, 124–125
   problem solving applications, 127
   quarter hour, 122–123
Trading
   in addition, 60–63
   in multiplication, 276–279
   in subtraction, 92–93, 96–99
   1 hundred for 10 tens, 96–97
   1 ten for 10 ones, 90–91
   10 hundreds for 1 thousand, 66–67
   10 ones for 1 ten, 58–59
   10 tens for 1 hundred, 62–63
Triangle, 204–205
Two-step problems, 188, 272, 274–275, 303

V

Volume, measurement, 140–141

W

Weight
   customary units of measurement, 352
   metric units of measurement, 143

Y

Yard, 346–347

Z

Zero
   in division, 260
   as factor, 170
   in subtraction, 104–105